Electrocardiography
in Emergency, Acute, and Critical Care
SECOND EDITION

Amal Mattu, MD, FACEP
Professor of Emergency Medicine
Vice Chair, Department of Emergency Medicine
University of Maryland School of Medicine
Baltimore, Maryland

Jeffrey A. Tabas, MD, FACEP
Professor of Emergency Medicine
Director of Faculty Development, UCSF Department of Emergency Medicine
Director of Outcomes and Innovations for Continuing Medical Education
UCSF School of Medicine
San Francisco, California

William J. Brady, MD, FACEP, FAAEM
Professor of Emergency Medicine and Internal Medicine
The David A. Harrison Distinguished Educator
Departments of Emergency Medicine & Internal Medicine
University of Virginia School of Medicine
Operational Medical Director, Albemarle County Fire Rescue
Charlottesville, Virginia

PUBLISHER'S NOTICE

The American College of Emergency Physicians (ACEP) makes every effort to ensure that contributors and editors of its publication are knowledgeable subject matter experts and that they used their best efforts to ensure accuracy of the content. However, it is the responsibility of each reader to personally evaluate the content and judge its suitability for use in his or her medical practice in the care of a particular patient. Readers are advised that the statements and opinions expressed in this publication are provided as recommendations of the contributors and editors at the time of publication and should not be construed as official College policy. ACEP acknowledges that, as new medical knowledge emerges, best practice recommendations can change faster than published content can be updated. ACEP recognizes the complexity of emergency medicine and makes no representation that this publication serves as an authoritative resource for the prevention, diagnosis, treatment, or intervention for any medical condition, nor should it be used as the basis for the definition of or the standard of care that should be practiced by all health care providers at any particular time or place. To the fullest extent permitted by law, and without limitation, ACEP expressly disclaims all liability for errors or omissions contained within this publication, and for damages of any kind or nature, arising out of use, reference to, reliance on, or performance of such information.

Copyright 2019, American College of Emergency Physicians, Dallas, Texas. All rights reserved. Printed in the United States of America. Except as permitted under the United States Copyright Act of 1976, no part of this publication may be reproduced or distributed in any form or by any means or stored in a database or retrieval system without prior written permission of the publisher.

To contact ACEP, call 800-798-1822 or 972-550-0911, or write to PO Box 619911, Dallas, TX 75261-9911, or visit bookstore.acep.org. Your comments and suggestions are always welcome.

First Printing: January 2019
ISBN: 978-1-7327486-0-6

Senior Editor, Marta Foster
Managing Editor, Ram Khatri
Design and Production, Kevin Callahan
Cover Design, James Normark
Copyediting, Mary Anne Mitchell, ELS
Proofreading, Wendell Anderson
Indexing, Judith McConville
Printing, Modern Litho

About the Editors

Amal Mattu, MD, FACEP

Dr. Mattu completed an emergency medicine residency at Thomas Jefferson University Hospital in Philadelphia, after which he completed a teaching fellowship with a special focus on emergency cardiology. Since joining the faculty at the University of Maryland in 1996, he has received more than 20 teaching awards including national awards from the American College of Emergency Physicians, the American Academy of Emergency Medicine, the Council of Residency Directors in Emergency Medicine, and the Emergency Medicine Residents' Association; and local honors including the Teacher of the Year for the University of Maryland at Baltimore campus and the Maryland State Emergency Physician of the Year Award. He is a frequent speaker at major conferences on topics pertaining to emergency cardiology and electrocardiography, having provided over 2,000 hours of instruction to providers in different specialties at national and international meetings. Dr. Mattu has authored or edited 20 textbooks in emergency medicine, and he is the editor-in-chief of ACEP's text *Cardiovascular Emergencies*. Dr. Mattu is currently a tenured professor, vice chair, and director of the Faculty Development Fellowship and co-director of the Emergency Cardiology Fellowship for the Department of Emergency Medicine at the University of Maryland School of Medicine.

Jeffrey A. Tabas, MD, FACEP

Dr. Tabas is a professor of emergency medicine at University of California San Francisco (UCSF) School of Medicine and practices in the emergency department at San Francisco General Hospital. He is an active educator and researcher in electrocardiography and cardiovascular emergencies, having lectured and published extensively on these topics. Dr. Tabas serves as a director in the UCSF Office of Continuing Medical Education and as director of faculty development for the UCSF Department of Emergency Medicine. He received his undergraduate training at Brown University and his medical training at the University of Pennsylvania. He trained in both internal medicine and emergency medicine at the University of California Los Angeles. He is a member of the UCSF Academy of Medical Educators and is past chair of the Education Committee of the American College of Emergency Physicians (ACEP). He has been recognized with numerous teaching awards, including the 2013 ACEP Outstanding Contribution in Education Award, a career achievement award presented to the ACEP member who has made a significant contribution to the educational aspects of the specialty. He previously served as editor of an electrocardiography section for *JAMA Internal Medicine* and currently serves as editor of an electrocardiography section for *Annals of Emergency Medicine*.

William J. Brady, MD, FACEP, FAAEM

Dr. Brady is a practicing emergency physician at the University of Virginia in Charlottesville; he is residency trained in emergency medicine and internal medicine. He is a tenured professor of emergency medicine, internal medicine, and nursing as well as the David A. Harrison Distinguished Educator at the University of Virginia School of Medicine (UVA). At UVA, he serves as the medical director of Emergency Management and chair of the Resuscitation Committee; in the community, he functions as the operational medical director of Albemarle County Fire Rescue. He is the associate editor of the *American Journal of Emergency Medicine*. Dr. Brady is actively involved in the instruction of health care providers on many topics, with a particular focus on the electrocardiogram in the prehospital, emergency department, and other acute/critical care settings with lectures delivered regionally, nationally, and internationally. He has also published numerous scholarly works (original research, reviews, annotated bibliographies, invited editorials, guidelines, book chapters, and textbooks), addressing the electrocardiogram and its use by emergency physicians. Additionally, he has contributed to clinical policy guidelines for the American College of Emergency Physicians and the American Heart Association. Dr. Brady lives in Charlottesville, Virginia, with his family; he is active in the community, working in volunteer capacities in public safety and community athletics.

Dedications

I would like to thank my wife, Sejal, for her constant support and encouragement; I thank my children, Nikhil, Eleena, and Kamran, for always reminding me of my proper priorities in life; I thank the residents, and students at the University of Maryland School of Medicine for providing me the inspiration for the work I do every day; I thank Dr. Brian Browne for being the most supportive chairman an educator could wish for; and finally, thanks to my colleagues and mentors, who continue to exemplify what I hope one day to become.
—**Amal Mattu**

This work is dedicated to my family who has supported and inspired me through my career, and to my colleagues, residents, and students, who have supported and inspired me as well.
—**Jeffrey A. Tabas**

I would like to thank my wife, King, for her support, guidance, and patience; my children, Lauren, Anne, Chip, and Katherine, for being awesome; my mother, Joann Brady, for everything she has given me; and to emergency physicians throughout the world, for being there, every day.
—**William J. Brady**

Acknowledgments

We wish to acknowledge and thank Linda J. Kesselring, ELS, MS, the technical editor for the Department of Emergency Medicine at the University of Maryland, for her enormous assistance in preparing this textbook. We also wish to acknowledge the incredible support and contributions of freelance copyeditor Mary Anne Mitchell, ELS, and of ACEP staff members Marta Foster and Ram Khatri. Finally, we wish to acknowledge the tireless work and dedication of emergency care providers around the world. May this textbook contribute to your continued success. —**The Editors**

Contributors

Benjamin S. Abella, MD, MPhil, FACEP
Professor and Vice Chair for Research
Department of Emergency Medicine
Center for Resuscitation Science
University of Pennsylvania
Philadelphia, Pennsylvania

Fredrick M. Abrahamian, DO, FACEP, FIDSA
Health Sciences Clinical Professor of Emergency Medicine
David Geffen School of Medicine at UCLA
Los Angeles, California

Leen Alblaihed, MBBS, MHA
Clinical Instructor and Faculty Development Fellow
Department of Emergency Medicine
University of Maryland School of Medicine
Baltimore, Maryland

Michael C. Bond, MD, FACEP, FAAEM
Associate Professor
Department of Emergency Medicine
University of Maryland School of Medicine
Residency Program Director, Emergency Medicine
University of Maryland Medical Center
Baltimore, Maryland

William J. Brady, MD, FACEP, FAAEM
Professor of Emergency Medicine & Internal Medicine
The David A. Harrison Distinguished Educator
Departments of Emergency Medicine & Internal Medicine
University of Virginia School of Medicine
Operational Medical Director, Albemarle County Fire Rescue
Charlottesville, Virginia

Kevin R. Brown, MD, MPH, FACEP, FAAEM, EMT-P
Attending Physician
NY Presbyterian-Lawrence Hospital
Bronxville, New York
Bassett Medical Center
Cooperstown, New York
Assistant Clinical Professor of Medicine
Columbia University, College of Physicians & Surgeons
New York, New York
Assistant Professor of Family Medicine
New York Medical College
Valhalla, New York

Jayaram Chelluri, MD, MHSA
Assistant Professor
Department of Emergency Medicine
Department of Surgery, Division of Traumatology, Critical Care, Emergency Surgery
Hospital of the University of Pennsylvania
Philadelphia, Pennsylvania

Stephanie J. Doniger, MD, RDMS, FAAP, FACEP
Pediatric Emergency Medicine
Emergency Ultrasound
Department of Emergency Medicine
NYU Winthrop Hospital
Mineola, New York
St. Christopher's Hospital for Children
Philadelphia, Pennsylvania

Suzanne Doyon, MD, MPH, FACMT, ASAM
Assistant Professor
Department of Emergency Medicine
University of Connecticut School of Medicine
Medical Director, Connecticut Poison Control Center
Farmington, Connecticut

Ali Farzad, MD, FAAEM, FACEP
Clinical Assistant Professor, Texas A&M College of Medicine
Assistant Emergency Department Medical Director
Observation Unit Medical Director
Department of Emergency Medicine
Baylor University Medical Center
Dallas, Texas

CONTRIBUTORS

Gus M. Garmel, MD, FACEP, FAAEM
Clinical Professor (Affiliate) of Emergency Medicine, Stanford University
Senior Staff Emergency Physician, TPMG, Kaiser
Santa Clara, California
Senior Editor, *The Permanente Journal*
Portland, Oregon
Chair, Faculty Development Subcommittee, Kaiser Permanente
Oakland, California

George Glass, MD
Assistant Professor
Department of Emergency Medicine
University of Virginia School of Medicine
Charlottesville, Virginia

Malkeet Gupta, MD, MS, FACEP
Associate Clinical Professor
UCLA Medical Center
Los Angeles, California
Managing Partner, AVEMA, Inc.
Lancaster, California

Richard A. Harrigan, MD, FAAEM
Professor of Emergency Medicine
Department of Emergency Medicine
Lewis Katz School of Medicine at Temple University
Philadelphia, Pennsylvania

Tarlan Hedayati, MD, FACEP
Assistant Professor
Associate Program Director
Department of Emergency Medicine
Cook County Health and Hospitals System
Chicago, Illinois

Maite Anna Huis in 't Veld, MD, FAAEM
Assistant Professor
Department of Emergency Medicine
University of Maryland School of Medicine
Baltimore, Maryland

ELECTROCARDIOGRAPHY IN EMERGENCY, ACUTE, AND CRITICAL CARE

Elizabeth Kwan, MS, MD
Assistant Professor
Department of Emergency Medicine
UCSF School of Medicine
San Francisco, California

Joel T. Levis, MD, PhD, FACEP, FAAEM
Chief, Department of Emergency Medicine
Kaiser Santa Clara Medical Center
Santa Clara, California
Clinical Assistant Professor (Affiliate) of Emergency Medicine
Stanford University School of Medicine
Medical Director, Foothill College Paramedic Program
Los Altos, California

Stephen Y. Liang, MD, MPHS, FACEP
Assistant Professor of Medicine
Divisions of Emergency Medicine and Infectious Diseases
Washington University School of Medicine
St. Louis, Missouri

Amal Mattu, MD, FACEP
Professor and Vice Chair
Department of Emergency Medicine
University of Maryland School of Medicine
Baltimore, Maryland

Andrew D. Perron, MD, FACEP
Professor and Residency Program Director
Department of Emergency Medicine
Maine Medical Center
Portland, Maine

Christopher H. Ross, MD, FACEP, FAAEM, FRCPC
Associate Professor of Emergency Medicine
Mercyhealth
Department of Emergency Medicine
Rockton Campus
Rockford, Illinois

CONTRIBUTORS

Theresa M. Schwab, MD
Advocate Christ Medical Center
Oak Lawn, Illinois
Assistant Clinical Professor of Emergency Medicine
University of Illinois Chicago
Chicago, Illinois

Ghazala Q. Sharieff, MD, MBA, FAAEM, FAAP
Clinical Professor, Rady Children's Hospital and Health Center
University of California San Diego
Corporate Vice President, Chief Experience Officer, Scripps Health
San Diego, California

Amandeep Singh, MD
Department of Emergency Medicine
Highland Hospital, Alameda Health System
Oakland, California
Assistant Clinical Professor Emergency Medicine
UCSF School of Medicine
San Francisco, California

Jeffrey A. Tabas, MD, FACEP
Professor
Department of Emergency Medicine
UCSF School of Medicine
San Francisco, California

Semhar Z. Tewelde, MD, FACEP, FAAEM
Assistant Professor
Department of Emergency Medicine
University of Maryland School of Medicine
Assistant Residency Program Director
University of Maryland Medical Center
Baltimore, Maryland

Contents

Foreword — xv

Preface — xvii

Fundamentals

CHAPTER ONE
The ECG and Clinical Decision-Making in the Emergency Department — 1

Abnormalities of Rhythm and Conduction

CHAPTER TWO
Intraventricular Conduction Abnormalities — 15

CHAPTER THREE
Bradycardia, Atrioventricular Block, and Sinoatrial Block — 29

CHAPTER FOUR
Narrow Complex Tachycardias — 53

CHAPTER FIVE
Wide Complex Tachycardias — 69

Acute Coronary Syndromes and Mimics

CHAPTER SIX
Acute Coronary Ischemia and Infarction — 91

CHAPTER SEVEN
Additional-Lead Testing in Electrocardiography — 117

CHAPTER EIGHT
Emerging Electrocardiographic Indications for Acute Reperfusion — 129

CHAPTER NINE
ACS Mimics Part I: Non-ACS Causes of ST-Segment Elevation — 141

CHAPTER TEN
ACS Mimics Part II: Non-ACS Causes of ST-Segment Depression and T-Wave Abnormalities — 159

Other Cardiac Conditions

CHAPTER ELEVEN
Pericarditis, Myocarditis, and Pericardial Effusions — 171

CHAPTER TWELVE
Preexcitation and Accessory Pathway Syndromes — 187

CHAPTER THIRTEEN
Inherited Syndromes of Sudden Cardiac Death — 199

CHAPTER FOURTEEN
Pacemakers and Pacemaker Dysfunction — 213

CHAPTER FIFTEEN
Metabolic Abnormalities: Effects of Electrolyte Imbalances and Thyroid Disorders on the ECG — 237

CHAPTER SIXTEEN
The ECG in Selected Noncardiac Conditions — 247

CHAPTER SEVENTEEN
The ECG and the Poisoned Patient — 265

Pediatric Considerations

CHAPTER EIGHTEEN
The Pediatric ECG — 281

Index — 297

Foreword

The ECG is by no means a new diagnostic technology in medicine; however, it remains among the most ubiquitous of tests, essential in the assessment, diagnosis, and treatment of patients—especially as they present in an emergency department. The foundational skills and knowledge necessary to appropriately interpret the rhythms and readings are refined through constant practice and experience. This interpretation (or misinterpretation) can have dramatic effect on the course of care provided to a patient. So, it is critical that the experienced physicians of today offer as much knowledge and support as possible for others in our clinical community to feel confident in their ECG skills and knowledge.

As an emergency physician, I have experienced first-hand a broad spectrum of environments for the assessment of ECGs and the critical nature of proper interpretation. From my earliest introduction as a medical student, resident, faculty, and ultimately becoming the chief of emergency medicine at the University of Maryland School of Medicine, I know that mastering this fundamental skill remains critically important to inform medical decision making.

Drs. Mattu, Tabas, and Brady are renowned clinicians and educators who are experts in the science and art of applying ECG interpretations across a wide variety of clinical settings. Through their years of instruction, they have demonstrated this expertise and commitment to quality educational resources for medical students, residents, physicians, and other health care providers. By providing this updated edition of *Electrocardiography in Emergency Medicine*, they have set out to convey their combined experience with refined methodology to guide appropriate ECG interpretations.

This textbook is certain to continue to be an essential resource for emergency physicians and others within the health care community. We thank Drs. Mattu, Tabas, and Brady for sharing their expertise through the material presented in this book. This contribution to the modern body of medical knowledge will improve outcomes for our patients and ultimately save lives.

Robert A. Barish, MD, MBA
Vice Chancellor for Health Affairs
University of Illinois at Chicago
Professor of Emergency Medicine
University of Illinois College of Medicine Chicago
Chicago, Illinois

Preface

We are very pleased to present this second edition of what we hope will continue to be the consummate "practitioners' guide" to electrocardiography for emergency physicians and other acute, critical, and emergency health care providers. The text is geared toward clinicians who evaluate the ECG in real time, with decisions made based on those interpretations—and medical care rendered. Much of the knowledge and inspiration for this book has come from our interactions rendering emergency care over the past three decades, as well as our extensive experience teaching ECG evaluation to a range of practitioners, including emergency and other acute care physicians, medical students, residents of many specialties, EMS personnel, and nurses—all aware of the importance of electrocardiographic interpretation in the emergency care setting. From these broad experiences, we have learned what works and doesn't work, what clinicians want and don't want, and, most importantly, what is needed to correctly and appropriately care for patients in the emergency department and related settings. This is how we have put this book together.

The health care practitioner in these settings *must* be the expert in emergency interpretation of the ECG—and there is considerable evidence to support this contention. Emergency physicians interpret the ECG, frequently, very early in the patient's course of care and usually before other information is available and related diagnostic test results are available. For instance, studies have shown that initiation of reperfusion therapy by emergency practitioners, based on the ECG and clinical interpretation of STEMI decreases time-to-therapy, with related improvements in patient outcome.

Our goal is to provide an easily understood, highly visual resource that is readable from cover to cover. The information is presented from the perspective of the clinician at the bedside: what he or she must recognize, how to discern the important findings, and what to consider doing with this information. In other words, this book is a highly practical reference guide to the management of the patient. In addition, this text can also be used as a "bookshelf reference," a very readable reference, written for the clinician at the bedside. We stress recognition of the various ECG diagnoses considering the electrocardiographic differential diagnosis when appropriate.

Many electrocardiographic presentations are interpreted relative to the individual patient. One important aspect of this book considers this issue—the interpretation of the ECG within the context of the individual patient presentation—which is best performed real time, by the clinician caring for that person.

We hope you enjoy your reading and look forward to any and all of your feedback. We would especially like to thank Linda Kesselring and Mary Anne Mitchell for their editorial expertise, support, and guidance. We would also like to thank our families for their patience and understanding while we worked on this project, and we thank our colleagues, our students, and our residents who have been—and continue to be—a constant source of inspiration for our work for you.

Amal Mattu
Jeffrey A. Tabas
William J. Brady

CHAPTER ONE

The ECG and Clinical Decision-Making in the Emergency Department

WILLIAM J. BRADY, JEFFREY A. TABAS, AND AMAL MATTU

KEY POINTS

- The ECG must be interpreted within the context of the clinical presentation, including information such as the patient's age, chief and secondary complaints, physical examination, and other diagnostic test results.
- Clinical judgment has a very important role in the interpretation of the ECG within the individual clinical event.
- The ECG can provide information to confirm a diagnosis, rule out a diagnosis, risk stratify certain conditions, provide an indication for therapy, and predict complications.
- The ECG has numerous limitations in the various clinical scenarios in which it is used. An awareness of these limitations is vital to the correct application of the ECG in clinical care.

Electrocardiography is performed widely throughout emergency medicine, in emergency departments and observation units as well as in the prehospital environment and other out-of-hospital medical settings. In fact, it is appropriate to state that electrocardiographic monitoring is one of the most widely applied diagnostic tools in clinical emergency medicine today. Electrocardiography allows rhythm monitoring using single or multiple leads as well as the 12-lead ECG used to assess patients with a range of primary and secondary cardiopulmonary illnesses. Numerous situations in the emergency department warrant an electrocardiographic evaluation.[1]

The ECG can assist in establishing a diagnosis, ruling out various ailments, guiding diagnostic and management strategies, providing indication for certain therapies, determining inpatient disposition location, and assessing the end-organ impact of a syndrome (Table 1.1). Unfortunately, in the emergency department environment, the ECG does not usually provide a specific diagnosis in isolation. When combined with the clinical presentation, however, ECGs are far more useful. In a study of ECGs obtained in an emergency department, only 8% of the ECGs were diagnostic, but when interpreted within the context of the presentation, they much more frequently were able to help in ruling out various syndromes.[1] The most frequent reasons for obtaining an ECG were chest pain and dyspnea (Figure 1.1). In this same investigation, the ECG influenced the diagnostic approach in one-third of patients; additions included repeat ECGs, serum markers, and rule-out MI protocol. Alterations in therapy were made almost as often with the addition of antiplatelet, anticoagulant, or anti-anginal medication or reperfusion. Disposition was changed in approximately 15% of patient presentations with an inpatient location selected based on the electrocardiographic interpretation. The effects of 12-lead electrocardiographic findings on diagnostic, therapeutic, and dispositional issues in this emergency department population are summarized in Figure 1.2.[1]

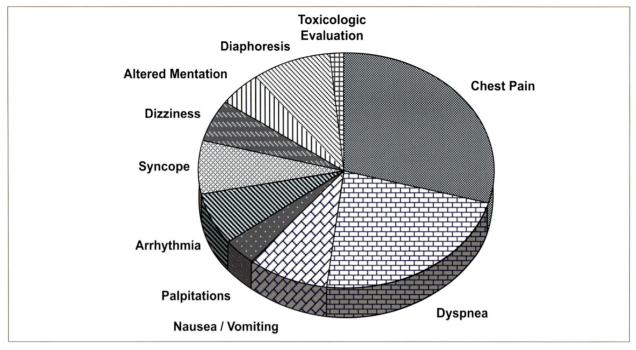

FIGURE 1.1. Clinical reasons for obtaining a 12-lead ECG.[1]

INTERPRETATION OF THE ECG WITHIN THE CLINICAL PRESENTATION

As with other diagnostic evaluations, the ECG must be interpreted within the context of the clinical presentation (ie, age, gender, chief complaint, comorbid medical illness, and results of the physical examination). An understanding of this concept and its application at the bedside is crucial for the appropriate use of ECGs in clinical practice. For instance, the meaning of a 12-lead ECG demonstrating normal sinus rhythm with normal ST segments and T waves (a normal ECG) (Figure 1.3) will differ depending on the patient being evaluated. Patient-based issues are the most important and common considerations in the interpretation of an ECG. A normal ECG from a stable 34-year-old man experiencing pleuritic chest pain will be interpreted very differently than a normal reading from a 64-year-old diaphoretic woman with chest pressure, dyspnea, and pulmonary congestion. The young man's presentation induces less concern than the middle-aged woman's; she is in the early stages of acute coronary syndrome (ACS). In these two scenarios, different evaluation and management pathways will be followed even though both patients have a "normal" ECG.

In scenario-based interpretations, the ECG is interpreted within the context of the circumstances leading to the patient's presentation. For example, the presence of a first-degree atrioventricular

TABLE 1.1. Clinical applications of the ECG.
Assessing the end-organ impact of a syndrome
Assessing the impact of therapy
Continuous or intermittent cardiac monitoring
Determining inpatient disposition location
Establishing a diagnosis
Guiding additional diagnostic studies
Guiding management
Predicting risk of cardiovascular complication
Providing an indication for certain therapies
Ruling out a syndrome

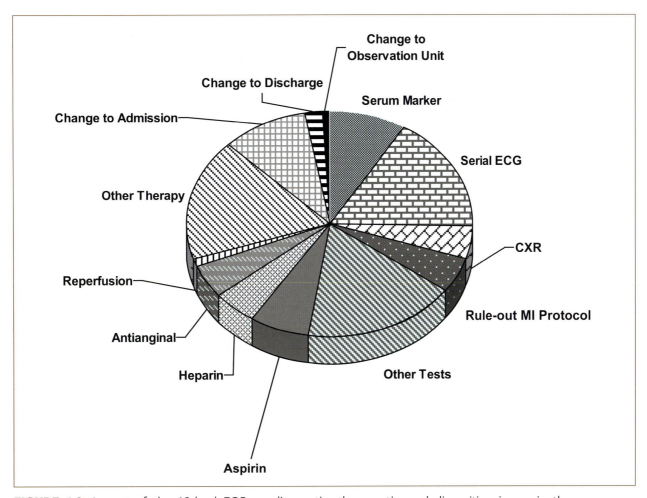

FIGURE 1.2. Impact of the 12-lead ECG on diagnostic, therapeutic, and disposition issues in the emergency department. Note that all changes in evaluation and therapy were additions.[1]

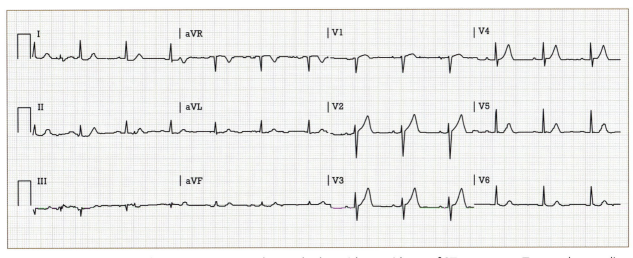

FIGURE 1.3. 12-lead ECG demonstrating normal sinus rhythm with no evidence of ST-segment or T-wave abnormality. A normal 12-lead ECG.

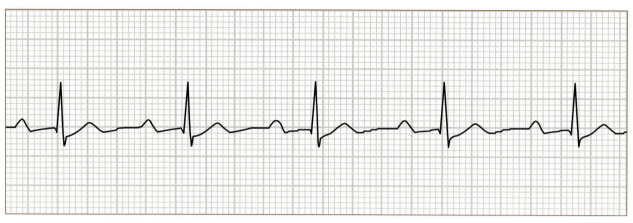

FIGURE 1.4. Normal sinus rhythm with first-degree atrioventricular block.

block (Figure 1.4) induces widely different levels of concern and medical management decisions. It has different meanings in a 27-year-old athletic woman undergoing electrocardiographic evaluation for operative "clearance" after sustaining a trimalleolar fracture of the ankle in a ground-level fall and in a 19-year-old man who ingested a large amount of metoprolol. The same electrocardiographic finding suggests significantly different levels of cardiovascular risk, mandating markedly different management strategies.

The basic, vital message is this: *Interpret the ECG within the context of the clinical presentation evolving before your eyes.* That statement captures the message of this chapter.

CLINICAL SCENARIOS AND THE ECG

The ECG is employed in different situations in the emergency department on a regular basis, including in the evaluation of patients presenting with chest pain, dyspnea, syncope, palpitations, altered mentation, and toxic ingestion and following resuscitation after cardiac arrest. The ECG can be used for many purposes: providing a diagnosis, indicating the extent of an illness, suggesting a therapy, and predicting risk. For instance, in the evaluation of a patient experiencing chest pain and thus suspected of having a coronary event, the ECG is used to help establish that diagnosis or, alternatively, to direct attention to a noncoronary condition. The electrocardiographic findings can also be helpful in selecting appropriate therapy, such as determining the patient's candidacy for fibrinolysis or percutaneous coronary intervention. And the ECG can be used to determine the patient's response to treatments delivered in the emergency department. Lastly, the ECG can help predict the risk of both cardiovascular complications and death.

When a 12-lead ECG is requested in the emergency department, the patient typically has three simultaneous indications.[1] An adult experiencing chest pain (the chest pain is the first indication) is evaluated according to the "rule-out MI" protocol (the rule-out protocol is the second indication) in consideration of ACS (the ACS evaluation is the third indication). In fact, the most frequent indication for an ECG in the emergency department is chest pain; others are dyspnea and syncope. Symptom-based considerations are the most common reasons for obtaining a 12-lead ECG, but patients can have diagnosis-based (eg, ACS and suspected pulmonary embolism [PE]) and system-related indications (eg, "rule-out myocardial infarction" protocol, admission purposes, and operative clearance) as well.[1] These indications involve consideration of a complaint, but the ECG is performed in a process, following the rule-out MI protocol. Although the value of electrocardiographic rhythm monitoring has not been studied, it is reasonable to assume its usefulness in the emergency department, especially for patients who are ill or who could become quite ill quickly.

Chest Pain

The 12-lead ECG is used widely in the evaluation of patients with chest pain. In fact, the most frequent clinical scenario in which an ECG is obtained is an adult patient with chest pain in whom ACS is being considered or to rule out MI.[1] In this application of the ECG, the clinician is attempting to rule in an ACS event with the demonstration of significant ST-segment and T-wave abnormalities. This same symptom-based approach can involve the 12-lead ECG for the diagnosis of other chest syndromes such as acute myopericarditis.

The ECG has a central role in the diagnostic evaluation of patients with chest discomfort. In fact, it is the major criterion for the diagnosis of STEMI, and it often provides information regarding the anatomic location of the infarct-related artery. In presentations of non-ST-segment elevation acute MI and unstable angina, the ECG provides important diagnostic information, yet less than for STEMI. The information provided by the ECG is less straightforward in that the range of abnormality (from minimal nonspecific ST-segment abnormality to obvious ST-segment depression and T-wave inversion) is quite broad.

Clearly, therapeutic interventions can be suggested or indicated based on the 12-lead ECG from a patient with chest pain suspected of ACS. For instance, the individual with chest discomfort who demonstrates anatomically oriented T-wave inversion or ST-segment depression can be a candidate for anticoagulant, antiplatelet, and antianginal therapies. In fact, the ECG provides clinical information that influences management strategies in one-third of ED patients with chest pain.[1]

The 12-lead ECG provides the major indication for acute reperfusion therapy (fibrinolysis or percutaneous coronary intervention [PCI]) in the STEMI patient. The electrocardiographic indications for acute reperfusion are:

- ST-segment elevation in two or more anatomically contiguous leads or
- left bundle-branch block (LBBB) with Sgarbossa criteria. These both are described in more detail in Chapter 6.

No evidence of benefit from fibrinolytic therapy has been found for patients with ACS presentations who lack either appropriate ST-segment elevation or the LBBB findings. For instance, the Fibrinolytic Therapy Trialists Collaborative Group analyzed randomized fibrinolytic therapy trials of more than 1,000 patients and found benefit of fibrinolytic therapy only in those with ST-segment elevation or LBBB.[2] Patients with an acute MI in anterior, inferior, or lateral anatomic locations benefitted from administration of fibrinolytic therapy if it was administered within 12 hours after onset. Benefit was greatest in patients with LBBB and anterior acute MI and least in those with inferior acute MI. Patients with inferior acute MI and right precordial ST-segment depression (presumably acute posterior wall STEMI) or elevation in the right ventricular leads (right ventricular STEMI) have a worse prognosis and benefit more from fibrinolytic agents than patients with isolated inferior ST-segment elevation.[3-12] Inferior acute MI patients with coexisting right ventricular infarctions, as detected by additional-lead ECGs, are likely to benefit because of the large amount of jeopardized myocardium. Acute, isolated posterior wall MI, diagnosed by posterior leads, could represent yet another electrocardiographic indication for fibrinolysis for the same reason (unproven in large fibrinolytic agent trials).[3-12]

Risk stratification is of great importance to emergency physicians. In broad terms, low-risk patients can be discharged safely for outpatient evaluation while high-risk patients generally require more extensive assessment. A more challenging category of patients is those who are at moderate (or intermediate) risk for ACS. In those chest pain patients, a new electrocardiographic abnormality, a positive cardiac biomarker, or acute heart failure represent high-risk features in the evaluation.[13] The ECG has a central role in the risk assessment strategy.

Clinical decision tools have been suggested as an adjunct in risk stratification of emergency department chest pain patients suspected of ACS. It is extremely important to note that clinical decision tools assist in decision-making, but they do not make decisions for the clinician. And, of course, the

ECG has a pivotal role in each of these tools. Most of these tools, when used alone without other clinical data, cannot clearly demarcate levels of risk, that is, they cannot distinctly separate low-risk from intermediate- and high-risk groups, and thus are of limited value to the clinician. Furthermore, the use of risk scoring systems based on inpatient populations (eg, TIMI) is not appropriate for identifying patients who can be discharged safely from an emergency department.

The HEART score is an exception because it identifies a discrete population that has a very low rate of adverse events within 4 to 6 weeks.[14-16] The score has five components: history of the chest pain, the ECG, the patient's age, coronary artery disease risk factors, and initial troponin value. Each variable is given three point values (0, 1, and 2). The ECG points are based on the interpretations of normal, nonspecific repolarization disturbance, and significant ST-segment depression, respectively. A score of 3 or lower is associated with a low risk of a major adverse cardiac event (0.9% to 1.7%).[14-16] The American Heart Association Guidelines 2015 recommend combining serial troponin testing with the HEART score or other clinical decision rules. With negative troponin serial test results and a low-risk HEART score (or an equivalent low-risk score from another decision rule), the adverse event rate is less than 1% at 30 days.[17]

The initial ECG correlates well with patient prognosis after acute MI based on the heart rate, QRS duration, infarct location, and amount of ST-segment deviation.[18-20] The initial 12-lead ECG obtained in the emergency department can be a helpful guide for determining cardiovascular risk and therefore in-hospital admission location. Brush and colleagues classified initial ECGs into high- and low-risk groups. Their low-risk group had absolutely normal ECGs, nonspecific ST-T wave changes, or no change from a previous ECG. The high-risk ECGs had a significant abnormality or confounding pattern such as pathologic Q waves, ischemic ST-segment or T-wave changes, left ventricular hypertrophy, LBBB, or ventricular paced rhythm. Patients with initial ECGs classified as low risk had a 14% incidence of acute MI, a 0.6% incidence of life-threatening complications, and a 0% mortality rate. Patients with initial ECGs classified as high risk had a 42% incidence of acute MI, a 14% incidence of life-threatening complications, and a 10% mortality rate.[21] Another approach to risk prediction involves a simple calculation of the number of electrocardiographic leads with ST-segment deviation (elevation or depression), with an increasing number of leads being associated with higher risk. Risk can also be predicted with a summation of the total millivolts of ST-segment deviation; once again, higher totals are associated with greater risk.[21]

The presence of left ventricular hypertrophy on the ECG is associated with an increased long-term risk of sudden death, acute heart failure, angina, and acute MI.[22] The ECG has been shown to predict adverse cardiac events as well as the release of cardiac serum markers in patients with chest pain and new LBBB, ST-segment elevation, or ST-segment depression. Blomkalns and colleagues raised awareness about the potential for adverse events when pathologic Q waves or T-wave inversion is seen on the ECG, so these abnormalities should be considered in treatment decisions regarding patients with risk factors for coronary disease.[19]

To further evaluate risk for ACS, some authors use standardized electrocardiographic classification systems based on the initial ECG. One example was created by the Standardized Reporting Criteria Working Group of the Emergency Medicine Cardiovascular Research and Education Group to determine whether the initial ECG can predict risk of death, acute MI, or need for revascularization at 30 days after presentation.[23] It has demonstrated high reliability in predicting adverse outcomes and presented the hope that it could lead to better risk stratification for low-risk patients with a normal or nondiagnostic ECG.[20,23]

Dyspnea

Dyspnea is the second most frequently encountered indication for ECG performance in the emergency department population. In this complaint-based situation, the clinician considers not only the anginal-equivalent ACS presentation but also other cardiorespiratory ailments such as PE. Electrocardiographic issues in the setting of ACS are reviewed above in the Chest Pain section.

The diagnosis of PE relies predominantly on the magnitude of clinical suspicion and the interpretation of various diagnostic investigations at that level of diagnostic concern. The diagnosis should be considered in the patient with unexplained dyspnea; certainly, the acute onset of additional symptoms such as pleuritic chest pain and hemoptysis suggest the possibility of PE, yet, as with most classic symptom constellations, these complaints rarely occur simultaneously. In this evaluation, a myriad of tests may be performed, including initial "screening" studies (chest radiography, 12-lead ECG, arterial blood gas measurement) and more advanced diagnostic investigations (chest computed tomography with angiography, ventilation-perfusion imaging). Along with the chest radiograph, the ECG is often obtained as an initial diagnostic test. Despite this widespread application of the ECG, its diagnostic performance in the patient with suspected PE is rather inadequate. In fact, the most common use of the ECG in this presentation is the exclusion of other diagnoses such as ACS. The ECG should not be used as a primary study to rule in PE because its sensitivity is quite low.

In patients with PE, the ECG might be entirely normal or could show any number of rhythm or morphologic abnormalities. The ECG can deviate from the norm with alterations in rhythm; in intraventricular conduction; in the axis of the QRS complex; and in the morphology of the P wave, QRS complex, and ST segment/T wave. The classic electrocardiographic finding of PE was first reported in 1935 by McGinn and White,[24] who described the traditional $S_1Q_3T_3$ pattern in acute cor pulmonale. However, this "classic" electrocardiographic finding is actually not often seen in patients with PE and is occasionally present in those without it, so its diagnostic power has been described as quite poor. The numerous electrocardiographic findings associated with PE include arrhythmias (sinus tachycardia, atrial flutter, atrial fibrillation, atrial tachycardia, and atrial premature contractions), nonspecific ST-segment/T-wave changes, and findings of acute cor pulmonale (including $S_1Q_3T_3$ pattern, T-wave inversions in the right precordial leads, right axis deviation, and right bundle-branch block).[25] The most common are nonspecific ST-segment/T-wave changes with sinus tachycardia. Unfortunately, these findings are extremely nonspecific.[26]

The relatively low sensitivities of these electrocardiographic presentations limit our ability to use the ECG as a sole diagnostic tool. Electrocardiographic changes are seen most frequently in patients with massive or submassive embolization; smaller PEs less often produce significant electrocardiographic abnormality. Various studies have shown that 15% to 30% of ECGs are normal in patients with established PE. Perhaps as a partial explanation of this relatively high rate of the "normal" ECG, it has been noted that the range of electrocardiographic findings in PE is transient, usually appearing during the acute phase of the illness.[27] As an independent marker, the ECG continues to be a limited study due to its poor sensitivity. The transient nature of electrocardiographic abnormalities and the often nonspecific changes reduce the effectiveness of the test as a single agent. The clinician must be aware of these electrocardiographic limitations in the application of the 12-lead ECG in the patient suspected of having PE.

Syncope

The patient with syncope presents a significant challenge to emergency physicians; this scenario is yet another common indication for electrocardiography in the emergency department. Most of these patients ultimately will have a favorable outcome; a significant minority, however, will be diagnosed with a life- or limb-threatening event or will die. Several clinical variables have demonstrated utility in the evaluation of patients with syncope; the ECG, of course, is one of them.

Certain obvious electrocardiographic presentations in the syncope patient will not only provide a reason for the loss of consciousness but also guide early therapy and disposition. Bradycardia, atrioventricular block, intraventricular conduction abnormality, and tachyarrhythmia in the appropriate clinical setting provide an answer for the syncopal event. Morphologic findings suggesting the range of cardiovascular malady are also encountered; they are far ranging, including the various ST-segment and T-wave abnormalities of ACS, ventricular hypertrophy suggestive of hypertrophic cardiomyopathy, ventricular preexcitation as seen in the Wolff-Parkinson-White syndrome, prolonged QT interval common in the diverse long QT interval presentations, and Brugada syndrome with the associated tendency for sudden death. Of course, this list is by no means inclusive.

Investigators have studied ECGs from patients with syncope with the aim of identifying individuals at risk for adverse outcome. For instance, Martin and colleagues endeavored to develop and validate a risk classification system for patients presenting to the emergency department with syncope. In a two-step analysis, they reviewed the presentations of 612 patients and found that an abnormal ECG was associated with arrhythmia or death with an odds ratio (OR) of 3.2. Other factors suggestive of poor outcome included histories of acute heart failure (AHF) (OR 3.2) and ventricular arrhythmia (OR 4.8).[28] Additional work by Sarasin and colleagues[29] considered the subset of patients with unexplained syncope after an initial emergency department evaluation. In 344 patients, those investigators found that an abnormal ECG was a predictor of arrhythmia, with an OR of 8.1. Other factors of significance associated with arrhythmic syncope included older age (OR 5.4) and a history of AHF (OR 5.3). In patients with one risk factor, arrhythmia was encountered rarely (0–2%). In patients with identified risk factors, arrhythmia occurred at the following frequencies: one risk factor, 0 to 2%; two, 35% to 41%; and three, 27% to 60%. The San Francisco Syncope Rule incorporates the ECG into the evaluation of patients with syncope. Quinn and associates considered 684 presentations of syncope and reviewed clinical variables with the intent of identifying patients at risk of poor short-term outcome.[30] An abnormal ECG was associated with an increased risk of short-term adverse event, and dyspnea, low hematocrit, and hypotension were predictors of poor outcome.

The most appropriate electrocardiographic approach to these patients is an initial review aimed at the detection of malignant arrhythmia. This first evaluation most often involves the rhythm strip. The detection at this stage of the evaluation is diagnostic of the cause and will mandate therapy. If the electrocardiographic rhythm strip does not yield an answer, then a 12-lead ECG can be performed. It can provide a more detailed review of a challenging rhythm presentation as well as the various morphologic findings noted above. Of course, a "negative" ECG itself does not rule out cardiac pathology.

Toxic Ingestion

The clinician approaches the poisoned patient with numerous important diagnostic tools, including the history of the ingestion, the physical examination demonstrating various toxidrome findings, and selected investigative tools. One of these tools is the ECG. In the poisoned patient, the ECG takes the form of the electrocardiographic rhythm strip and the 12-lead ECG. The ECG is used to establish the diagnosis, assess for end-organ toxicity, and guide therapeutic interventions. Not unlike patients with syncope, individuals presenting with significant cardiotoxicity manifested by arrhythmia will be assessed with an electrocardiographic monitor. Further diagnostic and management decisions will be suggested based on bedside interpretation of the rhythm strip.

For "stable" patients (ie, patients with a perfusing, stable cardiac rhythm), a 12-lead ECG is obtained. In addition to rhythm interpretation, this ECG is reviewed for abnormalities of the various structures, intervals, complexes, and axes. Beyond rhythm considerations, the primary electrocardiographic determinants of impending or established cardiotoxicity include the PR interval, the QRS complex, the T wave, the ST segment, and the QT interval.

Numerous authorities have explored the ECG in patients with suspected or known toxic diagnoses. It has been thoroughly explored in presentations after tricyclic antidepressant (TCA) ingestion and digoxin exposure, but little clinical information is available about the general use of the ECG in poisoned patients. Homer and associates undertook such a study,[31] with the goal of reviewing the range of electrocardiographic abnormalities encountered in poisoned patients. All patients evaluated for poisoning by the toxicology service at a tertiary referral center who underwent electrocardiographic analysis within 6 hours after ingestion were entered in the study. Each ECG was reviewed for rhythm and morphological diagnoses as well as interval/complex duration. Two hundred seventy-seven patients underwent electrocardiographic evaluation; 32% of them had a normal ECG. Of the patients (68%) with abnormal ECGs, 62% had a rhythm abnormality and 38% had morphologic abnormality. Rhythm disturbances included sinus tachycardia (51%), sinus bradycardia (7%), atrioventricular block (7%), non-sinus atrial tachycardias (3%), and nodal bradycardia (3%). Morphologic abnormalities included abnormal QRS configuration (35%), QRS complex widening (33%), QT-interval prolongation (33%), PR-interval prolongation (12%), ST-segment abnormality (9% elevated, 25% depressed), and T-wave inversion (20%). Interestingly, the degree of abnormality was directly related to the number of toxins ingested, but the cardiovascular agents (beta-adrenergic blockers and calcium channel antagonists) were no more likely to produce electrocardiographic abnormality than were noncardiovascular substances (sedative-hypnotic medications and stimulants). Importantly, this analysis did not include patients who underwent electrocardiographic rhythm analysis via the monitor. It likely would have missed the more malignant rhythm presentations, such as ventricular tachycardia or complete atrioventricular block. This study demonstrated that the ECG is, in fact, frequently abnormal in the poisoned patient. It did not explore the impact of an abnormal ECG on medical decision-making and patient management.

The ECGs of patients exposed to sedative-hypnotic or psychotropic medications have been explored thoroughly; importantly, the impact of the electrocardiographic findings has also been reviewed in various studies. For instance, patients with TCA poisoning have a range of electrocardiographic abnormalities, including arrhythmia, QRS-complex widening, QRS-complex configuration (prominent, terminal R wave in lead aVR, and S wave in lead I), and QT-interval prolongation. Specific electrocardiographic findings have different clinical implications; for example, sinus tachycardia, although present in many TCA-poisoned patients, is a nonspecific finding. Widening of the QRS complex, a more specific finding suggestive of TCA cardiotoxicity, is more useful. QRS complexes more than 100 milliseconds in duration are predictive of convulsion.[32] Conversely, a normal QRS complex duration is not "protective" in that convulsion and malignant arrhythmia can be seen in this group as well.[32,33] In general, with increasing QRS complex duration, the clinician is more likely to encounter significant end-organ toxicity. Rightward deviation of the terminal 40 milliseconds of the QRS complex frontal plane axis is also associated with both neurotoxicity and cardiotoxicity. A rightward axis of the terminal QRS complex is easily detected on the 12-lead ECG via observation of a prominent R wave in lead aVR and a deep S wave in lead I. This finding is reasonably predictive of either seizure or ventricular arrhythmia, with a sensitivity of 81%. As with increasingly wider QRS complexes, progressively larger R waves are associated with greater toxicity.[34] QTc interval prolongation is also seen in these patients but is not necessarily indicative of TCA cardiotoxicity or predictive of an impending adverse event.

Numerous studies[35,36] have noted that these and other electrocardiographic abnormalities occur commonly in the TCA-poisoned patient. The authors also point out that, even when these electrocardiographic findings are applied in collective fashion, they demonstrate less-than-reliable sensitivity and specificity for both the diagnosis as well as the occurrence of convulsion or malignant arrhythmia, meaning that the clinician should not employ these criteria alone as the reason to either rule in or rule out TCA poisoning. Baily and colleagues performed a meta-analysis of electrocardiographic prognostic indicators[37] and reported the frequent occurrence of these electrocardiographic abnormalities in the

ill TCA-poisoned patient. Unfortunately, these abnormalities were not entirely predictive of the development of significant end-organ toxicity, with sensitivities and specificities ranging from 69% to 81% and 46% to 69%, respectively.

When these electrocardiographic findings are interpreted within the context of the clinical presentation, they are markedly more powerful. In the TCA-poisoned patient who is fully alert and oriented, sinus tachycardia is an abnormal but nonspecific finding that is not necessarily indicative of impending cardiotoxicity. On the other hand, the same finding in a lethargic TCA-overdosed patient, is a stronger predictor of significant toxicity. If sinus tachycardia is complicated by a widened QRS complex and prominent R wave in lead aVR, the patient's mental status (normal or altered) does not significantly influence interpretation of the ECG: in both scenarios, the patient is at extreme risk of an adverse event.

The 12-lead ECG can be applied in serial fashion as a screening tool in the patient who is asymptomatic at presentation. This use of the ECG in the diagnosis of an asymptomatic patient (ie, fully alert with normal mentation and the absence of tachycardia) can aid the clinician in ruling out significant TCA poisoning. This type of patient can be monitored over a 6-hour period. If serial electrocardiography does not demonstrate tachycardia, QRS-complex widening, terminal QRS-complex rightward axis shift, or QT-interval prolongation, then the patient is unlikely to have significant TCA poisoning.[38]

Other Scenarios

Presentations involving metabolic abnormality, altered mentation, cardiorespiratory arrest, or blunt chest trauma are evaluated with numerous diagnostic studies. In the renal failure patient, hyperkalemia can be diagnosed early, even before serum laboratory test results become available, with the ECG. Obviously, abnormalities of the T wave and/or QRS complex suggest the diagnosis and allow potentially life-saving therapy to be delivered expeditiously. The ECG provides the reason for altered mental status in 7% of patients presenting to the emergency department with abnormal mentation.[39] Patients experiencing cardiorespiratory arrest are managed with the ECG while in active arrest; after resuscitation, the ECG continues to guide therapy; and after stabilization, a 12-lead ECG might yield clues as to the cause of the hemodynamic collapse such as STEMI or PE. Unexplained hypotension in the blunt trauma patient can result from myocardial contusion; the ECG can confirm the diagnosis during the early phase of the trauma evaluation.[40]

LIMITATIONS OF THE ECG

The ECG has numerous limitations when used in the patient suspected of ACS or another acute event. For instance, the adult with chest pain who is ultimately diagnosed with STEMI can demonstrate a normal or minimally abnormal ECG on presentation; the ECG then evolves over minutes to hours into STEMI. In non-ACS scenarios, the initial ECG after TCA ingestion might not reveal pathologic abnormality in a patient with impending toxicity, and the ECG from a patient found to have PE might show nonspecific findings such as sinus tachycardia. These clinical situations demonstrate the importance of having a sound understanding of the ECG's limitations, which will guide emergency physicians in appropriate applications of the 12-lead ECG.

For potential ACS patients, the ECG has additional shortcomings in the following scenarios: "normal" and "nondiagnostic" electrocardiographic presentations; evolving, confounding, and mimicking syndromes; and the "electrocardiographically silent" areas of the heart (eg, isolated acute posterior wall STEMI). The ECG that is diagnostic for acute MI at emergency department presentation is seen in only 50% of patients ultimately diagnosed with acute MI. The remaining patients have ECGs that are entirely normal, nonspecifically abnormal, or clearly abnormal yet without pathologic ST-segment elevation indicative of STEMI. Lee and colleagues[41] reported that a significant portion of emergency department patients suspected of ACS had a normal or minimally abnormal ECG yet were ultimately diagnosed with ACS (4%–20% had unstable angina and 1%-4% had acute MI). Pope and colleagues,[22] in a description of emergency department patients with the missed ACS diagnosis (2.1% unstable angina and 2.3% acute MI), noted a number of factors that could have contributed to the initial incorrect assessment; one was a normal ECG on presentation. Overreliance on a normal or nonspecifically abnormal ECG from a patient with potential ACS who is currently pain free should be avoided. Furthermore, the elapsed time from chest pain onset in patients with these nondiagnostic electrocardiographic patterns does not assist in ruling out the possibility of acute MI with a single ECG.[42]

It is important to understand that the single, initial emergency department ECG is merely a "snapshot" of the status of coronary perfusion and its effect on the myocardium, that is, an electrocardiographic abnormality that suggests ACS. Patients with nondiagnostic ECGs have probably presented during an early phase of their syndrome. ACS is a dynamic, evolving process—it follows that the ECG will change and evolve over time as the syndrome progresses. The history and other clinical data must be relied on heavily in patients with either normal or minimally abnormal ECGs and a convincing description of ischemic chest discomfort; in these patients with reasonable clinical suspicion for ACS, serial ECGs might reduce the initial relatively poor sensitivity for acute MI. Management and disposition decisions must be based on the total clinical picture, not on a nondiagnostic ECG.

A broad range of electrocardiographic abnormalities is encountered in adult emergency department patients with chest pain, some of whom are presenting with ACS while others are experiencing a noncoronary ailment. Certain electrocardiographic syndromes commonly mimic ischemia such as benign early repolarization, acute pericarditis, left ventricular hypertrophy, and bundle-branch block. For instance, ST-segment elevation in an adult with chest pain does not equate with STEMI. In fact, a minority of chest pain patients with ST-segment elevation are diagnosed with STEMI; most of them are ultimately diagnosed with non-STEMI syndromes. This observation has been noted in prehospital, emergency department, and coronary care unit populations.[43-46] A sound, thorough understanding of the various electrocardiographic syndromes encountered in the emergency department is crucial in the initial evaluation and subsequent management of these patients.[47,48] The electrocardiographic abnormalities associated with acute MI can be masked by the altered patterns of ventricular conduction encountered in patients with confounding patterns, including LBBB, ventricular paced rhythm, and left ventricular hypertrophy. These electrocardiographic syndromes produce ST-segment and T-wave changes that are the new "normal" findings in these patients. These electrocardiographic findings can obscure or mimic the typical electrocardiographic findings of ACS, including STEMI. Emergency physicians must approach these patients with the realization that the ECG is of limited diagnostic power. Further diagnostic and management decisions must be made with this caveat in mind.

The limitations of the ECG in ACS patients are well known and reasonably well elucidated in the literature. Other clinical scenarios, as described above in the Clinical Scenarios section, demonstrate similar limitations, ranging from major to minor. For instance, the 12-lead ECG in a patient suspected of having PE offers very little diagnostic information; conversely, the ECG in a patient with hyperkalemia provides evidence of the degree of cardiotoxicity in most instances, whether it demonstrates prominent T waves or QRS-complex abnormalities.

The important issue to consider is the presence of these limitations and their magnitude. With this knowledge in mind, the clinician is able to approach the patient and use the ECG in appropriate fashion.

REFERENCES

1. Benner JP, Borloz MP, Adams M, Brady WJ. The impact of the 12-lead electrocardiogram on emergency department evaluation and management. *Am J Emerg Med.* 2007;25:942-948.
2. Fibrinolytic Therapy Trialists (FTT) Collaborative Group. Indications for thrombolytic therapy in suspected acute myocardial infarction: collaborative overview of early mortality and major morbidity results from all randomized trials of more than 1000 patients. *Lancet.* 1994;343:311-322.

3. Bates ER, Clemmensen PM, Califf RM, et al. Precordial ST-segment depression predicts a worse prognosis in inferior infarction despite reperfusion therapy. *J Am Coll Cardiol.* 1990;16:1538-1544.
4. Willems JL, Willems RJ, Willems GM, et al. Significance of initial ST-segment elevation and depression for the management of thrombolytic therapy in acute myocardial infarction. *Circulation.* 1990;82:1147-1158.
5. Wong C, Freedman B, Bautovich G, et al. Mechanism and significance of precordial ST-segment depression associated with severe narrowing of the dominant right coronary artery. *Am J Cardiol.* 1993;71:1025-1030.
6. Zehender M, Kasper W, Kauder E, et al. Right ventricular infarction as an independent predictor of prognosis after acute inferior myocardial infarction. *N Engl J Med.* 1993;328:981-988.
7. Zehender M, Kasper W, Kauder E, et al. Eligibility for and benefit of thrombolytic therapy in inferior myocardial infarction: focus on the prognostic importance of right ventricular infarction. *J Am Coll Cardiol.* 1994;24:362-369.
8. Edmonds JJ, Gibbons RJ, Bresnahan JF, et al. Significance of anterior ST depression in inferior wall acute myocardial infarction. *Am J Cardiol.* 1994;73:143-148.
9. Wong C, Freedman SB. Precordial ST change and site of the infarct-related lesion in right coronary artery-related inferior wall acute myocardial infarction. *Am J Cardiol.* 1995;75:942-943.
10. Birnbaum Y, Herz I, Sclarovsky S, et al. Prognostic significance of precordial ST-segment depression on admission electrocardiogram in patients with inferior wall myocardial infarction. *J Am Coll Cardiol.* 1996;28:313-318.
11. Peterson ED, Hathaway WR, Zabel KM, et al. Prognostic significance of precordial ST-segment depression during inferior myocardial infarction in the thrombolytic era: results in 16,521 patients. *J Am Coll Cardiol.* 1996;28:305-312.
12. Schroder K, Wegscheider K, Neuhaus KL, et al. Significance of initial ST-segment changes for thrombolytic treatment in first inferior myocardial infarction. *Heart.* 1997;77:506-511.
13. Braunwald E, Mark DB, Jones RH, et al. Unstable angina: diagnosis and management. Rockville MD: Agency for Health Care Policy and Research and the National Heart, Lung, and Blood Institute, US Public Health Service, US Department of Health and Human Services; 1994.
14. Six AJ, Backus BE, Kelder JC. Chest pain in the emergency room: value of the HEART score. *Neth Heart J.* 2008;16:191-196.
15. Backus BE, Six AJ, Kelder JC, et al. A prospective validation of the HEART score for chest pain patients at the emergency department. *Int J Cardiol.* 2013;168:2153-2158.
16. Backus BE, Six AJ, Kelder JC, et al. Chest pain in the emergency room: a multicenter validation of the HEART Score. *Crit Pathw Cardiol.* 2010;9:164-169.
17. O'Connor RE, Al Ali AS, Brady WJ, et al. Part 9: Acute coronary syndromes - 2015 American Heart Association Guidelines Update for Cardiopulmonary Resuscitation and Emergency Cardiovascular Care. *Circulation.* 2015;132:s483-500.
18. Hathaway WR, Peterson ED, Wagner GS, et al. Prognostic significance of the initial electrocardiogram in patients with acute myocardial infarction. *JAMA.* 1998;279(5):387-391.
19. Blomkalns AL, Lindsell CJ, Chandra A, et al. Can electrocardiographic criteria predict adverse cardiac events and positive cardiac markers? *Acad Emerg Med.* 2003;10(3):205-210.
20. Zalenski R, Sloan E, Chen E, et al. The emergency department ECG and immediately life-threatening complications in initially uncomplicated suspected myocardial ischemia. *Ann Emerg Med* 1988;17:221-226.
21. Brush JE, Brand DA, Acamparo D, et al. Use of the initial electrocardiogram to predict in-hospital complications of acute myocardial infarction. *N Engl J Med.* 1985;312:1137-1141.
22. Pope JH, Ruthazer R, Kontos MC, et al. The impact of left ventricular hypertrophy and bundle branch block on the triage and outcome of ED patients with a suspected acute coronary syndrome: a multicenter study. *Am J Emerg Med.* 2004;22(3):156-163.
23. Forest RS, Shofer FS, Sease KL, et al. Assessment of the standardized reporting guidelines ECG classification system: the presenting ECG predicts 30-day outcomes. *Ann Emerg Med.* 2004;44(3):206-212.
24. McGinn S, White PD. Acute cor pulmonale resulting from pulmonary embolism. *JAMA.* 1935;104:1473.
25. Ullman E, Brady WJ, Perron AD, et al. Electrocardiographic manifestations of pulmonary embolism. *Am J Emerg Med.* 2001;19(6):514-519.
26. Petruzzelli S, Palla A, Pieraccini F, et al. Routine electrocardiography in screening for pulmonary embolism. *Respiration.* 1986;50(4):233-243.
27. Panos RJ, Barish RA, Whye DW, et al. The electrocardiographic manifestations of pulmonary embolism. *J Emerg Med.* 1988;6(4):301-307.

28. Martin TP, Hanusa BH, Kapoor WN. Risk stratification of patients with syncope. *Ann Emerg Med.* 1997;29(4):459-466.
29. Sarasin FP, Hanusa BH, Perneger T, et al. A risk score to predict arrhythmias in patients with unexplained syncope. *Acad Emerg Med.* 2003;10(12):1312-1317.
30. Quinn JV, Stiell IG, McDermott DA, et al. Derivation of the San Francisco Syncope Rule to predict patients with short-term serious outcomes. *Ann Emerg Med.* 2004;43(2):224-232.
31. Homer A, Brady WJ, Holstege C. The Association of Toxins and ECG Abnormality in Poisoned Patients. Presented at the Mediterranean Emergency Medicine Congress, Nice, France, September 2005.
32. Boehnert MT, Lovejoy FH. Value of the QRS complex duration versus the serum drug level in predicting seizures and ventricular arrhythmias after an acute overdose of tricyclic antidepressants. *New Engl J Med.* 1985;313(8):474-479.
33. Foulke GE, Albertson TE. QRS interval in tricyclic antidepressant overdose: inaccuracy as a toxicity indicator in emergency settings. *Ann Emerg Med.* 1987;16(2):160-163.
34. Liebelt EL, Francis PD, Woolf AD. ECG lead aVr versus QRS interval in predicting seizures and arrhythmias in acute tricyclic antidepressant toxicity. *Ann Emerg Med.* 1995;26(2):195-201.
35. Lavoie FW, Gansert GG, Weiss RE. Value of initial ECG findings and plasma drug levels in cyclic antidepressant overdose. *Ann Emerg Med.* 1990;19(6):696-700.
36. Buckley NA, Chevalier S, Leditschke IA, et al. The limited utility of electrocardiography variables used to predict arrhythmia in psychotropic drug overdose. *Crit Care.* 2003;7(5):R101-R107.
37. Bailey B, Buckley NA, Amre DK. A meta-analysis of prognostic indicators to predict seizures, arrhythmias or death after tricyclic antidepressant overdose. *J Toxicol Clin Toxicol.* 2004;42(6):877-888.
38. Banahan BF Jr, Schelkun PH. Tricyclic antidepressant overdose: conservative management in a community hospital with cost-saving implications. *J Emerg Med.* 1990;8(4):451-458.
39. Kanich W, Brady WJ, Huff JS, et al. Altered mental status: evaluation and etiology in the emergency department. *Am J Emerg Med.* 2002;20(7):613-617.
40. Plautz C, Perron AD, Brady WJ. Electrocardiographic ST-segment elevation in the trauma patient: acute myocardial infarction vs myocardial contusion. *Am J Emerg Med.* 2005;23(4):510-506.
41. Lee TH, Rouan GW, Weisberg MC, et al. Clinical characteristics and natural history of patients with acute myocardial infarction sent home from the emergency room. *Am J Cardiol.* 1987;60(4):219-224.
42. Singer AJ, Brogan GX, Valentine SM, et al. Effect of duration from symptom onset on the negative predictive value of a normal ECG for exclusion of acute myocardial infarction. *Ann Emerg Med.* 1997;29(5):575-582.
43. Otto LA, Aufderheide TP. Evaluation of ST segment elevation criteria for the prehospital electrocardiographic diagnosis of acute myocardial infarction. *Ann Emerg Med.* 1994;23(1):17-24.
44. Brady WJ, Syverud SA, Beagle C, et al. Electrocardiographic ST-segment elevation: the diagnosis of AMI by morphologic analysis of the ST segment. *Acad Emerg Med.* 2001;8(10):961-967.
45. Brady WJ, Perron AD, Martin ML, et al: Cause of ST segment abnormality in ED chest pain patients. *Am J Emerg Med.* 2001;19(1):25-28.
46. Miller DH, Kligfield P, Schreiber TL, et al. Relationship of prior myocardial infarction to false-positive electrocardiographic diagnosis of acute injury in patents with chest pain. *Arch Intern Med.* 1987;147(2):257-261.
47. Michelson EA, Brady WJ: Emergency physician interpretation of the electrocardiogram. *Acad Emerg Med.* 2002;9(4):317-319.
48. Brady WJ, O'Connor RE. Interpretation of the electrocardiogram: clinical correlation suggested. *Eur Heart J.* 2008;29(1):1-3.

CHAPTER TWO

Intraventricular Conduction Abnormalities

RICHARD A. HARRIGAN

KEY POINTS

- All complete bundle-branch block patterns feature QRS complexes with a duration of more than 0.12 second.
- Bundle-branch block typically features discordant ST-T-wave changes, meaning that the ST segment and T wave are directed opposite the major polarity of the QRS complex. In leads with positive QRS complexes, ST-segment depression and T-wave inversion are expected, and in leads with a primarily negative QRS complex, ST-segment elevation and an upright T wave are anticipated.
- Right bundle-branch block typically has an rSR' complex in leads V_1 and V_2; qR and notched R complex variants can occur.
- Signs of incomplete right bundle-branch block might result from incorrect positioning of leads V_1 and V_2.
- Left bundle-branch block might not show the characteristic slurred monophasic R wave in all lateral leads.
- The PR interval is used to differentiate incomplete left bundle-branch block from Wolff-Parkinson-White syndrome.
- Right bundle-branch block plus left anterior fascicular block is the most common bifascicular block.
- Left posterior fascicular block is rare and resembles right ventricular hypertrophy on the ECG.
- Intraventricular conduction delay is at times a benign electrocardiographic finding but is also seen with more important entities such as hyperkalemia, hypothermia, and preexcitation syndromes. Beware of the computerized interpretation "nonspecific intraventricular conduction delay."

Recognizing the electrocardiographic manifestations of intraventricular conduction abnormalities begins with an understanding of the basics of cardiac impulse conduction and the realization that a delay in a phase of the conduction sequence will lead to a lengthening, and distortion, of the corresponding portion of the waveform. Normally, the cardiac impulse begins at the sinoatrial node and then depolarizes the atria (right before left); on the surface ECG, this event is manifested by the P wave. Internodal fibers connect the sinoatrial node to the atrioventricular node, which serves as the gateway to the ventricles. Impulse conduction to the atrioventricular node, passing through the atrial tissues, is represented by the PR interval (which includes the P wave and the PR segment).

Ventricular activation, or depolarization, is represented on the ECG by the QRS complex.[1] Abnormalities of conduction within the ventricle, referred to as intraventricular conduction abnormalities, are manifested by anomalies of this complex. The Q wave represents septal depolarization, while the R and S waves represent the main and terminal phases of ventricular wall depolarization, respectively. Thus, a delay in impulse conduction down a part of the bundle-branch system will lead to

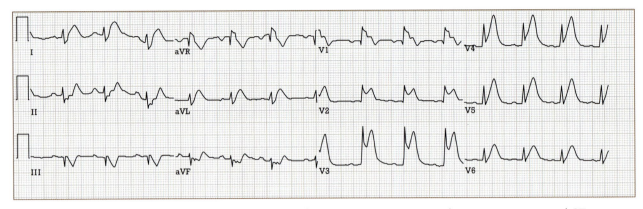

FIGURE 2.1. Acute MI in a patient with RBBB. One of the keys to recognizing the acute anteroseptal ST-segment elevation MI on this ECG is being comfortable with the appearance of RBBB at baseline. Note the qR pattern (with a notched R wave) in lead V_1 and the relatively deep, widened S wave in leads I and aVL—consistent with RBBB. However, the ST segment rapidly elevates across the precordium (V_1 through V_6), with bulky T waves evident in leads V_4, V_5, I, and aVL, signaling an injury current. During cardiac catheterization, this patient was found to have left anterior descending coronary artery occlusion.

a partial delay in ventricular activation; the impulse will reach the ventricles via the bundle branches at different times, leading to their asynchronous activation. Normally, the ventricles depolarize simultaneously, with the dominant left ventricle overshadowing the smaller right ventricle as the QRS waveform is generated. In bundle-branch block, the affected ventricle depolarizes after the unaffected ventricle. It follows that the cardinal manifestation of any complete bundle-branch block would be both widening and distortion of the QRS complex. It also makes interpretation of the ECG more difficult, demanding a working knowledge of the expected changes of bundle-branch block to recognize abnormalities such as acute cardiac ischemia (Figure 2.1).

All intraventricular conduction abnormalities feature widening and distortion of the QRS complex; the degree of widening and the variations in distortion make the various abnormalities distinct. Bundle-branch blocks are the widest and are of two varieties: right and left. Fascicular blocks, previously referred to as hemiblocks, do not significantly prolong the QRS complex duration but are important because they can cause changes that mimic previous infarction and, in certain circumstances, identify patients at greater risk of acute decompensation. Because the left bundle branch splits into two fascicles, two fascicular blocks are possible: the more common left anterior and the relatively rare left posterior. Finally, ventricular conduction can be delayed in ways that do not meet the morphologic criteria of the four major intraventricular conduction abnormalities described above. They are classified as nonspecific intraventricular conduction delays.

Any intraventricular conduction abnormality on the ECG must be recognized and interpreted with consideration of the individual patient's circumstances. An intraventricular conduction abnormality can signal a new or important disease process. The presence of these abnormalities also makes interpretation of the ECG more difficult because clinicians must be comfortable with how an intraventricular conduction abnormality "normally" manifests so as to recognize pathologic changes (eg, identifying acute cardiac ischemia, injury, or infarction in the presence of a bundle-branch block) (Figure 2.1). The causes of intraventricular conduction abnormalities are myriad[1,2] (Table 2.1) and should be considered in medical decision-making.

BUNDLE-BRANCH BLOCKS

The normal QRS complex seen in the precordial leads results from initial depolarization of the septum from left to right and subsequent depolarization of the left ventricle from right to left (overshadowing the smaller right ventricle). Consider the two precordial electrodes, V_1 and V_6, as being essentially opposite each other (in the horizontal plane) in a vector representation of ventricular depolarization. Also remember that a waveform (eg, a Q, an R, or an S wave) is positive if the depolarization vector is coming toward that electrode. Lead V_1, the right chest lead, demonstrates a small R wave followed by a large S wave. Lead V_6, the left chest lead, demonstrates a small initial Q wave (termed a "septal" Q wave) followed by a large R wave.

Bundle-branch block should be considered whenever the QRS complex exceeds 0.12 second; moreover, there are pathologic triggers to consider when scanning the ECG for an intraventricular conduction abnormality (Table 2.1).

Right Bundle-Branch Block

In right bundle-branch block (RBBB), the septum depolarizes normally, from left to right, but the time of depolarization is prolonged. Next, left ventricular depolarization proceeds relatively normally, but the resultant wave is diminished by prolonged septal depolarization in the opposite direction. The right ventricle then depolarizes, delayed and unopposed. In lead V_1, this depolarization pattern generates a normal, initial, small R wave; a subsequent S wave that can be small or even absent if significantly diminished; and a terminal R' wave. In lead V_6, there is a small initial Q wave from the septum, with a significant R wave caused by the proximity of the left ventricle to the electrode, followed by a wide S wave from delayed depolarization of the right ventricle. Recognition of a dominant R wave in lead V_1 should prompt consideration of RBBB, although other entities are associated with this phenomenon of "R>S wave amplitude in V_1" (Table 2.2). The key morphologic changes in RBBB therefore are: the appearance of a widened QRS complex (>0.12 sec), usually with an rSR' pattern in the right precordial leads (V_1 and V_2), and a prominent, wide S wave in the left precordial leads (V_5 and V_6). See Table 2.3 for the electrocardiographic criteria for RBBB (Figure 2.2)

In addition to the classic "rabbit ear" rSR' pattern, lead V_1 can demonstrate a "qR" pattern (Figure 2.3). The qR variant of RBBB should be differentiated from a qR complex in V_1 signaling right ventricular hypertrophy. Although the ECG is not sensitive for the latter, other findings such as right QRS axis deviation of more than 110°, right atrial

TABLE 2.1. Causes of intraventricular conduction abnormalities.[1,2]
Atherosclerotic heart disease
Congenital heart disease
Connective tissue disease (eg, scleroderma)
Electrolyte abnormalities (eg, hyperkalemia)
Fibrotic heart disease (eg, Lev syndrome, Lenègre syndrome)
Iatrogenic (eg, right heart catheterization/RBBB)
Infectious disease (eg, Lyme disease, Chagas disease, myocarditis)
Infiltrative cardiomyopathy (eg, sarcoidosis, hemochromatosis, amyloidosis)
Normal variant
Pulmonary embolism
Toxicologic (eg, sodium channel blocker toxicity)

TABLE 2.2. Causes of R-wave amplitude greater than S-wave amplitude in lead V_1.
Duchenne-type pseudohypertrophic muscular dystrophy
Hypertrophic cardiomyopathy
Normal variant (especially children and adolescents)
Pulmonary hypertension
Right bundle-branch block
Right ventricular hypertrophy
True posterior MI
Wolff-Parkinson-White syndrome

enlargement, S wave larger than 0.7 mV in lead V_6, and an R:S ratio of less than 1 in V_5 or V_6 all favor right ventricular hypertrophy. Alternatively, RBBB could appear as a notched R wave in the right precordial leads. In these cases, the S wave has been reduced to a mere hitch in the ascending limb of the R wave[1,3] (Figure 2.4).

It is important to recognize the ST-segment and T-wave changes that are a normal consequence of RBBB. These "expected abnormalities" occur in the right precordial leads with primarily positive QRS complexes (V_1 to V_3). In these leads, repolarization changes result in ST segments and T waves that are opposite to (discordant with) the overall direction of the QRS—in other words, ST-segment depression with T-wave inversion. Any ST-segment elevation in these leads, however slight, could suggest acute myocardial injury (Figures 2.1, 2.5). The ST segments in other leads are largely unaffected by RBBB, and any deviations should be assessed as usual. Importantly, RBBB does not reduce the ECG's ability to demonstrate abnormalities indicative of acute coronary syndrome.

ECGs that demonstrate the morphologic changes of RBBB yet do not feature a QRS complex width of more than 0.12 second are classified as having *incomplete RBBB* or *right-sided conduction delay* (Figure 2.6). Incomplete RBBB is a relatively

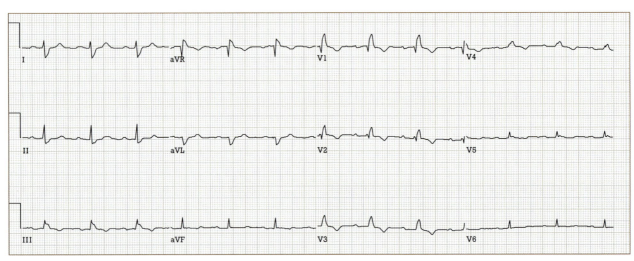

FIGURE 2.2. RBBB. This tracing features the rSR' and discordant (principally downward deflection of the) ST-T-wave complex classic for RBBB. The rSR' is more obvious in lead V_2 than in lead V_1, which is at times the case. The relatively deep and wide S waves appearing in leads I and/or V_6 are also typical of RBBB.

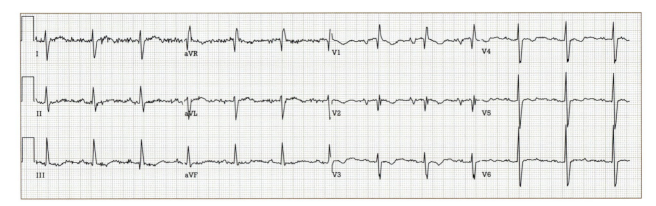

FIGURE 2.3. RBBB—qR variant. RBBB can appear without the characteristic rSR' in lead V_1. In this tracing, there is a qR complex in lead V_1. Note the discordant ST-T complex in the right-sided precordial leads and the deep, wide S wave laterally (both classic for RBBB).

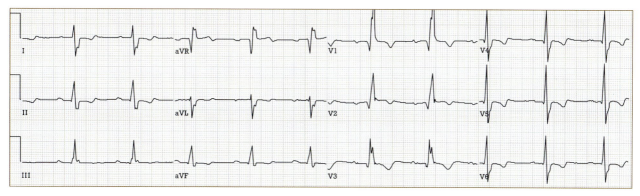

FIGURE 2.4. RBBB—notched R-wave variant. RBBB can present as a notched R wave in lead V_1 rather than the classic rSR'. The notched R wave might or might not have a preceding q wave (in this tracing, the q wave is evident). Note the discordant ST-T complex in the right-sided precordial leads (which in this case continues across the precordium) and the deep, wide S wave laterally (both classic for RBBB). Although the R-wave amplitude in lead V_1 exceeds 7 mm, suggesting right ventricular hypertrophy, echocardiography did not demonstrate that entity in this patient, providing evidence that the ECG is not specific for right ventricular hypertrophy.

common and benign finding in children and young adults. Liao and colleagues[4] found middle-aged men with incomplete RBBB to be roughly seven times more likely to develop complete RBBB over 11 years of follow-up; however, 95% of patients found to have incomplete RBBB did not progress to complete RBBB during that time. Incomplete RBBB might also arise as an artifact if the precordial leads V_1 and V_2 are inadvertently placed one interspace too high on the chest.[5]

TABLE 2.3. Electrocardiographic criteria for RBBB.

QRS complex >0.12 sec
Abnormal QRS morphology in right precordial leads (V_1, V_2)
rSR' / rsr' / RsR' wave ("rabbit ear" or "M-shaped" QRS complex)
qR variant
Single R-wave variant (wide and notched)
Deep, wide S wave in left precordial leads (V_5, V_6) and possibly left-sided leads I and aVL
Late intrinsicoid deflection (time to peak of R wave) in lead V_1 (>0.05 sec)

Left Bundle-Branch Block

In left bundle-branch block (LBBB), septal depolarization is delayed and proceeds abnormally from right to left. Ventricular wall depolarization is also delayed but proceeds in the normal right-to-left direction. The right-to-left depolarizations of both the septum and the ventricular free wall generate wide and primarily monophasic QRS complexes in LBBB—a QS wave in lead V_1 and a monophasic R wave in lead V_6 (Figure 2.7). Large negative QRS complexes in leads V_1, V_2, or V_3 are seen in only a few conditions (Table 2.4). The key morphologic findings with LBBB are a wide, slurred R wave in the left-sided leads (some combination of I, aVL, V_5, and V_6) as well as a QS (single negative deflection)

TABLE 2.4. Differential diagnosis of large-amplitude negative QS or rS complexes in leads V1 and V2 (right precordial leads).

Athlete's heart
LBBB
Left ventricular hypertrophy
Right ventricular paced rhythm
Ventricular tachycardia

or an rS complex in the right precordial leads (V₁ and V₂). Also characteristic of LBBB is the absence of the customary "septal" q wave in lead V₆. Since this q wave results from normal left-to-right septal depolarization (thus a negative, or rightward, spike in this left precordial lead), which is lost with LBBB, V₆ will demonstrate only an initial R wave in uncomplicated LBBB. The electrocardiographic criteria for LBBB are listed in Table 2.5.

Variations of this typical pattern can occur. For example, the slurred monophasic R wave in V₅ and occasionally V₆ might be absent but will typically be present in leads I and aVL. Left QRS axis deviation is not a prerequisite for diagnosis of LBBB but can occur with it (Figure 2.8); in fact, the axis is more often normal in LBBB. It has been suggested that such a finding, especially if the axis is quite superior (leftward and more toward −90°), suggests LBBB

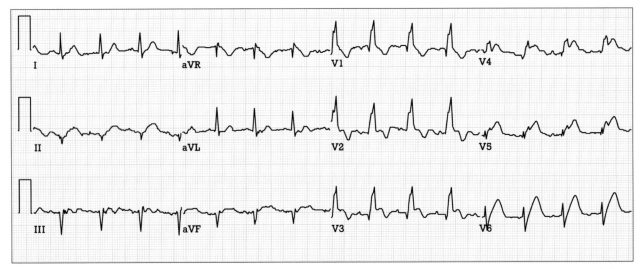

FIGURE 2.5. STEMI with RBBB. The qR variant of RBBB is present here. ST-segment elevation is somewhat subtle in leads V1 and V2; however, it is more noticeable in leads V3 and V4 and extends across the precordial leads. ST-segment elevation is even seen in lead II, the most leftward of the inferior leads, suggesting left anterior descending artery occlusion in a vessel responsible for significant myocardial territory.

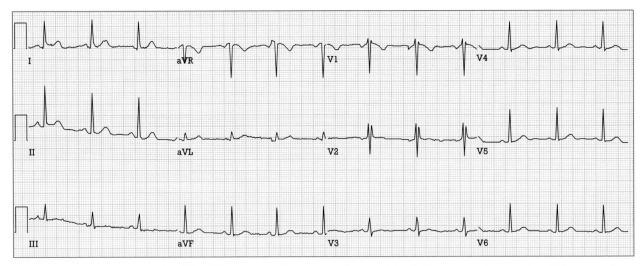

FIGURE 2.6. Incomplete RBBB. The QRS complex is less than the requisite 0.12 sec, so, despite the rSR' morphology in leads V₁ and V₂, this is merely an incomplete RBBB or right-sided conduction delay. At times, incomplete RBBB will show discordant ST-T complexes and a significant left-sided S wave as well.

with a preexisting or coincident left anterior fascicular block.[6] Other clinicians have found that patients with LBBB plus left-axis deviation are more likely to have organic heart disease than those with LBBB and a normal QRS axis.[1,7]

It is important to recognize the expected ST-segment changes that occur with LBBB. ST-segment deviation is opposite to (discordant with) the predominant direction of the QRS complex. Therefore, in leads with a predominantly positive QRS complex, the ST segments (and T waves) are isoelectric or depressed. In leads with a predominantly negative QRS complex, the ST segments are isoelectric or elevated (Figure 2.7). Only the transition leads, in which the overall QRS complex is neutral, do not necessarily follow this pattern. Deviations from this expected pattern of ST-segment change can suggest acute myocardial

TABLE 2.5. Electrocardiographic criteria for LBBB.

QRS complex >0.12 sec

Abnormal QRS morphology in left precordial leads (V_5, V_6) and/or left limb leads (I, aVL)

    Monophasic, slurred, or notched R wave

    Absence of septal q wave (although can be seen in aVL)

    QS or rS pattern in right precordial leads (V_1, V_2)

    Late intrinsicoid deflection (or time to peak of R wave) in V_5 and V_6 (0.06 sec)

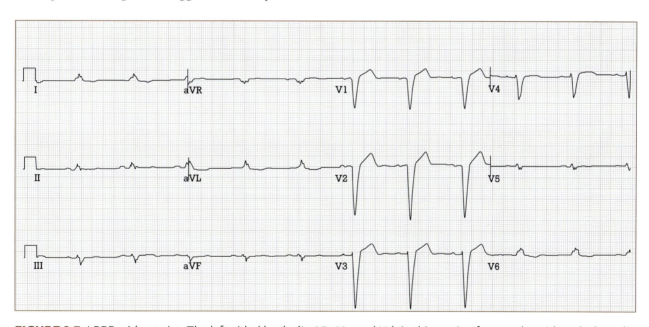

FIGURE 2.7. LBBB with a twist. The left-sided leads (I, aVL, V_5, and V_6) in this tracing feature the widened, slurred R wave seen in LBBB, as well as the discordant (principally downward deflection of the) ST-T-wave complex classic for LBBB, although these ST-T-wave findings are subtle. There is a good reason for this: the tracing has been recorded at "half standard." Note the vertical box to the far left of the tracing, immediately preceding leads I, II, and III. It is only 5 mm in height, as opposed to the customary 10 mm, signaling that all complexes are half the expected amplitude and thus the ST-segment changes are minimized. The computer within the electrocardiograph does this automatically, at times, to enable large-amplitude QRS complexes to be reasonably displayed on the tracing (most commonly seen in tracings with extreme left ventricular voltage and in LBBB). The clinician must note when tracings are "half standard" because when comparing them with tracings that are "full standard," the ST-T changes will be relatively but predictably different. The deep and wide S waves following the small r waves in leads V_1 and V_2 are also typical of LBBB. Note the absence of septal q waves in the left-sided leads.

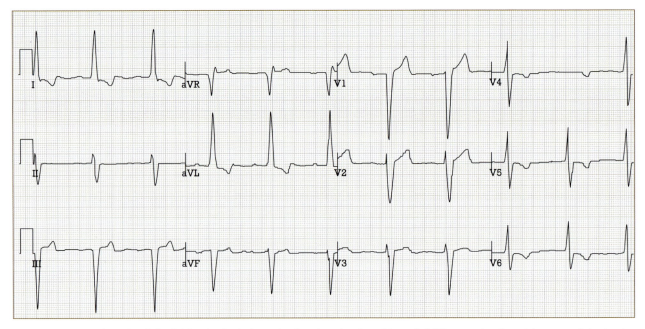

FIGURE 2.8. LBBB plus left QRS axis deviation. Again, the classic widened QRS complex is evident, upright in the left-sided leads (I, aVL, V$_5$, and V$_6$), although the characteristic LBBB morphology is more obvious in leads I and aVL than in leads V$_5$ and V$_6$. Note that these leads do not demonstrate an initial q wave. The right-sided precordial leads (and indeed all the way through lead V$_4$ in this case) show the rS pattern typical of LBBB. The ST-T-wave complexes are appropriately discordant in the affected leads. Lastly, there is left QRS axis deviation (roughly −50°). A pseudoinfarction pattern is evident on this tracing. The left-axis deviation can be mistaken for an age-indeterminate inferior infarction, in that leads III and aVF mimic QS complexes (yet there is a small r wave preceding the downward deflection, so this presentation is not truly consistent with an age-indeterminate inferior infarction).

ischemia (see Chapter 6) in the appropriate clinical presentation. Importantly, the ability of the ECG to identify changes of acute coronary syndrome in the setting of LBBB is significantly reduced. An ECG from a patient with LBBB and suspected acute coronary syndrome should be interpreted with consideration of the modified Sgarbossa rule.[11,12]

ECGs that demonstrate the morphologic changes of LBBB yet do not feature a QRS complex width larger than 0.12 second are classified as having *incomplete LBBB* or left-sided conduction delay (Figure 2.9). This finding can be difficult to distinguish from Wolff-Parkinson-White (WPW) syndrome (type B—no prominent R wave in lead V$_1$). This difficulty is not surprising, considering the pathophysiology. In incomplete LBBB, the left ventricle is activated in a delayed fashion; in type B WPW syndrome, the right ventricle is preexcited. A shortened PR interval favors the latter diagnosis, whereas a normal PR segment is more consistent with incomplete LBBB (or the relatively rare normal PR variant of WPW syndrome).[8] Consideration of the PR interval can aid in this identification, with shortening of the PR interval occurring in WPW syndrome. Clinical correlation with the patient's presentation can assist in the electrocardiographic distinction between incomplete LBBB and WPW type B pattern.

FASCICULAR BLOCKS

The left bundle branch divides into two fascicles soon after it arises from the bundle of His. The left anterior fascicle courses toward the anterior-superior papillary muscle, and the left posterior fascicle runs toward the posterior-inferior papillary muscle. In the past, conduction delay in these fascicles was referred to as left anterior or left posterior hemiblock; the term *fascicular block* is now

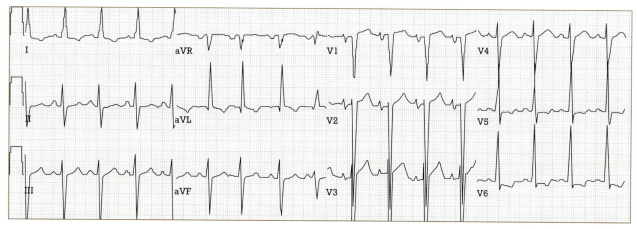

FIGURE 2.9. Incomplete LBBB. This tracing does not show complete LBBB, because the QRS complex is not wider than 0.12 sec. The ST-T-wave changes seen in leads I, aVL, V₅, and V₆ should invoke the differential diagnosis of incomplete LBBB, left ventricular hypertrophy with repolarization abnormality, and coronary ischemia. The delayed intrinsicoid deflection (time to peak height of the R wave) in the left-sided leads—a feature of incomplete LBBB—bears a resemblance to the slurred upstroke of the QRS complex (the delta wave) of WPW syndrome. Note, however, that the PR interval is not less than 0.12 sec, as would be expected in patients with WPW syndrome.

used more commonly. Compared with complete bundle-branch blocks, fascicular blocks are less often of vital clinical significance to emergency physicians, but they should be recognized to avoid misinterpretation of associated electrocardiographic findings. The emergency physician must realize, however, that the presence of a fascicular block does increase the chance of more pronounced conduction abnormality, particularly in acute presentations such as MI.

Left Anterior Fascicular Block

This intraventricular conduction abnormality is the more common of the two fascicular blocks, owing to the more delicate nature of the left anterior fascicle. Delayed conduction down this fascicle means that the left ventricle is depolarized in an asynchronous fashion. The anterior fascicle activates the anterior and lateral walls of the left ventricle. In left anterior fascicular block, this means the depolarization wave courses from an inferoposterior region (the posterior fascicle's territory) in an anterolateral direction.[1] Therefore, the inferior leads show an initial upward deflection followed by a larger downward deflection, as depolarization spreads first in an inferoposterior direction (along the left posterior fascicle and toward the inferior leads) and then subsequently toward the anterior and lateral walls of the left ventricle (and toward the lateral leads and away from the inferior leads). This depolarization pattern should shift the overall QRS axis leftward. These concepts should be kept in mind when reviewing the criteria for left anterior fascicular block (Table 2.6).

The trigger for recognition of a left anterior fascicular block is leftward QRS complex axis deviation, which is a criterion for the electrocardiographic diagnosis of left anterior fascicular block.

TABLE 2.6. Electrocardiographic criteria for left anterior fascicular block.
Left QRS axis deviation (generally considered to be >−45°)
Slightly widened QRS complex (but <0.12 sec unless coincident RBBB)
rS pattern in the inferior leads (II, III, and aVF)
qR pattern in the lateral limb leads (I and aVL)
Delayed intrinsicoid deflection in lead aVL (>0.045 sec)

The degree of left axis deviation necessary for left anterior fascicular block is debatable. In fact, the concept that some number serves as the criterion threshold between those with and those without left anterior fascicular block does not make clinical sense. It is generally accepted that the degree of deviation should exceed −45°, although a more liberal definition would begin at −30°.[1]

Once left axis deviation is noted, the next step focuses on analysis of the limb leads, not the precordial leads. QRS complex morphologic changes include an rS (small r, deep S wave) pattern inferiorly (leads II, III, and aVF) and a qR (small-to-absent q, tall R wave) in the lateral leads (I and aVL).

A key result of the presence of left anterior fascicular block is poor precordial R-wave progression, or displacement of the transition zone (where R equals S in amplitude, as one moves across the precordium from right to left). This pattern can mimic age-indeterminate anteroseptal MI (Figure 2.10). The strong shift in the lateral direction of ventricular depolarization forces also causes the R wave in lead aVL to be bigger than normal. Thus, left ventricular hypertrophy should not be diagnosed by aVL R-wave amplitude (>11 mm) in the presence of left anterior fascicular block.[1]

Although left anterior fascicular block is the most common intraventricular conduction abnormality seen in acute MI, isolated left anterior fascicular block has been found in only 4% of acute MIs. Left anterior fascicular block is also associated with:

- hypertensive heart disease,
- aortic valvular disease,
- cardiomyopathy, and
- degenerative disease of the cardiac conduction system.[1,3]

Left Posterior Fascicular Block

This entity is relatively rare, owing to the dual blood supply of the left posterior fascicle. The posterior fascicle activates the inferior and posterior walls of the left ventricle. Delayed conduction along this fascicle means the left ventricle is again depolarized in an asynchronous fashion. In left posterior fascicular block, the depolarization wave spreads from the anterolateral region (the domain of the left anterior fascicle) in an inferoposterior direction.[1] The electrocardiographic findings are perhaps best remembered as the "opposite" of left anterior fascicular block. The lateral limb leads (I and aVL) show an initial upward deflection followed by a larger downward deflection, as depolarization

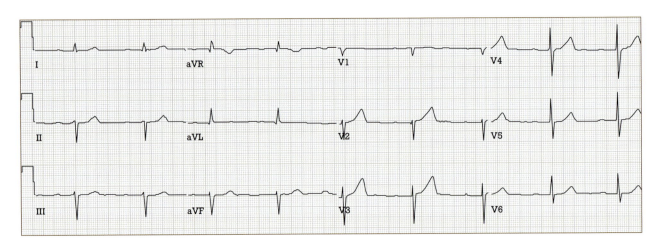

FIGURE 2.10. Left anterior fascicular block. The ECG trigger is the leftward deviation of the QRS axis in the frontal plane, here seen to be approximately −75° degrees. The rS pattern inferiorly (leads II, III, and aVF) and the qR pattern laterally (leads I and especially aVL) are part of the electrocardiographic definition of left anterior fascicular block. The poor R-wave progression across the precordium simulates age-indeterminate anteroseptal MI.

spreads first in an anterolateral direction (along the left anterior fascicle and toward the lateral leads) and then subsequently toward the inferior and posterior walls of the left ventricle (and toward the inferior leads [II, III, and aVF] and away from the lateral leads). This should shift the overall QRS axis rightward. These concepts should be kept in mind when reviewing the criteria for left posterior fascicular block (Table 2.7).

Just as the trigger to look for left anterior fascicular block is a left QRS axis deviation, the key with its "opposite," left posterior fascicular block, is the presence of a rightward QRS axis deviation—between +90° and +180°. The key morphologic changes include this rightward QRS complex axis deviation plus an rS (small r, deep S wave) pattern laterally (I and aVL) and a qR (small-to-absent q, tall R wave) inferiorly (III and perhaps II and aVF). As with left anterior fascicular block, left posterior fascicular block is defined by findings in the limb leads, not the precordial leads. Again, the precordial transition zone can be displaced to the left as the left ventricle is activated sequentially, simulating an age-indeterminate anteroseptal MI (Figure 2.11).

TABLE 2.7. Electrocardiographic criteria for left posterior fascicular block.

Right QRS axis deviation (between +90° and +180°; usually >+120°)

Slightly widened QRS complex (but <0.12 sec, unless coincident RBBB)

qR pattern in lead III; q waves might or might not be present in leads II and aVF

rS pattern in the lateral limb leads (I and aVL)

Right QRS complex axis deviation—the trigger to look for left posterior fascicular block—is itself rather rare, and there are other more common causes of this abnormality. The differential diagnosis includes:

- right ventricular hypertrophy,
- lateral wall MI (indicated by large Q waves in leads I and aVL),
- dextrocardia,
- ventricular tachycardia,

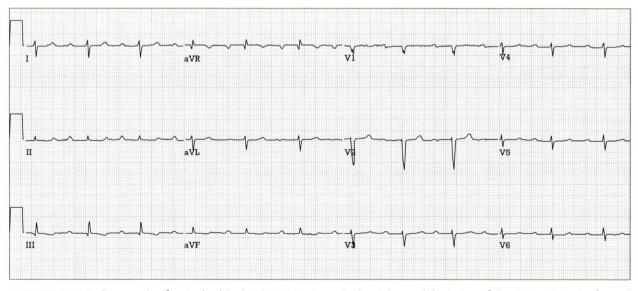

FIGURE 2.11. Left posterior fascicular block. The ECG trigger is the rightward deviation of the QRS axis in the frontal plane, here seen to be approximately +130°. The rS wave laterally (leads I and aVL) and the qR pattern inferiorly (best seen in lead III) are typical of left posterior fascicular block. It is difficult to discern if there has been a prior anteroseptal MI or if the poor R-wave progression is a result of the fascicular block. An echocardiogram looking for wall motion abnormality would be helpful in this regard and in excluding right ventricular hypertrophy as a cause of right axis deviation. A first-degree atrioventricular block is evident as well.

- limb electrode misconnection, and
- pulmonary disease (including acute pulmonary embolism as well as other diseases that could increase pressure in the pulmonary circuit such as chronic obstructive pulmonary disease and primary pulmonary hypertension).

Right axis deviation can be a normal finding in younger populations. Overdose with cyclic antidepressants and other sodium channel blocking agents can also cause a rightward shift in the QRS complex axis, particularly the terminal portion. Although the key to recognizing this toxicologic entity is a large R wave in lead aVR with or without widening of the QRS complex,[9] a deep S wave can emerge in lead I as well, causing a rightward shift in the QRS axis, if the S wave exceeds the amplitude of the R wave in lead I and the major QRS vector in lead aVF remains upright. This R wave in lead aVR and S wave in lead I are manifestations of terminal QRS complex right axis deviation.

Left posterior fascicular block is the least likely intraventricular conduction abnormality to be found in acute MI. It is associated with hypertensive heart disease, aortic valvular disease, and fibrotic changes of the heart. It is seldom seen in isolation, commonly occurring with coexistent RBBB[1,3] (Figure 2.12).

Multifascicular Blocks

Multifascicular block occurs when more than one fascicle is dysfunctional. By definition, a bifascicular block involves a conduction delay in two fascicles, and a trifascicular block involves three. Definitive diagnosis of the latter requires that recordings be made from the bundle of His.[1] Left bundle-branch block can be thought of as a bifascicular block if the conduction delay occurs in both the anterior and posterior fascicles; it can be considered a unifascicular block if the delay is more proximal.[1,3] Right bundle-branch block occurring with left anterior fascicular block is the most common type of bifascicular block (Figure 2.13), whereas RBBB plus left posterior fascicular block—although more common than left posterior fascicular block alone—is the rarest. In one series of 277 patients with bifascicular block, 196 had RBBB plus left anterior fascicular block, 60 had LBBB, and 21 had RBBB with left posterior fascicular block. Multifascicular block is a marker of advanced disease of the cardiac conduction system and is associated with higher rates of sudden cardiac death over time.[1,3,10]

The electrocardiographic diagnosis of bifascicular block is based on the individual criteria for RBBB, left anterior fascicular block, and left posterior fascicular block. As with unifascicular blocks (left anterior and left posterior fascicular blocks), recognition

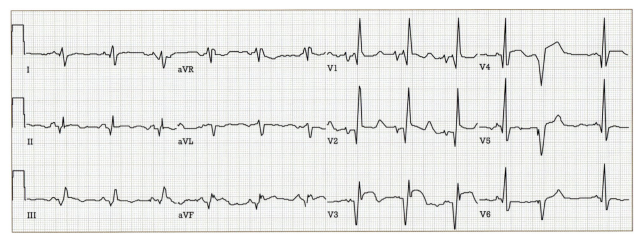

FIGURE 2.12. Left posterior fascicular block plus RBBB. This is a relatively uncommon bifascicular block. Note the rightward axis—a cue to look for left posterior fascicular block. Notice also the ST-segment elevation MI manifesting anteriorly. On cardiac catheterization, this patient was found to have critical stenosis of the left anterior descending artery.

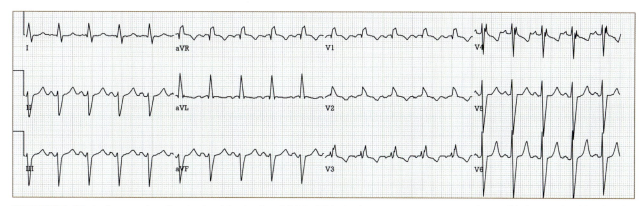

FIGURE 2.13. Left anterior fascicular block plus RBBB. This is the most common variety of bifascicular block. The trigger is to see RBBB morphology together with left QRS axis deviation, here between −60° and −90°. The criteria for left anterior fascicular block are also met (rS wave inferiorly; qR wave in lead aVL).

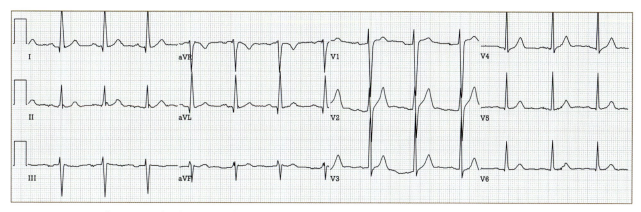

FIGURE 2.14. Left ventricular hypertrophy with QRS widening. Voltage criteria for left ventricular hypertrophy are met in this tracing (ie, the R wave amplitude in lead aVL exceeds 11 mm). Yet there is also QRS complex widening, which can be seen in left ventricular hypertrophy. Here, QRS duration is just shy of 120 milliseconds.

of axis deviation in the setting of RBBB is vital. Remember that the anticipated QRS complex axis is normal with RBBB; therefore, left or right axis deviation in the patient with RBBB can indicate an abnormality such as bifascicular block.

NONSPECIFIC INTRAVENTRICULAR CONDUCTION DELAY

When the QRS complex duration exceeds 0.11 second yet the criteria for LBBB or RBBB are not met, a nonspecific intraventricular conduction delay exists.[1] This entity might be encountered as is, or it could manifest secondarily to a disease process or syndrome. Nonspecific widening of the QRS complex can also be seen with anything that delays ventricular depolarization such as left ventricular hypertrophy with QRS complex widening (Figure 2.14), functioning artificial cardiac pacemaker with isoelectric (ie, undetectable) spikes, preexcitation syndromes (eg, WPW syndrome), ventricular tachycardia, hypothermia, hyperkalemia, and sodium channel blocker poisoning.

REFERENCES

1. Surawicz B, Knilans TK, eds. *Chou's Electrocardiography in Clinical Practice: Adult and Pediatric.* 6th ed. Philadelphia, PA: WB Saunders; 2008.
2. Mattu A, Rogers RL. Intraventricular conduction abnormalities. In: Chan TC, Brady WJ, Harrigan RA, et al, eds. *ECG in Emergency Medicine and Acute Care.* Philadelphia, PA: Elsevier Mosby; 2005:89-95.

3. Mirvis DM, Goldberger AL. Electrocardiography. In: Mann DL, Zipes DP, Bonow RO, Braunwald E, eds. *Braunwald's Heart Disease: A Textbook of Cardiovascular Medicine.* 6th ed. Philadelphia, PA: WB Saunders; 2014:114-154.
4. Liao Y, Emidy L A, Dyer A, et al. Characteristics and prognosis of incomplete right bundle-branch block: an epidemiologic study. *J Am Coll Cardiol.* 1986;7:492-499.
5. Harper RJ, Richards CF. Electrode misplacement and artifact. In: Chan TC, Brady WJ, Harrigan RA, et al, eds. *ECG in Emergency Medicine and Acute Care.* Philadelphia, PA: Elsevier Mosby; 2005:16-21.
6. Lichstein E, Mahapatra B, Gupta PK, Chadda KD. Significance of complete left bundle-branch block with left axis deviation. *Am J Cardiol.* 1979;44:239-242.
7. Parharidis G, Nouskas G, Efthimiadis J, et al. Complete left bundle-branch block with left QRS axis deviation: defining its clinical importance. *Acta Cardiol.* 1997;52:295-303.
8. Barold SS, Linhart JW, Hildner FJ, et al. Incomplete left bundle-branch block: a definite electrocardiographic entity. *Circulation.* 1968;38:702-710.
9. Liebelt EL, Francis PD, Woolf AD. ECG lead aVR versus QRS interval in predicting seizures and arrhythmias in acute tricyclic antidepressant toxicity. *Ann Emerg Med.* 1995;26:195-201.
10. Denes P, Dhingra RC, Wu D, et al. Sudden cardiac death in patients with chronic bifascicular block. *Arch Intern Med.* 1977;137:1005-1010.
11. Sgarbossa EB, Pinski SL, Barbagelata A, et al. Electrocardiographic diagnosis of evolving acute MI in the presence of left bundle-branch block. *N Engl J Med.* 1996;334:481-487.
12. Smith SW, Dodd KW, Henry TD, et al. Diagnosis of ST elevation MI in the presence of left bundle branch block using the ST elevation to S-wave ratio in a modified Sgarbossa rule. *Ann Emerg Med.* 2012;60:766-776.

CHAPTER THREE

Bradycardia, Atrioventricular Block, and Sinoatrial Block

KEVIN R. BROWN

KEY POINTS

- Symptomatic bradycardias are heart rates that are slow enough to cause hypotension, lightheadedness, altered mental state, near syncope, angina, shortness of breath, and, occasionally, loss of consciousness. Therapy for symptomatic bradycardia arrhythmias is based on the adequacy of the ventricular rate. Bradycardic rates above 45 beats/min generally do not cause hypotension.
- Asymptomatic bradycardias occur when the pacemaker slows but does not result in a clinically significant reduced cardiac output. They are benign and do not require emergent treatment.
- Common toxicologic causes of atrioventricular (AV) heart blocks and bradycardia are beta-adrenergic blocking agents, calcium channel blockers, and the now-seldom-used digoxin preparations.
- First-degree AV block involves only a delay in AV conduction—without nonconducted P wave—and is reflected in a constant prolongation of the PR interval of more than 0.2 seconds that is asymptomatic.
- Sinus bradycardia, second-degree AV block Mobitz type I (Wenckebach), and third-degree AV block with a narrow QRS complex (≤0.1 sec) generally have a good prognosis. They involve a block within the AV node and do not require permanent pacemakers.
- Second-degree block Mobitz type II and third-degree AV block with slow ventricular rates having wide (≥0.12 sec) distorted QRS complexes (ie, ventricular escape complexes) indicate *infra*nodal disease. They are not vagal induced and have a serious prognosis that likely requires a permanent pacemaker.
- Although AV dissociation involves independent atrial and ventricular activity, it is not synonymous with complete AV heart block. Atrioventricular dissociation can occur in the absence of heart block. It is a secondary electrocardiographic rhythm that results from sinus slowing or increased automaticity in a junctional or ventricular pacemaker.
- Sinoatrial (SA) blocks, in contrast to AV blocks, occur in the atria at the sinus node region. These blocks are caused by either unresponsiveness of the atrial tissue around the sinus node ("exit block" or conduction disorder) or failure of the sinus node to initiate a pacemaker impulse ("generator failure" or automaticity failure). The electrocardiographic sign of SA block is the absence of one or more complete cardiac cycles (P-QRT-T complexes). The electrocardiographic pause caused by sinus block is typically terminated by an escape beat—a junctional or lower pacemaker.
- A blocked premature atrial complex is the most common cause of a pause—not a sinus block/arrest.
- The most likely cause of bradycardia in atrial fibrillation and flutter is overtreatment of the rapid ventricular response. Withholding the offending medication usually corrects the problem. Atrial fibrillation with a slow *regular* ventricular rhythm (constant R-R intervals) indicates complete AV block, which is usually medication induced.

Bradyarrhythmias involve conduction and rhythm abnormalities that are "too slow" and might also be "too irregular." They are commonly encountered by emergency physicians and range from insignificant to life-threatening. Clinically significant bradyarrhythmias (Table 3.1) usually have rates slower than 45 beats/min; more rapid rates (>45 bpm) seldom have significant hemodynamic consequences. This concept is important for emergency physicians who aim to avoid unnecessary treatment while not delaying intervention when needed. This chapter describes the significant bradyarrhythmias that require assessment and intervention.

Atrioventricular heart blocks are a major cause of clinically significant bradyarrhythmias. The prognosis of a patient with an AV heart block caused by acute MI is related to:

- the site of the infarction (whether the block occurred at the AV node or below the node within the His-Purkinje system),
- the type of escape rhythm that develops, and
- the hemodynamic response to the escape rhythm.

Treatment is warranted when:

- the rate remains persistently slow,
- when the person is symptomatic, or
- when the likelihood is that the heart block will progress to a complete type.

The types of AV heart block and their clinical significance, as well as sinoatrial (SA) blocks, are also discussed in this chapter. Atrioventricular dissociation is an important concept in that it is sometimes confused with complete AV heart block; in fact, complete heart block is a form of AV dissociation. Yet, not all cases of AV dissociation involve a heart block.

BRADYCARDIAS

Slow ventricular rates in adults are those less than 60 beats/min. Some bradycardias are not even noticed by the individual, and others can threaten survival. Certain instances are caused by ischemic heart disease, whereas others are merely incidental findings. Unstable bradycardias generally have ventricular rates below 45 beats/min with resultant decreased cardiac output, producing a range of symptoms—lightheadedness, chest pain, syncope, generalized weakness, fatigue, shortness of breath. Syncope in the setting of AV heart block has been called a Stokes-Adams attack.

Electrocardiographic clues that can help sort out the various bradycardic arrhythmias can be found in the P waves, the QRS complexes, and the relationship between the two. Finding fixed P waves in association with bradycardia is useful in identifying the origin of the slow rhythm. P waves with a constant PR interval before each QRS complex indicate either sinus or supraventricular rhythm. P waves with regular progression of the PR-interval prolongation point toward second-degree Wenckebach AV heart block (Mobitz type I). When P waves occur helter-skelter across the QRS-T complexes and disrupt the isoelectric baseline, it suggests that complete heart block or AV dissociation is responsible. Fixed PR intervals before intermittent or regular nonconducted P waves indicate a non-Wenckebach form of second-degree block, namely Mobitz type II—the more serious type. When more than one consecutive P wave is blocked, an advanced AV block or AV dissociation such as a third-degree block is present.

Other clues can be gleaned from observing the width, rate, and shape of the QRS complex to determine whether the rhythm originated from a supraventricular focus or a ventricular site. Rhythms with a QRS duration of 0.1 second or less must have arisen from a supraventricular focus (above

TABLE 3.1. Types of bradycardias.
Atrial fibrillation or flutter with slow ventricular response
Complete heart block with idioventricular (escape) rhythm
Idioventricular (escape) rhythm
Junctional (escape) rhythm
Sinus block/sinus arrest
Sinus bradycardia

the bifurcation of the AV bundle). Many, but not all, rhythms with a wide distorted QRS complex have a ventricular focus in the His-Purkinje system. In many cases, supraventricular impulses that follow aberrant paths or are due to a block in the bundle branches cause a prolonged QRS duration (≥0.12 sec) with a distorted shape. A QRS complex that lacks an associated P wave and has a duration of 0.12 seconds or more with wide and distorted shapes indicates an ectopic pacemaker in the ventricle. Narrow QRS complexes lacking P waves are junctional beats or rhythms.

Sinus Bradycardia

Sinus bradycardia is a variant of normal sinus rhythm consisting of normal P-QRS-T complexes with the sinus node discharging at a rate below 60 beats/min (Figure 3.1). The SA node can depolarize more slowly than usual in several situations:

- the person is a well-conditioned athlete,
- as a normal variant,
- due to increased vagal tone, or
- from the use of beta-blocking or calcium channel–blocking medication.

In the setting of MI, mild slowing is protective: it lessens myocardial oxygen demand and limits infarct size (Figure 3.2). Sinus bradycardia is relatively common in an inferior wall MI and is often accompanied by a prolonged PR interval because of increased vagal tone. Sinus bradycardia is well tolerated unless the rate drops below 45 beats/min, in which case reduced stroke volume can cause symptoms.

Sinus bradycardias rarely need emergent treatment unless the patient is symptomatic. In that scenario, atropine is usually effective because the sinus node is innervated with parasympathetic nerves. The rare exception is found in patients who have had denervation postcardiac surgery (transplant), for whom atropine will not be effective, and an epinephrine infusion or pacing might be required.

Slow resting heart rates are normal in well-conditioned individuals, during sleep, in the elderly, and, not infrequently, in patients experiencing severe visceral pain, who are typically pale and diaphoretic as well. Vasovagal near-syncope episodes, which are not uncommon occurrences in the emergency department during suturing or blood drawing, involve transient slowing of the sinus node as the patient becomes pale and clammy and almost faints.

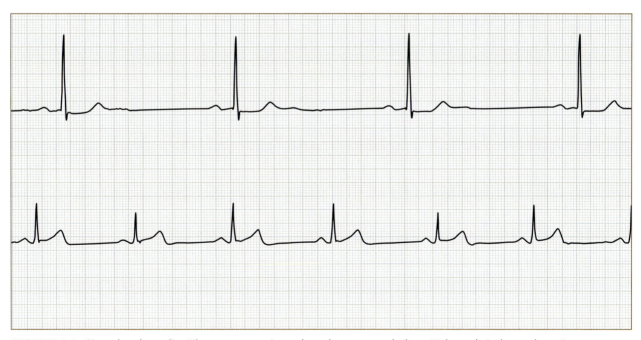

FIGURE 3.1. Sinus bradycardia. These two tracings show heart rates below 60 beats/min but otherwise appear to have normal P-QRS-T complexes.

A slow sinus rhythm can also accompany hypoglycemia, hypothyroidism, hypothermia, and increased intracranial pressure. But, in most cases, a slow sinus rhythm:

- is an incidental finding,
- has an excellent prognosis, and
- requires no treatment.

Blocked Premature Atrial Complexes Mimicking Bradycardia or Heart Blocks

Regularly blocked premature atrial complexes (PACs) (every other or every third PAC is not conducted) commonly masquerade as either sinus bradycardia or sinus block (Figure 3.3). Nonconducted PACs are benign and transient, yet the ECG can mimic a serious rhythm disorder. Premature atrial complexes are blocked when they occur so early during the cardiac cycle that the AV node remains refractory and unable to transmit the premature impulse. Clues to blocked PACs can be found hidden in the ST segments and T waves of the sinus beats preceding the cardiac pauses: the T waves have a slightly taller and altered configuration than the baseline T waves. The following Marriott[1] adage should be kept in mind: nonconducted PACs that occur after every sinus beat (bigeminy) are often misdiagnosed as sinus bradycardia.

Escape Pacemakers

When the ventricles are not stimulated because of AV conduction failure or automaticity problems, a slower escape (back-up) rhythm emerges to pace the heart (Table 3.2). These are called "escape" complexes or rhythms because they are normally suppressed by higher pacemakers with faster discharge rates—discharging or "escaping" suppression only when there is a pause in or failure of higher pacemakers. Escape pacemakers are "friendly" ectopic beats that rescue a silent heart. In the rare case that an escape pacemaker fails to develop, fatal ventricular asystole ensues (Figure 3.4). Fortunately, escape rhythms usually rescue the silent heart unless the patient has diffuse heart disease. When the sinus node fails to discharge or the AV node fails to conduct sinus impulses, escape

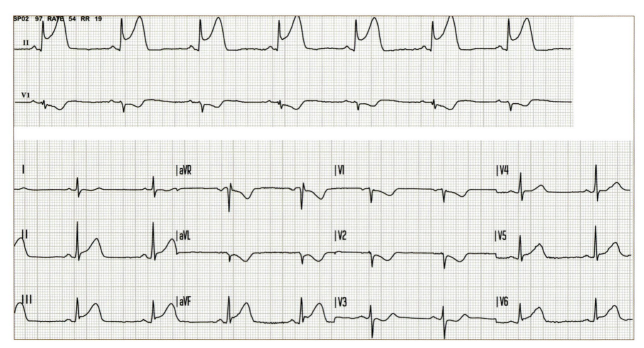

FIGURE 3.2. Sinus bradycardia in the setting of an acute myocardial injury. Top figure shows an inferior wall MI. The heart rate of 54 beats/min is protective in lowering myocardial oxygen demand. Efforts to increase the rate should be avoided. Bottom figure shows an inferior-lateral wall MI with a sinus rate of 50 beats/min.

TABLE 3.2. Escape pacemaker rhythms.				
SITE	QRS COMPLEX DURATION	RATE (BEATS/MIN)	REGULARITY	PACEMAKER SITE RELIABILITY
Idioventricular (bundle of His)	Wide	20–40	Regular	Poor
Idioventricular (Purkinje)	Wide	10–20	Irregular	Poor
Junctional	Narrow	40–55	Regular	Good

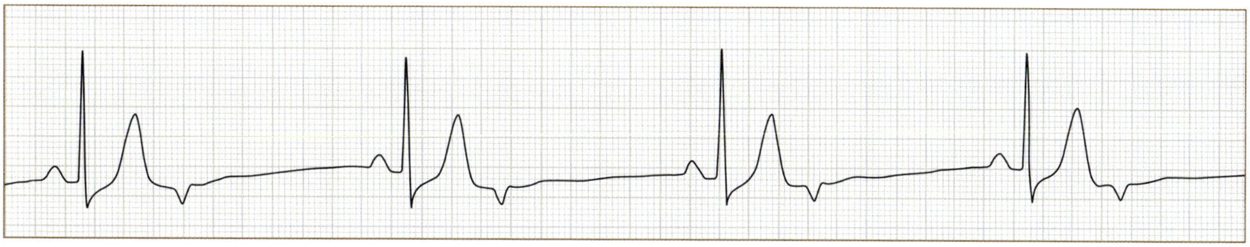

FIGURE 3.3. Blocked PACs mimic sinus bradycardia. The inverted P wave following each T wave is a nonconducted PAC. This benign finding is short-lived and requires no treatment.

rhythms discharge in the AV junction at a rate in the range of 40 to 60 beats/min. Junctional escape QRS complexes are similar in appearance to those complexes originating from the sinus node. If the AV junctional backup pacemaker also fails, a pacemaker located more distally in the conduction system such as in the bundle branches or His-Purkinje fibers stimulates the heart but at a rate much slower than normal, in the range of 20 to 40 beats/min. The QRS complexes of the more distal escape pacemakers are wide and distorted. The more distal an escape pacemaker develops, the more extensive the heart disease is and the less reliable the pacemaker. Slow idioventricular rhythms in the range of 10 to 20 beats/min seldom generate an adequate stroke volume and are likely to cease functioning abruptly (Figure 3.5).

Atrioventricular junctional (nodal) escape rhythm (Figure 3.6), a narrow QRS complex bradycardia, is regular and occurs at a rate around 50 beats/min. P waves either are typically missing, as they are obscured by the larger QRS complexes, or they can be observed immediately following the QRS complex (due to retrograde conduction) and are seen in the early phase of the ST segment. Patients with AV junctional rhythms are usually not symptomatic because the ventricular rate is fast enough (45-55 bpm) to generate an adequate stroke volume and perfuse organs despite the loss of atrial filling "kick." Junctional escape bradycardic rhythms are "secondary" cardiac rhythms that develop because of sinus node depression or complete failure.

Idioventricular escape rhythms (or beats) (Figure 3.7) occur in the setting of sinus node failure coupled with failure of the AV junctional escape to rescue the asystolic heart. Idioventricular escape rhythms are considerably less dependable than junctional escape rhythms and could fail abruptly, hence, the need for prompt application of an artificial pacemaker—either a transcutaneous one on standby or preferably by a transvenous route. These rhythms are easy to identify because their wide and distorted QRS complexes are coupled with missing P waves. These characteristics easily distinguish them from a sinus beat with a narrow QRS-T complex. The idioventricular pacemaker rate is between 20 and 40 beats/min. Idioventricular escape rhythms typically result when a conduction disturbance occurs simultaneously in both bundle branches or in three fascicles (the right bundle and both divisions of the left bundle).

Idioventricular bradyarrhythmias usually cause lightheadedness, dizziness, and near syncope because of diminished cerebral perfusion. An artificial pacemaker is generally required to stabilize this rhythm.

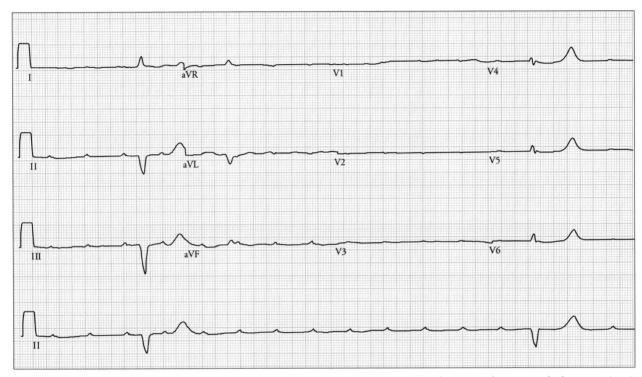

FIGURE 3.4. Complete AV heart block with ventricular asystole. This perimortal tracing shows regularly occurring P waves at a rate of 100 beats/min, but an effective escape pacemaker fails to develop. Occasional agonal idioventricular complexes are seen, but no cardiac output was generated.

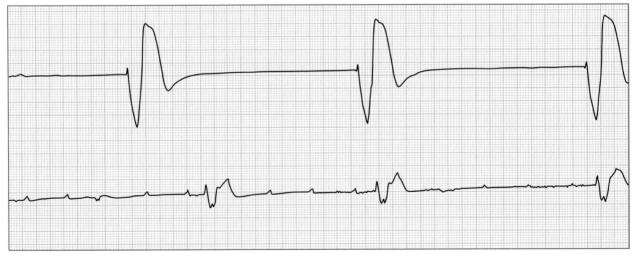

FIGURE 3.5. Idioventricular pacemakers. Top tracing shows a lone ventricular rhythm at 20 beats/min with very wide and distorted QRS-T complexes. Bottom tracing shows a slow ventricular escape rhythm at a rate of 20 beats/min in the setting of complete AV heart block.

Agonal Idioventricular Rhythms

Distorted QRS-T complexes, in a slow, irregular pattern, are commonly observed during the final phase of cardiopulmonary resuscitation and do not generate a cardiac output. During agonal idioventricular rhythm, the pacemaker is unreliable and degenerates abruptly into asystole (Figure 3.8).

Atrial Fibrillation or Flutter with a Bradycardic Ventricular Response

A bradycardic ventricular response in the setting of a tachycardic arrhythmia occurs secondary to the administration of medication that is intended to slow the ventricular response but that overshoots the mark and induces AV nodal refractoriness

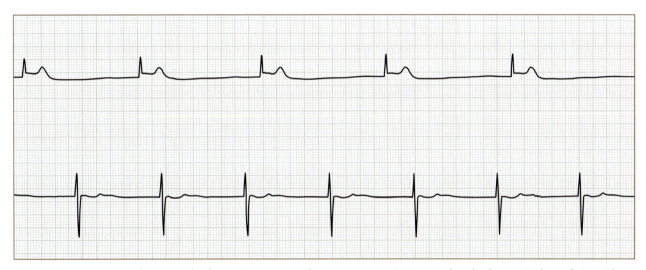

FIGURE 3.6. Junctional escape rhythms. Top tracing shows a narrow QRS complex rhythm at 33 beats/min with an elevated ST segment. There is no evidence of sinus pacemaker activity. Bottom tracing shows a junctional escape rhythm at 50 beats/min and sinus arrest.

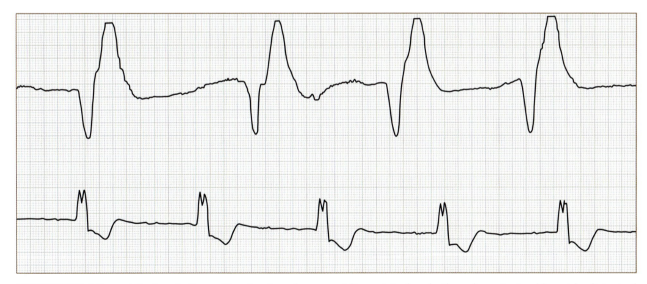

FIGURE 3.7. Idioventricular rhythms. Top tracing shows an idioventricular rhythm characterized by wide distorted QRS-T complexes at a rate of 38 beats/min. Occasional P waves, which are not conducted, are seen after the second QRS-T and before the fourth QRS-T complex. Bottom tracing shows atrial fibrillation with a regular ventricular rhythm that is slow and distorted. A slow regular rhythm in the setting of what would normally be a tachycardic arrhythmia can occur only in the setting of complete AV heart block.

(Figure 3.9). As a result, most of the atrial waves are blocked, inducing iatrogenic bradycardia. Transient third-degree AV block can also occur in atrial fibrillation and is recognized by regular R-R intervals instead of the classically irregularly irregular ventricular rhythm.

HEART BLOCKS

There are two types of heart block:

- AV and
- SA and sinus block.

Atrioventricular heart blocks are encountered much more commonly than are SA blocks. Atrioventricular blocks (except first-degree block) have more P waves than QRS complexes because some of the P waves are not conducted and therefore not followed by QRS-T complexes. In SA blocks, entire cardiac cycles (P-QRS-T complexes) are missing (Table 3.3).

Atrioventricular Blocks

The AV heart blocks can be divided into incomplete (first and second degree) and complete (third degree) (Table 3.4). First-degree block and the Mobitz type I (Wenckebach) form of second-degree AV block can occur in healthy individuals and do not usually require emergent treatment because patients tolerate them well. The conduction delay for first-degree and Wenckebach heart block forms occurs mostly in the AV node, and the QRS complexes are narrow (<0.12 sec). These forms are not likely to progress to more advanced blocks.

Second-degree Mobitz type II (non-Wenckebach form) and third-degree (complete) blocks are clinically significant. Their causes are listed in Table 3.5.

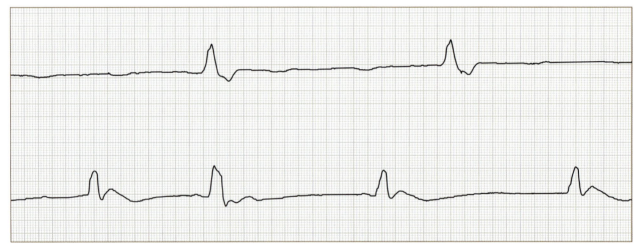

FIGURE 3.8. Agonal idioventricular complexes. Both tracings show occasional ventricular beats that are very distorted. These are perimortal tracings.

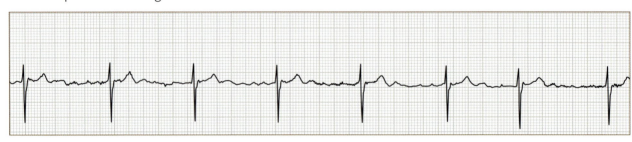

FIGURE 3.9. Atrial fibrillation with a bradycardic ventricular response. The tracing shows a bradycardic ventricular response of 45 beats/min resulting from overmedication. The patient had mistakenly taken extra beta-blocking medication. Treatment consisted of monitoring in a telemetry unit until the heart rate improved as the drug was metabolized.

These blocks are never normal and always require emergent treatment. Mobitz type II and complete AV blocks cause slow heart rates and induce effects due to hypoperfusion, such as syncope, near syncope, and myocardial ischemia. Stokes-Adams attacks are syncopal episodes caused by transient heart blocks. High-grade AV heart block refers to an advanced form of Mobitz type II, in which consecutive P waves are blocked—an ominous sign that complete AV heart block will soon follow.

FIRST-DEGREE AV HEART BLOCK. First-degree block involves a delay in impulse conduction between the sinus node and the ventricles. The hallmark is a sinus rhythm having a PR interval prolonged beyond 0.2 seconds (Figure 3.10). P waves are all conducted on the ECG tracing. Since the PR interval includes transmission in the atria, AV node, and His-Purkinje system, increased refractoriness in any of these areas could cause first-degree block. However, in most cases, a prolonged PR interval involves slowed conduction in the AV node. First-degree block has no cardiovascular consequences and is simply a benign PR interval delay. First-degree block is relatively common in inferior wall MIs (Figure 3.11) because the right coronary artery

TABLE 3.3. Heart blocks.

TYPES OF HEART BLOCKS	COMMENTS
Atrioventricular blocks	More common than SA blocks
	Characterized by the presence of more P waves than QRS complexes (except for first-degree block)
First-degree AV block	PR interval prolonged beyond 0.2 sec Usually does not require treatment
First-degree AV block with wide QRS complexes	QRS complex is beyond 0.10 sec
Second-degree AV block	Can result from dysfunction in the AV node or in the His-Purkinje conduction system
Mobitz type I (Wenckebach)	Often does not require treatment
Mobitz type II	Always requires treatment; can progress to third-degree block
2:1 AV block	Can be difficult to determine whether this block is a Mobitz type I or Mobitz type II (requiring treatment)
High-grade second-degree AV block	Highly unstable Typically progresses to complete AV block
Third-degree AV block (complete)	Initially stable patients can abruptly decompensate
Sinoatrial blocks	Less common than AV blocks; characterized by the absence of complete P-QRS-T complexes
Incomplete SA block	Involves an occasionally blocked P wave
Complete SA block (arrest)	A sustained failure of the sinus node to pace the heart
Sick sinus syndrome (tachy-brady syndrome)	Characterized by frequent periods of pronounced bradycardia, tachycardia, and sinus block

supplies the AV node 90% of the time, and the PR prolongation resolves as AV nodal edema subsides. First-degree AV block can also be seen along with the Wenckebach second-degree AV block. In such cases, the PR interval for the first beat following the dropped QRS-T complex will be the shortest of the group but can still be longer than 0.2 second.

The PR interval varies inversely with heart rate. In sinus tachycardia, the PR interval shortens. In sinus bradycardia caused by increased vagal tone, the PR interval is prolonged as the sinus node discharge also slows. It is estimated that 1.6% of the healthy population has a prolonged PR interval and experiences no adverse results. For that reason, some clinicians

TABLE 3.4. AV block electrocardiographic findings.

First-degree AV block

Simple prolongation of PR interval

No nonconducted P waves

All P waves are conducted

Second-degree AV block (intermittent P-wave blockage)

Mobitz type I (Wenckebach)

    PR interval increases progressively until a nonconducted P wave occurs

    Initial PR interval of each group is shortest

    Initial PR interval can be prolonged beyond 0.2 sec

    Intermittent nonconducted P waves

    QRS complex is usually narrow, as the AV block is *intra*nodal

    Usually fixed AV conduction ratio (3:2 or 4:3 but can be 5:4, 6:5, or even higher)

    R-R intervals crowd closer together before the nonconducted P wave occurs

    Typically does not progress to third-degree block

Mobitz type II

    Fixed PR interval before the nonconducted P waves

    Might be grouped beating (groups of QRS complexes) or occasional pauses in the QRS rhythm

    Wide and distorted QRS complexes due to *infra*nodal blockage

    Typically degenerates into third-degree block

Third-degree (complete) AV block

Complete interruption of atrial conduction

Independent atrial and ventricular activity

Atrial rate is faster than ventricular rate, so more P waves than QRS complexes

P waves march through the QRS complexes

Width and rate of QRS complexes indicate escape pacemaker site:

    if narrow and normal and 40–50 beats/min → junctional escape

    if wide and distorted and 20–40 beats/min → ventricular escape

prefer to use the term *prolonged PR interval* rather than *first-degree AV heart block* to describe such an electrocardiographic finding.

FIRST-DEGREE AV BLOCK WITH WIDE QRS COMPLEXES. When QRS duration is prolonged (≥0.12 sec), delayed AV conduction can be the result of dysfunction in the AV node (more proximal) or lower (more distal) in the His-Purkinje conduction system. In most patients with first-degree block, the QRS complexes are narrow or normal, and the dysfunction is in the AV node.

The prognosis for a patient with first-degree block is excellent, and the condition is typically benign. Even in the setting of bundle-branch block, the likelihood of progression to more advanced forms of heart block is low.

SECOND-DEGREE AV HEART BLOCK. Second-degree AV block involves intermittent conduction failure between the atria and ventricles, resulting in nonconducted P waves and longer-than-baseline R-R intervals (pauses). Some P waves fail to be conducted, resulting in QRS complexes being dropped. Second-degree AV block has two forms:

- Mobitz type I (Wenckebach form), which is less serious and typically does not require emergent treatment and
- Mobitz type II, which is serious and does require emergent therapy (Table 3.6).

Bradycardia can result from both forms if a significant number of (nonconducted) QRS complexes have been dropped. The ventricular rate depends on the inherent sinus rate coupled with the AV conduction ratio. For instance, when the sinus rate is 60 beats/min, a 3:2 AV conduction will yield a ventricular rate of 40 beats/min, which is likely to be symptomatic. The same AV conduction ratio of 3:2 will not cause symptoms if the sinus rate is 90 beats/min for the same conduction ratio because the resultant ventricular rate of 60 will generate a normal cardiac output.

SECOND-DEGREE AV HEART BLOCK MOBITZ TYPE I (WENCKEBACH TYPE). Mobitz type I is

TABLE 3.5. Causes of clinically significant AV block.

Age-associated AV nodal degeneration fibrosis
Age-associated His-Purkinje degeneration fibrosis
Amyloidosis, sarcoidosis
Aortic or mitral valve surgery (proximity to His-Purkinje fibers)
Calcific aortic stenosis
Cardiomyopathy
Congenital heart disease
Drug toxicity (calcium channel blocker, digitalis, and beta blocker toxicity)
Endocarditis
Lyme carditis
Myocardial ischemia/injury (especially inferior and anterior)
Rheumatic heart disease
Viral myocarditis

characterized by cycles of intermittent nonconducted P waves that are preceded by increasing PR intervals. Most, but not all, cases of Mobitz type I are caused by a blockage in the AV node. The classic pattern shows grouped beats until a nonconducted P wave occurs, resulting in a dropped QRS complex, and the cycle begins over (Figure 3.12). After the dropped QRS complex of each cycle, the next PR interval is the shortest of the bunch. The greatest increase in the PR prolongation is seen between the first and second PR intervals following the dropped QRS complex. The sinus impulse encounters a progressively more refractory AV node (slowed conduction) in the succeeding beats, eventually resulting in a dropped QRS complex.

The ECG shows a predictable pattern of "grouped beating" with progressive prolongation of the PR interval until a P wave is nonconducted and followed by a pause. The QRS complexes fall further behind

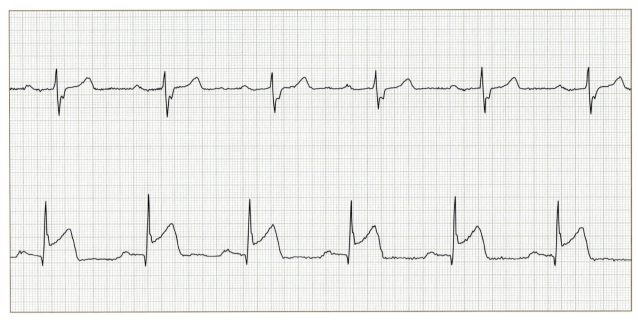

FIGURE 3.10. Sinus bradycardia with first-degree AV heart block. Top tracing shows a sinus bradycardia at 50 beats/min with a prolonged PR interval of 0.32 sec. Bottom tracing shows a sinus bradycardia at 52 beats/min and a prolonged PR interval of 0.28 sec. Both ECGs show an acute injury pattern.

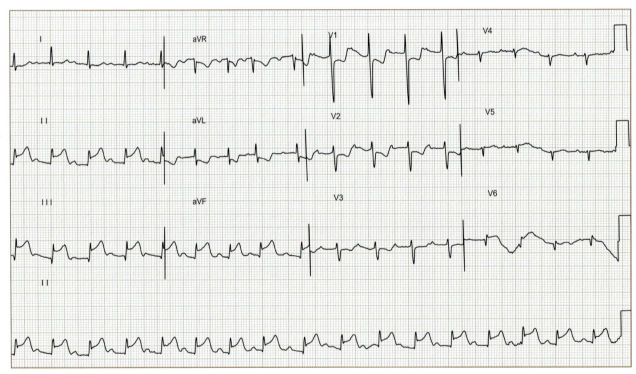

FIGURE 3.11. Acute inferior-posterior-lateral wall MI with first-degree AV heart block. The PR interval is prolonged to 0.28 sec.

TABLE 3.6. Types of second-degree AV heart block.

TYPE	SITE OF BLOCK	QRS COMPLEX DURATION	DEPENDABILITY OF ESCAPE RHYTHM	LIKELIHOOD OF PROGRESSION TO COMPLETE HEART BLOCK	BLOCK DURATION
Mobitz I (Wenckebach)	AV node	Narrow	Reliable	Rare	Transient
Mobitz II	Infra-His bundle	Narrow or wide (most common)	Unreliable	Frequent	Permanent

the P waves, appearing as a shortening of the R-P and R-R intervals. The most frequent AV conduction ratios are 3:2 or 4:3, but higher ratios, even 7:6 and 6:5 or greater, are seen.

Patients with Mobitz type I AV block are usually asymptomatic. Wenckebach block occurs in about 10% of patients with acute MI, especially those with inferior wall MIs. Mobitz type I also occurs in healthy individuals with high vagal tone. A clue to increased parasympathetic tone is a slow sinus rhythm along with prolonged PR interval. A Wenckebach block:

- does not usually cause symptoms,
- does not usually have an adverse effect on cardiac output, and
- does not usually progress to more serious forms of AV block.

Marriott[2] spoke of recognizing the "footprints" of Wenckebach:

- the grouped beating,
- the dropped QRS complexes, and
- the shortening of R-R intervals as the QRS falls farther behind the P wave.

Treatment is usually not needed, as Wenckebach is rarely symptomatic, and it is distinctly unusual for Mobitz type I to progress to higher degrees of AV block.

SECOND-DEGREE AV HEART BLOCK MOBITZ TYPE II. This is the serious form of second-degree block, in which there is underlying disease of the AV conduction system bundle branches or His-Purkinje fibers. The hallmark findings are constant PR intervals with the concurrent presence of some nonconducted P waves. Stokes-Adams syncope is associated with Mobitz type II when the dropped beats cause hypoperfusion of the brain. There is a sudden blockage of AV conduction without being preceded by gradually progressive increases in the PR interval, as in Mobitz type I. Mobitz type II is a partial block consisting of abruptly or regularly dropped QRS complexes with constant PR intervals before the dropped QRS complexes (Figure 3.13). Type II block is identified when at least two consecutive atrial impulses are conducted with constant PR intervals before the dropped QRS complex occurs. The QRS complexes are usually wide and distorted: the conduction disturbance is located *infra*nodally, that is, within the Purkinje fibers in the bundle branches. Such patients have bundle-branch blocks with prolonged and distorted QRS complexes.

Second-degree AV block Mobitz type II is important to identify because:

- it is associated with advanced disease of the conduction system,
- it causes symptoms, and
- it can abruptly progress to third-degree AV block.

It should be identified quickly because an artificial pacemaker is needed to stabilize the rhythm. Because of the likelihood of progression to

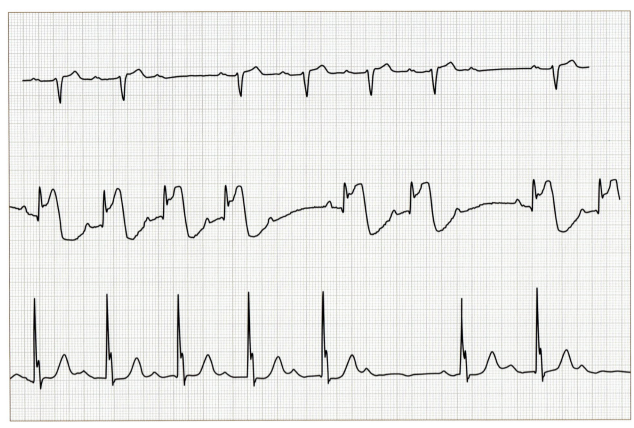

FIGURE 3.12. Second degree AV heart block Mobitz type I (Wenckebach). The top tracing shows nonconducted P waves in the setting of grouped beating and prolonging PR intervals. The third and eighth P waves are nonconducted and QRS complexes are dropped. The middle tracing shows an acute injury pattern with variable AV conduction. The first grouped beating has 5:4 AV conduction and the second group has 3:2 AV conduction. The bottom tracing has a 6:5 AV conduction ratio followed by 3:2 AV conduction.

third-degree AV block, urgent pacemaker insertion is generally needed even if the patient's condition is stable. In contrast to the treatment of Wenckebach block, atropine is not effective because of the lack of parasympathetic fibers in the ventricle. If transcutaneous pacing is ineffective or transvenous pacing is delayed, an epinephrine infusion at 2 to 10 mcg/min or dopamine infusion at 2 to 10 mcg/kg/min is needed.

2:1 AV HEART BLOCK: A SPECIAL FORM OF SECOND-DEGREE CONDUCTION.

Since two consecutive PR intervals before a nonconducted P wave need to be observed to determine if the PR interval is increasing or remaining constant, it is difficult to label 2:1 conduction as either as Mobitz I or II. There has been confusion over whether a 2:1 AV block is Mobitz type I or II. Some have argued that 2:1 block is a Wenckebach form of block while others cite it as an example of Mobitz type II (Figures 3.14, 3.15). This is not just an academic point: the two types of second-degree block represent distinctly different causes, require different treatment, and have different prognoses. Depending on the circumstances, each advocate is sometimes correct.

Because every other P wave is blocked, the surface ECG in 2:1 conduction does not show two consecutive PR intervals, so it is not clear whether the PR interval is increasing or staying the same. As a result, the lack of PR progression before the dropped QRS complex could signify a Mobitz type II block. This is the more serious of the two forms and usually requires a permanent pacemaker. The most useful clinical clue is obtained

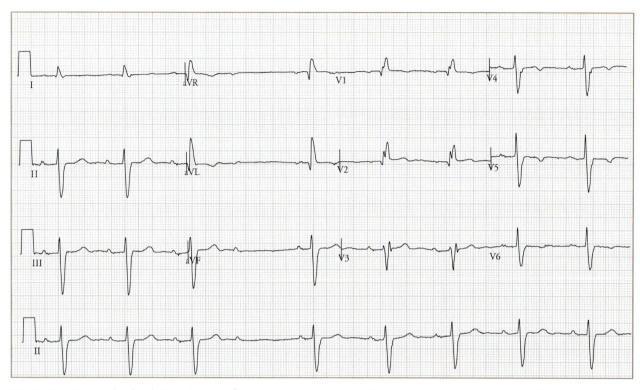

FIGURE 3.13. Twelve-lead ECG showing first- and second-degree AV heart block, Mobitz type II. The fourth P wave is not conducted, and a QRS-T complex is dropped. The PR intervals before and after the nonconducted P wave are constant, thereby differentiating this AV block from the Wenckebach type. *Fixed* PR intervals define Mobitz type II. Other conduction abnormalities are seen as well: right bundle-branch block and a left anterior hemiblock along with first-degree AV heart block. The AV conduction is tenuous at best and will shortly progress to complete heart block.

by inspecting the width of the QRS complexes. Atropine is also sometimes helpful in sorting between these possibilities. If atropine corrects the block, it suggests that the block was at the AV node, typical of Wenckebach. However, if atropine is not effective in eliminating the 2:1 block, the disorder is likely infranodal, where there are no parasympathetic fibers.

Another electrocardiographic characteristic that can help localize the block is the QRS duration. A Wenckebach-type AV block is usually located in the AV node and will usually have a QRS complex of normal shape and duration (<0.12 sec). In contrast, Mobitz type II AV block generally occurs below the AV node within the bundle branches and has wide (≥0.12 sec) and distorted QRS complexes.

Figure 3.16 is a continuous tracing that illustrates the rule in 2:1 block: the QRS complexes are narrow, indicating this is likely a Mobitz type I (Wenckebach block). In the author's experience, most 2:1 AV conduction cases are intranodal blocks with narrow QRS complexes; therefore, they usually do not need treatment. But if the patient is symptomatic, atropine is usually successful because increased vagal tone is most often the offending cause. In Figure 3.10, the QRS complexes are narrow, and the AV block is probably located in the AV node.

HIGH-GRADE SECOND-DEGREE AV HEART BLOCK. Advanced AV block is present when two or more consecutive P waves are blocked (Figure 3.17). For this diagnosis, however, the atrial rate must not be too fast (>140 bpm); if it is rapid, a physiologic cause for the nonconduction (such as atrial flutter with 3:1 AV conduction) is likely present rather than a true heart block. High-grade AV block is the most serious form of second-degree

AV block. Its identification is important because the rhythm disturbance is unstable and advances to complete AV block within a short period. This advanced form of Mobitz type II occurs when two or more consecutive P waves are nonconducted, leading to a pause in ventricular activity. Rather than every third or fourth QRS complex being dropped, as in other forms of second-degree block, two or more consecutive P waves are blocked.

High-grade AV block is a highly unstable form of second-degree block and requires urgent insertion of a permanent pacemaker.

THIRD-DEGREE (COMPLETE) AV HEART BLOCK. This manifestation of heart block has total interruption of AV conduction—no P waves are conducted, and atrial and ventricular activity have become independent (Figure 3.18). The hallmark

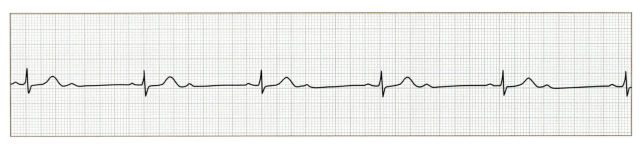

FIGURE 3.14. Sinus rhythm with second-degree AV heart block with 2:1 AV conduction. The sinus rate of 75 beats/min has every other P wave nonconducted, leading to a bradycardic ventricular rate of 37 beats/min. The QRS is narrow, indicating that the conduction problem is within the AV node.

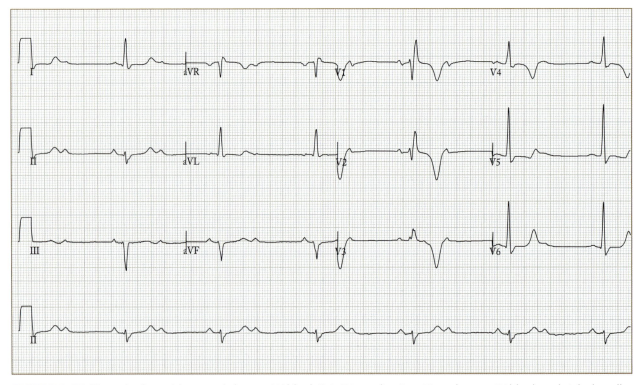

FIGURE 3.15. Sinus rhythm with second-degree AV block 2:1 AV conduction. First-degree AV block and right bundle-branch block are also present. The atrial rate is 75 beats/min, and the ventricular rate is 37 beats/min. The QRS duration is prolonged, indicating that the block is likely below the bundle of His and is a Mobitz type II AV block. The sharply inverted anterior T waves (arrowhead shape) indicate ischemia and left ventricular hypertrophy coupled with left axis deviation.

findings of third-degree AV heart block are regular P-P intervals that are unrelated to regular R-R intervals, with P waves appearing to "march through" the QRS-T complexes. There are two independent pacemakers:

- one in the SA node and
- one either in the AV junction or within the Purkinje/bundle-branch fibers in the ventricles.

The ventricular escape rhythm must be slow enough (usually 45 bpm) to permit an atrial beat to be conducted if conduction is possible. The ventricular rate depends on whether the block is in the AV junction (less common) or the bundle branches (more common). The more distal the blockage is in the conduction system, the lower the escape pacemaker rhythm will be and the less dependable it is compared to more proximal escape pacemakers. Slow and wide idioventricular escape rhythms ranging from 20 to 40 beats/min are generally caused by trifascicular blockage. Narrow and normal-appearing AV junctional rhythms range from 40 to 50 beats/min. The escape rhythm, whether junctional or ventricular, is regular (equal R-R intervals). The atrial rate is usually regular and considerably faster than the escape rhythm.

The most common causes of third-degree block are:

- age-associated fibrosis of the AV conduction system and
- MI (inferior and anterior types).

Fibrosis and an anterior wall MI are permanent, whereas the heart block caused by an inferior wall MI can subside as the edema resolves in 24 to 48 hours. Other causes of third-degree AV block are listed in Table 3.7.

Although patients can be hemodynamically stable initially, they have the potential for abrupt hemodynamic decompensation due to the questionable reliability of the escape pacemaker.

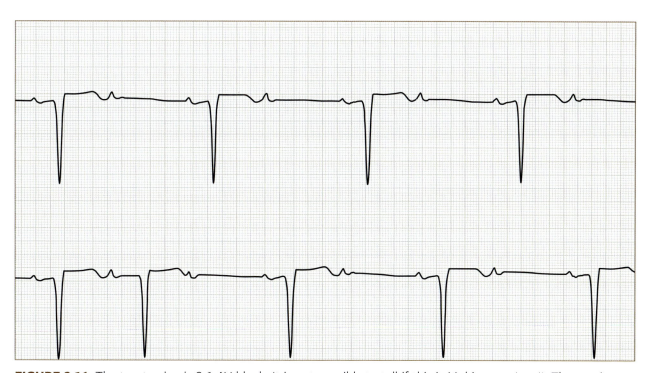

FIGURE 3.16. The top tracing is 2:1 AV block. It is not possible to tell if this is Mobitz type I or II. The continuous tracing lets us see a change in conduction in the bottom tracing and permits identification of the type of Mobitz block. In the bottom tracing, the initial portion has 3:2 AV conduction, confirming that this arrhythmia is a Wenckebach type (at least two PR intervals are needed to make the determination).

Cardiac output is usually impaired, resulting in lightheadedness, near syncope, dizziness, palpitations, angina, and even syncope and cardiovascular collapse. Surprisingly, some elderly patients with complete AV block complain only of fatigue, a lack of energy, or general malaise but have a pulse rate of 35 beats/min.

The treatment for these patients is transvenous pacemaker insertion. Temporizing measures until transvenous pacemaker insertion for unstable patients include:

- transcutaneous pacing,
- dopamine infusion (2–20 mcg/kg/min titrated to response), and
- epinephrine infusion (2–10 mcg/min infusion titrated to response).

For narrow-complex escape rhythms, atropine in 0.5-mg boluses may be attempted but is usually ineffective. Atropine may be given every 3 to 5 minutes to a maximum of 3 mg.

RISK OF PROGRESSION FROM FIRST- AND SECOND-DEGREE TO THIRD-DEGREE AV BLOCK IN ACUTE MI. Atrioventricular heart blocks are not uncommon in patients with acute MI, but most of them are first- and second-degree Mobitz type I that do not progress to third degree. Emergency physicians should learn to predict which acute MI patients might develop the unstable third-degree block. The following electrocardiographic findings have been used to estimate the likelihood of developing third-degree block:

- first-degree AV heart block,
- second-degree AV heart block (both type I and type II),
- right bundle-branch block,
- left bundle-branch block,
- left anterior hemiblock (common), and
- left posterior hemiblock (rare).[3]

Each of these findings on a 12-lead ECG counts for 1 point, and the total score indicates the risk for

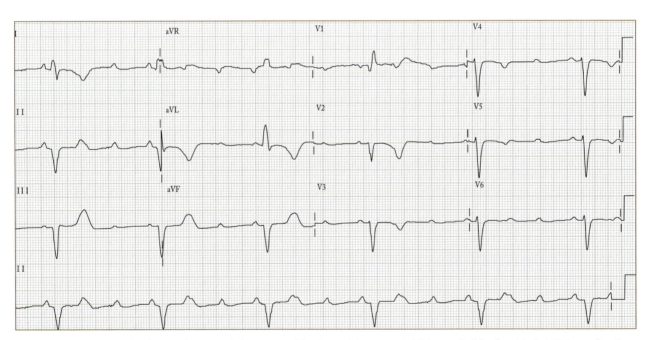

FIGURE 3.17. Sinus rhythm with second-degree AV block, Mobitz type II, high-grade block with 3:1 AV conduction. Only one-third of the P waves (at a rate of 100 bpm) are conducted, leading to a ventricular rate of 33 beats/min. The PR intervals are fixed, identifying this as the more serious form of second-degree AV heart block. Advanced or high-grade AV heart block is defined as two or more consecutive nonconducted P waves and is very unstable, as it abruptly deteriorates into complete heart block.

TABLE 3.7. Causes of third-degree AV heart block.
Amyloid/sarcoid/scleroderma
Calcific aortic stenosis
Cardiac surgery
Cardiomyopathy
Chagas disease
Drug toxicity (beta blocker, calcium channel, digoxin)
Fibrotic degeneration of conduction system
Hypothyroidism
Lyme disease
Myocardial injury
Rheumatic fever
Rheumatoid nodules
Viral myocarditis

third-degree AV heart block for an acute MI patient. The higher the score, the greater the likelihood that the patient will develop complete AV heart block. A score of:

- 0 indicates a 1.2% risk,
- 1, a 7.8% risk, and
- 2, a 25% risk.
- A score of 3 or more conveys a 36.4% risk of complete AV heart block.

Therefore, an apparently stable acute MI patient with sinus rhythm and first-degree AV heart block and right bundle-branch block (RBBB) with left anterior hemiblock has greater than a one-in-three chance of developing an unstable third-degree AV heart block and should undergo urgent transvenous pacemaker placement.[4]

DIFFERENTIATING AV DISSOCIATION FROM COMPLETE HEART BLOCK.
Independent atrial and ventricular rhythms occur in AV dissociation, but their occurrence does not imply that a complete AV block is present. Third-degree block is only one of several causes of a dissociated state between the atria and ventricles. Dissociation can occur in the absence of a heart block when either of two conditions exists:

- the sinus rhythm is slower than that of an escape junctional or ventricular backup pacemaker, causing rhythm "interference," or
- the ventricular rhythm accelerates faster than normal due to increased ectopic automaticity and competes with the sinus node.

In both cases, there is a lack of coordination (a dissociation) between the atrial and ventricular rhythm but not an AV heart block.

The most common form of AV dissociation is *isorhythmic AV dissociation,* which occurs when the atria and ventricles are paced independently but at almost the same rate. Its usual cause is a transient decrease in the sinus rate to below 60 beats/min (usually around 50 bpm), inducing an AV junctional escape rhythm (Figures 3.19, 3.20). The escape pacemaker can be faster than the sinus rate, causing the R-R intervals to be shorter than the P-P interval. The P waves and QRS complexes are briefly dissociated from one another; however, there is no actual AV conduction disorder. The dissociated rhythm results from close discharge rates of the sinus and junction escape pacemakers. The isorhythmic dissociation subsides as soon as the sinus node accelerates and regains control. Patients with isorhythmic dissociation are usually asymptomatic, unlike those with complete AV heart block. This is referred to as "AV dissociation by default" because the backup pacemaker emerges due to slowing of the sinus node.

A less common cause is AV dissociation by competition from the usually slower escape pacemaker: the accelerated junctional rhythm speeds up due to increased automaticity and overtakes a normally functioning sinus node. This has been referred to as "AV dissociation by usurpation" because the sinus's pacemaker role is taken over by competition from a lower pacemaker. Fusion and capture beats can be seen in AV dissociation.

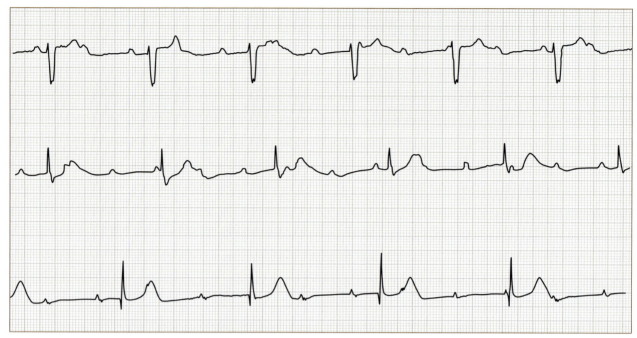

FIGURE 3.18. Third-degree (complete) AV heart block. The three examples show independent atrial and ventricular rhythm with no association between them. The P waves appear to "march through" the QRS-T complexes. The P waves appear helter-skelter among the QRS-T complexes and along baseline. The atrial rate is faster than the ventricular rate. Note that the ventricular rhythms are regular, but the rates of the escape pacemakers vary among the three tracings.

- *Fusion* beats, which occur because of depolarization from opposite directions, result in P-QRS-T complexes that share components of atrial and ventricular pacemaker rhythms.
- *Capture* beats occur when the sinus impulse finds a nonrefractory AV conduction, resulting in a normal QRS-T complex.

Fusion and capture beats can happen only if AV nodal conduction exists (therefore, there is no complete AV block).

Sinoatrial Blocks

An SA block is characterized by the sudden loss of sinus activity, recognized as absent P-QRS-T complexes. The sinus node fails to discharge (automaticity failure), or it might fire, but the impulse is blocked from stimulating the atrial tissue (conduction failure). Sinus block is easy to identify because of the dramatic disruption in cardiac rhythm (Figure 3.21). Patients with sinus block typically have a history of sudden syncopal episodes, generalized weakness, or lightheadedness. Sinus pauses are terminated by an escape beat or rhythm. Sinus node failure has three possible mechanisms:

- the sinus node generates the impulse, but it fails to be transmitted out of the node,
- the sinus node impulse occurs, but the atrial tissue fails to respond because of increased refractoriness of atrial tissue, or
- the sinus node fails to form an impulse.

Regardless of the mechanism, one or more P-QRS-T complexes are absent, resulting in a pause in the cardiac rhythm. In most cases, a junctional escape beat or rhythm ends the pause after a second or more and is recognized by its narrow QRS complex and absent or retrograde P wave. Sinus block is classified as either incomplete, in which an occasional sinus impulse is nonconducted, or complete, in which no P waves are visible at all and an escape rhythm occurs. Sinus block differs from AV block in that there are "lone" P waves in AV block but no extra P waves in sinus block. Complete P-QRS-T complexes are absent in SA block.

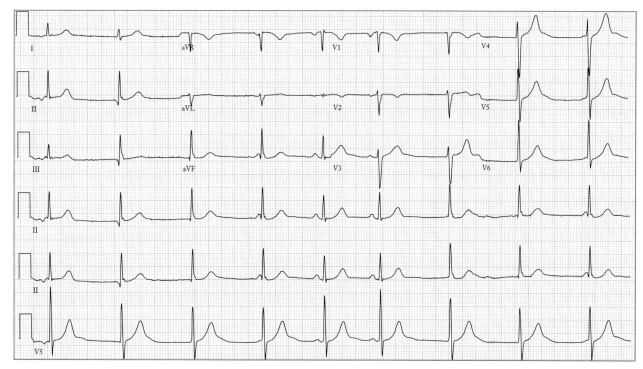

FIGURE 3.19. Sinus rhythm with isorhythmic AV dissociation. No AV heart block is present, yet AV dissociation does exist. AV dissociation occurs when the sinus rate slows to approximately 50 beats/min and approaches the discharge rate, when an escape pacemaker will emerge. The discharge of a junctional escape pacemaker is also in the range of 50 beats/min, leading to brief periods of AV dissociation. The P waves are dissociated from the QRS-T complexes at some points; at other times, the rhythm is a sinus bradycardia with fixed PR intervals.

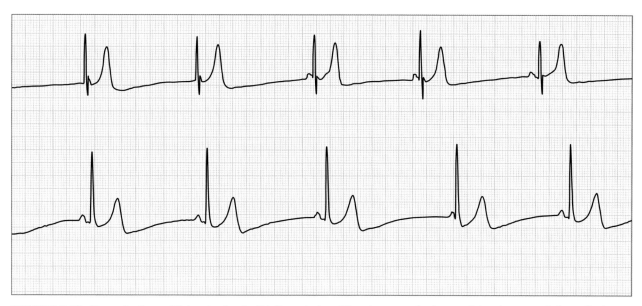

FIGURE 3.20. Sinus rhythm with isorhythmic AV dissociation. The sinus rate is slow and the depressed sinus discharge puts it in the range of the junctional escape rhythms. QRS-T looks the same in all complexes, but P waves are present for only some complexes and are missing with others.

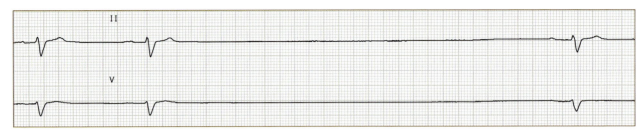

FIGURE 3.21. Sinus rhythm with sinus block. The initial portion of the tracing shows a slow sinus rhythm with first-degree AV block. A prolonged pause of at least 5 seconds occurs after the two beats and is terminated by a sinus beat.

INCOMPLETE SA BLOCK. Incomplete SA block involves an occasionally blocked P wave (Figure 3.22). It is sometimes possible to detect a relationship with the underlying P-P interval and to determine that the pause consists of multiple P-P cycles, but this is usually not the case. It is best to describe the electrocardiographic findings rather than try to find the precise term. "Sinus rhythm with a 3-and-a-half-second pause" conveys all the crucial information that is needed when discussing the ECG with a cardiologist.

COMPLETE SA BLOCK (ARREST). In complete SA block, there is a sustained failure of the sinus node to pace the heart (Figure 3.23). Management of complete SA block involves applying an external pacemaker. Atropine can sometimes help temporarily. It is rare to encounter a hypotensive patient who is refractory to external pacing and atropine, but when this clinical presentation arises, epinephrine infusion is indicated.

Sick Sinus Syndrome

Sick sinus syndrome is actually a group of arrhythmias that share the hallmarks of alternating bradycardia and tachycardia (Figure 3.24). Their presentation is characterized by frequent periods of pronounced bradycardia, tachycardia, and sinus block. Sinus node dysfunction has also been referred to as tachy-brady syndrome due to the alternating fast and slow rates.

MANAGEMENT

Hollander[5] provided a useful review of bradyarrhythmias occurring during an acute coronary event. The mortality rate is increased in AV heart block associated with an acute MI; however, artificial pacing has not been shown to improve survival. The heightened risk of death is probably related to more extensive myocardial damage rather than the heart block itself.

The 2015 advanced cardiac life support guidelines[6,7] are the same as the earlier 2005 edition and advise observation and monitoring in the setting of slow cardiac rhythms *with adequate perfusion*. If the patient looks well, observation is more appropriate than trying to accelerate the rhythm, and in the setting of an acute coronary syndrome with adequate perfusion, accelerating the heart rate could worsen the ischemia. Hypoxemia can cause bradycardia, so supplemental oxygen administration to maintain an oxygen saturation of at least 94% is appropriate. The standard approach to acute coronary syndrome patients should include:

- continuous cardiac, blood pressure, and pulse oximetry monitoring,
- a saline lock IV access, and
- rapid 12-lead ECG to identify a myocardial infarction.

For bradycardic patients who have signs and symptoms of poor perfusion (altered mental state, acute heart failure, angina, and pale, diaphoretic skin), permanent pacing is the definitive treatment. While pacing equipment is being prepared, atropine, a vagolytic drug that can temporarily speed up a slow heart rate, may be considered. It is given as 0.5-mg rapid boluses every 3 to 5 minutes as needed to a maximum dose of 3 mg. If atropine is administered but does not induce the intended result, external pacing should be commenced along with analgesia if the pacer causes pain. Second-line medications to consider are dopamine infused at 2 to 10 mcg/kg/min or epinephrine infused at 2 to 10 mcg/min titrated to effect (heart rate of 55 bpm or systolic blood pressure of 100 mm Hg). Expert cardiology consultation should be obtained and preparations made for transvenous pacemaker insertion.

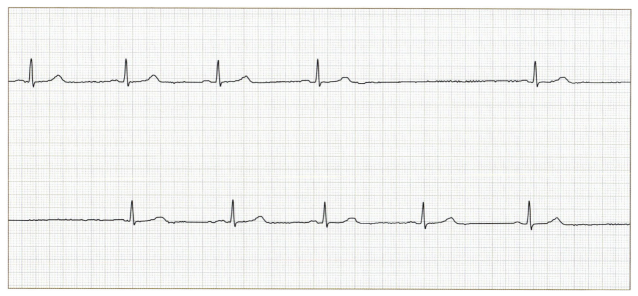

FIGURE 3.22. Sinus block. The sinus rhythm is disrupted by a sinus block, with an entire P-QRS-T complex missing. There is a 2-second pause as the sinus impulse fails to stimulate the atria. A junctional beat fails to develop.

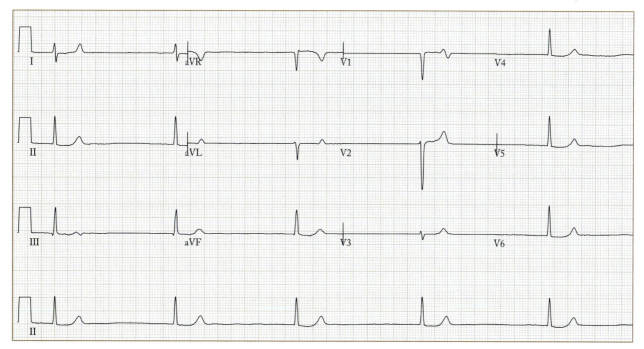

FIGURE 3.23. Sinus arrest with a slow junctional escape rhythm. This tracing is from a woman with renal failure who missed several dialysis appointments. Her potassium level had risen to 9 mEq/L, causing a heart rate of 20 to 30 beats/min. Following treatment with insulin, dextrose, albuterol, calcium, sodium bicarbonate, and sodium polystyrene sulfonate, her ECG returned to a normal sinus rhythm.

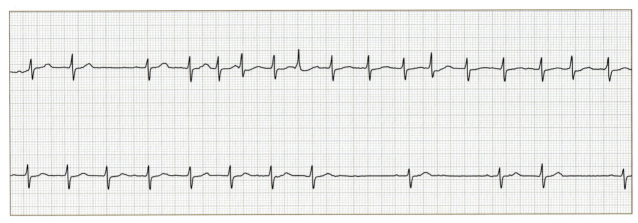

FIGURE 3.24. Tachy-brady syndrome. The top tracing shows an initial sinus rhythm that converts to rapid atrial fibrillation. The bottom tracing shows the resumption of a slow sinus rhythm. The pacemaker's stability is in question. Inserting a permanent pacemaker guarantees a backup pacemaker. *Tachy-brady syndrome* is another term for *sick sinus syndrome*, in which the pacemaker is stable one minute but unstable the next.

In the setting of beta blocker or calcium channel-blocker toxicity, intravenous administration of glucagon can be useful if atropine and a beta-adrenergic infusion fail to increase the heart rate. Bradycardia due to digoxin toxicity can be treated with a specific digitalis-binding antidote. Treatment of toxicologic causes of bradycardia should be guided by a toxicologist at a poison control center (1-800-P-O-I-S-O-N-S or 1-800-222-1222).

Atropine exerts its vagolytic effect at the sinus and AV nodes. It is effective for sinus bradycardia and Wenckebach second-degree AV block (narrow QRS complexes). Atropine is not effective if the block is at or below the bundle of His (which is typified by wide QRS complexes). Since advanced blocks (second-degree Mobitz type II and complete AV heart block) occur at lower sites in the ventricular system that lack parasympathetic innervation, a vagolytic drug such as atropine will not accelerate the ventricular rate nor will it correct an AV heart block. Atropine will likewise not be useful for the rare cardiac transplant patient with advanced AV heart block.

REFERENCES

1. Wagner GS, Strauss DG, eds. *Marriott's Practical Electrocardiography*. 12th ed. Baltimore, MD: Lippincott Williams & Wilkins; 2014:320.
2. Marriott HJL. *Rhythm Quizlets: Self Assessment*. 2nd ed. Baltimore, MD: Williams & Wilkins; 1996:115.
3. Harrigan RA, Perron AD, Brady WJ. Atrioventricular dissociation. *Am J Emerg Med*. 2001;19:218-222.
4. Lamas FA, Muller JE, Turi ZG, et al. A simplified method to predict occurrence of complete heart block during acute myocardial infarction. *Am J Cardiol*. 1986;57:1213-1219.
5. Hollander JE, Diercks DB. Acute coronary syndromes. In Tintinalli JE, ed. *Tintinalli's Emergency Medicine: A Comprehensive Study Guide*, 8th ed. New York: McGraw-Hill; 2016:332-348.
6. Pozner CN. Advanced Cardiac Life Support (ACLS) in Adults. UpToDate, January 3, 2018. Available at https://www.uptodate.com/contents/advanced-cardiac-life-support-acls-in-adults. Accessed January 17, 2018.
7. Link MS, Berkow LC, Kudenchuck PJ, et al. Part 7: Adult Advanced Cardiovascular Life Support. 2015 American Heart Association Guidelines Update for Cardiopulmonary Resuscitation and Emergency Cardiovascular Care. *Circulation*. 2015;132(18 Suppl 2):S444-S464.

ADDITIONAL READING

Brady WJ, Harrigan RA. Evaluation and management of bradyarrhythmias in the emergency department. *Emerg Med Clin North Am*. 1998;16(2):361-388.

CHAPTER FOUR

Narrow Complex Tachycardias

CHRISTOPHER H. ROSS AND THERESA M. SCHWAB

KEY POINTS
- The initial assessment of patients with narrow complex tachycardia should determine hemodynamic status, focusing on the presence or absence of stability.
- The differential diagnosis for regular narrow complex tachycardia can generally be categorized into sinus, atrial (atrial tachycardia and atrial flutter), or atrioventricular (AV) nodal (AVRT and AVNRT) sources.
- Initial assessment of the ECG from a patient with narrow complex tachycardia should determine the regularity of the ventricular response. A P wave originating from the sinus node will be upright in limb lead II and inverted in aVR.
- Atrial tachycardia with AV block, an uncommon arrhythmia, is classically associated with digoxin toxicity.

Narrow QRS complex tachycardias, often simply referred to as narrow complex tachycardias, are defined as arrhythmias with a rate faster than 100 beats/min and a QRS duration of 120 milliseconds or less. The normal QRS duration indicates normal activation of both ventricles through the atrioventricular (AV) junction, the bundle of His, the bundle branches, and the terminal Purkinje conduction system. This synchronous activation of the ventricles requires initial depolarization proximal to the ventricular tissue using the atrial or AV junctional tissue.[1] Narrow complex tachycardias comprise a variety of rhythms (Table 4.1). An understanding of the interpretation and classification of these entities can direct clinicians to the most appropriate diagnoses and treatments. Correct identification can be challenging, however, because "distinguishing" electrocardiographic findings are not always present.

The terminology used in clinical practice for narrow complex tachycardias is often imprecise and confusing. It is based on both occurrence patterns (paroxysmal, nonparoxysmal, persistent, permanent, sustained, or nonsustained) and mechanism (automatic, accelerated, focal, ectopic, reentrant, or reciprocating). This rather broad terminology has led to several terms that are imprecise, based on antiquated understanding (or misunderstanding) of presentation or mechanism. *Supraventricular tachycardia* (SVT) is a generalized term used to describe tachycardias (atrial or ventricular rates in excess of 100 bpm at rest), the mechanism of which involves a focus in tissues at or above the lower AV node or His bundle. Supraventricular tachycardias include inappropriate sinus tachycardia, atrial tachycardia (including focal and multifocal atrial tachycardia), macroreentrant atrial tachycardia (including typical atrial flutter), junctional tachycardia, atrioventricular node reentrant tachycardia (AVNRT), and various forms of accessory pathway-mediated reentrant tachycardias. *Paroxysmal supraventricular tachycardia* (PSVT) is a clinical syndrome characterized by the presence of a regular and rapid tachycardia of abrupt onset and termination. These features are characteristic of AVNRT and atrioventricular reentrant tachycardia via an accessory pathway (AVRT) and, less frequently, of atrial tachycardia. Paroxysmal supraventricular tachycardia is a subset of SVT.[2] *Atrial tachycardia* means any tachycardia originating in the atrium, although it commonly refers to tachycardia arising from an ectopic atrial area of enhanced automaticity or, occasionally, reentry. *Junctional tachycardia* means any tachycardia that involves the AV node and thus includes AVNRT, AVRT, and accelerated junctional tachycardias, usually arising from discreet foci of increased automaticity in the AV node or bundle of His (variously called focal junctional, paroxysmal junctional, nonparoxysmal junctional, automatic junctional, accelerated AV junctional, and junctional ectopic tachycardia). In this chapter, we have chosen to use terminology defined in the 2015 guidelines from the American College of Cardiology/American Heart Association for the management of patients with supraventricular arrhythmias.[2]

The basic mechanisms of all tachyarrhythmias fall into three classic categories: reentrant, automatic, and triggered (Table 4.2)[3]:

- Reentry (or circus movement) is the most common mechanism, involving conduction down an anterograde path and back up a retrograde path. It occurs either within a single locus (such as within the sinus node, the atria, or the AV node) or across multiple sites, as with AVRT (anterograde through the AV node and His-Purkinje system to the ventricles and then retrograde over an accessory AV pathway to the atrium). It is typically associated with rhythms arising from the AV node and the immediately surrounding tissues. For a reentrant circuit to occur, two pathways must exist with different rates of conduction and recovery. The initial electrical impulse, often a premature complex, depolarizes one limb of the circuit while the other is refractory after the previous depolarization. When the impulse completes its transit down the first limb (anterograde), which is now refractory, it travels back up the now recovered second limb (retrograde) to the initiation point. The cycle continues until this balance

TABLE 4.1. Narrow complex tachycardias.

Atrial fibrillation
Atrial flutter
AV nodal reentrant tachycardia
AV reentrant tachycardia
Focal and nonparoxysmal junctional tachycardia
Focal atrial tachycardia
Inappropriate sinus tachycardia
Multifocal atrial tachycardia
Sinoatrial nodal reentrant tachycardia
Sinus tachycardia

TABLE 4.2. Mechanisms of tachyarrhythmias and their characteristics.

Reentry

Often precipitated by premature contraction

Begin at their maximal rate, no warm-up period

Fixed rate (no beat-to-beat variability)

Cease abruptly, no slow-down period

Examples: atrial flutter, AV reentrant tachycardia, AV nodal reentrant tachycardia, sinoatrial nodal reentry

Enhanced automaticity

Often precipitated by adrenergic stimulation or medications such as digoxin

Exhibit warm-up and slow-down periods

Beat-to-beat variability

Examples: sinus tachycardia, multifocal atrial tachycardia, focal atrial tachycardia, focal and nonparoxysmal junctional tachycardia

Triggered (early or late afterdepolarization)

Often caused by conditions that increase the QT interval

More likely to occur when sinus rate is slow

Often associated with digoxin

Examples: focal atrial tachycardia, torsades de pointes

of depolarization and refractoriness is altered by a change in conduction properties. This pattern establishes the characteristics of reentrant circuits: the arrhythmias are often precipitated by a premature contraction, begin immediately at their maximal rate, are fixed (no beat-to-beat variability), and cease completely (no slow down of the arrhythmia). The response of these rhythms to medications and electrical interventions depends on the location of the circuit. If the AV node is involved, the reentrant circuit can be terminated by interventions that slow AV nodal conduction such as vagal maneuvers and adenosine. If the AV node is not involved, as with atrial flutter, the rhythm will not change when AV nodal conduction is blocked, although the ventricular rate will slow transiently.

- Enhanced automaticity occurs when arrhythmias arise from diseased tissue (abnormal automaticity) or from fibers that have pacemaker capability but do not normally function in this manner (enhanced automaticity). Rhythms associated with enhanced automaticity are often precipitated by adrenergic stimulation, tend to accelerate to their maximal rate, and are not initiated by premature contractions. They have beat-to-beat variability and decelerate gradually. They often do not respond predictably to pharmacologic or electrical interventions but can respond to overdrive pacing. Examples of narrow complex tachycardias caused by both abnormal and enhanced automaticity are focal atrial tachycardia and nonparoxysmal junctional tachycardia.
- Triggered arrhythmias are caused by early or late afterdepolarizations, depending on when they arise in the action potential. Ventricular arrhythmias associated with QT prolongation such as torsades de pointes are commonly caused by this mechanism, as are tachyarrhythmias associated with digoxin toxicity.

These mechanisms are illustrated in Figure 4.1.

SINUS TACHYCARDIA

Sinus tachycardia is a regular narrow complex tachycardia characterized by:

- normal AV conduction, with a P wave before every QRS complex and a fixed PR interval and
- an impulse that originates from the sinus node with uniform P-wave morphology that is upright in leads I, II, and aVF and inverted in lead aVR.

Physiologic sinus tachycardia can be a reaction to a stressor such as infection, dehydration, fever, anemia, heart failure, or hyperthyroidism or to exposure to exogenous substances such as caffeine, cocaine, or beta-agonists. The rate varies and often shows gradual variation over time and in response to treatment of the underlying physiology or pathology. A general guideline for predicting a patient's maximum sinus heart rate is 220 beats/min minus years of age.

Sinus tachycardia can be challenging to diagnose at rates of 150 beats/min or higher when the P wave is "buried" in the terminal portion of the T wave. A diligent search for the buried P wave often reveals the definitive diagnosis (Figure 4.2). Small decreases in rate such as occur with fluid resuscitation or fever reduction can sometimes "uncover" the buried P wave. Inappropriate sinus tachycardia (sometimes called nonparoxysmal sinus tachycardia) is a condition without apparent heart disease or other cause. It is a difficult diagnosis to make, not from the electrocardiographic perspective but from the clinical standpoint. The label "inappropriate" assumes that no physiologic stressor exists; thus, the diagnosis is, by definition, one of exclusion. The cause of inappropriate sinus tachycardia is unknown, but abnormal autonomic control is inherent in this disease. In addition, certain individuals probably have a higher rate of "normal" sinus rhythm, so even though they might have tachycardia according to its standard definition, they are actually clinically stable without being under physiologic stress. Sinoatrial nodal reentrant tachycardia is quite uncommon and accounts for fewer than 5% of patients referred for electrophysiologic studies and therefore is uncommon in the emergency department.[4]

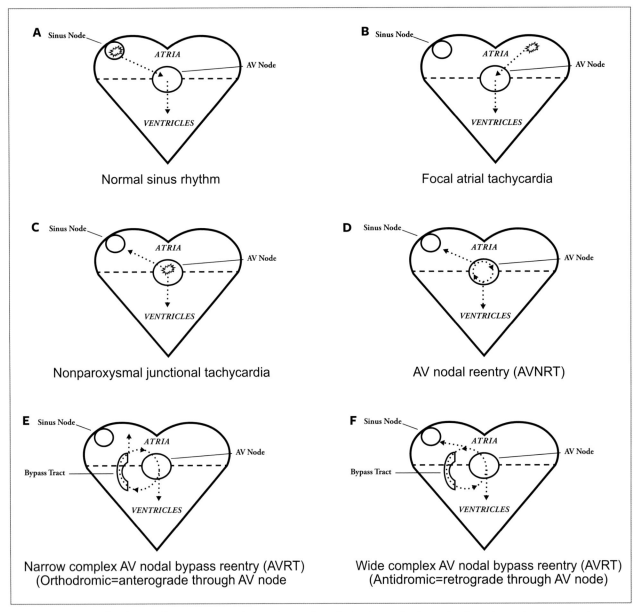

FIGURE 4.1. Mechanisms of narrow complex tachycardias. **A.** In sinus rhythm, the impulse originates in the sinus node and travels through the AV node and His-Purkinje system to the ventricle. This generates a P wave, which is upright in lead II and inverted in aVR. **B.** In focal atrial tachycardia, an ectopic atrial focus provides source of impulse formation. The P wave often appears ectopic but will appear sinus in origin if the focus is near the sinus node. **C.** In nonparoxysmal junctional tachycardia, the ectopic focus originates in the AV node or His bundle, generating a retrograde P wave, which is inverted in II and upright in aVR. **D.** In AVNRT, a reentrant circuit in the AV node generates a retrograde P wave (inverted in II and upright in aVR) that is often obscured within the QRS complex. **E.** In the narrow complex form of AVRT, the impulse travels anterograde through the AV node and retrograde through the accessory pathway. **F.** In the wide complex form of AVRT, the impulse travels anterograde through the accessory pathway and retrograde through the AV node. Reproduced with permission from: Jeffrey A. Tabas, MD, FACEP.

NARROW COMPLEX TACHYCARDIAS

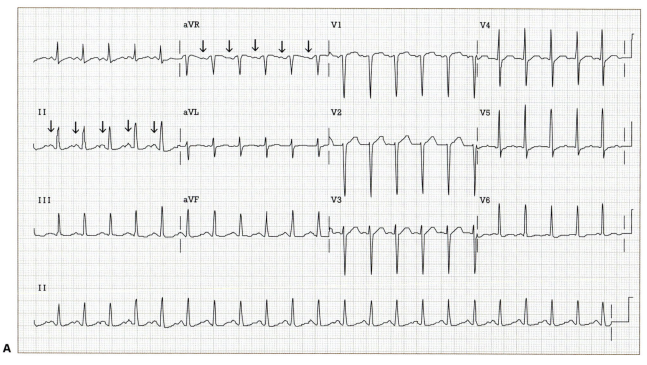

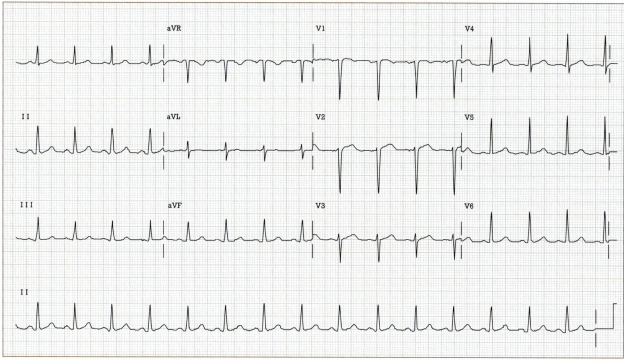

FIGURE 4.2. Sinus rhythm. **A.** This ECG reveals rapid narrow complex tachycardia at a rate of 134 bpm. An initial search reveals P waves that are obscured by the T wave because of the rapid rate. Further inspection reveals a P wave that is upright in lead II and inverted in aVR, highly suggestive of sinus tachycardia (*arrows*). **B.** After fluid resuscitation and antipyretic therapy, the sinus tachycardia resolved. Inspection reveals easily identifiable P waves, which are separated from the T waves at the slower rate and clearly of sinus origin. Reproduced with permission from: Jeffrey A. Tabas, MD, FACEP.

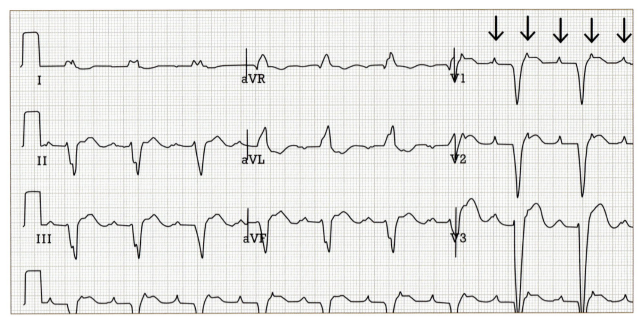

FIGURE 4.3. Atrial tachycardia with AV block. This ECG demonstrates rapid, regular narrow complex tachycardia with P waves that precede each QRS complex. The P-wave morphology is inverted in lead II and upright in lead aVR, demonstrating an ectopic atrial focus. In addition, in leads V_4 and V_5, P waves are easily observed (*arrows*). Note that every other P wave is conducted to the ventricle, producing a QRS complex. Every second P wave is not conducted, hence, the AV block descriptor. Reproduced with permission from: Stahmer SA, Cowan R. Tachydysrhythmias. *Emerg Med Clin North Am*. 2006;24:11-40. Copyright 2006 Elsevier Inc.

FOCAL ATRIAL TACHYCARDIA

Focal atrial tachycardia is one of the less common causes of regular narrow complex tachycardias. It is most often caused by enhanced automaticity but is occasionally the result of reentry or triggering.[5] It is characterized as a fast rhythm from a discrete origin external to the sinus node, discharging at a rate that is generally regular and conducting in a centrifugal manner throughout the atrial tissue. In general, a positive P wave in lead V_1 and negative P waves in leads I and aVL correlate with atrial tachycardia arising from the left atrium. Positive P waves in leads II, III, and aVF suggest that the origin is the cranial portion of either atrium.[6] Shorter P-wave duration correlates with atrial tachycardia arising from the paraseptal tissue versus the right or left atrial free wall. In atrial tachycardia, a single atrial focus takes over pacing from the sinoatrial node, typically at a rate of 150 to 250 beats/min (Figure 4.3). As with other arrhythmias caused by enhanced automaticity, this rhythm tends to accelerate at initiation to its maximal rate and is not initiated by a premature contraction. It has beat-to-beat variability and decelerates gradually. It generally does not respond to vagal maneuvers. In the group of arrhythmias commonly referred to as PSVT, atrial tachycardia accounts for approximately 10% of cases (Table 4.3).

MULTIFOCAL ATRIAL TACHYCARDIA

Multifocal atrial tachycardia (MAT) classically occurs as a complication of chronic pulmonary disease with acute decompensation, but it can also be seen in patients with acute heart failure, sepsis, MI, and hypokalemia and in those with methylxanthine (eg, theophylline) toxicity. In MAT, multiple atrial foci occur as a result of abnormal automaticity, causing an irregular rhythm. The criteria for MAT include at least three P-wave morphologies in a single ECG lead, with varying PR intervals (Figure 4.4, Table 4.4). The rate varies between 100 and 200 beats/min. The QRS complexes do not vary in morphology. It can be difficult to distinguish MAT from atrial fibrillation on physical examination or even on a single tracing, so a 12-lead ECG is indicated to

TABLE 4.3. Electrocardiographic characteristics of focal atrial tachycardia caused by enhanced automaticity.
100–250 bpm
Warm-up at onset and slow-down at offset (if captured on monitoring)
Lack of sawtooth flutter waves
AV nodal blockade does not terminate tachycardia
Classic rhythm of digoxin toxicity, especially with AV nodal block
Occasionally caused by reentry

TABLE 4.4. Electrocardiographic characteristics of multifocal atrial tachycardia.
Irregularly irregular rhythm, usually faster than 100 bpm
At least three P-wave morphologies
Varying P-P, RP, and PR intervals

TABLE 4.5. Causes of atrial fibrillation.
Alcohol intake
Autonomic dysfunction
Cardiac or thoracic surgery
Cardiomyopathy of any cause
Congenital heart disease
Heart failure
Hypertension
Hyperthyroidism
Myocardial infarction/ischemia
Pericarditis
Pulmonary disease
Rheumatic heart disease
Sick sinus syndrome
Supraventricular arrhythmias
Valvular heart disease

confirm the diagnosis. Unlike atrial fibrillation (see below), there is a distinct isoelectric period between P waves. The P-P, PR, and R-R intervals are variable. Treatment focuses on correcting the underlying disease that is creating the rhythm disturbance. Rarely is this rhythm responsible for a patient's symptoms.[7] Antiarrhythmic medications are usually not helpful for this rhythm, so the primary mode of therapy should focus on management of the underlying pathologic process. Cardioversion is not indicated in MAT.[8]

ATRIAL FIBRILLATION

After sinus tachycardia, atrial fibrillation is the second most common sustained arrhythmia encountered in the ED; it is increasing in frequency as the population ages. Atrial fibrillation can occur in persons without intrinsic cardiac or systemic disease as well as in association with various clinical states (Table 4.5).[9] It is characterized by uncoordinated atrial activation and, consequently, ineffective atrial contraction. The atria are stimulated and depolarized at rates ranging from 300 to 600 beats/min, resulting in fibrillatory activity. This activity produces characteristic fibrillatory waves that can be coarse or fine. There are no discrete P waves, and the fibrillatory pattern is evident in the ECG baseline (Figure 4.5). The AV junction is stimulated in a random fashion, resulting in an irregular ventricular rate that varies from 100 to 240 beats/min, usually approximately 170 beats/min. Electrocardiographic characteristics include:

- irregular R-R intervals (when AV conduction is present),
- absence of distinct P waves, and
- irregular atrial activity.[10]

The ventricular rate during atrial fibrillation can be quite variable, depending on autonomic tone, the electrophysiologic properties of the AV node, and the effects of medications that act on the AV conduction system. Untreated ventricular responses of less than 100 beats/min suggest the presence of coexistent AV node disease. The QRS complex is narrow unless

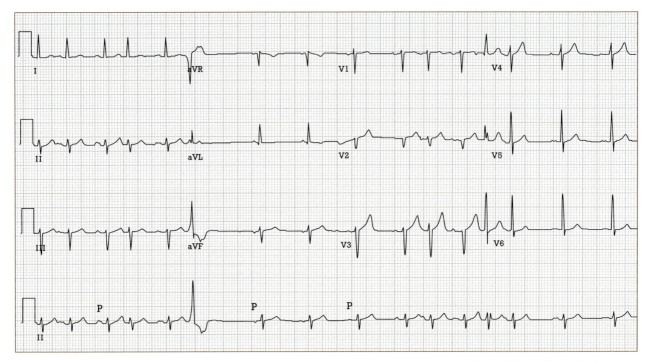

FIGURE 4.4. Multifocal atrial tachycardia. This ECG reveals narrow complex irregular tachycardia with three or more P-wave morphologies (p) and varying PR intervals. Reproduced with permission from: Stahmer SA, Cowan R. Tachydysrhythmias. *Emerg Med Clin North Am*. 2006;24:11-40. Copyright 2006 Elsevier Inc.

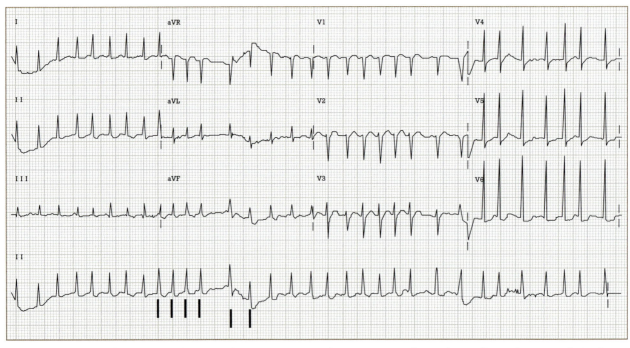

FIGURE 4.5. Atrial fibrillation. This ECG demonstrates rapid, narrow complex tachycardia at the rate of 204 bpm. On initial review, the rhythm appears to be regular. On closer review, however, some irregularity is noted. At very rapid rates, atrial fibrillation can appear regular unless care is taken to assess the regularity of ventricular response. Reproduced with permission from: Jeffrey A. Tabas, MD, FACEP.

there is a preexisting or rate-related bundle-branch block or conduction down an accessory pathway, as is seen in atrial fibrillation in the Wolff-Parkinson-White (WPW) syndrome.

The differential diagnosis for irregularly irregular narrow complex tachycardia includes MAT and any regular tachycardia arising from the atrium that is associated with variable AV block or frequent premature ventricular beats (eg, atrial flutter with variable block). The hallmark features of atrial fibrillation are the marked irregularity and absence of distinct atrial activity (Table 4.6).

ATRIAL FLUTTER

Atrial flutter is an arrhythmia characterized by rapid, regular atrial depolarizations, usually at approximately 300 beats/min, and with a ventricular response typically of 150 ± 20 beats/min in patients not using AV nodal blocking agents. It typically occurs by a macroreentrant mechanism that runs a circuit from the right atrium to the left in a counterclockwise direction. Other mechanisms of atrial flutter such as reentry in the left atrium and reentry around surgical incisions in the atria are seen less commonly. As in atrial fibrillation, the ventricular response depends on the status of AV function.

On the ECG, the "flutter waves" create a "sawtooth" pattern and are best seen in leads II, III, aVF, and V$_1$ (Figure 4.6). These flutter waves appear as atrial complexes of constant morphology, polarity, and cycle length, with a rate typically around 300 beats/min (ranging from 240 to 340 beats/min). The sawtooth pattern is pathognomonic and characterized by a positive P-wave deflection alternating with a negative P-wave deflection in conducted and nonconducted beats. These appear because of rotation of the circuit along the base of the atrium. This pattern can distort the ST segment, which provides a clue to the diagnosis. Inability to identify the isoelectric point in lead II is highly suggestive of atrial flutter since the circuit is almost never perpendicular to lead II. There is often an AV block associated with this rhythm because the AV node cannot conduct at these rapid rates (>220 bpm). The resultant ventricular rate is therefore often at 150 (2:1 block) or 100 (3:1 block) beats/min (Table 4.7). The block can also be variable, leading to an irregularly irregular rhythm, clinically similar to atrial fibrillation although electrocardiographically distinct. To differentiate atrial flutter from atrial fibrillation, review the ECG for inverted P waves (flutter waves) in leads II, III, and aVF with an atrial rate of approximately 300 beats/min. In addition, look at the R-R intervals to see if they are occurring in divisibles of 300 (for example, a rhythm with two beats at a rate of 75 beats/min, followed by several beats at a rate of 100 beats/min, and subsequently by several additional beats at a rate of 150 beats/min would produce conduction patterns of 4:1, 3:1, and 2:1 conduction, respectively). Clinically, however, this pattern is usually not relevant to treatment, because atrial flutter and atrial fibrillation have similar primary management considerations.

Transient blockade of the AV node with vagal maneuvers or adenosine will slow the ventricular rate, allowing the flutter waves to be visualized

TABLE 4.6. Electrocardiographic characteristics of atrial fibrillation.

Rapid and irregular atrial fibrillatory activity with an atrial rate typically faster than 300 bpm
Irregularly irregular ventricular response, with rate of 90–200 bpm
No detectable P waves

TABLE 4.7. Electrocardiographic characteristics of atrial flutter.

Narrow complex tachycardia of 250–350 bpm
Usually abrupt onset and offset (if captured on monitor)
Flutter waves visualized as sawtooth pattern, best seen in leads II, III, aVF, and V$_1$
ST-segment distortion such that no isoelectric point is clearly identified in lead II

more clearly (Figure 4.6B). Because the AV node is not part of the reentrant circuit, administration of adenosine will not terminate this rhythm, although it can aid in the diagnosis.[11]

NONPAROXYSMAL JUNCTIONAL TACHYCARDIA

Nonparoxysmal junctional tachycardia refers to focal sites of enhanced automaticity/triggered activity in the

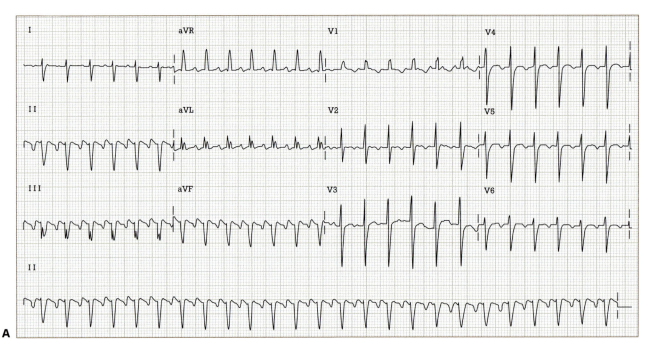

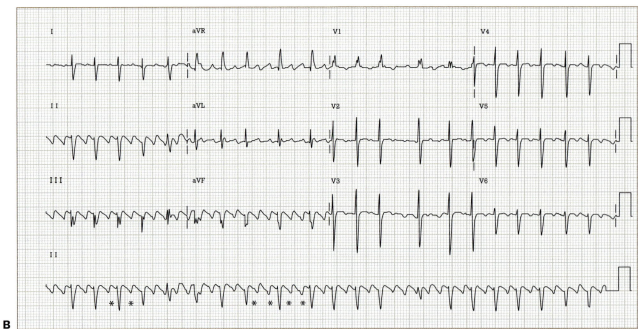

FIGURE 4.6. Atrial flutter. **A.** Rapid, regular, narrow complex tachycardia at a rate of 154 bpm. Flutter waves are apparent in leads in II, III, aVF, and V₁. **B.** After treatment with adenosine, AV conduction slows transiently and flutter waves are more apparent when ventricular response is slower. Conduction decreases transiently from 2:1 to 3:1 AV block (*stars*). Reproduced with permission from: Jeffrey A. Tabas, MD, FACEP.

AV node or the bundle of His. These sites of enhanced automaticity are uncommon in adults; when they do occur, they are usually associated with ischemia, infarction, cardiomyopathy, or digoxin toxicity.[12] This rhythm is also referred to as accelerated AV junctional tachycardia (Table 4.8). Electrocardiographic findings include rates ranging from 70 to 130 beats/min.[12] Retrograde activation of the atria results in a retrograde P wave that is often obscured by the QRS complex, but it can be seen following or, rarely, preceding the QRS complex. As with other automatic rhythms, there are usually "warm-up" and "cool-down" phases. Atrioventricular dissociation might be seen as the result of a functional AV node that is made refractory to sinus impulses by continuing partial or complete depolarizations from the competing junctional pacemaker, identified by a difference in the sinus and ventricular rates without a clear association between the P waves and the QRS complexes. This arrhythmia generally does not terminate with vagal stimulation or adenosine. Focal junctional tachycardia (also known as paroxysmal junctional, junctional ectopic, or automatic junctional tachycardia) occurs primarily in children, at rates up to 250 beats/min, and can show periods of irregularity.

ATRIOVENTRICULAR NODE REENTRY TACHYCARDIA

Atrioventricular node reentry tachycardia is a regular SVT resulting from a reentry circuit formation in the AV node and perinodal atrial tissue. It has an abrupt onset and termination, hence the "paroxysmal" in PSVT. Atrioventricular node reentry tachycardia is the most common PSVT, accounting for 60% of cases.[13] The rate is regular, usually 140 to 220 beats/min (Table 4.9), and the QRS complex is narrow, unless there is aberrant conduction such as in a preexisting or rate-related bundle-branch block. Following an initiating premature complex, subsequent atrial depolarizations are retrograde. The P wave is either partially or completely obscured within the QRS complex in 90% to 95% of cases (Figure 4.7). If the P wave is visualized, it will appear retrograde. Atrioventricular node reentry tachycardia displays the typical characteristics of reentrant arrhythmias. It is rarely life-threatening and is usually well tolerated. It will terminate via AV nodal blocking with vagal stimulation, adenosine, or other similar agents.[2]

ATRIOVENTRICULAR REENTRY TACHYCARDIA VIA AN ACCESSORY PATHWAY

Wolff-Parkinson-White syndrome, the most commonly encountered form of ventricular preexcitation, can present with narrow complex tachycardia. This is termed atrioventricular reentry tachycardia and occurs via an accessory pathway. It involves a reentrant circuit that includes the AV node as well as an accessory pathway, a short muscle bundle that directly connects the atria and ventricles. In the

TABLE 4.8. Electrocardiographic characteristics of nonparoxysmal junctional tachycardia (also known as accelerated AV junctional tachycardia).

Rates of 70–130 bpm
Uncommon in adults
Retrograde activation of the atria might be seen with P waves inverted in lead II and upright in aVR
Might see AV dissociation
Most often caused by enhanced automaticity
Can occur in association with digitalis toxicity, postcardiac surgery, electrolyte abnormalities, myocarditis, or myocardial ischemia
Focal junctional tachycardia (also known as paroxysmal junctional, junctional ectopic, and automatic junctional tachycardia) occurs primarily in children, occurs at rates up to 250 bpm, and can be erratic

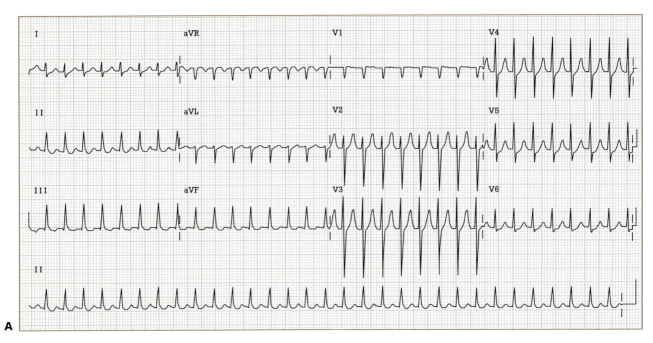

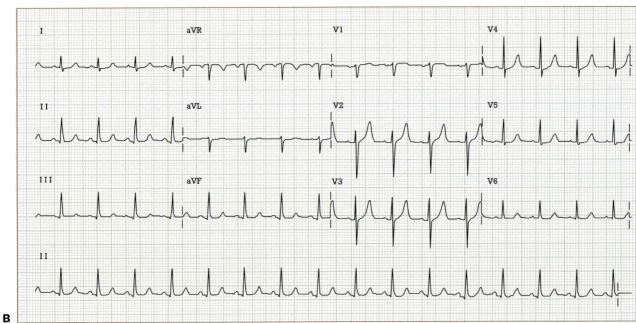

FIGURE 4.7. AVNRT with no underlying accessory pathway. **A.** This ECG reveals regular, narrow complex tachycardia at a rate of 191 bpm. At this rate, several causes, including AVNRT, AVRT, atrial flutter, and focal atrial tachycardia, must be considered. P waves are not clearly visible, although there is a suggestion of an inverted P wave in limb lead III that occurs roughly 120 milliseconds after the R wave. This suggests AVRT, although in the acute situation, this diagnosis could not be determined with certainty, and, in fact, electrophysiologic testing confirmed AVNRT. **B.** An ECG obtained after treatment with 6 mg of adenosine, showing resolution of the tachycardia. The patient is now in sinus rhythm. There is no evidence of accessory conduction in this resting tracing. Reproduced with permission from: Jeffrey A. Tabas, MD, FACEP.

TABLE 4.9. Electrocardiographic characteristics of atrioventricular nodal reentry tachycardia (AVNRT).
Fast, regular, narrow, without variation in ventricular rate
Rates often between 140 and 250 bpm, usually 180–200 bpm
P waves are often concealed within in the QRS complex; the RP interval is usually <70 ms
Concealed P waves can cause a pseudo S wave in inferior leads and pseudo R wave in V_1; recognized only in comparison with the QRS complex in normal sinus rhythm
Atypical form with P wave preceding QRS complex is uncommon (<5%)

TABLE 4.10. Electrocardiographic characteristics of atrioventricular reentry tachycardia via accessory pathway (AVRT).
Fast, regular, narrow, without variation in ventricular rate
Retrograde P waves are more delayed and therefore more often distinct from the QRS complex than in AVNRT. The RP interval is usually >70 ms
Rates of 140–280 bpm; usually 200 bpm

narrow complex tachycardia form (orthodromic reciprocating tachycardia), the impulse travels anterograde (from atria to ventricles) down the AV node, through the His-Purkinje system, and then retrograde (from ventricles to atria) up the accessory pathway, ultimately completing the circuit back to the AV node. Within the group of arrhythmias commonly referred to as PSVT, AVRT constitutes 5% of cases of narrow complex tachycardia encountered in the emergency department; in the electrophysiology community, it accounts for approximately 30% of cases of SVT.[14]

Atrioventricular reentry tachycardia is often seen in patients younger than those with AVNRT. It is similar to AVNRT in that it is a reentrant loop tachycardia initiated by a premature contraction. A retrograde P wave is more commonly visible on the ECG with AVRT than with AVNRT because of greater differences in time to depolarization of the ventricle and retrograde depolarization of the atria (Table 4.10). Here, the PR interval is *longer* than the RP interval, compared with normal atrial impulse conduction through the AV node to the ventricle, in which the PR interval is *shorter* than the RP interval (Figure 4.8). Due to retrograde activation, the P waves in AVNRT are inverted in the inferior leads and upright in aVR. QRS alternans (alternating amplitude of the QRS complex) can be seen, but it is associated with all atrial tachycardias and could simply be related to faster rates.[14]

Visible conduction through the accessory pathway manifests as a short PR interval and a delta wave (slurring of the initial portion of the R wave). This presentation constitutes WPW syndrome (see Chapter 12). In approximately 30% of patients with accessory pathways, however, there is no evidence of accessory pathway conduction on the baseline ECG in sinus rhythm. This "concealed bypass tract," also called concealed conduction, often conducts in a retrograde fashion, allowing generation of an orthodromic, reentrant tachyarrhythmia.

APPROACH TO EVALUATION AND DIAGNOSIS

The initial step in the evaluation of any patient with narrow QRS tachycardia is to determine whether symptoms or signs of inadequate organ perfusion attributable to the rapid heart rate are present. If so, and if they are severe (and the rhythm is not sinus tachycardia or atrial fibrillation/flutter), then immediate cardioversion should be considered. If the patient is hemodynamically stable, then treatment can include consideration of medication or electrical interventions. The consideration of instability is not binary, meaning that the patient should not be considered stable or unstable as the only clinical choices. Rather, stability, or lack thereof, should be

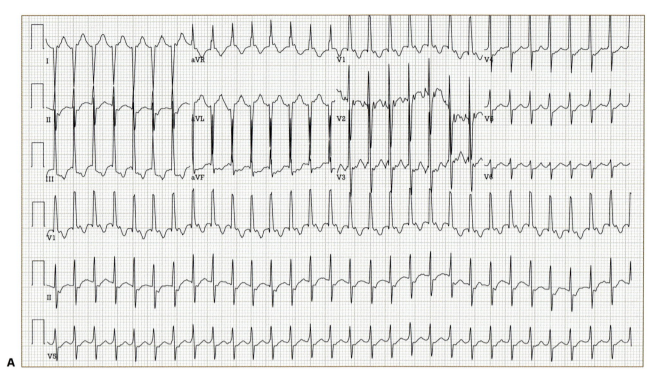
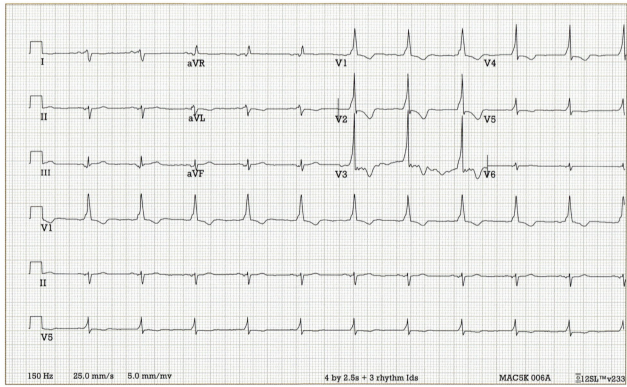

FIGURE 4.8. AVNRT with an underlying accessory pathway. **A.** This ECG reveals regular, narrow complex tachycardia at a rate of 176 bpm. P waves are not clearly visible, although there is a suggestion of an inverted P wave at the beginning of the T wave. **B.** An ECG obtained after treatment with 6 mg of adenosine, showing resolution of the tachycardia. The patient is now in sinus rhythm. Evidence of accessory conduction in this resting tracing is found in the slurred upstroke of the QRS complexes, consistent with WPW syndrome.

considered across a spectrum of clinical conditions, with varying degrees of instability, ranging from minimally to maximally unstable. Treatment should be chosen from this perspective of stability.

In the absence of instability, assessment of narrow complex tachycardia should begin with determination of ventricular rate and regularity (Table 4.11). An irregularly irregular rhythm is usually atrial fibrillation, although MAT, atrial flutter with variable block, and sinus tachycardia with frequent premature complexes can be mistaken for it. At rapid rates, the irregularity of atrial fibrillation can be difficult to observe with the naked eye; therefore, care should be taken to assess the regularity of the R-R interval using calipers or other measuring devices.

Once the clinician has determined that the rhythm is a regular narrow complex tachycardia, the evaluation should proceed with a search for sinus tachycardia. Treatment of the underlying cause such as hypovolemia, hypoxia, elevated body temperature (ie, fever), pharmacologic effect, pain, or anxiety should follow as appropriate for the clinical situation.

If sinus tachycardia is not suspected, the evaluation should proceed with assessment of atrial activity for rate, P-wave morphology, the relationship between atrial and ventricular rates, and the position of the P wave in relation to the preceding and following QRS complexes. This approach will assist in identifying the origin of the arrhythmia as the sinus node (sinus tachycardia), the atria (atrial flutter or atrial tachycardia), or an AV nodal source

TABLE 4.11. Diagnostic approach to narrow complex tachycardias.

Determine if QRS complex is narrow (<120 ms)

Determine if ventricular response is irregularly irregular

    Atrial fibrillation

    Multifocal atrial tachycardia

    Any atrial tachycardia with variable block or premature ventricular beats

    Focal junctional tachycardia (rarely)

Determine if the regular narrow complex tachycardia is sinus tachycardia

    Uniform P wave before every QRS complex

    P-wave morphology upright in lead II, inverted in aVR

    Fixed PR interval

    Rate is not fixed

Determine if the regular narrow complex tachycardia terminates with AV nodal blocking

    AVNRT

    AVRT

Determine if the ventricular response of the regular narrow complex tachycardia slows with AV nodal blocking but fails to terminate

    Sinus tachycardia

    Atrial flutter

    Focal atrial tachycardia

    Focal and nonparoxysmal junctional tachycardia

(AVRT, AVNRT, or accelerated junctional tachycardia). With rapid rates, atrial activity can be difficult to discern. Maneuvers to slow the rate or ventricular response are often diagnostic and can be therapeutic.

A search should be made for P waves being obscured by the QRS complex or T waves. Increasing the paper speed during ECG recording might improve identification of P waves. Limb lead II and precordial lead V_1 are often optimal for identification of the P wave. If the P-wave morphology is not characteristic of sinus rhythm, then an ectopic atrial focus, a retrograde conducted P wave, or limb lead misplacement should be considered. A sawtooth pattern, best seen in lead II, is characteristic of atrial flutter. A regular narrow complex tachycardia with a P wave preceding the QRS that demonstrates abnormal morphology is usually caused by atrial tachycardia, especially if the presence of flutter waves can be excluded. A retrograde P wave arising from the AV node can be identified if it follows the QRS complex (described as a PR interval *longer* than the RP interval) and shows reversal of P-wave morphology, being inverted in lead II and upright in aVR. Retrograde P waves indicate that the rhythm arises from the AV node and is most likely AVRT (or AVNRT), which will convert to sinus rhythm when the AV node is blocked. It is rare but possible for a retrograde P wave to precede the QRS complex.

With regular narrow complex tachycardia, the diagnosis is often achieved with vagal maneuvers or adenosine treatment to block the AV node (Table 4.11). Atrial or automatic tachycardias will persist despite slowed ventricular conduction, whereas the reentry tachycardias—AVRT and AVNRT—will terminate. More prolonged AV nodal blockade can be achieved with calcium channel or beta-blocking agents for prolonged rate control.

REFERENCES

1. Ganz LI, Friedman PL. Supraventricular tachycardia. *N Engl J Med*. 1995;332(3):162-173.
2. Page RL, Joglar JA, Caldwell MA, et al. 2015 ACC/AHA/HRS Guideline for the Management of Adult Patients With Supraventricular Tachycardia: Executive Summary: A Report of the American College of Cardiology/American Heart Association Task Force on Clinical Practice Guidelines and the Heart Rhythm Society. *Circulation*. 2016;133(14):e471-e505.
3. Bibas L, Levi M, Essebag V. Diagnosis and management of supraventricular tachycardias. *CMAJ*. 2016;188(17-18):E466-E473.
4. Bauernfeind RA, Wyndham CR, Dhingra RC, et al. Serial electrophysiologic testing of multiple drugs in patients with atrioventricular nodal reentrant paroxysmal tachycardia. *Circulation*. 1980;62(6):1341-1349.
5. Roberts SA, Diaz C, Nolan PE, et al. Effectiveness and costs of digoxin treatment for atrial fibrillation and flutter. *Am J Cardiol*. 1993;72(7):567-573.
6. Doni F, Manfredi M, Piermonti C, et al. New onset atrial flutter termination by overdrive transoesophageal pacing: effects of different protocols of stimulation. *Europace*. 2000;2(4):292-296.
7. Kastor JA. Multifocal atrial tachycardia. *N Engl J Med*. 1990;322(24):1713-1717.
8. Deal BJ, Mavroudis C, Backer CL, et al. Comparison of anatomic isthmus block with the modified right atrial maze procedure for late atrial tachycardia in Fontan patients. *Circulation*. 2002;106(5):575-579.
9. McManus DD, Rienstra M, Benjamin EJ. An update on the prognosis of patients with atrial fibrillation. *Circulation*. 2012;126(10):e143-e146.
10. Camm AJ, Kirchhof P, Lip GY, et al. Guidelines for the management of atrial fibrillation: the Task Force for the Management of Atrial Fibrillation of the European Society of Cardiology (ESC). *Europace*. 2010;.12(10):1360-1420.
11. Wellens HJ. Contemporary management of atrial flutter. *Circulation*. 2002;106(6):649-652.
12. Surawicz B, Knilans TK, eds. *Chou's Electrocardiography in Clinical Practice: Adult and Pediatric*. 6th ed. 2008, Philadelphia: Saunders.
13. Goyal R, Zivin A, Souza J, et al. Comparison of the ages of tachycardia onset in patients with atrioventricular nodal reentrant tachycardia and accessory pathway-mediated tachycardia. *Am Heart J*. 1996;132(4):765-767.
14. Green M, Heddle B, Dassen W, et al. Value of QRS alteration in determining the site of origin of narrow QRS supraventricular tachycardia. *Circulation*. 1983;68(2):368-373.

CHAPTER FIVE

Wide Complex Tachycardias

GUS M. GARMEL

KEY POINTS[1,2]

- Hemodynamically unstable patients presenting with wide complex tachycardia require defibrillation or emergent cardioversion (with sedation considered).
- Treatment should be based on the individual's clinical or hemodynamic status, not on the ECG.
- The ECG in patients with wide complex tachycardia does not always allow determination of the cause of the rhythm disturbance. It might not even have clinical relevance in the emergent setting. It is therefore acceptable to interpret an ECG demonstrating wide complex tachycardia as "wide complex tachycardia of uncertain etiology."
- Algorithms and diagnostic criteria intended to help clinicians correctly interpret wide complex tachycardias are not always easy to apply (or remember). Most importantly, these do not always accurately identify the etiology. They should be used with caution (if at all).
- In a patient with regular wide complex tachycardia of uncertain cause, assume the diagnosis to be ventricular tachycardia (VT) and treat as such, given the probability of VT and the minimal negative consequences if the diagnosis is incorrect.
- If the clinical situation allows, compare a patient's current ECG to a previous ECG if one is available.
- ECG findings suggestive of VT (ie, capture and fusion beats, atrioventricular dissociation, and ventriculoatrial retrograde conduction) can be difficult to identify and are not 100% specific for VT.
- Treatments for torsades de pointes and drug toxicity (overdose) differ substantially from treatments for other causes of wide QRS complex tachycardia. When possible, identify these early and initiate appropriately directed therapy.
- Medications that block the atrioventricular node (other than adenosine) should be avoided in patients with wide complex tachycardia unless a supraventricular origin without accessory conduction is confirmed or the medication is recommended by expert consultation.

A QRS complex that is wide (greater than or equal to 120 milliseconds, or 3 small boxes on a typical 12-lead ECG) represents delayed or abnormal ventricular depolarization.[3] In normal ventricular depolarization, the QRS complex is generated when an electrical stimulus passes from the atrioventricular (AV) node to the ventricular conduction system, terminating in the ventricular myocardial cells. The term *wide complex tachycardia* (WCT) (also known as broad complex or wide QRS complex tachycardia) refers to a rhythm disturbance with a wide QRS complex and a rate of 100 beats/min or faster. An understanding of WCTs requires appreciation of whether the rhythm and its associated tachycardia originate from the ventricle itself (ventricular tachycardia [VT]) or from above the ventricle (supraventricular tachycardia [SVT]) in association with aberrant conduction, accessory pathway conduction, or an underlying (baseline) QRS prolongation.[4-6] There are a number of other entities that result in WCTs that are unrelated to these common causes, such as electrolyte abnormalities, structural irregularities, pacemakers, and toxins; these will be discussed later in this chapter[7-11] (Table 5.1). Some patients on certain antiarrhythmic agents can have their intrinsic cardiac rate slowed yet still demonstrate features of VT.

Patients in the emergency department with WCT present both diagnostic and therapeutic challenges.[17,18] The goal of this chapter is to remove the "complex" from WCT recognition, identification, and management. Controversies will also be described. Despite the desire to accurately interpret an ECG demonstrating a WCT, numerous stepwise approaches[19-22] and extensive criteria used to interpret this potentially lethal rhythm have failed to provide acceptable agreement among physicians regarding ECG diagnosis.[23-26] An understanding of the causes of WCT allows an appreciation of when recognition and accurate treatment selection are possible, or when empiric treatment is indicated because accurate diagnosis is not possible. This understanding is essential to prevent mismanagement and reduce morbidity and mortality.[27,28]

APPROACH TO WIDE COMPLEX TACHYCARDIA

The initial consideration in an individual with WCT should be assessment for hemodynamic instability, represented by inadequate end-organ perfusion attributable to the arrhythmia.[1] Manifestations of instability include hypotension, pulmonary edema, confusion, angina, and poor skin perfusion. An approach in which the clinician errs on the side of considering a patient "unstable" is most prudent. Instability is not determined by the rate or width of the QRS complex.

Distinguishing with certainty between supraventricular and ventricular etiologies using published

TABLE 5.1. Causes of wide complex tachycardia.

Preexcited tachycardias (accessory pathway) (Figures 5.2E, 5.5, 5.14)

SVT with aberrant conduction (aberrancy)

Ventricular fibrillation

Ventricular-paced rhythm (Figure 5.6)

VT (monomorphic or polymorphic) (Figures 5.1, 5.4)

Other[4,12]

    Acute ST-segment elevation MI, or STEMI[14] (Figure 5.2G)

    Atrial tachycardia (atrial fibrillation or atrial flutter) with wide QRS (Figure 5.2C)

    Drug toxicities or overdose (tricyclic antidepressants, cocaine,[13] lithium, phenothiazines, diphenhydramine, bupropion, those with quinidine-like effects, sodium channel blocking agents, digitalis, lamotrigine, citalopram, flecainide, propoxyphene) (Figure 5.2B)

    ECG artifact[15] (Figure 5.2H)

    Hyperkalemia

    Hypermagnesemia

    Hypothermia

    Left ventricular hypertrophy

    Malingering[16]

    Postresuscitation

    Sinus tachycardia with preexisting wide QRS (Figure 5.2A)

algorithms has proved challenging even for the most experienced cardiologists and electrophysiologists.[29] Although rates above 200 beats/min are more likely to represent SVT, heart rate is not diagnostic for SVT, nor does it determine the etiology of the WCT (Figure 5.1). An individual's hemodynamic status does not help determine the cause of the WCT (although this has been a common misconception).[17] In an emergency setting, it is best to assume a ventricular origin for WCTs[30] unless certainty exists that the abnormal ECG is the result of a supraventricular source.

Wide Complex Tachycardia of Supraventricular Origin

Supraventricular rhythm disturbances can be seen as irregularly irregular, as in atrial fibrillation and multifocal atrial tachycardia, or generally regular, as in sinus tachycardia, atrial flutter, focal atrial tachycardia, and reentrant circuits through the AV node (see Chapter 4). Three basic mechanisms for QRS widening should be considered in a patient with WCT from a supraventricular origin (Figure 5.2, Table 5.2):

- Preexisting bundle-branch block pattern or any intraventricular conduction delay should be suspected when the same QRS pattern is evident on a prior ECG demonstrating sinus rhythm.
- Widening can be caused by aberrant ventricular conduction. This is the abnormal intraventricular conduction of supraventricular impulses, usually due to a change in cycle length. This can be rate related, as is seen with the Ashman phenomenon (typically in atrial fibrillation).[31-33] Right bundle-branch block (RBBB) is most common in this scenario.
- Widening of the QRS can be caused by conduction through an accessory pathway.[4,5,34-36] In this situation, normal electrical impulses originating from the atria depolarize ventricular

TABLE 5.2. Supraventricular causes of wide QRS complex tachycardia.

Conduction through an accessory pathway
Preexisting bundle-branch block or intraventricular conduction delay
Rate-related bundle-branch block (Ashman phenomenon or Ashman aberrancy)

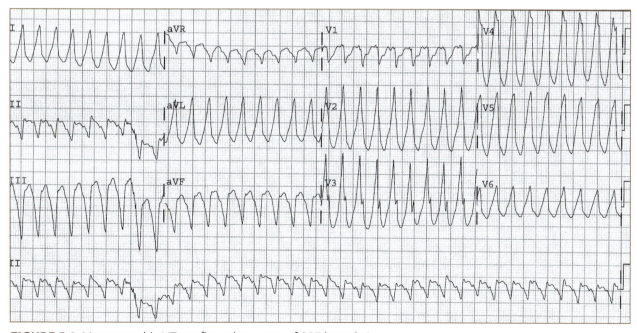

FIGURE 5.1. Monomorphic VT confirmed at a rate of 225 beats/min.

tissue earlier than normal conduction pathways. Conduction via an accessory pathway results in QRS widening due to *premature* activation of the ventricle. This differs from bundle-branch block, which causes widening due to *delayed* activation of the ventricle.[37,38]

Conduction down the accessory pathway typically occurs at faster rates than conduction through the AV node, which can result in an extremely rapid ventricular response and possible degeneration into ventricular arrhythmias. In patients with accessory pathways,

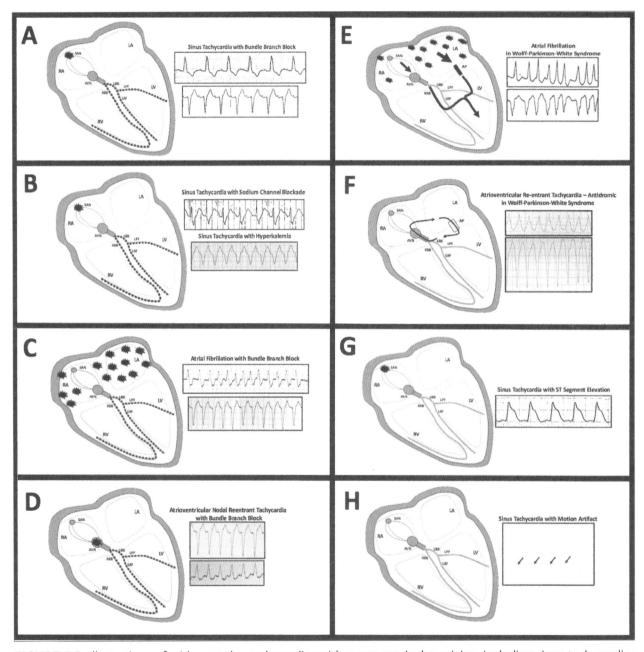

FIGURE 5.2. Illustrations of wide complex tachycardias with supraventricular origins, including sinus tachycardias (A, B, G, H), atrial tachycardias (C, E), and those with atrioventricular node reentry (D, F). Reproduced with permission from: Brady WJ, Mattu A, Tabas JA, Ferguson JD. The differential diagnosis of wide QRS complex tachycardia. *Am J Emerg Med*. 2017;35(10):1525-1529. Copyright 2017 Elsevier Inc.

impulse conduction can travel from the atria through the AV node alone, resulting in narrow complexes (unless there is preexisting conduction delay); through both the AV node and the accessory pathway simultaneously, resulting in fusion complexes of variable duration (a QRS complex with a delta wave is one example); or through the accessory pathway intermittently or exclusively, resulting in a prolonged QRS duration (Figures 5.2A-E). For reentrant circuits involving both an accessory pathway and the AV node, terminology is based on the direction of conduction through the AV node.[4,39-42] Conduction anterograde through the AV node and retrograde through the accessory pathway is termed *orthodromic*, resulting in a narrow QRS complex. Conduction retrograde through the AV node and anterograde through the accessory pathway is termed *antidromic*, resulting in a wide QRS complex (Figure 5.2F).

Other causes of QRS complex widening include the effect of medication toxicity, ingestion, and overdose (see Chapter 17), cardiac structural abnormalities, and electrolyte or metabolic abnormalities (see Chapter 15). Rapid identification of these causes should direct the initiation of life-saving therapeutic interventions.

Wide Complex Tachycardia of Ventricular Origin

Sustained VT has been defined as successive rapid ventricular complexes lasting more than 30 seconds or requiring intervention for termination. The heart rate for VT typically is faster than 120 beats/min. Exceptions are noted in patients taking oral (or being administered) antiarrhythmic agents that slow conduction and in patients with significant cardiomyopathy (because the heart is unable to increase its intrinsic rate). Nonsustained (intermittent) VT involves more than three successive rapid ventricular complexes lasting less than 30 seconds (Figure 5.3). Some cardiologists use the term *incessant* VT, which refers to hemodynamically stable

TABLE 5.3. Ventricular causes of wide QRS complex tachycardia.

Accelerated idiopathic ventricular rhythm

Monomorphic VT

Paced rhythm (including pacemaker-mediated tachycardia[43])

Polymorphic VT

    Bidirectional VT

    Multifocal VT

    Torsades de pointes

VT persisting longer than 1 hour. Ventricular tachycardia can be classified as monomorphic or polymorphic (Table 5.3); this distinction has important implications for identifying the underlying etiology and for assisting with therapeutic decisions.

In monomorphic VT, complexes of a single morphology occur at a rate classically between 120 and 200 beats/min (Figure 5.4A). Classic features of monomorphic VT include a predominantly regular rate, the presence of AV dissociation, capture or fusion beats, concordance of the QRS complexes across the precordium, and a left bundle-branch block (LBBB) pattern (see below). These classic features might not always be present or apparent, however, especially as the heart rate increases and baseline artifact occurs. Diagnostic algorithms based on the presence or absence of these features lack sufficient accuracy for use in the clinical setting. A novel score developed for the identification of VT has been recently introduced, but this scoring system has its challenges as well.[44,45]

Polymorphic VT includes torsades de pointes, multifocal VT, and bidirectional VT. Torsades de pointes[46] is characterized by ventricular complexes that vary in a sinusoidal pattern about the isoelectric line at a rate typically between 200 and 250 beats/min (Figures 5.4B, 5.5). It can develop with underlying QT prolongation, and is more likely to occur during episodes of bradycardia when the QT interval is prolonged.[47] It has been associated with congenital prolonged QT syndrome, multiple electrolyte abnormalities (especially those commonly related to alcoholism), many antiarrhythmic agents (ibutilide, sotalol, and Class Ia agents, for example), and other medications (phenothiazines, tricyclic antidepressants, and pentamidine).[48-50] Identification of polymorphic VT is essential because treatments appropriate for monomorphic VT can be ineffective in treating polymorphic VT, especially if torsades de pointes is present. Depending on the patient's hemodynamic status, treatment of torsades de pointes with magnesium infusion is recommended.[51] If magnesium is unsuccessful, attempts to increase the heart rate with beta-adrenergic or dopaminergic agents or overdrive pacing are recommended. Torsades de pointes that causes hemodynamic instability or is refractory to treatment should be managed with electrical cardioversion or defibrillation.

Multifocal VT refers to VT with two or more ventricular morphologies in a patient without QT-interval prolongation. It is less common than torsades de pointes, and occurs primarily in patients with previous MI and abnormal left ventricular function.

Bidirectional VT consists of alternating QRS complexes with opposite directions; it is one type of multifocal VT. It is typically associated with digoxin toxicity.[52-54] This WCT generally has RBBB pattern,

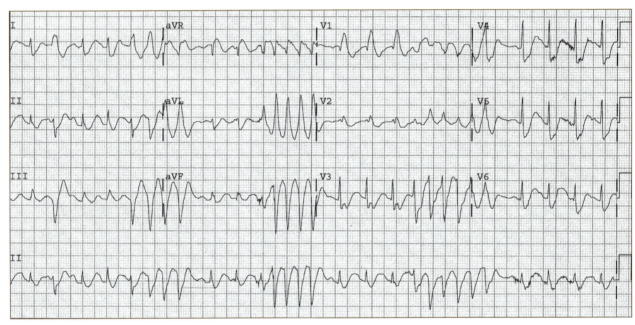

FIGURE 5.3. Nonsustained (intermittent) VT, not commonly identified on a 12-lead ECG.

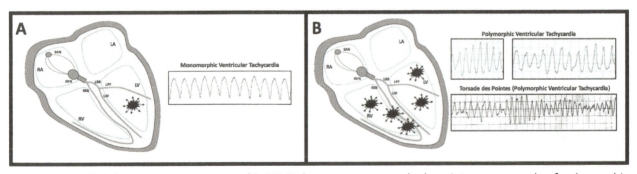

FIGURE 5.4. VT **A** demonstrates monomorphic VT; **B** demonstrates torsade de pointes, an example of polymorphic VT. Reproduced with permission from: Brady WJ, Mattu A, Tabas JA, Ferguson JD. The differential diagnosis of wide QRS complex tachycardia. *Am J Emerg Med.* 2017;35(10):1525-1529. Copyright 2017 Elsevier Inc.

with the QRS complexes alternating between right- and left-axis deviation in the limb leads.

An additional consideration for WCT with a ventricular origin is tachycardia caused by paced rhythms (Figure 5.6). With careful attention, one can identify pacer spikes at the top of the ECG or prior to pacemaker-generated ventricular capture (See Chapter 14).

Accelerated idiopathic ventricular rhythm is an enhanced ectopic ventricular rhythm with a maximum

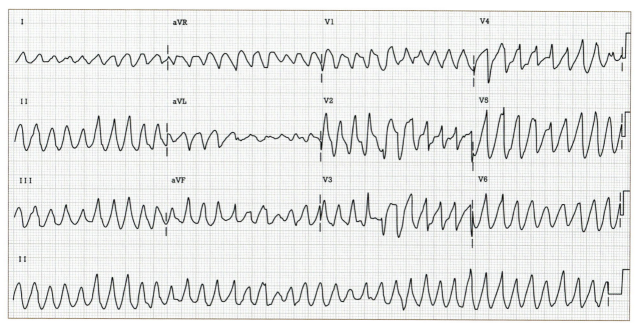

FIGURE 5.5. Torsades de pointes, a form of polymorphic VT. This is rare to be captured on a 12-lead ECG. The heart rate was 208 beats/min. The amplitude of the QRS complexes appears to expand and compress, best seen in the rhythm strip of lead II. Reproduced with permission from: Jeffrey A. Tabas, MD, FACEP.

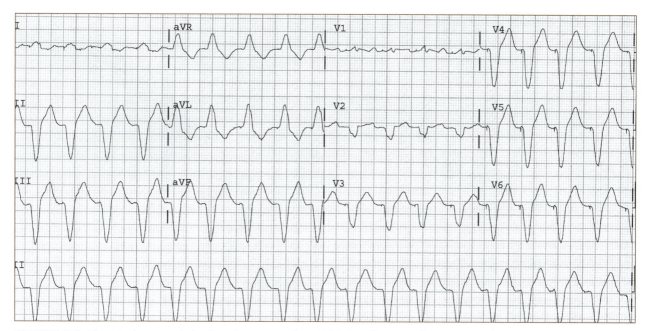

FIGURE 5.6. Ventricular-paced rhythm demonstrating WCT. Small pacemaker-generated impulses (spikes) can be recognized within the 12-lead ECG in leads V_3 through V_6 but are easily identified at the top of the ECG.

heart rate of 110 beats/min. It is a common reperfusion rhythm following cardiac arrest or MI, and it is generally well tolerated and self-limited in these settings. Incorrect or inappropriate treatment of this WCT can increase morbidity or mortality. The goals of treatment, if needed, are to increase the underlying atrial rate (with atropine, for example) and to suppress the enhanced ventricular automaticity.

DIFFERENTIATION BETWEEN VT AND SVT

Despite multiple attempts by researchers and clinicians, no elements of the patient's history, clinical characteristics, or ECG algorithm have been demonstrated to have acceptable precision in determining the cause of WCT.[23,25] In many cases, the "final" determination of the cause is not of utmost importance even for a stable patient in an emergency department. It is perfectly acceptable for an emergency physician to provide a final interpretation of the abnormal ECG with WCT as "wide complex tachycardia of uncertain (undetermined) etiology." In fact, not establishing a definitive diagnosis (ECG interpretation) might result in better patient care and outcomes, as the focus of care is directed toward the patient's clinical condition and hemodynamic status, not the correct ECG interpretation.

It has been reported that approximately 80% of patients who present with WCT will ultimately be diagnosed with VT,[55,56] although this frequency could be lower, as it is influenced by referral bias and dependence on older literature.[6,29,57]

Patient History

Elements of the patient's history that increase the likelihood of a ventricular focus of the WCT include prior MI, a history of acute heart failure, and a history of recent angina.[25] These findings can be related to the association between older age and increased likelihood of VT as the etiology. An age of 35 years or younger supports a supraventricular origin. Male sex, the presence of an implantable cardioverter defibrillator, and a low ejection fraction have also been shown to increase the likelihood of VT, although none of these is diagnostic.

A focused history should include current medications, ingestions (intentional or accidental), presence of a pacemaker or implantable cardioverter defibrillator, prior cardiac surgery (eg, coronary artery bypass graft, structural repair, cardiac tumor removal), electrophysiology studies (including ablation of an accessory pathway), and symptom duration (including previous episodes and management).

Clinical Features

Hemodynamic status does not help determine the etiology of the WCT. Patients with VT can be stable, and those with wide SVT can have hemodynamic compromise. Clues that support the diagnosis of SVT include a QRS complex pattern that is identical to a previously identified bundle-branch block, aberrant conduction, or SVT with an accessory pathway. Brief attempts to transiently block the AV node with adenosine in stable patients with regular rates and suspicion for SVT can reveal the underlying rhythm or even terminate the arrhythmia. However, this is not definitive for SVT because some cases of VT are adenosine sensitive and can be terminated following its administration. If the diagnosis of SVT with aberrant conduction rather than VT is incorrectly assigned, the clinician could fail to make an appropriate referral or might initiate inappropriate subsequent pharmacologic treatment.

Cannon A (atrial) waves in a hemodynamically stable patient can suggest an etiology of the WCT. These waves are associated with AV dissociation and occur when the atria (typically the right atrium) contracts against a closed AV (typically tricuspid) valve, resulting in large jugular vein pulsations. Atrioventricular dissociation, although suggestive, is not diagnostic of VT. Other clinical findings that have been associated with AV dissociation include variability or fluctuations in blood pressure, and variability in the occurrence of or intensity of heart sounds (especially S_1). This might be due to the loss of AV synchrony that can occur with AV dissociation.

ECG Findings

REGULARITY (TABLE 5.4). A regular WCT should be managed as VT—the diagnosis is rarely determined with certainty in clinical practice. An *irregular* WCT suggests a supraventricular source such as atrial fibrillation with an accessory pathway, especially in a young person with a fast rate (Figure 5.7). The R-R interval in VT is constant in more than 90% of cases.[58] Clinicians must recognize, however, that VT can manifest some irregularity because of changes in cycle length, fusion or capture beats, multifocal ventricular complexes, or intermittent episodes of the arrhythmia.

QRS COMPLEX AXIS, DURATION, AND MORPHOLOGY. QRS characteristics can provide additional support for the cause of the WCT but are not diagnostic. A QRS axis that is more negative than −90° or more positive than +180° strongly suggests VT, especially if this was not present on a prior ECG (Figure 5.8). QRS complexes with RBBB morphology and a duration greater than 140 milliseconds, or those with LBBB morphology and a duration greater than 160 milliseconds support VT. Careful review of a prior ECG to compare QRS duration can be helpful, as a preexisting bundle-branch block pattern with the identical QRS morphology and duration when tachycardia is not present supports an etiology other than VT (Figures 5.9, 5.10). Although previously thought

TABLE 5.4. Wide complex tachycardia by QRS regularity.

Irregular
Atrial fibrillation with aberrancy
Preexcited atrial fibrillation (accessory pathway for antegrade conduction)
Polymorphic VT
Torsades de pointes

Regular
SVT with aberrancy
VT

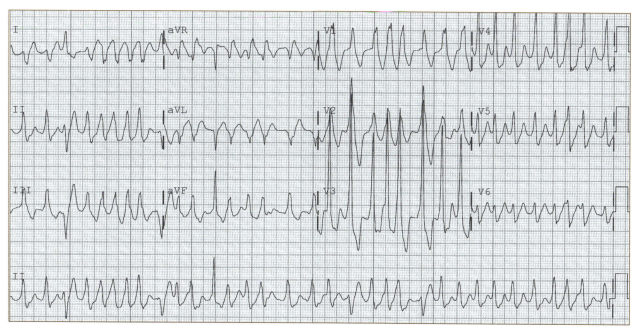

FIGURE 5.7. Atrial fibrillation with Wolff-Parkinson-White syndrome. This chaotic wide complex tachycardia is irregular. Delta waves can be identified, especially in leads V_4 through V_6. Recognition of several R-R intervals approaching 300 beats/min with this irregularly irregular rate is a strong clue for atrial fibrillation using the accessory pathway of Wolff-Parkinson-White syndrome. Reproduced with permission from: Joel T. Levis, MD, PhD, FACEP, FAAEM.

to predict SVT, a WCT with RBBB pattern is not predictive of etiology (Figure 5.11). QRS complex morphology suggestive of VT, such as a V_1 lead with an R-wave duration of more than 30 milliseconds, notching of the S wave and an S-wave duration of more than 70 milliseconds, is not reliable.

Many of these studies did not include WCTs with accessory pathways.

FUSION/CAPTURE BEATS. Fusion beats are hybrid QRS complexes resulting from simultaneous supranodal and infranodal (ventricular) activation

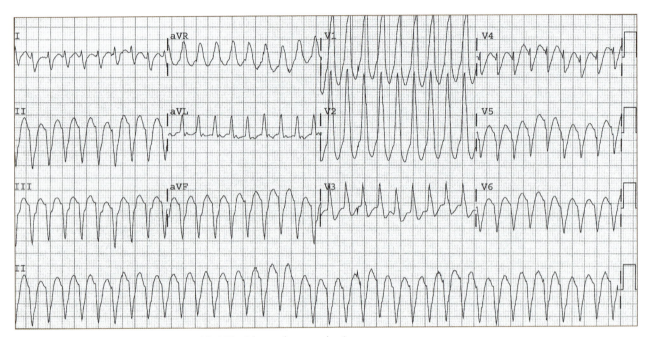

FIGURE 5.8. Incessant monomorphic VT with an abnormal axis.

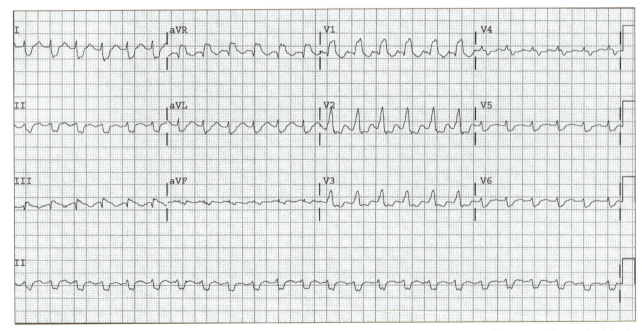

FIGURE 5.9. Wide complex tachycardia due to atrial fibrillation has RBBB pattern with a left anterior fascicular block. Atrial fibrillation was identified on previous ECGs, with identical QRS complexes.

of ventricular tissue. They are therefore intermediate in morphology and width from either a capture or ventricular beat (Figure 5.12). Capture beats are supraventricular impulses that travel through the normal conducting system, resulting in QRS complexes that are similar (or identical) to the "normal" QRS complex[57] (Figure 5.13). Neither fusion nor capture beats are diagnostic for VT despite

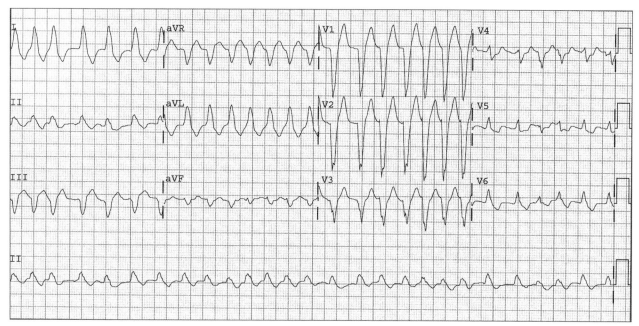

FIGURE 5.10. Wide complex tachycardia with atrial fibrillation and LBBB (both present in prior ECGs). This patient's tachycardia was due to sepsis.

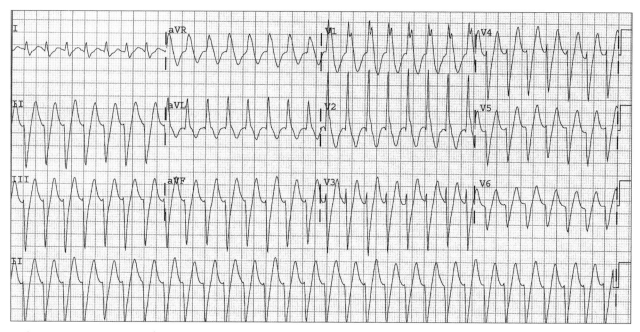

FIGURE 5.11. Monomorphic VT with RBBB configuration with a left superior axis. An electrophysiologic diagnosis of idiopathic left ventricular tachycardia was confirmed, caused by a reentry loop in the left ventricular apex. This particular etiology of VT is verapamil responsive, although treating patients presenting to the emergency department with wide complex tachycardia of uncertain etiology with calcium channel blockers is not recommended.

suggestions from older literature. They do favor VT as the mechanism for the WCT. However, similar complexes have been demonstrated in atrial fibrillation with conduction down an accessory pathway. In the setting of atrial fibrillation and an accessory pathway, an apparent capture complex represents exclusive conduction of an atrial impulse through the AV node, while an apparent fusion complex represents coincident conduction of the impulse through the AV node and the accessory pathway. The two can be distinguished by timing—fusion and capture beats occur prematurely in VT (Figure 5.14) but occur either prematurely or after a delay in atrial fibrillation with an accessory pathway (Figure 5.15).

AV DISSOCIATION AND VENTRICULOATRIAL CONDUCTION. The presence of AV dissociation (ie, atrial activity independent of ventricular activity) supports the diagnosis of VT. Atrioventricular dissociation is identified by detecting separate (or independent) rates for P waves and QRS complexes (Figure 5.16). However, AV dissociation has been identified in SVTs arising from the AV junction and is therefore not diagnostic of VT.

The presence of ventriculoatrial (VA) conduction, evident from a retrograde P wave seen in the QRS complex, also supports the diagnosis of VT. The use of sensitive esophageal lead recording devices has demonstrated that VA conduction occurs in as many as half of patients with VT.[58] Ventriculoatrial conduction is more common with slower rates (<200 beats/min). The RP interval of the retrograde atrial beat is generally 0.11 second or longer.[58] Both AV dissociation and VA conduction can be challenging to identify because the P wave is often obscured by the QRS complex and components of the QRS complex can resemble P waves. This is especially true with faster heart rates and technical artifact (such as a wandering baseline).

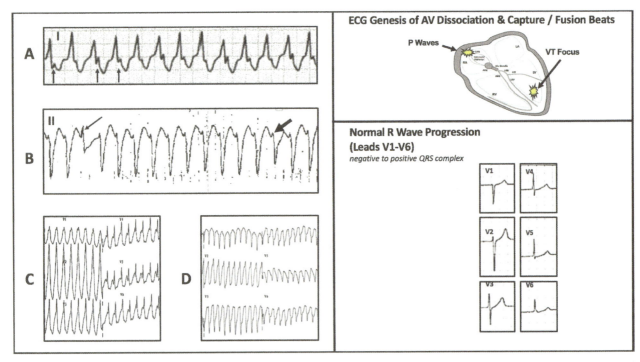

FIGURE 5.12. ECG findings suggestive of VT include AV dissociation (panel A), capture and fusion beats (small and large arrows, respectively, panel B), and examples of positive and negative precordial concordance (panels C and D, respectively). None of these findings confirms VT. Reproduced with permission from: Brady WJ, Mattu A, Tabas JA, Ferguson JD. The differential diagnosis of wide QRS complex tachycardia. *Am J Emerg Med*. 2017;35(10):1525-1529. Copyright 2017 Elsevier Inc.

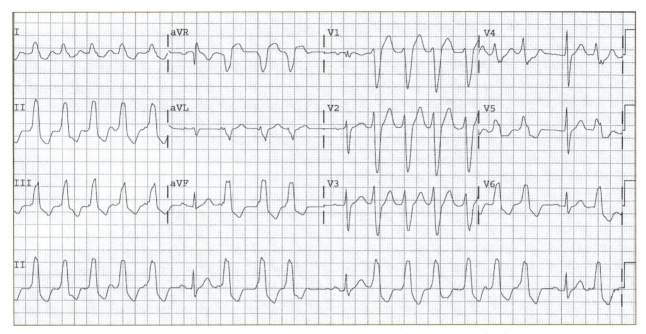

FIGURE 5.13. VT with clear demonstration of capture beats (QRS complexes 6, 10, and 17).

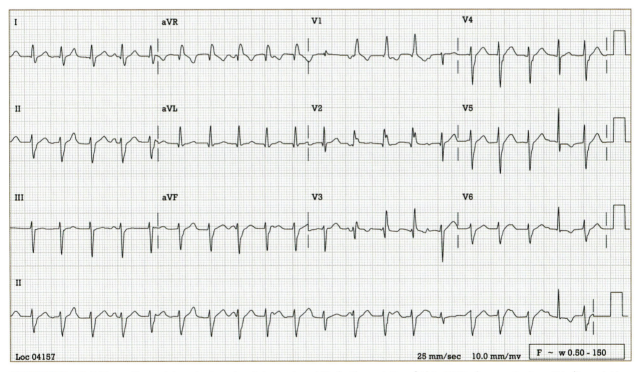

FIGURE 5.14. VT confirmed by electrophysiology. Lead II rhythm strip of this ECG demonstrates AV dissociation (best seen in beats 2-10), in which the P waves are independent of QRS complexes. Some P waves precede, fall within, or follow the QRS complex or T wave, slightly altering their appearance. Capture (QRS complex #19) and fusion (QRS complexes #11, 15, and 20) beats can be identified.

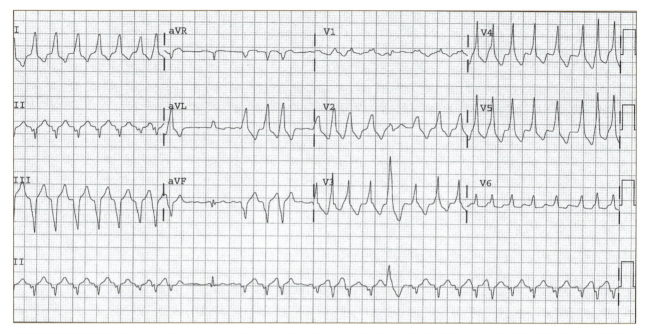

FIGURE 5.15. This irregularly irregular wide complex tachycardia is atrial fibrillation with Wolff-Parkinson-White syndrome due to a left posterior accessory pathway. QRS complex #9 is a minimally preexcited or fusion beat. QRS complex #17 is a premature ventricular contraction since it is upright and the other preexcited QRS complexes in lead II are negative. Delta waves can be identified on some QRS complexes, although these are much more apparent postcardioversion. Reproduced with permission from: Charlie Young, MD.

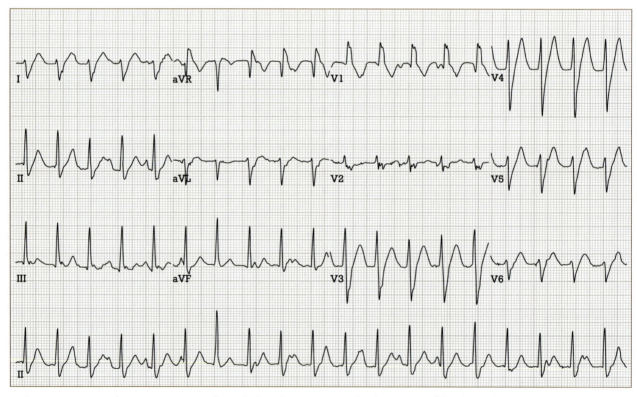

FIGURE 5.16. VT demonstrates AV dissociation, best seen in rhythm strip of lead II. The regular P wave rate is independent (and slower) than the ventricular rate. This ECG has right axis deviation and RBBB pattern. In lead V_1, the RSR' pattern has the initial R wave larger than the following R wave. The QRS complex #7 is likely a capture beat. Reproduced with permission from: Amal Mattu, MD, FACEP.

PRECORDIAL CONCORDANCE. Precordial concordance means that the main direction of the QRS complexes is the same in all precordial leads. Positive precordial QRS concordance can occur during VT or during SVT using a left posterior accessory pathway for AV conduction (Figure 5.17). Therefore, positive precordial concordance does not discriminate between VT and SVT with aberrant conduction. Negative precordial concordance is most predictive of VT due to the impulse originating from the apical area of the left ventricle. This "rule," however, is not perfect[59,60] (Figure 5.18, Table 5.5).

ALGORITHMS TO DETERMINE THE ORIGIN OF A WIDE COMPLEX TACHYCARDIA

Algorithms have been developed to help identify the correct etiology of WCTs.[19,20,30,61] Several recent algorithms have been proposed, in part because of the challenges inherent in using previous algorithms.[21,22,24,45] These earlier and new algorithms have been studied prospectively using real-time patient ECGs and sets of ECGs from teaching files.[6,26,44,62] Many of these algorithms are similar, and some even incorporate portions of prior algorithms in the new algorithm. This adds complexity and variability to the interpreter's efforts. One study reported difficulty applying an algorithm that analyzes lead aVR for its initial step because researchers could not apply the algorithm due to low amplitude and multiphasic QRS complexes in this lead in some cases.[29]

Given the many algorithms, their complexity, and their varied predictive accuracy to identify the etiology of WCTs, there is no single best algorithm to use when a patient needs medical intervention. Using these algorithms takes practice and does not consistently provide an accurate final diagnosis ultimately obtained from electrophysiology studies. Furthermore, there is a lack of strong interobserver agreement using these algorithms. Although it is helpful to know that these algorithms exist, they are an academic exercise that could lead to delays in patient care or inappropriate treatment with adverse outcomes. Therefore, it is best that an emergency physician errs on the side of treating the patient as if the WCT were ventricular rather than supraventricular in origin given the potential for adverse outcomes.[27,28]

OTHER APPROACHES TO DIAGNOSIS

The use of bedside ultrasound (transthoracic echocardiography [TTE]) is increasing in emergency practice. In stable patients and in experienced hands, TTE can help assess overall cardiac output, the relationship between atrial and ventricular activity, and the AV valves in relationship to contraction of the atria and ventricles. Transesophageal echocardiography (TEE) is generally not performed by emergency physicians and should not be done in clinically unstable or potentially unstable patients.[63] However, TEE does offer promise because images demonstrating the relationship between atrial and ventricular activity (looking for synchrony or asynchrony) are much better than those that can be obtained with TTE. Similar to TEE, transesophageal atrial "pill" electrodes can be used to record atrial activity, which can help identify AV dissociation or 1:1 VA conduction (both suggestive of VT). This approach is unlikely to have a place in emergency practice because of its lack of availability, cost, and difficulty of use. Furthermore, there are safety concerns given that these electrodes must be swallowed, and emergency physician experience with this technology is limited. The use of a pill electrode is contraindicated in patients experiencing hemodynamic compromise.

THERAPY

Initial management of patients presenting with WCT is based exclusively on patient stability, following the most current American Heart Association (AHA) advanced cardiac life support (ACLS) guidelines.[64,65] Although controversial, a precordial thump may be considered for patients with witnessed, monitored, unstable VT if a defibrillator is not immediately available. For unstable patients without a pulse, cardiopulmonary resuscitation and immediate defibrillation are warranted. For unstable patients with a

TABLE 5.5. Morphological criteria favoring VT.
RBBB-like QRS
Monophasic R, QR, or RS in V_1
R/S ratio less than 1, QS or QR in V_6
Triphasic QRS in V_1 or V_6 supports SVT with aberrant conduction
LBBB-like QRS
R >30 ms, >60 ms to nadir S, or notched S in V_1 or V_2
QR or QS in V_6
Monophasic R in V_6 not helpful
Using V1-positive and V1-negative QRS morphology characteristics
$V_1(V_2)$-positive (Figure 5.17):
$\quad V_1$
$\quad\quad$ Monophasic or biphasic QRS = VT
$\quad\quad$ Rabbit ear sign with first peak > second (L >R) = VT
$\quad\quad$ RSR' (triphasic) = SVT + RBBB
$\quad V_6$
$\quad\quad$ QS or deep S (R/S ratio <1) = VT
$\quad\quad$ QRS (triphasic) with R/S ratio >1 = SVT + RBBB
V_1-negative (Figure 5.18):
$\quad V_1(V_2)$
$\quad\quad$ Broad r >0.04 sec and/or slurred or notched S resulting in prolonged interval from beginning QRS to S nadir = VT
$\quad\quad$ Narrow r wave and quick S wave downstroke = SVT + LBBB
$\quad V_6$
$\quad\quad$ Any q wave = VT

pulse, synchronized cardioversion is warranted. In cases of irregular, wide complexes, defibrillation is recommended (*not* synchronized cardioversion).[64] Whether or not to use rapid-onset, short-acting, intravenous sedation prior to electrical cardioversion is at the discretion of the physician and the clinical situation. According to current guidelines, sedation should be considered only if the "unstable" patient would tolerate any (short) delay to cardioversion, the medication itself, and is not allergic to the medication.

Pharmacologic treatment of stable patients should also follow the most updated AHA/ACLS guidelines,[64,65] and expert consultation should be considered for all stable patients presenting with WCT.

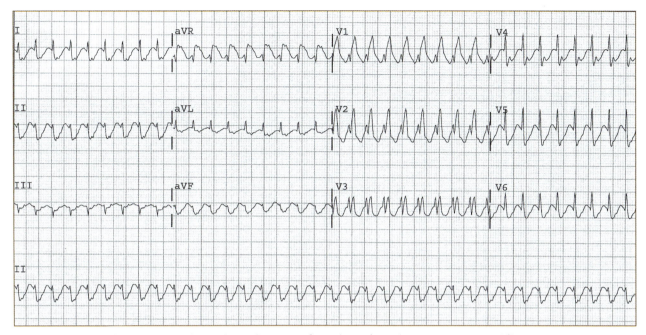

FIGURE 5.17. Wide complex tachycardia with a rate of 217 beats/min demonstrating atrial flutter with 2:1 AV block and RBBB. This ECG demonstrates positive precordial concordance.

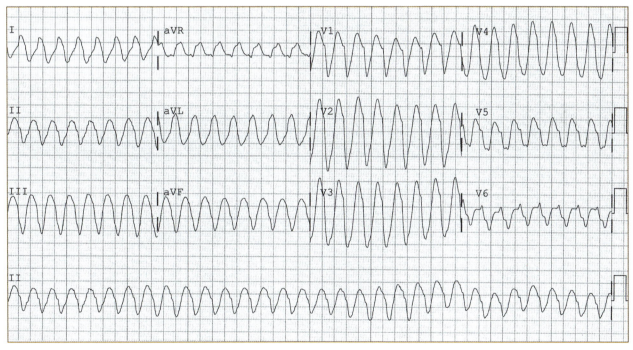

FIGURE 5.18. Wide complex tachycardia demonstrating negative precordial concordance was ultimately determined to be due to atrial flutter with aberrant conduction. Flecainide toxicity in this case resulted in a wider QRS complex due to a greater degree of aberration. Not all negative precordial concordance is the result of VT. Reproduced with permission from: Lisa Rapoport, MD.

SPECIAL PATIENT POPULATIONS

Pediatric Patients

Pediatric patients can present with WCT. Definitions for tachycardia in children vary with age. According to the 2015 AHA guidelines for pediatric advanced life support, WCT is defined by a QRS complex width of more than 0.09 seconds (90 milliseconds).[66] Wide complex tachycardia often originates in the ventricles (VT), but it might be supraventricular in origin. Early expert consultation is strongly recommended, particularly in hemodynamically stable patients. Adenosine can be useful both diagnostically and therapeutically, but it should be considered only in regular WCT where the QRS morphology is monomorphic. It should not be used in patients with known Wolff-Parkinson-White syndrome presenting with WCT. Amiodarone or procainamide should be considered, but not together, and not before expert consultation in this population. Synchronized electrical cardioversion, beginning at 0.5 to 1 joule/kg, increased to 2 joules/kg if unsuccessful, is part of the AHA's pediatric advanced life support algorithm.[66] Sedation should be considered based on the patient's stability, provided it does not delay cardioversion.

Patients with Cardiac Transplant, Ventricular Assist Device, or Other Implantable Cardiac Devices

Patients who have undergone cardiac transplant or who have ventricular assist or other implantable cardiac devices can present with a WCT. As with all patients, hemodynamic status should be assessed and treated as the first priority. Expert consultation should be sought immediately, regardless of hemodynamic status. Recipients of heterotopic hearts can have an ECG demonstrating WCT due to the native heart.[67,68] This can be identified in the ECG because some leads could show wide QRS complexes while others have a normal QRS complex (these can be misinterpreted as capture beats), or during confirmatory electrophysiology studies. With selective repositioning of the ECG leads, this situation can be confirmed. Patients with ventricular assist devices and implantable pacemakers or defibrillators can also present with a WCT. Although these patients have a high likelihood for VT, other etiologies (including those of supraventricular origin) should be considered and have been reported.[69–75]

CLINICAL MANAGEMENT ALGORITHM

A clinical-based three-step algorithm for the treatment of patients presenting with WCT published by an emergency physician in 1989 remains relevant today (with modification).[4,76]

1. If the patient is hemodynamically unstable, immediate synchronized graded cardioversion (defibrillation if pulseless) is warranted. Subsequent pharmacologic therapy may be guided by experienced consultants.
2. If the patient is symptomatic but otherwise hemodynamically stable, controlled graded cardioversion (consider sedation) or pharmacologic therapy (with preparation for cardioversion or defibrillation, if needed), is appropriate.
3. If the patient is asymptomatic or minimally symptomatic and hemodynamically stable, consult with an experienced cardiologist, (if one is available) while closely observing the patient.

ACKNOWLEDGMENTS

Dr. Garmel is grateful to the cardiology group at Kaiser Santa Clara and to Dr. Charlie Young, electrophysiologist at Kaiser Santa Teresa. Dr. Garmel appreciates the efforts of Evelyn Kobayashi, MILS, AHIP; Eve Melton, MLIS, MIS, AHIP; Elaine Barnes, MLS; and the staff in the Kaiser Permanente Health Sciences Library system. Finally, special thanks to Christopher Stave, MLS, research librarian at Lane Medical Library, Stanford University, for his continued support and expertise.

REFERENCES

1. Garmel GM. Wide complex tachycardias: understanding this complex condition: Part 2 - management, miscellaneous causes, and pitfalls. *West J Emerg Med.* 2008;9(2):97-103.
2. Garmel GM. Wide complex tachycardias. In: Mattu A, Tabas JA, Barish RA, eds. *Electrocardiography in Emergency Medicine.* Dallas, TX: American College of Emergency Physicians; 2007:59-72.
3. Garmel GM. Wide complex tachycardias. *Hosp Phys Emerg Med Board Rev Manual.* 1998;2(4):1-14.
4. Garmel GM. Wide complex tachycardias: understanding this complex condition: Part 1 - epidemiology and electrophysiology. *West J Emerg Med.* 2008;9(1):28-39.
5. Pollack ML, Chan TC, Brady WJ. Electrocardiographic manifestations: aberrant ventricular conduction. *J Emerg Med.* 2000;19(4):363-367.
6. Brady WJ, Mattu A, Tabas J, Ferguson JD. The differential diagnosis of wide QRS complex tachycardia. *Am J Emerg Med.* 2017;35(10):1525-1520. doi:10.1016/j.ajem.2017.07.056
7. Rajani AR, Murugesan V, Baslaib FO, Rafiq MA. Mitral valve prolapse and electrolyte abnormality: a dangerous combination for ventricular arrhythmias. *BMJ Case Rep.* 2014; May 14;2014. doi:10.1136/bcr-2014-205055
8. Reddy V, Shen YS, Kundumadam S, et al. A forgotten cause of wide complex tachycardia. *J Electrocardiol.* 2017;50(2):238-240. doi:10.1016/j.jelectrocard.2016.11.013
9. Nogar JN, Minns AB, Savaser DJ, Ly BT. Severe sodium channel blockade and cardiovascular collapse due to a massive lamotrigine overdose. *Clin Toxicol* 2011;49(9):854-857. doi:10.3109/15563650.2011.617307
10. Francis J, Hamzeh RK, Lantin-Hermoso MR. Lithium toxicity-induced wide-complex tachycardia in a pediatric patient. *J Pediatr.* 2004;145(2):235-240. doi:10.1016/j.jpeds.2004.05.028
11. Tsai C-F, Sia S-K, Lin M-C, et al. Unstable wide complex tachycardia during propafenone therapy. *Resuscitation.* 2010;81(8):1046-1047. doi:10.1016/j.resuscitation.2010.03.029
12. Bruccoleri RE, Burns MM. A literature review of the use of sodium bicarbonate for the treatment of QRS widening. *J Med Toxicol.* 2016;12(1):121-129. doi:10.1007/s13181-015-0483-y
13. Levis JT, Garmel GM. Cocaine-associated chest pain. *Emerg Med Clin North Am.* 2005;23(4):1083-1103. doi:10.1016/j.emc.2005.07.009
14. Li Y-C, Lin J-F, Chen P. An unusually wide QRS complex tachycardia in a patient with hemodynamic instability. *JAMA Intern Med.* 2016;176(12):1857–1859.
15. Knight BP, Pelosi F, Michaud GF, et al. Physician interpretation of electrocardiographic artifact that mimics ventricular tachycardia. *Am J Med.* 2001;110(5):335-338.
16. Kefalas S, Ezenkwele U. Wide-complex tachycardia as the presenting complaint in a case of malingering. *J Emerg Med.* 2006;30(2):159-161. doi:10.1016/j.jemermed.2005.09.002
17. Morady F, Baerman JM, DiCarlo LAJ, et al. A prevalent misconception regarding wide-complex tachycardias. *JAMA.* 1985;254(19):2790-2792.
18. Mason JW, Stinson EB, Winkle RA, Oyer PE. Mechanisms of ventricular tachycardia: wide, complex ignorance. *Am Heart J.* 1981;102(6 Pt 1):1083-1087.
19. Kindwall KE, Brown J, Josephson ME. Electrocardiographic criteria for ventricular tachycardia in wide complex left bundle branch block morphology tachycardias. *Am J Cardiol.* 1988;61(15):1279-1283.
20. Brugada P, Brugada J, Mont L, Smeets J, Andries EW. A new approach to the differential diagnosis of a regular tachycardia with a wide QRS complex. *Circulation.* 1991;83(5):1649-1659.
21. Vereckei A, Duray G, Szenasi G, et al. New algorithm using only lead aVR for differential diagnosis of wide QRS complex tachycardia. *Heart Rhythm.* 2008;5(1):89-98. doi:10.1016/j.hrthm.2007.09.020
22. Pava LF, Perafan P, Badiel M, et al. R-wave peak time at DII: a new criterion for differentiating between wide complex QRS tachycardias. *Heart Rhythm.* 2010;7(7):922-926. doi:10.1016/j.hrthm.2010.03.001
23. Gutierrez-Macias A, Sanz-Prieto JC, Aguirre-Herrero J, Varona-Peinador M. Wide-complex tachycardia: diagnostic value of the Brugada algorithm in emergency medicine. *Acad Emerg Med.* 2001;8(3):300-301.
24. Vereckei A, Duray G, Szenasi G, et al. Application of a new algorithm in the differential diagnosis of wide QRS complex tachycardia. *Eur Heart J.* 2007;28(5):589-600. doi:10.1093/eurheartj/ehl473
25. Baerman JM, Morady F, DiCarlo LAJ, de Buitleir M. Differentiation of ventricular tachycardia from supraventricular tachycardia with aberration: value of the clinical history. *Ann Emerg Med.* 1987;16(1):40-43.
26. Szelényi Z, Duray G, Katona G, et al. Comparison of the "real-life" diagnostic value of two recently published electrocardiogram methods for the differential diagnosis of wide QRS complex tachycardias. *Acad Emerg Med.* 2013;20(11):1121-1130. doi:10.1111/acem.12247

27. McGovern B, Garan H, Ruskin JN. Precipitation of cardiac arrest by verapamil in patients with Wolff-Parkinson-White syndrome. *Ann Intern Med.* 1986;104(6):791-794.
28. Stewart RB, Bardy GH, Greene HL. Wide complex tachycardia: misdiagnosis and outcome after emergent therapy. *Ann Intern Med.* 1986;104(6):766-771.
29. Jastrzebski M, Kukla P, Czarnecka D, Kawecka-Jaszcz K. Comparison of five electrocardiographic methods for differentiation of wide. *Europace.* 2012;14(8):1165-1171. doi:10.1093/europace/eus015
30. Griffith MJ, Garratt CJ, Mounsey P, Camm AJ. Ventricular tachycardia as default diagnosis in broad complex tachycardia. *Lancet.* 1994;343(8894):386-388.
31. Chenevert M, Lewis RJ. Ashman's phenomenon – a source of nonsustained wide-complex tachycardia: case report and discussion. *J Emerg Med.* 1992;10(2):179-183.
32. Harrigan RA, Garg M. An interesting cause of wide complex tachycardia: Ashman's phenomenon in atrial fibrillation. *J Emerg Med.* 2013;45(6):835-841. doi:10.1016/j.jemermed.2013.08.018
33. Smith DC. Ashman's phenomenon – a source of nonsustained wide complex tachycardia. *J Emerg Med.* 1993;11(1):98.
34. Deam AG, Burton ME, Walter PF, Langberg JJ. Wide complex tachycardia due to automaticity in an accessory pathway. *Pacing Clin Electrophysiol.* 1995;18(11):2106-2108.
35. Nelson JG, Zhu DW. Atrial flutter with 1:1 conduction in undiagnosed Wolff-Parkinson-White syndrome. *J Emerg Med.* 2014;46(5):e135-140. doi:10.1016/j.jemermed.2013.09.021
36. Nelson JA, Knowlton KU, Harrigan R, et al. Electrocardiographic manifestations: wide complex tachycardia due to accessory pathway. *J Emerg Med.* 2003;24(3):295-301.
37. Traykov VB, Pap R, Bencsik G, et al. Transition of narrow into wide complex tachycardia with left bundle branch block morphology and varying QRS duration: what is the mechanism? *Pacing Clin Electrophysiol.* 2007;30(4):547-550. doi:10.1111/j.1540-8159.2007.00707.x
38. Al Harbi M, Abdelwahab A, Gray C, Parkash R. Narrow, intermediate, and wide complex tachycardia: what is the mechanism? *J Cardiovasc Electrophysiol.* 2016;27(4):494-496. doi:10.1111/jce.12862
39. Oreto G, Smeets JL, Rodriguez LM, et al. Wide complex tachycardia with atrioventricular dissociation and QRS morphology identical to that of sinus rhythm: a manifestation of bundle branch reentry. *Heart.* 1996;76(6):541-547.
40. Goldberger JJ, Pederson DN, Damle RS, et al. Antidromic tachycardia utilizing decremental, latent accessory atrioventricular fibers: differentiation from adenosine-sensitive ventricular tachycardia. *J Am Coll Cardiol.* 1994;24(3):732-738.
41. Tutuianu C, Saghy L, Pap R. A wide complex left bundle branch block tachycardia in a patient with complete right bundle branch block: what is the mechanism? *J Cardiovasc Electrophysiol.* 2015;26(7):816-818. doi:10.1111/jce.12661
42. Khairy P, Guerra PG, Thibault B, et al. Alternating narrow and wide complex tachycardia. *Pacing Clin Electrophysiol.* 2002;25(1):103-104.
43. Barber CR, Garmel GM. Pacemaker-associated tachycardia. *Acad Emerg Med.* 1997;4(2):150-153.
44. Jastrzębski M, Kukla P, Czarnecka D. Ventricular tachycardia score – a novel method for wide QRS complex tachycardia differentiation – Explained. *J Electrocardiol.* 2017;50(5):704-709. doi:10.1016/j.jelectrocard.2017.04.003
45. Jastrzebski M, Sasaki K, Kukla P, et al. The ventricular tachycardia score: a novel approach to electrocardiographic diagnosis of ventricular tachycardia. *Europace.* 2016;18(4):578-584. doi:10.1093/europace/euv118
46. *Dorland's Illustrated Medical Dictionary.* 32nd ed. Philadelphia, PA: Elsevier, Saunders; 2012.
47. Vukmir RB. Torsades de pointes: a review. *Am J Emerg Med.* 1991;9(3):250-255.
48. Keren A, Tzivoni D. Torsades de pointes: prevention and therapy. *Cardiovasc Drugs Ther.* 1991;5(2):509-513.
49. Tzivoni D, Keren A, Banai S, Stern S. Terminology of torsades de pointes. *Cardiovasc Drugs Ther.* 1991;5(2):505-507.
50. Engrav MB, Coodley G, Magnusson AR. Torsade de pointes after inhaled pentamidine. *Ann Emerg Med.* 1992;21(11):1403-1405.
51. Tzivoni D, Banai S, Schuger C, et al. Treatment of torsade de pointes with magnesium sulfate. *Circulation.* 1988;77(2):392–397.
52. Kummer JL. Bidirectional ventricular tachycardia caused by digitalis toxicity. *Circulation.* 2006;113(7):e156-e157. doi:10.1161/CIRCULATIONAHA.105.557561
53. Piccini J, Zaas A. Cases from the Osler Medical Service at Johns Hopkins University. Digitalis toxicity with bidirectional ventricular tachycardia. *Am J Med.* 2003;115(1):70-71.

54. Ma G, Brady WJ, Pollack M, Chan TC. Electrocardiographic manifestations: digitalis toxicity. *J Emerg Med*. 2001;20(2):145-152.
55. Steinman RT, Herrera C, Schuger CD, Lehmann MH. Wide QRS tachycardia in the conscious adult. Ventricular tachycardia is the most frequent cause. *JAMA*. 1989;261(7):1013-1016.
56. Brady WJ, Skiles J. Wide QRS complex tachycardia: ECG differential diagnosis. *Am J Emerg Med*. 1999;17(4):376–381.
57. Akhtar M, Shenasa M, Jazayeri M, et al. Wide QRS complex tachycardia. Reappraisal of a common clinical problem. *Ann Intern Med*. 1988;109(11):905-912.
58. Surawicz B, Knilans TK, Chou T-C. *Chou's Electrocardiography in Clinical Practice: Adult and Pediatric*. Saunders; 2001.
59. Volders PGA, Timmermans C, Rodriguez L-M, et al. Wide QRS complex tachycardia with negative precordial concordance: always a ventricular origin? *J Cardiovasc Electrophysiol*. 2003;14(1):109-111.
60. Kappos KG, Andrikopoulos GK, Tzeis SE, Manolis AS. Wide-QRS-complex tachycardia with a negative concordance pattern in the precordial leads: Are the ECG criteria always reliable? *Pacing Clin Electrophysiol*. 2006;29(1):63-66. doi:10.1111/j.1540-8159.2006.00291.x
61. Wellens HJ, Bär FW, Lie KI. The value of the electrocardiogram in the differential diagnosis of a tachycardia with a widened QRS complex. *Am J Med*. 1978;64(1):27–33.
62. Kaiser E, Darrieux FCC, Barbosa SA, et al. Differential diagnosis of wide QRS tachycardias: comparison of two electrocardiographic algorithms. *Europace*. 2015;17(9):1422-1427. doi:10.1093/europace/euu354
63. Guidelines for the use of transesophageal echocardiography (TEE) in the ED for cardiac arrest. *Ann Emerg Med*. 2017;70(3):442-445. doi:10.1016/j.annemergmed.2017.06.033
64. Neumar RW, Otto CW, Link MS, et al. Part 8: Adult Advanced Cardiovascular Life Support: 2010 American Heart Association Guidelines for Cardiopulmonary Resuscitation and Emergency Cardiovascular Care. *Circulation*. 2010;122(18 suppl 3):S729-S767. doi:10.1161/CIRCULATIONAHA.110.970988
65. Link MS, Berkow LC, Kudenchuk PJ, et al. Part 7: adult advanced cardiovascular life support. *Circulation*. 2015;132(18 suppl 2):S444–S464.
66. De Caen AR, Berg MD, Chameides L, et al. Part 12: pediatric advanced life support. *Circulation*. 2015;132(18 suppl 2):S526–S542.
67. Vanderheyden M, de Sutter J, Goethals M. ECG diagnosis of native heart ventricular tachycardia in a heterotopic heart transplant recipient. *Heart Br Card Soc*. 1999;81(3):323-324.
68. Jayamaha JE, Dowdle JR. Acceleration of ventricular tachycardia following propofol in a patient with heterotopic cardiac transplant. Cardioversion of ventricular tachycardia in the native heart. *Anaesthesia*. 1993;48(10):889-891.
69. Abrams Mark P, William W, Vivek I, et al. A case of wide complex tachycardia in a patient with a biventricular assist device. *J Atr Fibrillation*. 2016;8(5):1364. doi:10.4022/jafib.1364
70. Noheria A, Mulpuru SK, Noseworthy PA, Asirvatham SJ. Incessant tachycardia in a patient with advanced heart failure and left ventricular assist device: What is the mechanism? *Indian Pacing Electrophysiol J*. 2016;16(1):34-39. doi:10.1016/j.ipej.2016.04.001
71. Thajudeen A, Kannarkat V, Noheria A, Shehata M. Wide complex tachycardia in a patient with a dual-chamber defibrillator: what is the rhythm? A tale of timing cycles. *Heart Rhythm*. 2013;10(8):1237-1239. doi:10.1016/j.hrthm.2013.03.047
72. Garan AR, Levin AP, Topkara V, et al. Early post-operative ventricular arrhythmias in patients with continuous-flow left ventricular assist devices. *J Heart Lung Transplant*. 2015;34(12):1611-1616. doi:10.1016/j.healun.2015.05.018
73. Wood MA. Pacing during a wide complex rhythm: implantable cardioverter defibrillator malfunction or not? *J Cardiovasc Electrophysiol*. 2004;15(1):114-115. doi:10.1046/j.1540-8167.2004.03387.x
74. Kantharia BK. Wide complex tachycardia and dual-chamber pacing. *Heart Rhythm*. 2005;2(9):1013-1014. doi:10.1016/j.hrthm.2005.03.018
75. Arias MA, Puchol A, Pachon M, Briz C. Wide QRS complex tachycardia in a patient with a biventricular implantable cardioverter defibrillator: what is the mechanism? *J Cardiovasc Electrophysiol*. 2014;25(3):334-337. doi:10.1111/jce.12324
76. Wrenn KD. Wide QRS-complex tachycardia. *Ann Intern Med*. 1989;110(5):412.

CHAPTER SIX
Acute Coronary Ischemia and Infarction

JOEL T. LEVIS AND GUS M. GARMEL

KEY POINTS

- In patients with a high likelihood of acute coronary syndrome and an initially normal or nondiagnostic ECG, serial ECGs should be performed at 15- to 30-minute intervals in the setting of ongoing or recurrent symptoms.
- STEMI can be diagnosed on the 12-lead ECG when there is new ST-segment elevation at the J point in two or more contiguous leads of 2 mm or more in men or 1.5 mm or more in women in leads V_2 to V_3, or elevation of 1 mm or more in at least two other contiguous leads.
- Early findings of STEMI on an ECG include hyperacute T waves (minutes), ST-segment elevation (minutes to hours), and evolving Q waves (hours).
- Late electrocardiographic changes after STEMI depend on multiple factors, such as treatment with reperfusion therapy, and location and degree of damage. These changes can include T-wave inversions and resolution of ST-segment abnormalities.
- An upwardly convex morphology of ST-segment elevation is more specific for STEMI and has been associated with greater infarct size and morbidity.
- Acute subendocardial ischemia due to a reduction of blood flow or an increase of demand results in primary ST-segment depression, which is an electrocardiographic sign of non–ST-segment elevation acute coronary syndrome.
- Reciprocal ST-segment depression improves the specificity for a STEMI diagnosis; however, the absence of reciprocal ST-segment depression does not rule out STEMI.
- In the setting of active anginal symptoms, new T-wave inversions in leads other than III, aVF, and aVR, particularly when accompanied by ST depression and QT prolongation, should raise suspicion for myocardial ischemia.
- Wellens syndrome, described in patients while they are symptom free, is a pattern of deeply inverted or biphasic T waves in leads V_2 to V_3, suggestive of a critical stenosis of the left anterior descending coronary artery. Typically, there is no (or minimal) elevation in cardiac biomarkers.
- Application of additional leads to the standard 12-lead ECG can assist in diagnosing isolated posterior STEMI (posterior leads V_7 through V_9) and right ventricular STEMI (V_1R through V_6R).
- The modified Sgarbossa criteria can be used to diagnose STEMI in the presence of left bundle-branch block or with a ventricular-paced rhythm.

The spectrum of acute coronary syndrome (ACS) includes STEMI, non–ST-segment elevation MI (NSTEMI), and unstable angina. Non–ST-segment elevation MI and unstable angina are currently referred to as non–ST-elevation ACS (NSTE-ACS).

In 2010, an estimated 625,000 patients were discharged from US hospitals with the diagnosis of ACS. When secondary discharge diagnoses for ACS in this same year were included, the corresponding number of hospital discharges was 1,141,000 for ACS.[1]

In light of the volume of emergency department patients presenting with ACS-related complaints (eg, chest pain, dyspnea, nausea, weakness, and fatigue), it is imperative that emergency physicians have an appreciation of the electrocardiographic changes that can establish these diagnoses so that rapid treatment and further risk stratification decisions can be made.

CORONARY BLOOD SUPPLY AND AREAS OF INFARCTION

The cardiac blood supply is delivered by the three main coronary arteries and their branches (Figure 6.1). The right coronary artery (RCA) supplies both the inferior (diaphragmatic) portion of the heart and the right ventricle. The left main coronary artery (LMCA) is short and divides into the left anterior descending (LAD) and left circumflex (LCx) coronary arteries. The LAD coronary artery generally supplies the ventricular septum and a large part of the left ventricular free wall. The LCx coronary artery supplies the lateral wall of the left ventricle. This circulation pattern is variable. Occasionally, the LCx also supplies the inferoposterior portion of the left ventricle. Acute MIs *tend* to be localized to the region (eg, anterior or inferior) of the heart supplied by one of these arteries or its branches (Table 6.1). For example, an acute anterior MI (resulting from occlusion of the LAD) is indicated by ST-segment elevation in leads V_1 through V_4 (at least two contiguous leads); an inferior MI (occlusion of the RCA or LCx artery) by ST-segment elevation in leads II, III, and aVF; a lateral MI (occlusion of a branch of the LAD or LCx artery) by ST elevation in leads V_5, V_6; or leads I and aVL (a "high lateral" MI). With careful analysis of the 12-lead ECG, one can predict not only the ischemic region of the heart, but also the affected coronary artery in most cases of STEMI (Table 6.1). Combinations of anatomic regions can be affected as indicated by ST-segment elevation in two anatomic areas on the ECG. For example, anterolateral wall MI presents with ST-segment elevation in leads V_1 through V_6, I, and aVL (Figure 6.2).

THE PREHOSPITAL ECG

The use of prehospital electrocardiography by trained EMS personnel, particularly with communication of STEMI diagnosis and preferential transport to a hospital capable of percutaneous coronary intervention (PCI), is associated with shorter reperfusion times, lower mortality rates, and improved clinical outcomes.[2-5] Prehospital ECG acquisition and hospital notification have been shown to reduce mortality by 32% when primary PCI is the reperfusion strategy, and by 24% when emergency department fibrinolysis is the reperfusion strategy.[6] Because of these data, prehospital ECG acquisition and transmission by EMS is recommended in the 2013 ACCF/AHA guidelines for the management of STEMI.[7]

TABLE 6.1. STEMI location, ST-segment elevation, and corresponding coronary artery.

STEMI LOCATION	ST-SEGMENT ELEVATION LEADS	CORRESPONDING CORONARY ARTERY
Anteroseptal	V_1 through V_4	LAD
Inferior	II, III, and aVF	RCA (80%), LCx (20%)
Lateral	I, aVL (high lateral), V_5–V_6	LCx, LAD and branches of either LCx or LAD
Posterior	ST-segment depression V_1–V_4 ST-segment elevation posterior leads V_7–V_9	LCx
Right ventricular	II, III, aVF, V_1, right precordial lead V_4R	RCA

NORMAL AND NONDIAGNOSTIC ECGS

In patients presenting with complaints suggestive of ACS, a 12-lead ECG should be performed and interpreted within 10 minutes of the patient's arrival to assess for cardiac ischemia or injury (American College of Cardiology-American Heart Association [ACC-AHA] class I recommendation, evidence level C).[8] The ECG can be relatively normal or initially nondiagnostic; in this case, the ECG should be repeated at 15- to 30-minute intervals during the first hour, especially if symptoms recur or the likelihood for ACS is high.[8] A normal ECG does not exclude ACS. It has been demonstrated that 1% to 6% of patients with ACS have a normal ECG,[9-11] and ECGs with nonspecific changes ccur in patients subsequently diagnosed with acute MI 22% to 35% of the time.[12] The overall missed rate of acute MI in emergency departments is estimated to be 2%, but this is based on data from more than two decades ago. In one study of emergency department patients with high-risk electrocardiographic findings that were initially missed (significant ST-segment depressions, ST-segment elevations, or T-wave inversions) and ultimately diagnosed with acute MI on the same emergency department visit, in-hospital mortality was 7.9% (compared to 4.9% among those without missed findings).[13]

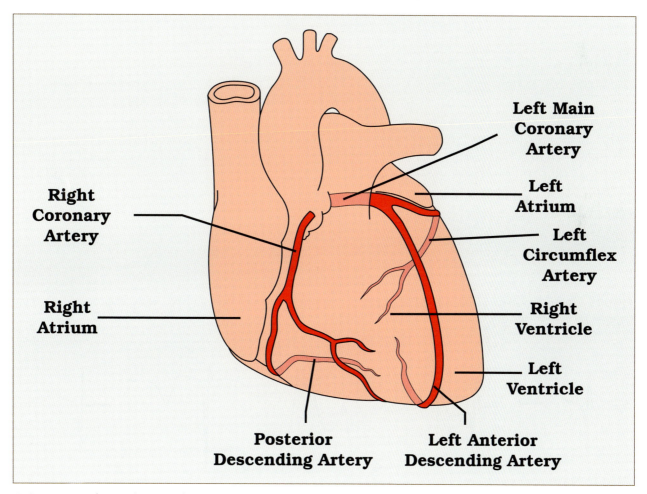

FIGURE 6.1. The cardiac circulation. The right coronary artery supplies both the inferior (diaphragmatic) portion of the heart and the right ventricle. The left anterior descending coronary artery generally supplies the ventricular septum and a large part of the left ventricular free wall. The left circumflex coronary artery supplies the lateral wall of the left ventricle. This circulation pattern can be variable (for example, the left circumflex artery might also supply the inferior portion of the left ventricle).

EVOLUTION OF STEMI

In the first minutes after acute coronary occlusion, changes that can be evident on the ECG include prolongation of the QT intervals, then the appearance of hyperacute T waves, followed by ST-segment elevation that occurs within the first 12 hours post-occlusion (Table 6.2, Figure 6.3).[14] If this occlusion persists, Q-wave formation can start within 1 hour and be completed within 8 to 12 hours.[15] Early Q waves presenting within the first hour of acute MI onset are caused by ischemia of the conduction system and not necessarily by irreversible infarction.[9] Within hours to days, an evolving acute MI will typically demonstrate T-wave inversions. These are initially shallow before progressing to deeper T-wave inversions.[16] This temporal development tends to make T-wave inversion a fairly late finding in an evolving acute MI. The inverted T waves generally appear in the same leads that demonstrated ST-segment elevation, and their morphology tends

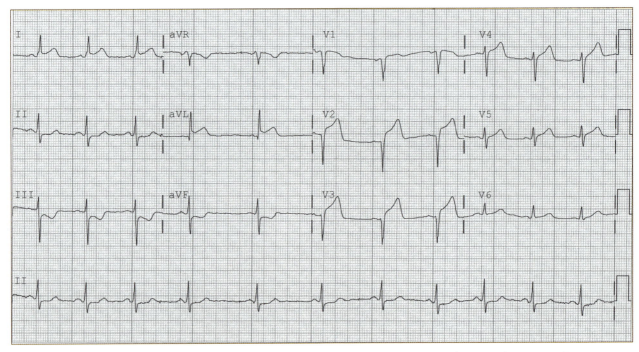

FIGURE 6.2. Anterolateral STEMI with ST-segment elevation in V_2 through V_4, I, and aVL, with reciprocal ST-segment depression in II, III, and aVF.

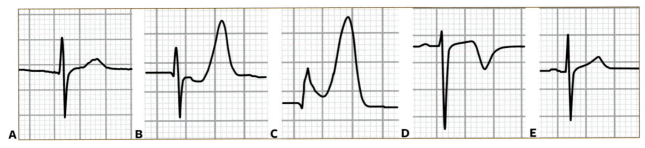

FIGURE 6.3. Evolution of anterior STEMI, lead V_2. **A.** Arrival at ED following 30 minutes of chest pain. **B.** 50 minutes following onset of symptoms, with hyperacute T waves. **C.** 62 minutes following onset of symptoms with ST-segment elevation; referred for emergent PCI with stent to proximal left anterior descending coronary artery (symptoms-to-balloon time 98 minutes). **D.** 3 hours postprocedure, ST segments have decreased, and T waves have inverted (markers of reperfusion). **E.** One month after PCI, ST segment has returned to baseline and T waves have normalized.

TABLE 6.2. Progression of electrocardiographic changes in STEMI.	
ECG CHANGE	TIME FRAME
QT prolongation	Minutes
Hyperacute T waves	Minutes
ST-segment elevation	Minutes to hours
Pathologic Q-wave formation	1 to 12 hours
T-wave inversions	Several hours to days
T-wave normalization	Weeks to months

to be symmetric.[17,18] In the absence of reperfusion therapy, which affects the time course of electrocardiographic changes, normalization of the T wave over weeks to months is part of the natural evolution of electrocardiographic changes with acute MI. Stabilization of the ST segment usually takes place within 12 hours, with or without ST-segment elevation resolution over the ensuing days to weeks, depending on location, severity, and presence or absence of reperfusion.[18-20] ST-segment elevation completely resolves within 2 weeks after 95% of inferior and 40% of anterior acute MIs.[20]

HYPERACUTE T WAVES

After QT prolongation, hyperacute T waves are the earliest described electrocardiographic sign of acute ischemia, preceding ST-segment elevation.[21] Hyperacute T waves are broad based and symmetrical, usually with increased amplitude and often associated with a depressed ST take off. They are most evident in the anterior chest leads and are more easily identified when a previous ECG is available for comparison (Figure 6.4A).[22] Hyperacute T waves can also be larger than the preceding QRS complex (Figure 6.4B). Hyperacute T waves are noted early after the onset of coronary occlusion and transmural infarction and tend to evolve rapidly into ST-segment elevation.[23] Experimentally in both animals and humans, hyperacute T waves can form as early as 2 minutes after coronary ligation, but they typically present within the first 30 minutes following acute coronary artery occlusion.[24-26] The differential diagnosis of hyperacute T waves includes transmural acute MI, hyperkalemia, early repolarization, left ventricular hypertrophy, and acute myopericarditis.[27] The principal entity to exclude is hyperkalemia—this T-wave morphology can be confused with hyperacute T waves of early transmural MI. The finding of hyperacute T waves on the ECG does not mandate acute reperfusion therapy; however, obtaining frequent serial 12-lead ECGs in this setting (every 5-15 minutes) is strongly recommended. Although hyperacute T waves are one of the earliest signs of acute MI, this early finding is not generally seen because patients do not frequently present to an emergency department at the onset of their ACS symptoms.

ST-SEGMENT ELEVATION AND CURRENT OF INJURY

The ST-segment elevation seen with acute STEMI is called a current of injury. This indicates that damage has occurred to the epicardial (outer) layer of the heart as a result of severe ischemia. The exact reason that acute MI produces ST-segment elevation is complex and not fully understood. Normally, the ST segment is isoelectric (neither positive nor negative) because net current flow is not occurring at this time. Acute MI alters the electrical charge on the myocardial cell membranes in a number of ways. As a result, current flow becomes abnormal (current of injury) and produces ST-segment deviations. The ST segment begins at the J point (the end of the QRS) and ends at the initiation of the T wave. Because the PR segment can be altered in the setting of atrial ischemia, acute pericarditis, or abnormal atrial depolarization, ST-segment deviation should be compared to the level of the TP segment at the isoelectric point or baseline. In the setting of atrial arrhythmias, when the TP segment is obscured (sinus tachycardia) or absent (atrial fibrillation), the PR segment is used as the isoelectric point. Diagnostic ST-segment elevation in the absence of left ventricular hypertrophy or left bundle-branch block (LBBB) is defined by the European Society of Cardiology/ACCF/AHA/World Heart Federation Task

Force for the Universal Definition of Myocardial Infarction as new ST-segment elevation at the J point in at least two contiguous leads of 1 mm; but in leads V2 and V3 of 1.5 mm in women, 2.5 mm in men younger than 40 years, and 2 mm in men 40 years old and older (Figures 6.5A, 6.5B, 6.6).[7,8] Leads I and aVL ("high lateral leads") are considered contiguous in the frontal plane, with elevation in these

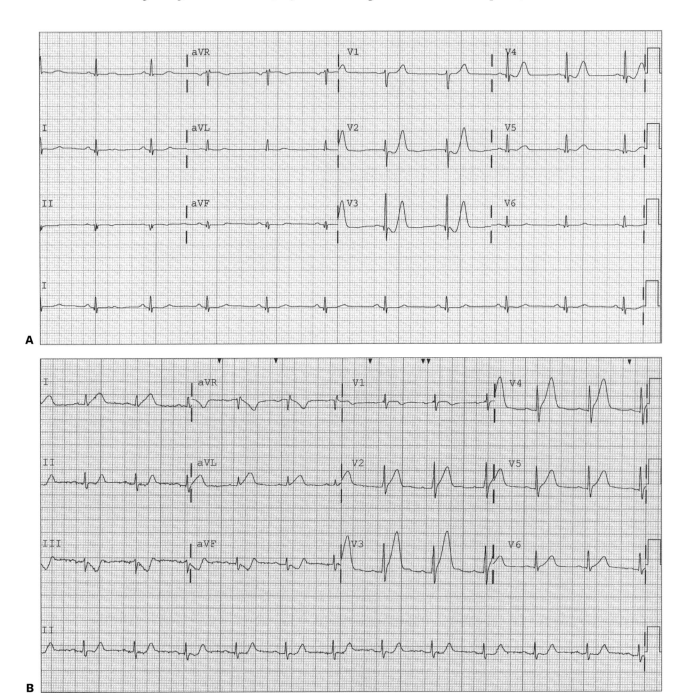

FIGURE 6.4. A. This ECG has hyperacute T waves in leads V_2 through V_4 with depressed take off at the initiation of the ST segment and straight uptake of the T wave. **B.** Another example of hyperacute T waves in V_2 through V_4. Note the broad-based, bulky T waves in the anterior leads, with T-wave height larger than the QRS complexes in V_2 and V_3. Adapted figure A with permission from: Levis JT. ECG diagnosis: hyperacute T waves. *Perm J.* 2015;19(3):79. Copyright 2015 The Permanente Press.

leads comprising a high lateral STEMI (Figures 6.7A, 6.7B). During prolonged ischemia, the ST segment can change from concave to straight and then convex morphology (Figure 6.8). In anterior MI, an upwardly concave waveform in V_2 through V_5 is common (Figure 6.9), although upwardly convex morphology is more specific for STEMI and has been associated with greater infarct size and morbidity.[28,29]

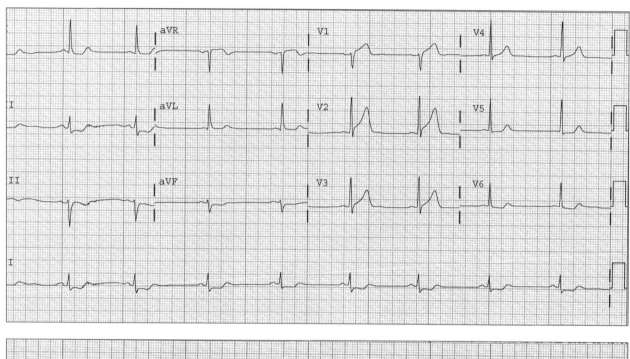

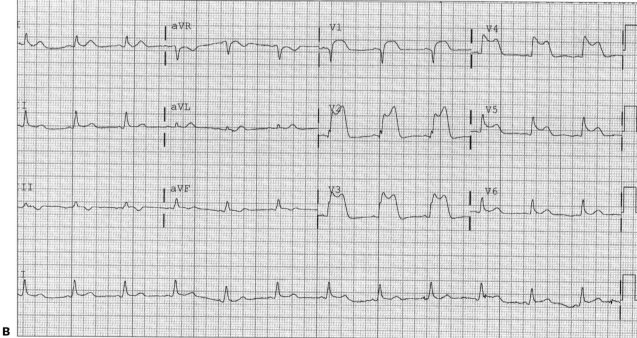

FIGURE 6.5. A. Early anterior STEMI. Note ST-segment elevation at the J-point in V_1 through V_3 (2 mm in leads V_1 and V_2), as well as reciprocal ST-segment depressions in the inferior leads II, III, and aVF. **B.** Anterior STEMI with significant ST elevation in V_1 through V_5.

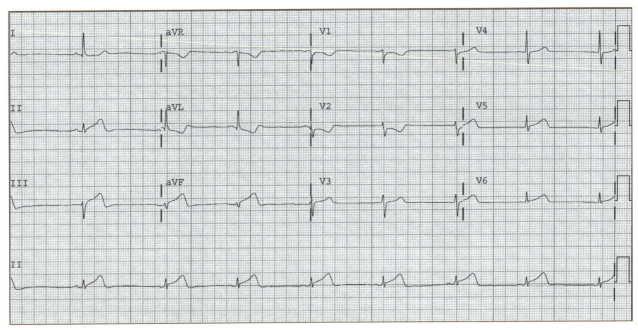

FIGURE 6.6. Inferior STEMI with ST-segment elevation of more than 1 mm in leads II, III, and aVF, with reciprocal ST-segment depression in I, aVL, V$_1$, and V$_2$.

ST-SEGMENT DEPRESSION

Acute subendocardial ischemia due to a reduction of blood flow or an increase in demand causes horizontal (flat) or downsloping ST-segment depression in the leads facing the involved area of the heart (Figure 6.10). Primary ST-segment depression is distinguished from reciprocal ST-segment depression seen in some STEMI ECGs, including posterior STEMI. In primary ST-segment depression, concurrent T-wave inversions might or might not be present. Primary ST-segment depression is an electrocardiographic sign of NSTE-ACS. ST-segment depression of only 0.5 mm, if unchanged from baseline, is associated with an increased mortality rate but is more specific for NSTE-ACS when it is greater than 1 mm (0.1 mV) in two or more contiguous leads.[30] In a study of more than 250,000 patients in the National Registry of Myocardial Infarction (NRMI) database, patients with ST-segment depression had an in-hospital mortality rate of 15.5%, which was equivalent to that of patients with STEMI.[31] ST-segment depression associated with NSTE-ACS can be transient and dynamic.[26] The proportionality of ST-segment depression in relation to the R wave is important, with 1 mm ST-segment depression following an R wave of less than 10 mm being more specific for ischemia but less sensitive than 1 mm of ST-segment depression following an R wave larger than 20 mm.[26] ST-segment depression larger than 2 mm in three or more leads is associated with a high probability that cardiac biomarkers will be elevated. Without primary PCI, the 30-day mortality rate in these patients is 35%.[32]

When reciprocal ST-segment depression occurs in the setting of anterior or lateral STEMI, it is typically found in the inferior leads. When reciprocal ST-segment depression occurs in the setting of inferior STEMI, it is typically found in the anterior leads. (Table 6.3, Figures 6.11, 6.12). Because a significant number of STEMIs do not develop reciprocal ST-segment depression, its absence does not rule out STEMI, but its presence increases the specificity of a STEMI diagnosis.[26,33,34]

T-WAVE INVERSIONS

T waves are typically upright except in aVR, where they are typically inverted, and in leads III, aVF, V$_1$,

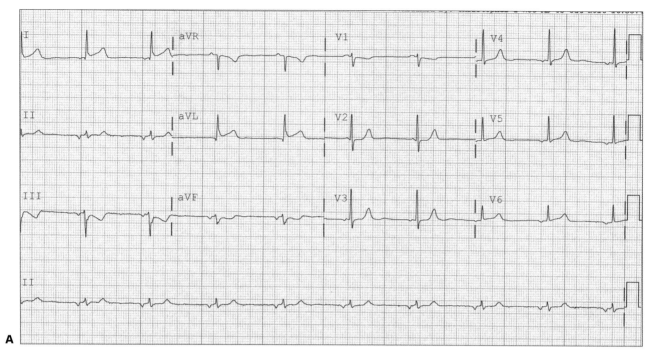

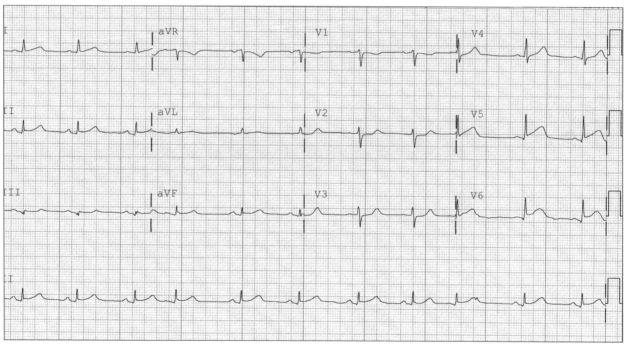

FIGURE 6.7. A. High lateral STEMI with ST-segment elevation in leads I and aVL (high lateral leads), with reciprocal ST-segment depression in III and aVF. **B.** Lateral STEMI with ST-segment elevation in lateral leads V_5 and V_6.

and V_2, where they can be inverted or upright.[35] In the setting of anginal symptoms, new T-wave inversions in leads other than III, aVF, and aVR, particularly when accompanied by ST-segment depression and QT prolongation, should raise suspicion for myocardial ischemia (Figures 6.13A, 6.13B). Patients with persistent T-wave inversions and suspected ACS will generally have troponin elevations,

TABLE 6.3. Reciprocal ST-segment depressions according to the area of infarction.

Anterior STEMI	Reciprocal ST-segment depressions in at least one of leads II, III, or aVF
Inferior STEMI	Reciprocal ST-segment depression generally present in leads I, aVL, and often precordial leads V_1-V_3
Lateral STEMI (ST-segment elevation leads I, aVL)	Reciprocal ST depressions in leads II, III, and aVF

leading to the diagnosis of NSTEMI. T-wave inversions without concomitant ST-segment depression are not typically a sign of ongoing ischemia but are usually seen after reperfusion.[36] T-wave inversions without associated ST-segment depression on an admission ECG are not independent predictors of adverse short- and long-term mortality in patients diagnosed with NSTE-ACS.[37]

WELLENS SYNDROME

Wellens syndrome is a pattern of deeply inverted or biphasic T waves in leads V2 to V3 that is specific for a critical stenosis of the LAD coronary artery (Figure 6.14).[38] Wellens syndrome is generally described in patients while they are symptom free and are subsequently found to have no (or minimal) elevations in cardiac biomarkers. These patients are at high risk for extensive anterior wall MI within the next few days to weeks.[39] Due to the critical LAD artery stenosis, these patients usually require invasive therapy, do poorly with medical management, and can suffer MI or cardiac arrest if stress tested. Therefore, stress testing is contraindicated.[40] Diagnostic criteria for Wellens syndrome are shown in Table 6.4.[41] The T-wave morphology present in Wellens syndrome is identical to the T-wave changes that occur during reperfusion. It most likely results from transient STEMI that has spontaneously reperfused or received collateral flow.

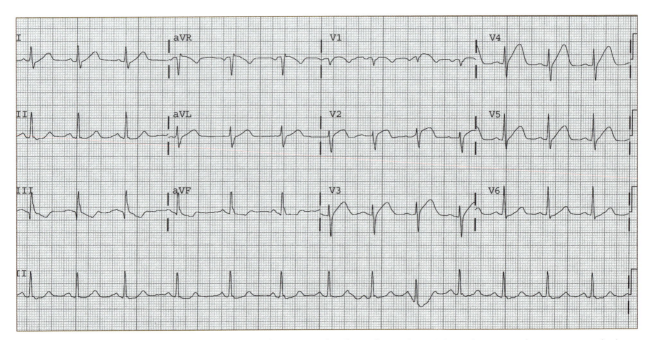

FIGURE 6.8. Anterior STEMI with ST-segment elevation in leads V_2 through V_4. Note the upward convex morphology in lead V_2, which increases the specificity for STEMI.

TABLE 6.4. Diagnostic electrocardiographic criteria for Wellens syndrome.[41]

Biphasic (type A) or deeply inverted (type B) T waves in V_2 and V_3

Isoelectric or minimally elevated (<1 mm) ST segments

Absence of precordial Q waves

Preserved precordial R-wave progression

Recent history of angina

ECG pattern present in pain-free state

Normal or slightly elevated serum cardiac biomarkers

LOSS OF PRECORDIAL T-WAVE BALANCE

Typically, the normal ECG shows progression of T-wave size across the precordial leads, with the T wave in V_1 inverted or flat. A large upright T wave in V_1 may be considered "normal" when there is high voltage, as in left ventricular hypertrophy or LBBB. However, a newly upright T wave in V_1 can indicate NSTE-ACS, particularly when the T wave is both upright and large.[42] A T wave in V_1 that is larger than the T wave in V_6 warrants a high degree of suspicion for myocardial ischemia.[43,44] A new, tall upright T wave in V_1 has been shown to have approximately 84% specificity for ischemic heart disease.[44]

Q WAVES

The Q wave is the initial negative deflection of the QRS complex. Q waves can be normal when found in the lateral and inferior leads. These represent the rapid depolarization of the thin septal wall between the two ventricles. Termed "septal" Q waves, they are of short duration (<0.04 seconds) and low amplitude. QS waves are QRS complexes without an R wave. Q waves in the anterior leads are always pathologic. Pathologic Q waves can be a consequence of MI, are generally wider (>30 ms in duration) and deeper (>25% of the following R wave in amplitude) than the normal "septal" Q wave (Figure 6.15). Leads III and aVR can have Q waves that are deep or 30 milliseconds or more in duration without underlying pathology. However, Q waves with a duration of 40 milliseconds or more in leads I, II, aVL, aVF, or V_3 through V_6 are considered abnormal.

Acute MI results in electrically inactive tissue that

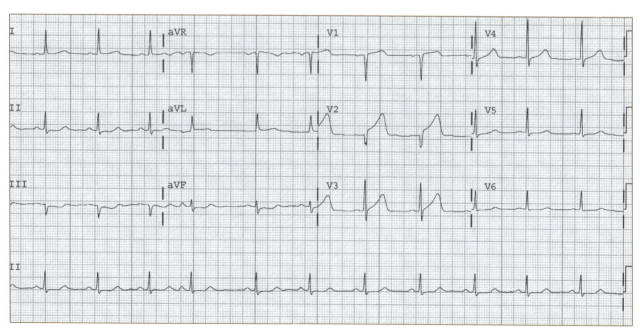

FIGURE 6.9. Anterior STEMI with ST-segment elevation in leads V_2 through V_4 with concave morphology to the ST-elevation segments in these leads. Also present is ST-segment depression in leads II, III, and aVF.

fails to produce an R wave in the overlying leads; depolarization of the opposite wall is recorded as a negative, pathologic Q wave.[26] Within 1 hour of onset of an anterior MI, QR waves can occur in the right precordial leads but frequently disappear after reperfusion. Such QR waves are caused by ischemia of the conducting system supplied by the LAD coronary artery and not necessarily by irreversible infarction.[45] Q waves

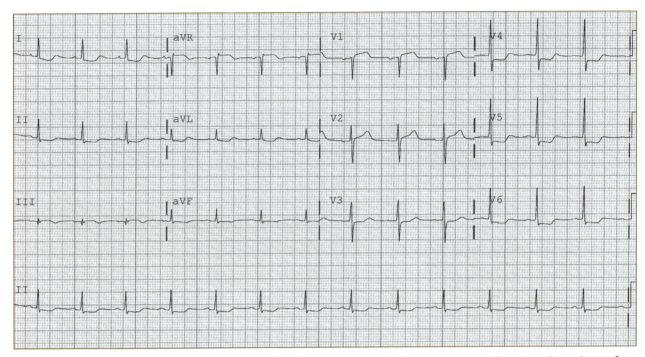

FIGURE 6.10. ST-segment depression in leads I, II, aVL, and V$_4$ through V$_6$ in a patient with active chest discomfort and an elevated troponin I.

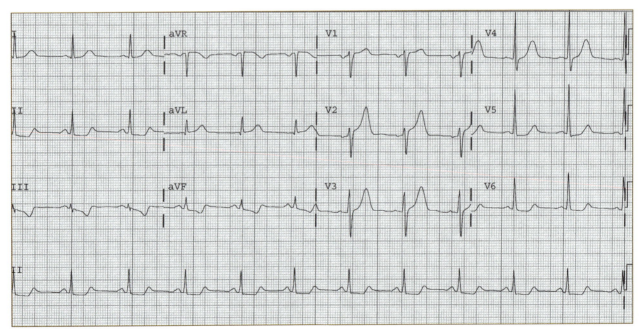

FIGURE 6.11. Anterior STEMI with ST-segment elevation in leads V$_2$ and V$_3$ with reciprocal ST-segment depression in II, III, and aVF.

signifying necrosis should be completely developed by 8 to 12 hours after the onset of persistent occlusion.[15,19] The presence of abnormal Q waves in the leads with ST-segment elevation on an admission ECG has been associated with larger infarct size and increased in-hospital mortality.[15] Patients with ECGs showing high ST segments and absent Q waves have the greatest benefit from reperfusion therapy.[15,46] However, patients with persistent ST-segment elevation and QR waves also receive significant benefit from reperfusion therapy.[15] Q waves eventually disappear within months to years in up to 30% of patients with acute MI who receive no reperfusion therapy, and within a few days to weeks in those who do receive early reperfusion therapy.[19,47] Q-wave equivalents suggestive of ischemia should also be identified on the ECG (Table 6.5). Q waves that are pathologic but not ischemic should be noted (Table 6.6).

TABLE 6.5. Q-wave equivalents in the precordial leads.

- R-wave diminution or poor R-wave progression
- Reverse R-wave progression, in which R waves increase then decrease in amplitude across the precordial leads
- Tall R waves in leads V_1 and V_2 representing Q waves of posterior infarction

Adapted with permission from: Haro LH. Acute coronary ischemia and infarction. In: Mattu A, Tabas JA, Barish RA, eds. *Electrocardiography in Emergency Medicine*. Dallas, TX: American College of Emergency Physicians; 2007:76. Copyright 2007 American College of Emergency Physicians.

TABLE 6.6. Differential diagnosis of pathologic Q waves.

- Chronic lung disease
- Dilated cardiomyopathy
- Hypertrophic cardiomyopathy
- Ischemic Q waves
- Left bundle-branch block
- Left ventricular hypertrophy

Adapted with permission from: Haro LH. Acute coronary ischemia and infarction. In: Mattu A, Tabas JA, Barish RA, eds. *Electrocardiography in Emergency Medicine*. Dallas, TX: American College of Emergency Physicians; 2007:77. Copyright 2007 American College of Emergency Physicians.

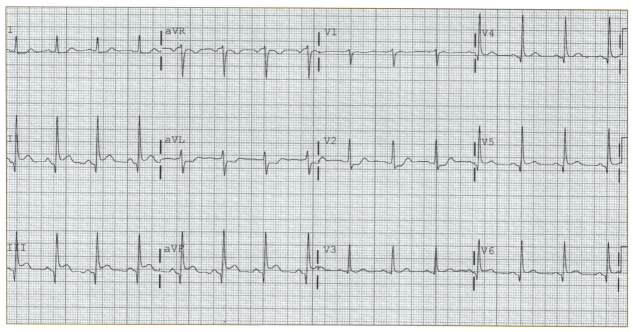

FIGURE 6.12. Inferior STEMI with ST-segment elevation in leads II, III, and aVF with reciprocal ST-segment depression in I, aVL, and V_2. Also present are developing Q waves in II, III, and aVF.

REPERFUSION

The rapid resolution of ST-segment elevation (ST resolution) with angiographic evidence for microvascular reperfusion is the best predictor of outcome from STEMI.[26] On continuous ST-segment monitoring after reperfusion therapy, a recovery of the ST segment to less than 50% of its maximal height by 60 minutes is strongly associated with Thrombolysis in Myocardial Infarction category 3 (TIMI-3) reperfusion and good microvascular perfusion (Figure 6.16).[48] A less sensitive but highly specific predictor of reperfusion is

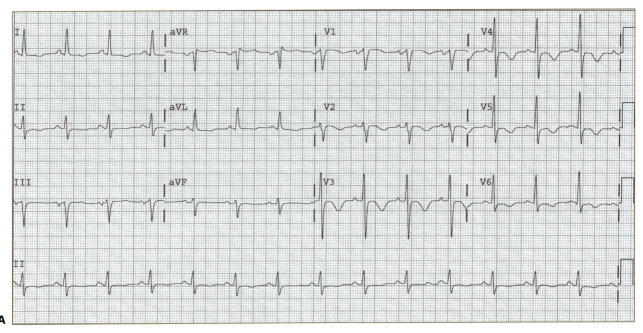

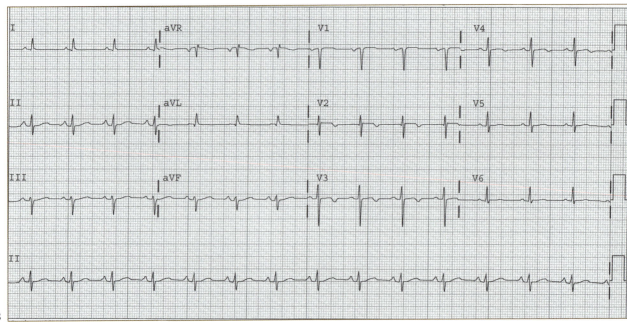

FIGURE 6.13. A. T-wave inversions in leads V_1 though V_6 in a patient with active chest discomfort. **B.** Less prominent T-wave inversions in V_2 through V_4 in a patient with active chest pain.

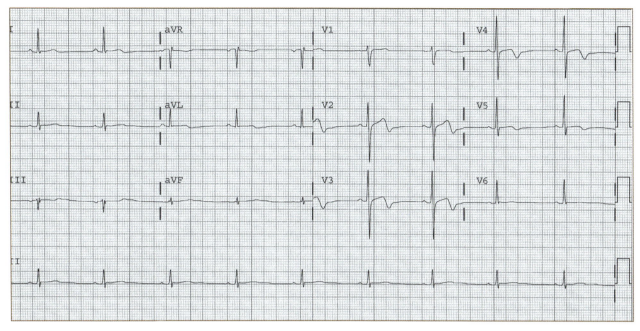

FIGURE 6.14. Wellens syndrome type A. Minimal ST-segment elevation in leads V_2 through V_4 with biphasic T waves in these leads. The patient was free of chest pain at the time of the ECG and was found to have 90% proximal LAD coronary artery stenosis.

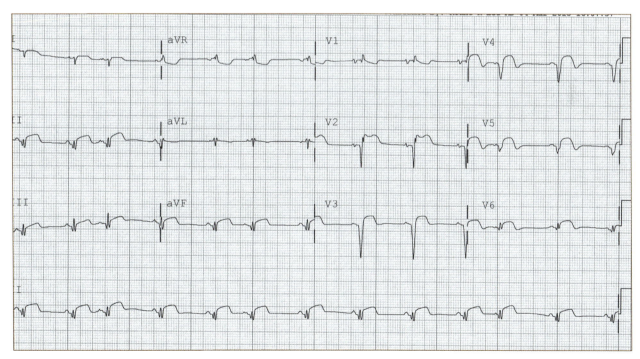

FIGURE 6.15. Anterior and inferior ST-segment elevation with pathologic Q waves in leads V_2 through V_4 indicating transmural MI.

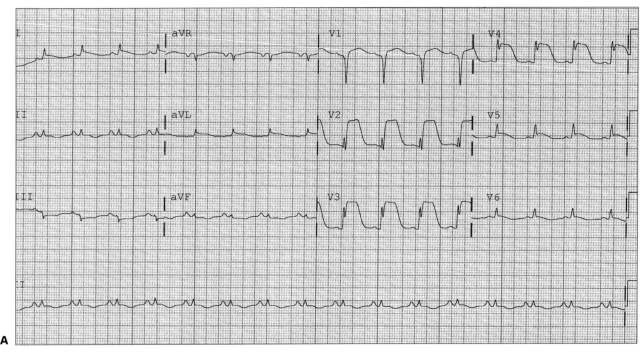
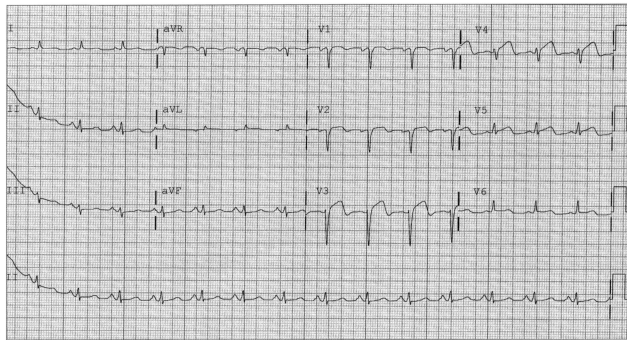

FIGURE 6.16. A. Anterior STEMI with significant ST-segment elevation in leads V_2 through V_4. **B.** An ECG from the same patient following PCI with stent to proximal LAD artery demonstrating more than 50% resolution in anterior ST-segment elevation indicating successful reperfusion of the occluded LAD artery.

terminal T-wave inversion identical to that of Wellens T waves. In STEMI patients, the presence of negative T waves early after presentation or soon after therapy is generally associated with a good prognosis.

POSTERIOR INFARCTIONS

Acute posterior wall MI occurs in up to 20% of acute MIs and is commonly associated with inferior or lateral acute MI.[49] Isolated posterior wall MI has an incidence of 3% to 4% of all acute MIs.[50] Most patients with electrocardiographic abnormalities of posterior wall MI have a stenosis or occlusion of the LCx coronary artery.[51] The electrocardiographic diagnosis of posterior wall MI is difficult because no leads of the standard ECG directly represent this area.[52] The typical infarction pattern appears only in posteriorly placed electrodes (ie, leads V_7 through V_9).

In posterior wall MI, there is an increase in the R/S ratio of more than 1 in leads V_1 and V_2.[52] This R wave is equivalent to a mirror image of the Q wave associated with STEMI in other locations. The ST segment points in the direction of the infarcted area, and ST-segment depression occurs in the precordial leads in the acute phase (Figure 6.17A). The T wave points away from the infarcted area. The combination of right precordial horizontal ST-segment depression with tall, upright T waves is an early sign of acute ischemia of the posterior wall during an evolving posterior wall MI.[53] The addition of posterior leads V_7 through V_9 significantly increases the detection of posterior injury patterns compared with the standard 12-lead ECG.[52,54] Using posterior leads to diagnosis posterior wall MI, ST-segment elevation in leads V_7 through V_9 is defined as elevation of at least 0.5 mm in two or more of these leads (Figure 6.17B). This reduced amplitude requirement is based on the increased distance between the posterior chest wall and the heart.[54]

RIGHT VENTRICULAR INFARCTION

Approximately 25% to 50% of cases of inferior wall MI are associated with a right ventricular MI (RVMI).[55,56] Right ventricular MI is often associated with hypotension, elevated venous pressures, and shock without evidence of acute heart failure.[57] The standard 12-lead ECG provides information on the left ventricle but yields limited information on the right side of the heart. Leads V_1 and V_2 on the standard ECG provide only a partial view of the right ventricle free wall.[55] Electrocardiographic findings suggestive of RVMI on the standard 12-lead ECG include ST-segment elevation in leads II, III, and aVF, with reciprocal ST-segment depression in the lateral leads (Figure 6.18A). Characteristically in RVMI, the ST-segment elevation in lead III is greater than in lead II, and the ST-segment elevation in lead aVF is greater than the ST-segment depression in lead V_2.[57] Using right-sided precordial leads, an ST-segmentt elevation in lead V_4R of 1 mm or more is diagnostic of RVMI (Figure 6.18B).[58] The ECG finding of ST-segment elevation in lead V_4R for diagnosis of RVMI has 100% sensitivity, 87% specificity, and 92% predictive accuracy.[58,59] Right precordial ST-segment elevation is a transient event that can be absent in up to half of patients with RVMI 12 hours after the onset of pain.[60,61] ST-segment elevation in right-sided precordial leads, especially in V_4R, correlates with reduced right ventricle ejection fraction; it is associated with major complications and in-hospital mortality.[60-62]

LEFT VENTRICULAR ANEURYSM

Persistent ST-segment elevation after a prior MI is clinically and pathologically manifested as a left ventricular aneurysm (LVA) and has been found in up to 60% of completed anterior STEMIs when there is no spontaneous or therapeutic reperfusion.[20] Anatomic LVA is defined as thinning and bulging of the myocardial wall, most commonly involving the anterior wall. This results in persistent ST-segment elevation, with QS waves in leads V_1 through V_4 (Figure 6.19). There are several electrocardiographic features of LVA that can help distinguish it from an acute MI, including:

- deep Q waves (usually QS waves),
- flattened T waves (often with some shallow T-wave inversions), and
- a lesser degree of ST-segment elevation.[63]

Echocardiography can be useful in distinguishing LVA from acute MI, which in the case of LVA could

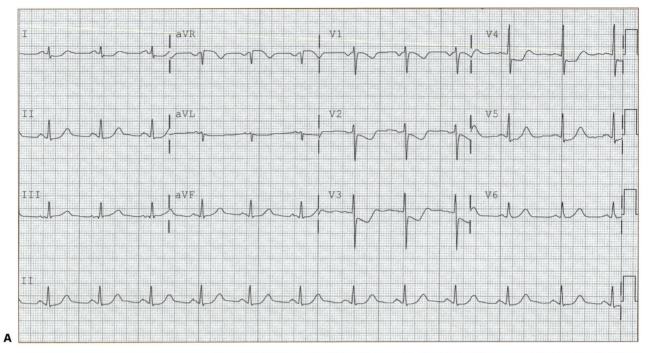
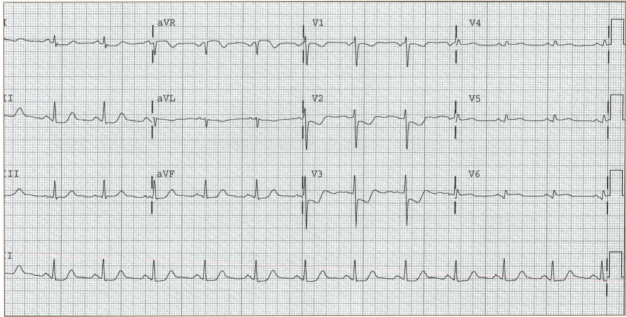

FIGURE 6.17. A. Isolated posterior STEMI from a 71-year-old woman with 90 minutes of chest discomfort. The ECG demonstrates deep ST-segment depression in leads V_2 through V_4. **B.** Posterior ECG including leads V_7 through V_9 (V_4 through V_6 on ECG) from the same patient, obtained shortly after the initial ECG (A), demonstrates 0.5 mm ST-segment elevation in posterior leads V_8 and V_9, confirming the posterior wall MI. The patient had 100% occlusion of the proximal LCx artery on coronary angiography. Adapted with permission from: Levis JT. ECG diagnosis: isolated posterior wall myocardial infarction. *Perm J.* 2015;19(4):e143-e144. Copyright 2015 The Permanente Press.

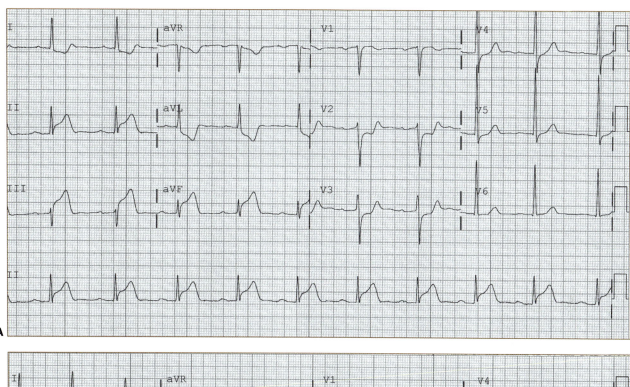
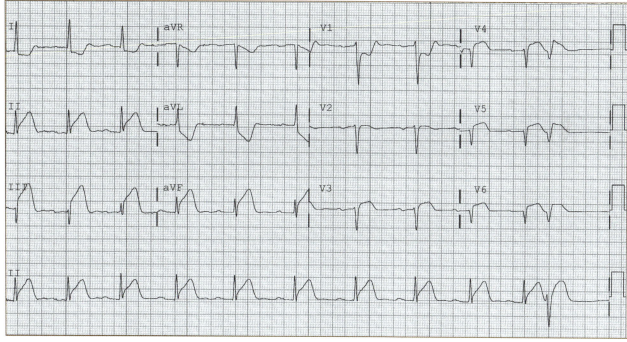

FIGURE 6.18. A. Acute inferoposterior STEMI with ST-segment elevation in leads II, III, aVF (ST-segment elevation in III > II); deep ST-segment depression in V_2 and V_3. **B.** ECG from same patient using right-sided leads (V_1R through V_6R are V_1 through V_6) with ST-segment elevation of more than 1 mm in V_3 through V_6 consistent with acute right ventricular infarction. The patient had 100% occlusion of proximal RCA on coronary angiography.

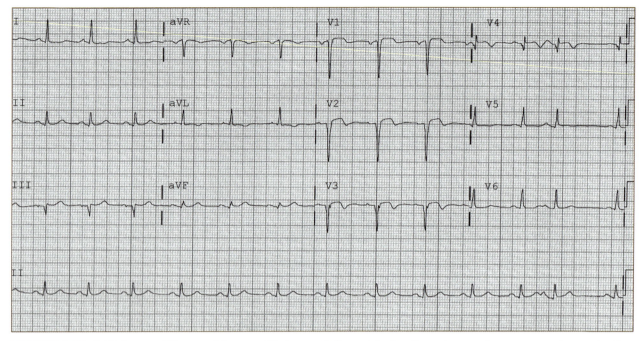

FIGURE 6.19. ECG from a 70-year-old man with known left ventricular thrombus and aneurysm, demonstrating convex ST-segment elevation in leads V_1 through V_4 with Q waves in these leads. The ECG was unchanged 5 days later; findings are consistent with left ventricular aneurysm.

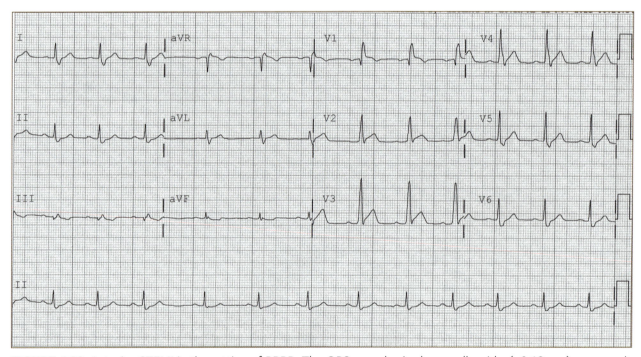

FIGURE 6.20. Anterior STEMI in the setting of RBBB. The QRS complex is abnormally wide (>0.12 sec) as a result of the bundle-branch block; lead V_1 shows a terminal positive deflection, and lead V_6 shows a wide S wave, with ST-segment elevation in V_2 through V_4.

demonstrate dyskinesis (diastolic dysfunction—the anatomic definition of aneurysm). Ventricular aneurysms can cause acute heart failure, ventricular arrhythmias, and thrombus formation, resulting in stroke and other embolic complications.

RIGHT BUNDLE-BRANCH BLOCK WITH MI

In right bundle-branch block (RBBB), the ST segment is as reliable in determining ST-segment deviation as it is in normal conduction.[26] However, the widened terminal portion of the QRS is frequently mistaken for the ST segment. The key to evaluating an ECG in the presence of RBBB is to find the true end of the QRS and the true beginning of the ST segment, so that the ST segment itself can be measured. When RBBB and an infarct occur together, a combination of patterns is seen: the QRS complex is abnormally wide (>0.12 sec) as a result of the bundle-branch block, lead V_1 shows a terminal positive deflection, and lead V_6 shows a wide S wave (Figure 6.20).

LEFT BUNDLE-BRANCH BLOCK WITH MI

In patients with LBBB, infarct diagnosis based on the ECG is challenging. The baseline ST segments and T waves tend to be shifted in a discordant direction (see Chapter 2), which can mask or mimic acute MI. The modified Sgarbossa criteria exhibit the best predictive values for identification of STEMI in the presence of LBBB.[64] In a study of 258 patients, the modified criteria were 80% sensitive and 99% specific for identification of acute coronary occlusion in the presence of LBBB. Positive and negative likelihood ratios for the modified criteria were 99.6 (95% CI 24.9-399.1) and 0.20 (95% CI 0.11-0.36), respectively.[65]

STEMI in the presence of LBBB is diagnosed if any one of the following three criteria is met:

- concordant (same direction as QRS complex) ST-segment elevation greater than 1 mm in leads with a positive QRS complex,
- concordant ST-segment depression larger than 1 mm in leads V_1 through V_3, or
- *excessively* discordant ST-segment elevation, defined by ST elevation equal to or greater than 25% of the depth of the S wave in leads with a negative QRS complex.

Figures 6.21, 6.22, and 6.23 demonstrate STEMI and LBBB with each of these three criteria.

Ventricular paced rhythms result in intraventricular conduction delays similar to LBBB. The modified Sgarbossa criteria have also been successfully used in the diagnosis of acute MI in patients with ventricular paced rhythms (Figure 6.24).[66]

REFERENCES

1. Benjamin EJ, Blaha MJ, Chiuve SE, et al. Heart Disease and Stroke Statistics - 2017 Update: A Report From the American Heart Association. *Circulation.* 2017;135:00–00.
2. Ting HH, Krumholz HM, Bradley EH, et al. Implementation and integration of prehospital ECGs into systems of care for acute coronary syndrome: a scientific statement from the American Heart Association Interdisciplinary Council on Quality of Care and Outcomes Research, Emergency Cardiovascular Care Committee, Council on Cardiovascular Nursing, and Council on Clinical Cardiology. *Circulation.* 2008;118:1066–1079.
3. O'Conner RE, Abdulaziz SAA, Brady WJ, et al. Part 9: Acute coronary syndromes. 2015 American Heart Association Guidelines Update for Cardiopulmonary Resuscitation and Emergency Cardiovascular Care. *Circulation.* 2015;132[suppl 2]:S483–S500.
4. Rokos IC, French WJ, Koenig WJ, et al. Integration of pre-hospital electrocardiograms and ST-elevation myocardial infarction receiving center (SRC) networks impact on door-to-balloon times across 10 independent regions. *JACC Cardiovasc Interv.* 2009;2:339–346.
5. Nam J, Caners K, Bowen JM, et al. Systemic review and meta-analysis of the benefits of out-of-hospital 12-lead ECG and advanced notification in ST-segment elevation myocardial infarction patients. *Ann Emerg Med.* 2014;64:176-186.
6. Welsford M, Nikolaou NI, Beygui F, et al; on behalf of the Acute Coronary Syndrome Chapter Collaborators. Part 5: acute coronary syndromes: 2015 International Consensus on Cardiopulmonary Resuscitation and Emergency Cardiovascular Care Science With Treatment Recommendations. *Circulation.* 2015;132(suppl 1):S146–S176.

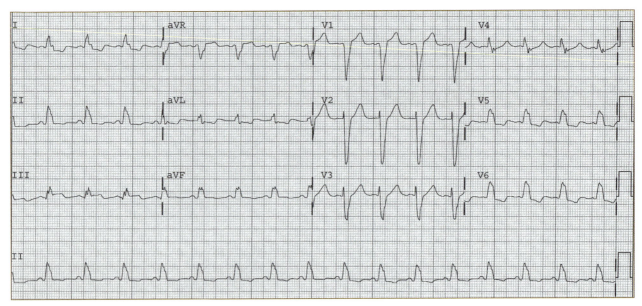

FIGURE 6.21. LBBB pattern with 1 mm concordant ST-segment elevation in lead III in a patient with active chest pain. Coronary angiography demonstrated 100% occlusion of the proximal RCA.

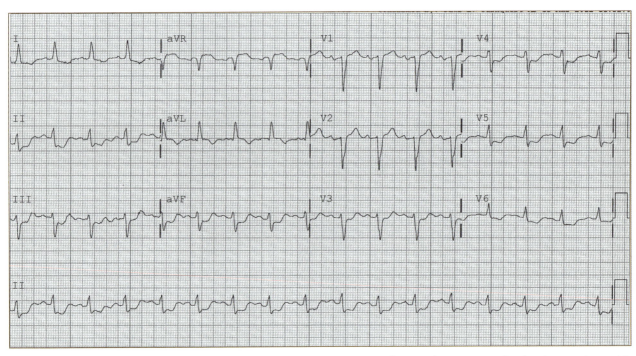

FIGURE 6.22. LBBB pattern with concordant ST-segment depression of more than 1 mm in lead V_3 in a patient with active chest pain. Coronary angiography demonstrated 100% occlusion of the mid LAD coronary artery.

ACUTE CORONARY ISCHEMIA AND INFARCTION

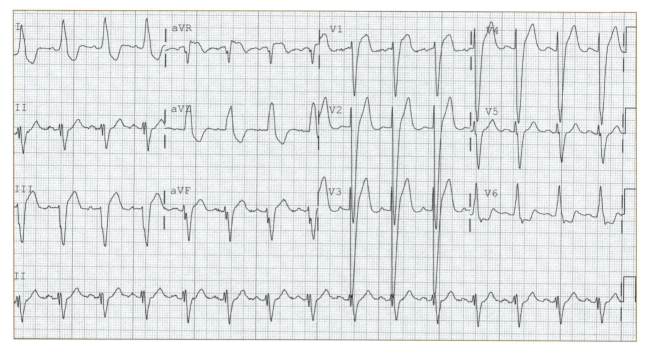

FIGURE 6.23. LBBB pattern with excessively discordant ST-segment elevation in a patient with active chest pain. Coronary angiography demonstrated 100% occlusion of the proximal LAD coronary artery.

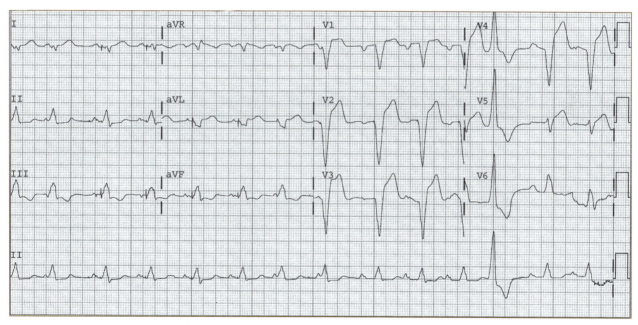

FIGURE 6.24. Paced ventricular rhythm with discordant ST-segment elevation greater than 25% of the S wave in leads V_2 through V_4 in a patient with active chest pain. Coronary angiography demonstrated 99% stenosis of the proximal LAD coronary artery.

7. O'Gara PT, Kushner FG, Ascheim DD, et al. American College of Cardiology Foundation/American Heart Association Task Force on Practice Guidelines. 2013 ACCF/AHA guideline for the management of ST-elevation myocardial infarction: a report of the American College of Cardiology Foundation/American Heart Association Task Force on Practice Guidelines. *Circulation*. 2013;127:e362–425.
8. Thygesen K, Alpert JS, Jaffe AS, et al. Third universal definition of myocardial infarction. *Circulation*. 2012;126:2020–2035.
9. Rouan GW, Lee TH, Cook EF, et al. Clinical characteristics and outcome of acute myocardial infarction in patients with initially normal or nonspecific electrocardiograms (a report from the Multicenter Chest Pain Study). *Am J Cardiol*. 1989;64:1087–1092.
10. McCarthy BD, Wong JB, Selker HP. Detecting acute cardiac ischemia in the emergency department: a review of the literature. *J Gen Intern Med*. 1990;5:365–373.
11. Slater DK, Hlatky MA, Mark DB, et al. Outcome in suspected acute myocardial infarction with normal or minimally abnormal admission electrocardiographic findings. *Am J Cardiol*. 1987;60:766–770.
12. Welch RD, Zalenski RJ, Frederick PD, et al. Prognostic value of normal or nonspecific initial electrocardiogram in acute myocardial infarction. *JAMA*. 2001;286:1977-1984.
13. Masoudi FA, Magid DJ, Vinson DR, et al. Implications of the failure to identify high-risk electrocardiogram findings for the quality of care of patients with acute myocardial infarction. Results of the Emergency Department Quality in Myocardial Infarction (EDQMI) study. *Circulation*. 2006;114:1565-1571.
14. Stellpflug SJ, Holger JS, Smith SW. What is the role of the ECG in ACS? In: Brady WJ, Truwit JD, eds. *Critical Decisions in Emergency and Acute Care Electrocardiography*. West Sussex, UK: Wiley-Blackwell; 2009:85-91.
15. Raitt MH, Maynard C, Wagner GS, et al. Appearance of abnormal Q waves early in the course of acute myocardial infarction: implications for efficacy of thrombolytic therapy. *J Am Coll Cardiol*. 1995;25:1084-1088.
16. Goldberger AL. *Myocardial Infarction: Electrocardiographic Differential Diagnosis*. 4th ed. St. Louis, MO: Mosby; 1991:17-312.
17. Oliva PB, Hammill SC, Edwards WD. Electrocardiographic diagnosis of postinfarction regional pericarditis. Ancillary observations regarding the effect of reperfusion on the rapidity and amplitude of T wave inversion after acute myocardial infarction. *Circulation*. 1993;88:896-904.
18. Goldschlager N, Goldman MJ. *Principles of Clinical Electrocardiography*. 13th ed. Norwalk, CT: Appleton and Lange; 1989:110-112.
19. Bar FW, Volders PG, Hoppener B, et al. Development of ST-segment elevation and Q- and R-wave changes in acute myocardial infarction and the influence of thrombolytic therapy. *Am J Cardiol*. 1996;77:337-343.
20. Mills RM, Young E, Gorlin R, et al. Natural history of S-T segment elevation after acute myocardial infarction. *Am J Cardiol*. 1975;35:609-614.
21. Goldberger AL. Hyperacute T waves revisited. *Am Heart J*. 1982;104:888-890.
22. Nable JV, Brady W. The evolution of electrocardiographic changes in ST-segment elevation myocardial infarction. *Am J Emerg Med*. 2009;27(6):734-746.
23. Morris F, Brady WJ. ABC of clinical electrocardiography: acute myocardial infarction—part I. *BMJ*. 2002;324:831.
24. Smith FM. The ligation of coronary arteries with electrocardiographic study. *Ann Intern Med*. 1918;5:1-27.
25. Graham GK, Laforet EG. An electrocardiographic and morphologic study of changes following ligation of the left coronary artery in human beings: a report of two cases. *Am Heart J*. 1952;43:42-52.
26. Smith SW, Whitman W. Acute coronary syndromes. *Emerg Med Clin North Am*. 2006;24(1):53-89.
27. Brady W, Morris F. Electrocardiographic abnormalities encountered in acute myocardial infarction. *J Accid Emerg Med*. 2000;17(1):40-45.
28. Smith SW. Upwardly concave ST segment morphology is common in acute left anterior descending coronary artery occlusion [abstract]. *Acad Emerg Med*. 2003;10:516.
29. Kosuge M, Kimura K, Ishikawa T, et al. Value of ST segment elevation pattern in predicting infarct size and left ventricular function at discharge in patients with reperfused acute anterior myocardial infarction. *Am Heart J*. 1999;137:522-527.
30. Hyde TA, French JK, Wong CK, et al. Four-year survival of patients with acute coronary syndromes without ST-segment elevation and prognostic significance of 0.5 mm ST-segment depression. *Am J Cardiol*. 1999;84:379-385.
31. Pitta SR, Grzybowski M, Welch RD, et al. ST-segment depression on the initial electrocardiogram in acute myocardial infarction-prognostic significance and its effect on short-term mortality: A report from the National Registry of Myocardial Infarction (NRMI-2, 3, 4). *Am J Cardiol*. 2005;95(7):843–848.

32. Lee HS, Cross SJ, Rawles JM, et al. Patients with suspected myocardial infarction who present with ST depression. *Lancet.* 1993;342:1204-1207.
33. Otto LA, Aufderheide TP. Evaluation of ST segment elevation criteria for the prehospital electrocardiographic diagnosis of acute myocardial infarction. *Ann Emerg Med.* 1994;23:17-24.
34. Brady WJ, Perron AD, Syverud SA, et al. Reciprocal ST segment depression: impact on the electrocardiographic diagnosis of ST segment elevation acute myocardial infarction. *Am J Emerg Med.* 2002;20:35-38.
35. Bertog SC, Smith SW. What ECG changes might myocardial ischemia cause other than ST segment elevation or Q waves, and what are the differential diagnoses of these changes? In: Brady WJ, Truwit JD, eds. *Critical Decisions in Emergency and Acute Care Electrocardiography*. West Sussex, UK: Wiley-Blackwell; 2009;103-114.
36. Birnbaum Y, Nikus K, Kligfield P, et al. The role of the ECG in diagnosis, risk estimation, and catheterization laboratory activation in patients with acute coronary syndromes: A consensus document. *Ann Noninvasive Electrocardiol.* 2014:19(5):412-425.
37. Tan SN, Goodman SG, Yan RT, et al. Comparative prognostic value of T-wave inversion and ST-segment depression on the admission electrocardiogram in non–ST-segment elevation acute coronary syndromes. *Am Heart J.* 2013;166:290-297.
38. de Zwaan C, Bär FW, Wellens HJ. Characteristic electrocardiographic pattern indicating a critical stenosis high in left anterior descending coronary artery in patients admitted because of impending myocardial infarction. *Am Heart J.* 1982;103(4 Pt 2):730-736. PMID:6121481
39. Chan TC, Brady WJ, Harrigan RA, et al. *ECG in Emergency Medicine and Acute Care.* St. Louis, MO: Mosby; 2005.
40. Rhinehardt J, Brady WJ, Perron AD, Mattu A. Electrocardiographic manifestations of Wellens' syndrome. *Am J Emerg Med.* 2002 Nov;20(7):638-643.
41. Tandy TK, Bottomy DP, Lewis JG. Wellens' syndrome. *Ann Emerg Med.* 1999;33:347-351.
42. Tewelde SZ, Mattu A, Brady WJ. Pitfalls in electrocardiographic diagnosis of acute coronary syndrome in low-risk chest pain. *West J Emerg Med.* 2017;18(4):601-606.
43. Stankovic I, Milekic K, Vlahovic SA, et al. Upright T-wave in precordial lead V_1 indicates the presence of significant coronary artery disease in patients undergoing coronary angiography with otherwise unremarkable electrocardiogram. *Herz.* 2012;37(7):756–761.
44. Barthwal SP, Agarwal R, Sarkari NB, et al. Diagnostic significance of T I < T III and TV_1 > TV_6 signs in ischaemic heart disease. *J Assoc Physicians India.* 1993;41(1):26–27.
45. Barold SS, Falkoff MD, Ong LS, et al. Significance of transient electrocardographic Q waves in coronary artery disease. *Cardiol Clin.* 1987;5:367-380.
46. Birnbaum Y, Chetrit A, Sclarovsky S, et al. Abnormal Q waves on the admission electrocardiogram of patients with first acute myocardial infarction: prognostic implications. *Clin Cardiol.* 1997;20:477-481.
47. Kaplan BM, Berkson DM. Serial electrocardiograms after myocardial infarction. *Ann Intern Med.* 1964;60:430-435.
48. Krucoff MW, Croll MA, Pope JE, et al. Continuous 12-lead ST segment recovery analysis in the TAMI 7 study. Performance of a non-invasive method for real-time detection of failed myocardial reperfusion. *Circulation.* 1993;88:437-446.
49. Zalenski RJ, Cooke D, Rydman R, et al. Assessing the diagnostic value of an ECG containing leads V_4R, V_8 and V_9: the 15-lead ECG. *Ann Emerg Med.* 1993;22:786-793.
50. Oraii S, Maleki M, Abbas Tavakolian A, et al. Prevalence and outcome of ST-segment elevation posterior electrocardiographic leads during acute myocardial infarction. *J Electrocardiol.* 1999;32:275-278.
51. Bough E, Korr K. Prevalence and severity of circumflex coronary artery disease in electrocardiographic posterior myocardial infarction. *J Am Coll Cardiol.* 1986;7:990-996.
52. Rich M, Erling B, King T, et al. Electrocardiographic diagnosis of remote posterior wall myocardial infarction using unipolar posterior lead V_9. *Chest.* 1989;96:489-493.
53. Agarwal J, Khaw K, Aurignac F, et al. Importance of posterior chest leads in patients with suspected myocardial infarction, but nondiagnostic, routine 12-lead electrocardiogram. *Am J Cardiol.* 1999;83:323-326.
54. Matetzky S, Freimark D, Feinberg MS, et al. Acute myocardial infarction with isolated ST-segment elevation in posterior chest leads V_{7-9}. *J Am Coll Cardiol.* 1999;34:748-753.
55. Nagam MR, Vinson DR, Levis JT. ECG diagnosis: right ventricular myocardial infarction. *Perm J.* 2017;21:16-105.
56. Kakouros N, Cokkinos DV. Right ventricular myocardial infarction: pathophysiology, diagnosis, and management. *Postgrad Med J.* 2010;86(1022):719-728.
57. Cohn JN, Guiha NH, Broder MI, Limas CJ. Right ventricular infarction. Clinical and hemodynamic features. *Am J Cardiol.* 1974;33(2):209-214.
58. Somers MP, Brady WJ, Bateman DC, et al. Additional electrocardiographic leads in the ED chest pain patient:

right ventricular and posterior leads. *Am J Emerg Med.* 2003;21(7):563-573.
59. Robalino BD, Whitlow PL, Underwood DA, Salcedo EE. Electrocardiographic manifestations of right ventricular infarction. *Am Heart J.* 1989;118(1):138-144.
60. Andersen HR, Nielsen D, Lund O, Falk E. Prognostic significance of right ventricular infarction diagnosed by ST elevation in right chest leads V_3R to V_7R. *Int J Cardiol.* 1989;23(3):349-356.
61. Shiraki H, Yokozuka H, Negishi K, et al. Acute impact of right ventricular infarction on early hemodynamic course after inferior myocardial infarction. *Circ J.* 2010;74(1):148-155.
62. Zehender M, Kasper W, Kauder E, et al. Right ventricular infarction as an independent predictor of prognosis after acute inferior myocardial infarction. *N Engl J Med.* 1993;328(14):981-988.
63. Klein LR, Shroff GR, Beeman W, et al. Electrocardiographic criteria to differentiate acute anterior ST-elevation myocardial infarction from left ventricular aneurysm. *Am J Emerg Med.* 2015;33:786-790.
64. Smith SW, Dodd KW, Henry TD, et al. Diagnosis of ST-elevation myocardial infarction in the presence of left bundle branch block with the ST-elevation to S-wave ratio in a modified Sgarbossa rule. *Ann Emerg Med.* 2012;60(6):766-776.
65. Meyers HP, Limkakeng AT, Jaffa EJ, et al. Validation of the modified Sgarbossa criteria for acute coronary occlusion in the setting of left bundle branch block: A retrospective case-control study. *Am Heart J.* 2015;170(6):1255-1264.
66. Schaaf SG, Tabas JA, Smith SW. A patient with a paced rhythm presenting with chest pain and hypotension. *JAMA Intern Med.* 2013;173(22):2082-2085.

CHAPTER SEVEN

Additional-Lead Testing in Electrocardiography

ANDREW D. PERRON AND WILLIAM J. BRADY

KEY POINTS

- The right ventricle and the posterior wall of the left ventricle are not well visualized on the standard 12-lead ECG.
- An additional-lead (15-lead) ECG can be obtained using a standard 12-lead ECG machine.
- ST-segment elevation in lead V_4R is indicative of a right ventricular infarction. Patients with this entity are at increased risk for morbidity and mortality from the MI. Preload-reducing medications should be used with caution, if at all.
- ST-segment elevation in leads V_8 and V_9 is indicative of a posterior left ventricular infarct. Patients with this entity are also at increased risk for morbidity and mortality from the MI.

The standard 12-lead ECG is a useful but clearly limited tool in the assessment of emergency department patients for acute coronary syndrome. For example, Rude and colleagues[1] examined the initial ECGs obtained from adult patients with chest pain, all of whom were subsequently shown to have had an acute MI. Less than 50% of these patients demonstrated ST-segment elevation on their initial ECG; the others manifested a variety of ischemic changes, including ST-segment depression and T-wave inversion. Perhaps of greatest concern to the emergency clinician is that, in 30% of patients, the initial ECG was normal or showed nonspecific changes only. This same study also demonstrated that ST-segment depression was a relatively poor indicator of acute MI; less than 50% of patients who presented with isolated precordial ST-segment depression were subsequently determined to have had an acute MI.

Some authors have suggested that the sensitivity of the 12-lead ECG can be improved if additional body surface leads are used for the evaluation of chest pain in selected individuals.[2-5] The two coronary syndromes that could be more easily identified by such a strategy are:

- acute posterior MI and
- right ventricular MI.

These syndromes are at risk of being underdiagnosed because placement for the standard 12-lead ECG does not allow these areas of myocardium to be assessed directly.[6] Additional leads that can be used to examine these "silent" areas include:

- the right-sided lead V_4R (also called RV4), which reflects electrical current changes in the right ventricle,[7] and
- the posterior leads V_8 and V_9, which image the posterior wall of the left ventricle.[6]

Posterior MI is the most commonly missed STEMI, so the use of additional posterior leads on patients with ST-segment depression in leads V_1 through V_3 can be particularly useful to identify this condition.

THE RIGHT VENTRICULAR LEADS

Cohn and associates[8] were the first to describe right ventricular infarction as the clinical syndrome of hypotension, elevated jugular venous pressure, and shock in the presence of clear lung fields. The true incidence of right ventricular infarction is uncertain. Reported rates vary depending on the method of detection used (eg, autopsy, invasive studies, or noninvasive imaging, including electrocardiography).[7] Although isolated right ventricular infarction is presumably a rare phenomenon, electrocardiographic studies have shown consistently that right ventricular infarction accompanies approximately one-third of inferior wall acute MIs.[9–11] The anatomic reason for this association with inferior ischemia is that most right ventricular infarctions result from occlusion of the right coronary artery proximal to the right ventricular branch. The left circumflex artery supplies the right ventricle in approximately 10% of patients and, in this situation, right ventricular infarction can present in the setting of a lateral wall acute MI, as opposed to inferior MI.

A number of findings on the standard 12-lead ECG are suggestive of right ventricular acute MI, including ST-segment elevation in the inferior leads (II, III, and aVF)[12] or in the right precordial chest leads, particularly V_1, the only one of the standard 12 leads that reflects the right ventricle.[10,13–15] On occasion, coexisting acute MI of the left ventricle's posterior wall can obscure the ST-segment elevation resulting from right ventricular infarction in lead V_1.[16–18] In particular, right ventricular acute MI should be suspected:

- when the combination of ST-segment elevation is noted in lead V_1 with concurrent ST-segment depression in lead V_2, or
- when ST-segment depression is noted in lead V_2 in conjunction with leads V_1 and V_3 demonstrating isoelectric ST segments.

In addition, a pattern of the relative magnitudes of the ST-segment elevation in the inferior leads could indicate right ventricular acute MI, that is, when ST-segment elevation is markedly greater in lead III compared with the other inferior leads, then right ventricular infarction is suggested. Other findings suggestive of right ventricular acute MI in the presence of inferior wall MI include:

- the presence of a right bundle-branch block,[19,20]
- second- and third-degree atrioventricular (AV) blocks,[21] and
- ST-segment elevation in lead V_2 50% greater than the magnitude of ST-segment depression in lead aVF.[22]

The addition of lead V_4R provides objective evidence of right ventricular involvement that can be noted on the 12-lead ECG. Right ventricular infarction can be diagnosed with 80% to 100% sensitivity by ST-segment elevation of more than 1 mm in lead V_4R.[7,10,11] Robalino and colleagues[20] found that ST-segment elevation above 1 mm in V_4R has 100% sensitivity, 87% specificity, and 92% predictive accuracy in detecting acute infarction of the right ventricle resulting from occlusion of the right coronary artery above its first ventricular branch.[20] As shown in Figure 7.1, the magnitude of the ST-segment elevation can be less pronounced than is usually seen in the standard 12 leads of the ECG. This finding results from the fact that the right ventricle is composed of considerably less muscle mass than is the left ventricle; with less myocardium manifesting a current of injury, the degree of ST-segment elevation is correspondingly less. In comparing the diagnostic performance of six right-sided leads (V_1R through V_6R) with a single lead V_4R, the literature has demonstrated similar rates of right ventricular infarction diagnosis.[4]

Identifying right ventricular involvement can be important because patients with coexisting inferior infarction have more jeopardized myocardium than do patients without right ventricular involvement. As a result, they are at increased risk for life-threatening complications, including high-grade AV blocks,[10] atrial fibrillation, symptomatic sinus bradycardia, atrial infarction, cardiogenic shock, cardiopulmonary arrest, and death.[7] In fact, the complication rate for this type of infarction is similar to that expected of anterior acute MIs.[23] Aggressive therapy is warranted to limit adverse events. Zehender and colleagues[24] showed that patients with right ventricular acute MI diagnosed by ST-segment elevation in V_4R had significantly reduced mortality rates and in-hospital complications if they received thrombolysis.

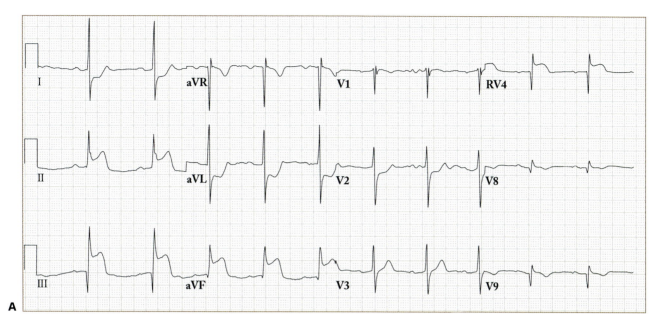

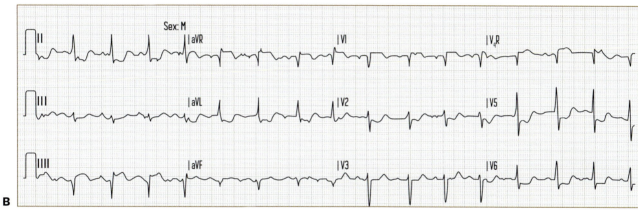

FIGURE 7.1. Two examples of inferior ST-segment MI with additional lead V_4R. Note the Q wave preceding the ST complex and the ST-segment elevation, confirming right ventricular MI in each. **A.** ST-segment depression in lead V_2 in conjunction with isoelectric ST segments in leads V_1 and V_3 is present in the standard leads, strongly suggesting right ventricular MI. **B.** ST-segment elevation in lead V_1 with concurrent ST-segment depression in lead V_2 on the standard leads is a strong indication of right ventricular MI.

Because patients with right ventricular acute MI are preload dependent for left ventricular filling, they are vulnerable to nitrate-induced hypotension. Under these circumstances, the usual treatment for acute MI can induce potentially dangerous hypotension. ST-segment elevation in lead V_4R should prompt the physician to avoid the use of nitrates and other vasodilating agents and to administer crystalloid infusions judiciously to avoid systemic hypotension. Negative inotropes (such as beta blockers) should be used with extreme caution (or not at all) in patients identified as having right ventricular acute MI because administration of these drugs could lead to severe hypotension.

THE POSTERIOR LEADS

The term *posterior myocardial infarction* refers to acute MI of the posterior wall of the left ventricle. This region is supplied by either the left circumflex artery or, less frequently, by a dominant right coronary artery with prominent posterolateral or posterior descending branches. Consequently, infarctions involving the posterior wall usually occur in conjunction with inferior or lateral MIs and are estimated to occur in 15% to 20% of all patients with infarction.[25] Isolated posterior MIs are less common. The rapid recognition of posterior MIs is important for several reasons. Patients with inferior or lateral wall acute MI with concomitant posterior MI are experiencing a larger infarction; in essence, two walls of the left ventricle are involved. The risks of arrhythmia, left ventricular dysfunction, and death increase proportionally with the size of the infarct. Therefore, the combination of inferior or lateral acute MI with posterior MI is a factor for a less favorable prognosis.[26-29] In a recent survey, many cardiologists and emergency physicians indicated they would be more likely to administer thrombolytic agents if they saw electrocardiographic evidence suggestive of posterior MI.[30] However, current protocols for the thrombolytic treatment of acute MI do not specifically address isolated posterior MI. As noted above, posterior MI is frequently under identified by clinicians during the identification and care of STEMI patients.

Using a standard 12-lead ECG to identify posterior MI can be challenging. Electrocardiographic changes occur primarily in V_1 and V_2, occasionally extending to V_3. These include:

- horizontal ST-segment depression,
- a tall, upright T wave, and
- an R/S wave ratio greater than 1.25.

These changes seem more familiar when thought of as a reversal of the electrocardiographic findings indicative of transmural acute MI. They are reversed for posterior MI because the endocardial surface of the posterior wall faces the anterior precordial leads. In other words, "when reversed," the ST-segment depression, prominent R waves, and tall, upright T waves in leads V_1 to V_3 represent the ST-segment elevation, prominent Q waves, and T-wave inversions of posterior MI (Figure 7.2). When viewed in this manner, the changes on the 12-lead ECG in posterior MI assume a more familiar, ominous significance. Indications of coexisting infarctions on the inferior or lateral walls of the left ventricle are other electrocardiographic features that should stimulate consideration of acute posterior MI, particularly if these findings are accompanied by ST-segment depression or prominent R waves in leads V_1 to V_3.

Evaluating the posterior wall through the 15-lead ECG is often more rewarding than is the 12-lead evaluation. ST-segment elevation greater than 1 mm in V_8 and V_9 confirms the diagnosis of posterior MI; such a finding is more indicative of acute MI than the anterior lead findings described above.[3,4,16] In fact, the sensitivity could be as high as 90% for identifying posterior acute MIs,[31] with a predictive accuracy up to 93.8%.[6] Notably, false-positive ST-segment elevation in V_8 and V_9 occurs at the same frequency encountered in the 12-lead ECG.[25] However, the degree of ST-segment elevation could be significantly less in the posterior leads than in the anterior leads because of the greater distance between the epicardial surface and the surface leads as well as the amount of interposed tissues (Figure 7.3).

A recent increase in the use of posterior chest leads indicates that the incidence of posterior MI is higher than once thought. Posterior MI was thought to be very rare, but it can be present in as many as 11% of cases of acute MI.[2,3,7,32] Similar to right ventricular acute MIs and V_4R, electrocardiographic changes in V_8 and V_9 might provide information about the amount of myocardium involved and the potential complications for isolated posterior MI and posterior MI associated with inferior or lateral acute MI. Oraii and colleagues[32] observed that patients with posterior MI who exhibit posterior-lead ST-segment elevation had more frequent in-hospital complications than did matched control subjects (odds ratio of 7).

Recently, valuable information regarding the pathophysiology and natural history of posterior MI has been revealed through electrocardiographic studies performed during coronary angiography. Khaw and colleagues[33] demonstrated improved detection of posterior MI using the 15-lead ECG during single-vessel percutaneous transluminal

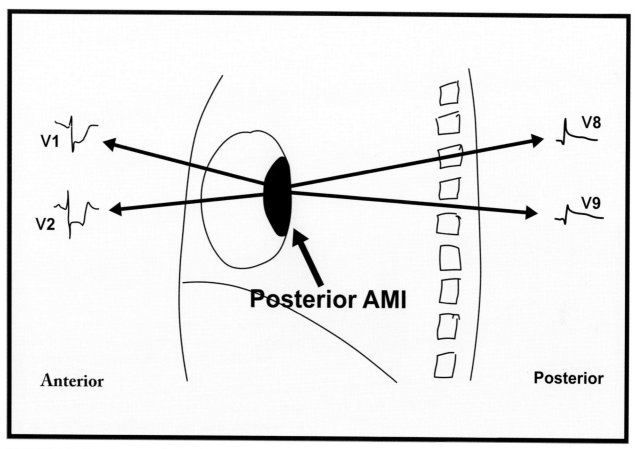

FIGURE 7.2. The electrocardiographic relationship between leads V_1 and V_2 and their posterior correlates (V_8 and V_9). A posterior wall MI will have a "reversal" of the findings typical for transmural MI in leads V_1 and V_2. Specifically, the standard ECG will demonstrate ST-segment depression, a prominent R wave, and upright T waves in these leads. When viewed with leads V_8 and V_9, these same findings are recognized as a typical transmural acute MI pattern, with ST-segment elevation, pathologic Q waves, and T-wave inversions. Reproduced with permission from: Brady WJ, Erling B, Pollack M, et al. Electrocardiographic manifestations: acute posterior wall myocardial infarction. *J Emerg Med.* 2001;20(4):397. Copyright 2001 Elsevier Inc.

coronary angioplasty of the right, circumflex, and left anterior descending coronary arteries. Overall sensitivity during circumflex occlusion was 32% for the 12-lead ECG versus 69% for the 15-lead ECG when maximal ST-segment depression in leads V_2 to V_3 was considered secondary to posterior wall injury. In a similar study, Wung and colleagues[34] showed that adjusting the ischemic threshold from 1 to 0.5 mm of ST-segment elevation in leads V_7 to V_9 improved sensitivity for diagnosing posterior MI from 49% with the 12-lead ECG to 94% with the 15-lead ECG. Future use of this lower criterion could increase the reported incidence of posterior MI from the 11% mentioned above.[2,3,7,32] Correale and colleagues[19] suggested that higher in-hospital mortality and complication rates found with right ventricular involvement are actually related more to posterior extension masked by right ventricular involvement than to right ventricular involvement itself. This study evaluated patients with inferior acute MI, using extra-lead ECGs (V_3R to V_5R and V_8 and V_9), cardiac enzymes, cardiac catheterization, and other methods. Comparing ECG markers, enzyme peaks, ejection fractions, and coronary scores, they concluded that the masking of markers of posterior extension by right ventricular involvement is likely the result of electrical balancing. All these studies affirm the usefulness of the 15-lead

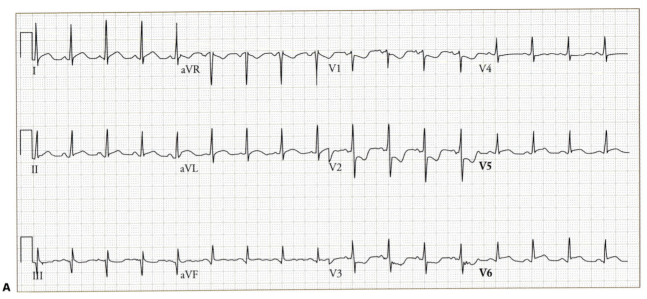

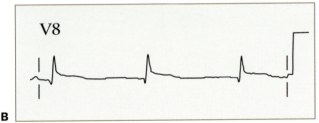

FIGURE 7.3. A. Standard 12-lead ECG from a patient experiencing a lateral acute MI. Note ST-segment depression in leads V_1 through V_3 and ST-segment elevation in leads V_5 and V_6. **B.** Posterior lead V_8 from the same patient as in Figure 7.3A. Note the subtle but definite ST-segment elevation in these leads, confirming posterior wall MI. Reproduced with permission from: Brady WJ, Erling B, Pollack M, et al. Electrocardiographic manifestations: acute posterior wall myocardial infarction. *J Emerg Med.* 2001;20(4):393. Copyright 2001 Elsevier Inc.

ECG for diagnosing posterior MI and predicting prognosis for patients in whom it develops.

LEWIS LEAD

The Lewis lead (also known as the S_5 lead) is a modified electrocardiographic lead used to augment analysis of atrial electrical activity when it is not definitely demonstrated on the standard 12-lead ECG. The most common clinical situation for its use is when a patient presents with a wide-complex tachycardia and the clinician wants to identify whether AV dissociation is present. To create the Lewis lead (described by Sir Thomas Lewis in 1931), the right arm electrode is moved to the manubrium next to the sternum. Then the left arm electrode is moved to the right fifth intercostal space next to the sternum. The left leg electrode is placed on the right lower costal margin. The Lewis lead is then read as lead I on the ECG and, since in most patients it will be roughly perpendicular to the wave of ventricular depolarization, atrial flutter waves can be more apparent. If AV dissociation is identified in wide-complex tachycardia using this technique, the diagnosis of ventricular tachycardia is secured (Figure 7.4).[35,36]

INDICATIONS FOR USING ADDITIONAL LEADS

It is important to maintain a high degree of suspicion for right ventricular or posterior wall involvement when evaluating emergency department patients at risk for acute coronary syndrome with the 12-lead ECG, particularly when only subtle abnormalities are present. A 15-lead ECG should be obtained when there is evidence of inferior acute MI, lateral acute MI, or ST-segment depression in V_1, V_2, or V_3[18,37] (Table 7.1). Although the following indications are less clearly established as emergency department indications, clinicians may consider using a 15-lead ECG in the following situations:

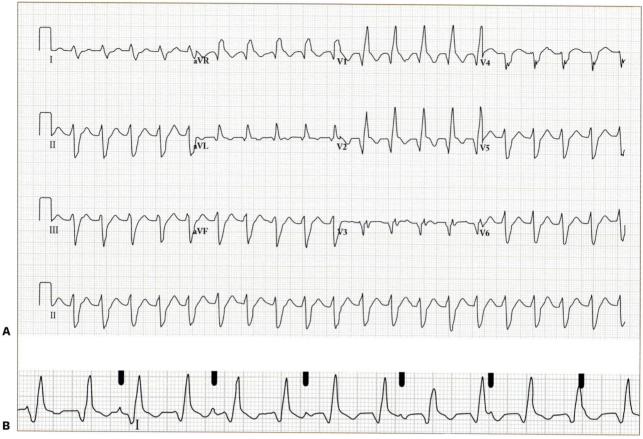

FIGURE 7.4. A. ECG from an older man presenting with wide complex tachycardia. The Lewis lead **B.** demonstrates P waves, indicative of AV dissociation. This finding strongly suggests ventricular tachycardia.

TABLE 7.1. Indications for obtaining additional-lead ECGs in emergency department patients.
ST-segment depression or suspicious isoelectric ST segments in leads V_1 to V_3
Borderline ST-segment elevation in leads V_5 and V_6 or in leads II, III, and aVF
ST-segment elevation inferior acute MIs (ST-segment elevation in leads II, III, and aVF)
ST-segment elevation in lead V_1 with concurrent ST-segment depression in lead V_2
ST-segment depression in lead V_2 in conjunction with isoelectric ST-segments in leads V_1 and V_3

- right bundle-branch block,
- second- and third-degree AV blocks, and
- ST-segment elevation in lead V_2 less than 50% the magnitude of ST-segment depression in aVF.

Additionally, inferior acute MI presenting with hypotension is a strong indicator of coexistent right ventricular infarction. Hemodynamic instability presents in the minority of right ventricular acute MI cases,[7] but hypotension can be precipitated in these patients if preload-reducing medications, such as nitroglycerin, are administered. Therefore, the findings of right ventricular infarction should alert providers to avoid these medications.

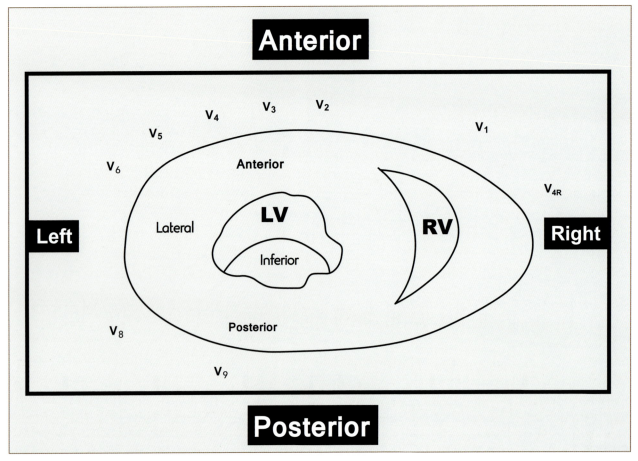

FIGURE 7.5. Axial depiction of the standard precordial leads as well as additional leads (V_4R, V_8, and V_9) and their relation to the myocardium. Note that lead V_1 shows only a small portion of the right ventricular muscle mass, whereas V_4R is positioned directly over this area to better identify the right ventricular infarct. Similarly, V_8 and V_9 directly show the posterior wall of the left ventricle. Reproduced with permission from: Somers MP, Brady WJ, Bateman DC, et al. Additional electrocardiographic leads in the ED chest pain patient: right ventricular and posterior leads. *Am J Emerg Med.* 2003;21:569. Copyright 2003 Elsevier Inc.

LIMITATIONS OF ADDITIONAL-LEAD ELECTROCARDIOGRAPHY

In a few situations, additional-lead electrocardiography might not yield an accurate diagnosis. Regarding right ventricular infarction, ST-segment elevation in lead V_4R is represented by a rightward and anteriorly oriented vector. Consequently, leftward ST-segment deviation, as seen in V_5 and V_6 during a lateral acute MI, could cancel the right-lead ST-segment elevation and obscure the diagnosis. Additionally, if ST-segment elevation is not prominent in the inferior leads, it will be less prominent in V_4R.

There are also cases of inferior wall acute MI with simultaneous right ventricular infarction but false-negative ST-segment elevation in lead V_4R. A study by Kosuge and colleagues[38] suggests that this phenomenon results from concomitant posterior wall ischemia with a resultant current of injury that attenuates ST-segment elevation otherwise observed in the right precordial leads. This study involved patients with first-time inferior wall acute MI and total occlusion of the right coronary artery proximal to its first ventricular branch. Patients *without* ST-segment elevation of more than 1 mm in V_4R had a higher frequency of dominant right coronary arteries in addition to greater levels of

ST-segment elevation in V_7, V_8, and V_9.

Several studies have suggested that the 15-lead ECG has greater sensitivity for identifying acute MIs than the standard 12-lead ECG.[2,3,6,16,17] Two of them are particularly noteworthy. Zalenski and colleagues[16] compared 12- and 15-lead ECGs in a prospective study that demonstrated an increase in sensitivity (from 47.1% to 58.5%) for the diagnosis of acute MI by ST-segment elevation with the use of additional leads. Specificity remained unchanged, and the odds of meeting electrocardiographic thrombolytic therapy criteria increased six-fold. Later work by Zelenski and colleagues[17] revealed that additional-lead analysis increased diagnostic accuracy modestly and influenced therapy by increasing the administration of fibrinolytic agents. These results, obtained in a patient population with a high suspicion for acute coronary disease, are promising.

More recent work by Brady and colleagues[39] involved emergency department patients with general chest pain, not just those with suspected acute MI or unstable angina, and therefore with a lower pretest probability for acute MI.[39] This prospective study with a real-time physician survey showed that the 15-lead ECG did not alter diagnostic and management decisions related to acute coronary ischemic syndromes (acute MI and unstable angina). However, physicians thought the 15-lead ECG provided a more complete anatomic picture of the ischemic events than did 12-lead ECGs. The authors concluded that all patients with chest pain in the emergency department do not require a 15-lead ECG and that more studies are needed to identify the patients who will truly benefit from 15-lead analysis. These are likely to be patients with right precordial lead ST-segment depression and inferior or lateral acute MIs, particularly those with hypotension, as discussed above.

Agarwal and colleagues[40] used posterior chest leads (V_7 through V_9) on patients with chest pain considered to have a cardiac cause but without ST-segment elevation on the 12-lead ECG. Of 58 such patients (the authors did not mention the total number of patients screened), 18 had posterior-lead ST-segment elevation of more than 1 mm or Q waves, and all 18 were confirmed to have had

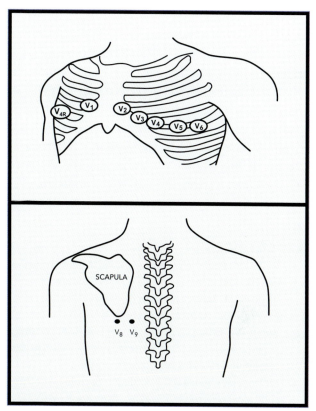

FIGURE 7.6. Proper placement of V_4R (top) and V_8 and V_9 (bottom) leads. V_4R is placed as a mirror image of the standard V_4 location. V_8 is placed on the patient's left back at the tip of the scapula, and V_9 is placed half the distance between lead V_8 and the paraspinal muscles. Reproduced with permission from: Somers MP, Brady WJ, Bateman DC, et al. Additional electrocardiographic leads in the ED chest pain patient: right ventricular and posterior leads. *Am J Emerg Med.* 2003;21:572. Copyright 2003 Elsevier Inc.

acute MI by creatine phosphokinase criteria or cardiac catheterization. The investigators concluded that all patients with suspected acute MI but nondiagnostic 12-lead results should receive posterior lead analysis. This conclusion can be extrapolated to suggest that strong consideration be given to the use of 15-lead ECGs for suspected acute MI despite a nondiagnostic 12-lead ECG.[4]

OBTAINING A 15-LEAD ECG

A 15-lead ECG can be obtained by moving the leads on a standard 12-lead machine or using a specialized 15-lead ECG machine. The least expensive method involves manipulating the leads on a 12-lead machine to evaluate additional areas of the heart. After a standard 12-lead ECG is obtained, the leads are moved as follows: the right ventricular (right-sided) lead V_4R is moved to the right side of the chest in a position analogous to the left-sided lead V_4 seen in Figure 7.5, and the posterior leads V_8 and V_9 are moved to the patient's left back at the tip of the scapula (V_8) and half the distance between lead V_8 and the paraspinal muscles (V_9) (Figure 7.6).

REFERENCES

1. Rude RE, Poole WK, Muller JE, et al. Electrocardiographic and clinical criteria for recognition of acute myocardial infarction based on analysis of 3,697 patients. *Am J Cardiol.* 1983;52:936-942.
2. Brady WJ, Erling BF, Pollack M, et al. Electrocardiographic manifestations: acute posterior wall myocardial infarction. *J Emerg Med.* 2001;20:391-401.
3. Melendez LI, Jones DT, Salcedo JR. Usefulness of three additional electrocardiographic chest leads (V_7, V_8 and V_9) in the diagnosis of acute myocardial infarction. *Can Med Assoc J.* 1978;119:745-748.
4. Somers MP, Brady WJ, Bateman DC, et al. Additional lead electrocardiographic leads in the ED chest pain patient: right ventricular and posterior leads. *Am J Emerg Med.* 2003;21:563-573.
5. Brady WJ, Morris F. The additional lead electrocardiogram in acute myocardial infarction. *J Accident Emerg Med.* 1999;16:202-207.
6. Rich MW, Imburgia M, King TR, et al. Electrocardiographic diagnosis of remote posterior wall myocardial infarction using unipolar posterior lead V_9. *Chest.* 1989;96:489-493.
7. Haji SA, Movahed A. Right ventricular infarction—diagnosis and treatment. *Clin Cardiol.* 2000;23:473-482.
8. Cohn JN, Guiha NH, Broder MI, et al. Right ventricular infarction: clinical and hemodynamic features. *Am J Cardiol.* 1974;44:209-214.
9. Zeymer U, Heuhaus KL, Wegscheider W, et al. Effects of fibrinolytic therapy in acute myocardial infarction with or without right ventricular involvement. *J Am Coll Cardiol.* 1998;32:876-881.
10. Braat SJ, Brugada P, DeZwaam C, et al. Value of the electrocardiogram in diagnosing right ventricular involvement in patients with acute inferior wall myocardial infarction. *Br Heart J.* 1983;49:368-372.
11. Klein HO, Tordjman T, Ninio R, et al. The early recognition of right ventricular infarction: diagnostic accuracy of the electrocardiographic V_4R lead. *Circulation.* 1983;67:558-565.
12. Andersen HR, Nielsen D, Falk E. Right ventricular infarction: diagnostic value of ST elevation in lead III greater than that of lead II during inferior/posterior infarction, and comparison with right chest leads V_3R to V_7R. *Am Heart J.* 1989;117:82-85.
13. Lopez-Sendon J, Coma-Canella I, Alcasena S, et al. Electrocardiographic findings in acute right ventricular infarction: sensitivity and specificity of electrocardiographic alterations in right precordial leads V_4R, V_3R, V_1, V_2, and V_3. *J Am Coll Cardiol.* 1985;6:1273-1279.
14. Croft C, Nicord P, Corbett JR, et al. Detection of acute right ventricular infarction by precordial electrocardiography. *Am J Cardiol.* 1982;50:421-427.
15. Coma-Canella I, Lopez-Sendon J, Alcasena S, et al. Electrocardiographic alterations in leads V_1 to V_3 in the diagnosis of right and left ventricular infarction. *Am Heart J.* 1986;112:940-946.
16. Zalenski RJ, Cooke D, Rydman RJ, et al. Assessing the diagnostic value of an ECG containing leads V_4R, V_8, and V_9: the 15-lead ECG. *Ann Emerg Med.* 1993;22:786-793.
17. Zalenski RJ, Rydman RJ, Sloan EP, et al. Value of posterior and right ventricular leads in comparison to the standard 12-lead electrocardiogram in evaluation of ST-segment elevation in suspected acute myocardial infarction. *Am J Cardiol.* 1997;79:1585-1597.
18. Aufderheide TP, Brady WJ. Electrocardiography in the patient in myocardial ischemia or infarction. In: Gibler WB, Aufderheide TP, eds. *Emergency Cardiac Care.* St Louis, MO: Mosby-Year; 1994:169-216.
19. Correale E, Battista R, Martone A, et al. Electrocardiographic patterns in acute inferior myocardial infarction with and without right ventricle involvement: classification, diagnostic and prognostic value, masking effect. *Clin Cardiol.* 1999;22:37-44.
20. Robalino BD, Whitlow PL, Underwood DA, et al. Electrocardiographic manifestations of right ventricular infarction. *Am Heart J.* 1989;118:138-144.
21. Zehender M, Kasper W, Kauder E, et al. Right ventricular infarction as an independent predictor of prognosis after acute inferior myocardial infarction. *N Engl J Med.* 1993;328:981-988.
22. Lew AS, Laramee P, Shah PK, et al. Ratio of ST-segment depression in lead V_2 to ST-segment elevation in lead aVF in evolving inferior acute myocardial infarction: an aid to the early recognition of right ventricular ischemia. *Am J Cardiol.* 1985;57:1047-1051.

23. Zalenski RJ, Rydman RJ, Sloan EP. ST-segment elevation and the prediction of hospital life-threatening complications. *J Electrocardiol*. 1998;31:164-171.
24. Zehender M, Kasper W, Kauder E, et al. Eligibility for and benefit of thrombolytic therapy in inferior myocardial infarction: focus on the prognostic importance of right ventricular infarction. *J Am Coll Cardiol*. 1994;24:362-369.
25. Boden WE, Kleiger RE, Gibson RS, et al. Electrocardiographic evolution of posterior acute myocardial infarction: importance of early precordial ST-segment depression. *Am J Cardiol*. 1987;59:782-787.
26. Brush JE, Brand DA, Acamparo D, et al. Use of the initial electrocardiogram to predict in-hospital complications of acute myocardial infarction. *N Engl J Med*. 1985;312:1137-1141.
27. Yusuf S, Pearson M, Sterry H, et al. The entry EKG in the early diagnosis and prognostic stratification of patients with suspected acute myocardial infarction. *Eur Heart J*. 1983;5:690-696.
28. Stark ME, Vacuum JL. The initial electrocardiogram during admission for myocardial infarction: use as a predictor of clinical course and facility utilization. *Arch Intern Med*. 1987;147:843-846.
29. Matetzky S, Freimark D, Chouraqui P, et al. Significance of ST-segment elevations in posterior chest leads (V_7 to V_9) in patients with acute inferior myocardial infarction: application for thrombolytic therapy. *J Am Coll Cardiol*. 1998;31:506-511.
30. Novak PG, Davies C, Ken GG. Survey of British Columbia cardiologists' and emergency physicians' practice of using nonstandard EKG leads (V_4R to V_6R and V_7 to V_9) in the diagnosis and treatment of acute myocardial infarction. *Can J Cardiol*. 1999;15:967-972.
31. Perloff JK. The recognition of strictly posterior myocardial infarction by conventional scale electrocardiography. *Circulation*. 1964;30:706-718.
32. Oraii S, Maleki M, Tavakolian AA, et al. Prevalence and outcome of ST-segment elevation in posterior electrocardiographic leads during acute myocardial infarction. *J Electrocardiol*. 1999;32:275-278.
33. Khaw K, Moreyra A, Tannenbaum A, et al. Improved detection of posterior myocardial wall ischemia with the 15-lead electrocardiogram. *Am Heart J*. 1999;138:934-940.
34. Wung S, Drew B. New electrocardiographic criteria for posterior wall acute myocardial ischemia validated by a percutaneous transluminal coronary angioplasty model of acute myocardial infarction. *Am J Cardiol*. 2001;87:970-974.
35. Holinda-Miranda WR, Furtado FM, Luciano PM, et al. Lewis lead enhances atrial activity detection in wide QRS tachycardia. *J Emerg Med*. 2012;43(2):e97-e99.
36. Bakker AL, Nijkerk G, Groenemeijer BE, et al. The Lewis lead: making recognition of P waves easy during wide QRS complex tachycardia. *Circulation*. 2009;119:e592-e593.
37. Selker HP, Zalenski RJ, Amman EM, et al. An evaluation of the technologies for identifying acute cardiac ischemia in the emergency department: a report from the National Heart Attack Alert Program Working Group. Nonstandard ECG leads and body surface mapping. *Ann Emerg Med*. 1997;29:28-33.
38. Kosuge M, Kimura K, Ishikawa T, et al. Implications of the absence of ST-segment elevation in lead V_4R in patients who have inferior wall acute myocardial infarction with right ventricular involvement. *Clin Cardiol*. 2001;24:225-230.
39. Brady WJ, Hwang V, Sullivan R, et al. A comparison of 12- and 15-lead ECGs in ED chest pain patients: impact on diagnosis, therapy, and disposition. *Am J Emerg Med*. 2000;18:239-243.
40. Agarwal J, Khaw K, Aurignac F, et al. Importance of posterior chest leads in patients with suspected myocardial infarction, but nondiagnostic routine 12-lead electrocardiogram. *Am J Cardiol*. 1999;83:323-326.

CHAPTER EIGHT

Emerging Electrocardiographic Indications for Acute Reperfusion

GEORGE GLASS

KEY POINTS

- Several ECG findings merit consideration of emergent catheterization without meeting traditional STEMI criteria. Emergency care providers should be familiar with them.
- In left bundle-branch block, Sgarbossa criteria are suggestive of acute coronary syndrome (ACS) in the presence of any of the following: a) concordant ST-segment elevation of 1 mm or more, b) concordant ST depression of 1 mm or more in V_1, V_2, or V_3, or c) discordant ST-segment elevation of 5 mm or more.
- Sgarbossa criteria are fairly specific but not completely sensitive for ACS.
- The modified Sgarbossa criteria replace the 5-mm cut-off for excessive discordant elevation with a proportional ratio of ST segment/S wave, with more than 0.25 being suggestive of acute MI. This ratio is more sensitive for ACS but slightly less specific.
- Limited data suggest that the Sgarbossa criteria are useful for diagnosing ACS in the setting of ventricular pacing.
- Chest pain accompanied by more than 1 mm of ST-segment elevation in lead aVR suggests occlusion of the left main coronary artery or the proximal left anterior descending artery (LAD), or triple-vessel disease, especially in the setting of diffuse ST-segment depressions elsewhere in the ECG.
- de Winter waves consist of upsloping ST-segment depression and large, symmetrically peaked T waves in the midprecordial leads. This pattern suggests an acutely unstable proximal LAD occlusion.
- Wellens waves take two forms—biphasic T waves and deeply inverted (>2 mm) T waves in V_2 and V_3. In the setting of unstable angina, these findings suggest proximal LAD disease.

One of the primary goals of electrocardiographic interpretation in the setting of suspected acute coronary syndrome (ACS) is to expedite appropriate care for the clinical situation. In addition to showing traditional indications for emergent catheter-based or fibrinolytic reperfusion therapy in patients with STEMI, an ECG can identify individuals with suspected ACS who are potential candidates for urgent or emergent intervention yet lack classic electrocardiographic STEMI findings. In this chapter, we discuss several "STEMI-equivalent" or "impending acute MI" electrocardiographic presentations that identify patients who are eligible for urgent or emergent reperfusion therapy.

LEFT BUNDLE-BRANCH BLOCK

Left bundle-branch block (LBBB), the failure to conduct supraventricular impulses through the left bundle, results in reversal of the normal pattern of ventricular activation. Normal ventricular depolarization occurs in a left-to-right pattern; however, in LBBB, left ventricular depolarization occurs secondarily through trans-septal activation, reversing the pattern. In general, the ECG is characterized by a broad (QRS >120 milliseconds) negative QS or rS complex in lead V_1 with poor R-wave progression through the precordium and a broad, notched R wave in the lateral leads V_5 and V_6. This characteristic conduction pattern results in ST segments that are discordant with (ie, directed opposite from) the predominant QRS complex (Figure 8.1). This characteristic electrocardiographic pattern has traditionally made diagnosis of acute ischemia in the presence of LBBB difficult, with resultant delays in appropriate therapy.[1] Unfortunately, potential ACS patients presenting with LBBB are at high risk of MI,[2,3] and those found to have ACS have worse outcomes in terms of 30-day and 1-year mortality and the development of new heart failure.[4] The left-sided conduction system is large, so LBBB resulting from true acute ischemia is often the result of a large infarction of the anterior or anteroseptal myocardium, portending a poor prognosis.[5]

In light of this concern, previous guidelines have recommended treating new or presumably new LBBB in a patient presenting with symptoms suggesting ACS as a "STEMI-equivalent," that is, with either percutaneous coronary intervention or fibrinolytic therapy.[6] Subsequent data, however, revealed the finding of a new or presumed new LBBB has a relatively low specificity for acute coronary occlusion.[7,8] Therefore, the 2013 American College of Cardiology Foundation/American Heart Association (ACCF/AHA) guidelines were revised to suggest that new or presumably new LBBB "should not be considered diagnostic of acute myocardial infarction (AMI) in isolation."[9] Nonetheless, expert opinion continues to suggest that such patients who have typical ACS symptoms and are clinically or hemodynamically unstable should be considered for immediate reperfusion therapy.[10] They often present with significant clinical decompensation in the setting of occlusion of the proximal left anterior descending artery (LAD), so definitive treatment should not be delayed. In fact, LBBB acute MI patients can derive significant benefit from rapidly delivered reperfusion therapy. Conversely, they can experience large MIs, significant cardiovascular complications, and high rates of death when definitive therapy is delayed.

In 1996, Sgarbossa and colleagues proposed

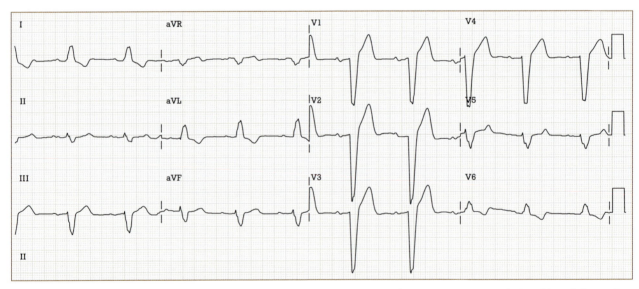

FIGURE 8.1. Expected orientation of the ST segment in LBBB. Expected, or appropriate, relationship of the major, terminal portion of the QRS complex with the ST segment. This relationship is characterized by the major, terminal portion of the QRS complex being opposite the ST segment relative to the isoelectric baseline. Thus, in leads with a primarily or entirely negatively oriented QRS complex (II, III, aVF, and V_1 through V_5), the ST segment is elevated; conversely, in leads with a primarily or entirely positively oriented QRS complex (I, aVL, and V_6), the ST segment is depressed.

criteria for the diagnosis of MI in patients with underlying LBBB.[11] These criteria use a point system based on electrocardiographic morphology to stratify patients according to their likelihood of having ACS. The three components of the system are:

- concordant ST-segment elevation of 1 mm or more (odds ratio, 25.2) (5 points),
- concordant ST-segment depression of 1 mm or more in any of leads V_1, V_2, or V_3 (odds ratio, 6.0) (3 points), and
- discordant ST-segment elevation of 5 mm or more (odds ratio, 4.3) (2 points) (Figure 8.2).

The presence of contiguous leads demonstrating the abnormalities is not required; that is, the presence of one of the criteria in a single lead is sufficient. The first criterion, concordant ST-segment elevation (Figure 8.3), is the most suggestive of acute MI, whereas isolated excessive discordance is less so. It should also be noted that, although the Sgarbossa criteria are specific for acute MI (96%), they are relatively insensitive (36%).[11] Subsequent studies demonstrated that patients with higher Sgarbossa scores have worse 30-day mortality rates[12] and validated the utility of a Sgarbossa score of 3 or above in the diagnosis of ACS.[13,14] These studies also confirmed that a score of 0 in the Sgarbossa system does not exclude the presence of ACS. These findings suggest that, in a patient with LBBB of unknown chronicity, the clinical presentation and other clinical data must be considered carefully before excluding ACS.

A more recent modification of the Sgarbossa criteria, the Smith-modified Sgarbossa criteria, demonstrated improved accuracy compared with the original.[15] The modification omits the third component of the original set (discordant ST-segment elevation ≥5 mm), using the ratio of discordant ST-segment elevation to S-wave depth instead (Figure 8.4). This criterion is considered "positive"

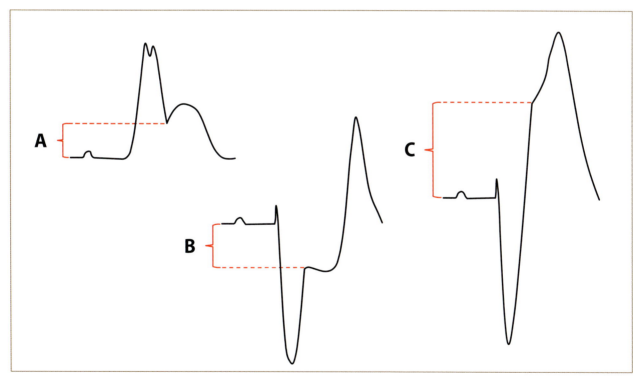

FIGURE 8.2. Sgarbossa criteria. Findings suggestive of acute MI. **A.** Concordant ST-segment elevation >1 mm. **B.** Concordant ST-segment depression >1 mm in any of leads V_1 through V_3. **C.** Discordant ST-segment elevation ≥5 mm. Of these, concordant elevation is the most specific for acute MI. Note that Sgarbossa criteria are met when a single lead demonstrates one of these abnormalities. Two contiguous leads with these abnormalities is not required.

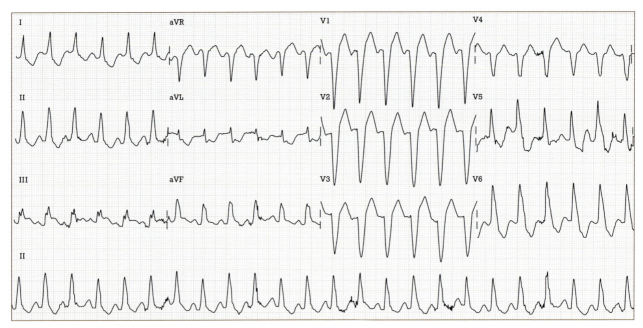

FIGURE 8.3. ECG with LBBB and ST changes that raise concern for acute MI. Note the concordant ST-segment elevations in lead III (positive Sgarbossa criterion). The patient was found to have severe three-vessel disease, with 99% occlusion of the proximal right coronary artery and a peak troponin elevation of 97 ng/mL.

for ratios less than −0.25 (or, for simplicity, if the absolute value is >0.25). In one validation study, use of the modified rule increased the sensitivity for acute MI (80% versus 49%) compared with the original weighted Sgarbossa criteria, with only a modest decrease in specificity (99% versus 100%).[16]

Although the 2013 ACCF/AHA guidelines briefly mention that "criteria for ECG diagnosis of acute STEMI in the setting of LBBB have been proposed,"[9] there is currently no consensus guideline regarding their use. Further validation of these criteria is warranted; however, current data suggest that their appropriate application can aid in the identification of patients in need of revascularization. Such patients are likely to benefit from emergent catheterization and therefore warrant timely evaluation by an interventional cardiologist or consideration for thrombolysis.

THE RIGHT VENTRICULAR-PACED ELECTROCARDIOGRAPHIC PATTERN

Interpretation of the ECG from a chest pain patient with an implantable cardiac device poses several

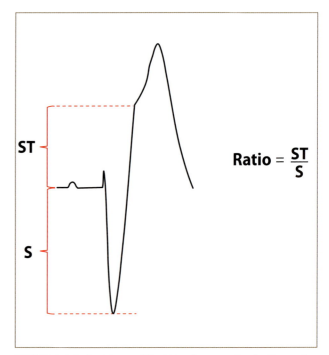

FIGURE 8.4. Smith-modified Sgarbossa criteria. Excessive discordant ST-segment elevation (ST/S>0.25) is used instead of a fixed cut-off of 5 mm (Figure 8.2C). The other criteria remain unchanged. Replacing the fixed cut-off increases the sensitivity for acute MI.

challenges for emergency care providers. The presence of a pacemaker adds a degree of historical complexity to the clinical scenario. For example, consistent pacing in a patient who is only sporadically paced at baseline can represent new underlying arrhythmia or bradycardia, possibly due to ischemia. Chest pain could also be the result of device complication, device migration, discharge of an implantable cardioverter defibrillator, or lead migration or perforation. Although the ECG in atrial-paced patients is not significantly altered and can be readily interpreted for standard signs of ischemia, ventricular pacing produces significant changes in the baseline ECG that confound interpretation. Ventricular pacing leads are most often located in the right ventricular apex, although placement in the right ventricular septum or outflow tract has also occurred.[17] Activation of the pacer causes initial right ventricular depolarization followed by trans-septal activation of the left ventricle and a resultant LBBB pattern on the ECG, once again with a broad (QRS >120 millisecond) negative QS or rS complex in V_1 with poor R-wave progression through the precordium.

Given the similarity of the electrocardiographic patterns in a ventricular-paced rhythm and LBBB, as well as their similar underlying electromechanical activation patterns,[18] it is logical to believe that similar patterns of change would be seen during ischemic insult (Figure 8.5). In 1996, Sgarbossa and colleagues applied the same three criteria used for LBBB in patients with ventricular-paced rhythm and found that ST-segment depression of 1 mm or more in lead V_1, V_2, or V_3 was 82% specific for acute MI; however, this finding did not reach statistical significance. The authors also reported that concordant ST-segment elevation of 1 mm or more was significantly specific for acute MI, but this finding did not reach statistical significance either. Excessive discordance (≥5 mm) was found to be 53% sensitive

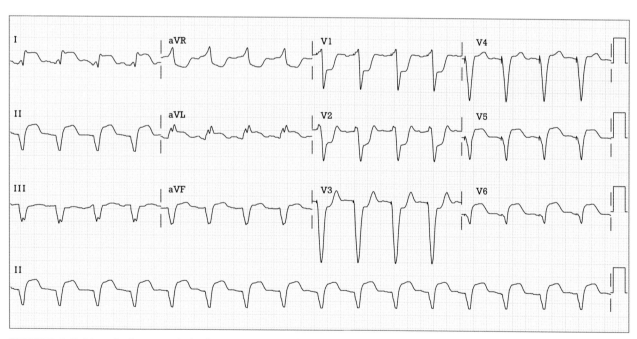

FIGURE 8.5. Ventricular-paced rhythm suggestive of acute MI. Following resuscitation, this patient, who initially presented in asystole, had intermittent sustained ventricular tachycardia requiring cardioversion. The post-resuscitation ECG suggested STEMI. (Concordant ST-segment elevation is present in leads I and aVL. Concordant ST-segment depression is present in leads V_1 through V_3. Excessive discordance is present in lead V_6.) The patient was found to have proximal LAD occlusion.

and 88% specific (p = 0.025). The study was limited by its relatively small sample size (n = 17).[19] A 2002 study, testing only discordant ST elevation above 5 mm, found this criterion to be predictive of severe underlying coronary disease but not of flow limitation caused by acute occlusion of a culprit artery.[20] The findings are again limited due to small sample size (5 of 20 patients with "positive" electrocardiographic findings) and the fact that concordant ST changes were not evaluated. A more recent (2016) study with a larger cohort (43 patients with ventricular-paced rhythm, 26 of them positive for STEMI) found the traditional Sgarbossa criteria to be 100% sensitive for acute MI—defined by either positive catheterization (TIMI grade flow 0 or 1) or peak troponin level of more than 10 ng/mL—but only 9.1% sensitive. The use of Smith's modified Sgarbossa criteria resulted in a significant increase in sensitivity (31.8%) but a slight loss in specificity (71.4%).[21] Given these findings, it seems that the Sgarbossa or the Smith-modified Sgarbossa criteria can be useful for identification of ventricular-paced rhythm patients with acute MI. Their use should be tied carefully to appropriate clinical context and understanding of the limitations in sensitivity.

ST-SEGMENT ELEVATION IN LEAD aVR

Lead aVR has historically been underutilized by many physicians. Although aVR has no conventional role in the diagnosis of STEMI, over the past 15 years, ST-segment changes in this lead have found increasing use as markers of critical illness and potentially severe coronary disease requiring emergent intervention. Lead aVR, an augmented limb lead with positive deflection toward the atria at the ventricular apex, has been described as an "intracavitary lead."[22] ST-segment elevation in this lead represents global subendocardial ischemia.[23] In the setting of ACS, such ischemia raises concern about left main coronary artery or proximal LAD occlusion or triple-vessel disease. It should, however, be noted that it can be the result of many other forms of diffuse ischemia, thoracic aortic dissection, massive pulmonary embolism, profound hemorrhage, and shock (Figure 8.6).

In 2003, Barrabés and colleagues reported significant correlation between the level of ST-segment elevation in lead aVR and in-hospital mortality in patients with non-STEMI: for elevations of less than 0.5 mm, 0.5 to 1 mm, and 1 mm or more, the mortality rates were 1.3%, 8.6%, and 19.4%, respectively.[24] This association was thought to be related to severe underlying cardiovascular disease, so early invasive therapy was proposed for this subset of patients. Follow-up data have demonstrated that elevation in aVR is often associated with severe left main coronary artery insufficiency or three-vessel disease, with specificity increasing with the degree of elevation (≥ 1 mm 93% specific; ≥ 1.5 mm 98% specific).[23] Diffuse ST-segment depression is also highly suggestive of critical left main coronary artery disease, proximal LAD disease, or three-vessel disease.[25] This finding in tandem with aVR elevation should raise significant concern.[25,26]

Left main coronary artery occlusion is a true emergency because complete occlusion will result in rapid decompensation, cardiogenic shock, and death. In fact, patients with true complete occlusion of this artery are unlikely to survive to hospital presentation. Therefore, presenting patients are probably more accurately described in terms of incomplete left main coronary occlusion or left main coronary insufficiency. Appropriate identification of left main coronary disease and prompt intervention are crucial in optimizing outcomes for these patients.

A few caveats should be noted in the diagnostic evaluation of suspected left main coronary artery disease. As stated above, the associated electrocardiographic findings (notably ST-segment elevation in lead aVR with diffuse ST-segment depression) suggest it, but these findings can also be found in proximal LAD occlusion and diffuse coronary artery disease, either of which might be treated quite differently than left main coronary artery occlusion. Additionally, patients with chest pain and these characteristic findings on the ECG could have another underlying disease process causing subendocardial ischemia such as pulmonary embolism[27] or type A aortic dissection with coronary involvement.[28]

Global ischemia due to hemorrhage or septic shock can produce similar findings. Additionally, elevation in lead aVR can be seen in several other conditions unrelated to acute ischemia, including LBBB and left ventricular hypertrophy. ST-segment elevation in lead aVR should therefore be interpreted in the appropriate clinical context. Certainly, in patients with an appropriate clinical context, elevation of more than 1 mm and associated diffuse ST-segment elevation, concern for left main coronary artery occlusion is high. In such cases, emergent interventional cardiology consultation or cardiac catheterization lab activation should be considered. Depending on the cardiologist's preference and patient stability, a trial of medical therapy might be reasonable, but if signs of ischemia are ongoing or if the patient becomes unstable, emergent revascularization is warranted.[29]

THE DE WINTER PATTERN

The de Winter T-wave pattern, first described in 2008, is a unique constellation of electrocardiographic findings that heighten concern for acute proximal LAD occlusion.[30] The pattern consists of the following:

- pronounced upsloping ST-segment depression in leads V_2 through V_4,
- prominent symmetrically enlarged T waves in the same distribution, and
- ST-segment elevation in lead aVR (Figure 8.7).

The mechanism for these changes is currently unclear, but it might be related to ischemic effects on cardiac ATP-sensitive potassium channels in the setting of anatomic variance of the Purkinje system.[30,31] Patients presenting with de Winter waves tend to be younger, are more often male, and are more often

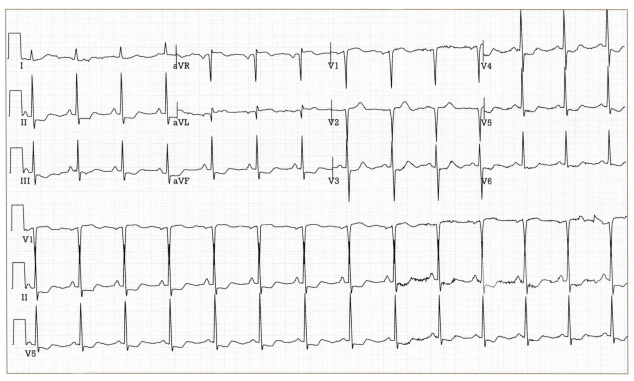

FIGURE 8.6. ST-Segment elevation in lead aVR with associated precordial ST-segment depressions. ST-segment elevations in lead aVR >1 mm with associated diffuse ST-segment depressions are highly suggestive of left main coronary artery occlusion, proximal LAD occlusion, or acute triple-vessel disease. This patient had a 95% left main coronary occlusion as well as significant disease in two other major vessels and required urgent bypass surgery. Reproduced with permission from: Joseph Young, DO.

hypercholesterolemic than those with traditional electrocardiographic findings of STEMI.[32]

In a series of 1,890 patients undergoing primary percutaneous coronary intervention of the LAD, de Winter reported that 35 (2%) had electrocardiographic changes characteristic of de Winter waves and were subsequently found to have significant myocardial injury.[32] Although progression of de Winter waves to classic anterior STEMI has been described,[33] lack of progression from the de Winter pattern has also been reported in the setting of complete proximal LAD occlusion.[34] The need for prompt recognition and reperfusion of these patients is apparent, and treatment of de Winter waves as a STEMI equivalent has been advocated. Unfortunately, typical findings are easily overlooked given their relatively low incidence and lack of "eye-catching" ST-segment elevation. The electrocardiographic findings are easily mistaken for the prominent T waves of hyperkalemia, but they can be distinguished by their J-point depression and the potassium concentration. To expedite appropriate therapy, emergency physicians should be vigilant in their identification of these findings in patients presenting concerns for acute MI.

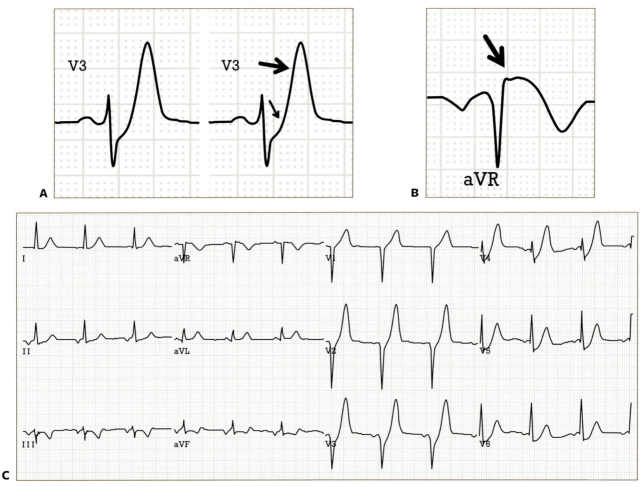

FIGURE 8.7. de Winter ECG abnormalities. Findings typical of the de Winter ECG presentation. **A.** Upsloping J-point depression with prominent T waves in the right to midprecordial leads. **B.** ST-segment elevation in lead aVR. **C.** 12-lead ECG demonstrating the de Winter ECG presentation as described in images A and B. Reproduced with permission from: Goebel M, Bledsoe J, Orford JL, et al. A new ST-segment elevation myocardial infarction equivalent pattern? Prominent T wave and J-point depression in the precordial leads associated with ST-segment elevation in lead aVR. *Am J Emerg Med.* 2014;32:287.e5-287.e8. Copyright 2014 Elsevier Inc.

WELLENS SYNDROME

Wellens syndrome, initially described in 1982, is a pattern of unstable anginal-type pain associated with characteristic electrocardiographic changes heralding significant LAD obstruction and impending infarction (Figures 8.8, 8.9). Without revascularization, 75% of patients with the syndrome will progress to large anterior MI within the course of

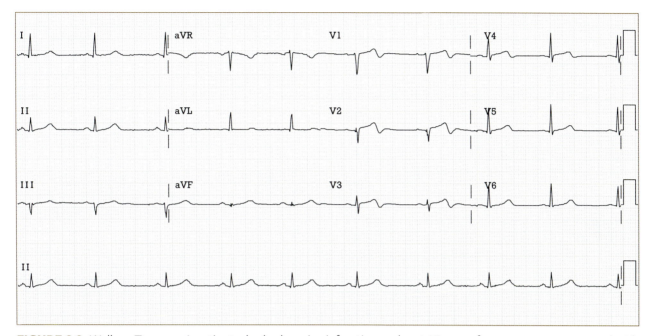

FIGURE 8.8. Wellens T waves. A patient who had a prior infarction and an LAD stent for many years presented with substernal chest pain invoked by activity. The biphasic T waves in the midprecordial leads are indicative of Wellens T waves (type A Wellens waves). The patient underwent angiography and was found to have 75% in-stent stenosis.

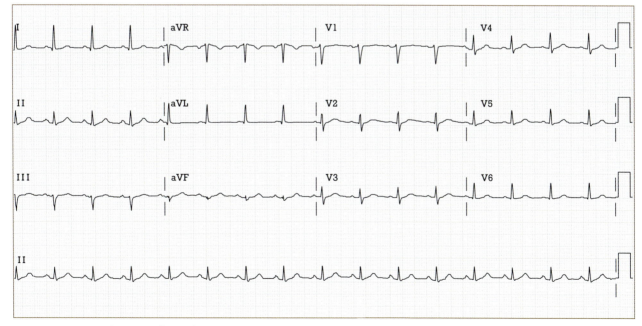

FIGURE 8.9. Baseline ECG from the patient in Figure 8.8.

1 to 2 weeks regardless of appropriate medical therapy and initial resolution of symptoms.[35] It is therefore imperative that emergency physicians be proficient in recognizing the electrocardiographic findings suggestive of this entity and understand its implications for morbidity and mortality.

Characteristic electrocardiographic findings of Wellens syndrome take one of two forms:

- type A, biphasic T waves with an initial positive deflection and negative terminal portion, representing about 25% of cases or
- type B, deeply, symmetrically inverted T waves (>2 mm), comprising the remaining 75%.[35]

Evidence of Wellens syndrome is most often found in leads V_2 and V_3, but it can also appear in other precordial leads. Most patients with these findings are not experiencing pain, but their pain can return with normalization of the ECG or progression to STEMI.[36] Type A morphology can progress to type B. Type B findings can be distinguished from benign T-wave inversion by location (in V_2 through V_4 as opposed to V_3 through V_5) and the QT interval (generally >425 milliseconds in Wellens syndrome).[37]

This syndrome is relatively common—a prospective study of 1,260 patients with unstable angina found that 14% of them had characteristic electrocardiographic changes. Of these 14%, all were found to have a 50% or larger stenosis of the LAD.[38] Although not a true STEMI equivalent—it does not involve plaque rupture and subsequent thrombosis—Wellens syndrome nevertheless must be recognized and treated urgently. Treatment of patients with symptoms of unstable angina and electrocardiographic findings of Wellens syndrome consists of initiation of appropriate medical therapy followed by urgent catheterization. Initiation of therapy should be predicated on the clinical context, as several other entities can present with T-wave inversions or "pseudo-Wellens waves." Mimics include benign T-wave inversion,[37] electrocardiographic changes of intracranial hemorrhage,[39] hypertrophic cardiomyopathy,[40] cocaine-induced coronary vasospasm,[41] digitalis effect, Brugada syndrome, and persistent juvenile T-wave pattern.[42] Most of them have characteristic historical features suggestive of the appropriate clinical entity. In unclear cases, stress imaging is discouraged because of the potential for precipitating acute MI[36]; however, nonstress echocardiography might be reasonable if done in consultation with an interventional cardiologist.

REFERENCES

1. Barron HV, Bowlby LJ, Breen T, et al. Use of reperfusion therapy for acute myocardial infarction in the United States: data from the National Registry of Myocardial Infarction 2. *Circulation*. 1998;97(12):1150-1156.
2. Alkindi F, El-Menyar A, Al-Suwaidi J, et al. Left bundle branch block in acute cardiac events: insights from a 23-year registry. *Angiology*. 2015;66(9):811-817.
3. Bansilal S, Aneja A, Mathew V, et al. Long-term cardiovascular outcomes in patients with angina pectoris presenting with bundle branch block. *Am J Cardiol*. 2011;107(11):1565-1570.
4. Al Rajoub B, Noureddine S, El Chami S, et al. The prognostic value of a new left bundle branch block in patients with acute myocardial infarction: a systematic review and meta-analysis. *Heart Lung J Acute Crit Care*. 2017;46(2):85-91.
5. Sgarbossa EB, Pinski SL, Topol EJ, et al S. Acute myocardial infarction and complete bundle branch block at hospital admission: clinical characteristics and outcome in the thrombolytic era. *J Am Coll Cardiol*. 1998;31(1):105-110.
6. Antman EM, Anbe DT, Armstrong PW, et al. ACC/AHA Guidelines for the Management of Patients With ST-Elevation Myocardial Infarction—executive summary: a report of the American College of Cardiology/American Heart Association Task Force on Practice Guidelines (Writing Committee to Revise the 1999 Guidelines for the Management of Patients With Acute Myocardial Infarction). *J Am Coll Cardiol*. 2004;44(3):671-719.
7. Chang AM, Shofer FS, Tabas JA, et al. Lack of association between left bundle-branch block and acute myocardial infarction in symptomatic ED patients. *Am J Emerg Med*. 2009;27(8):916-921.
8. Jain S, Ting HT, Bell M, et al. Utility of left bundle branch block as a diagnostic criterion for acute myocardial infarction. *Am J Cardiol*. 2011;107(8):1111-1116.
9. O'Gara PT, Kushner FG, Ascheim DD, et al. 2013 ACCF/AHA Guideline for the Management of ST-Elevation Myocardial Infarction: a report of the American College of Cardiology Foundation/American Heart Association

Task Force on Practice Guidelines. *J Am Coll Cardiol.* 2013;61(4):e78-e140.

10. Neeland IJ, Kontos MC, de Lemos JA. Evolving considerations in the management of patients with left bundle branch block and suspected myocardial infarction. *J Am Coll Cardiol.* 2012;60(2):96-105.

11. Sgarbossa EB, Pinski SL, Barbagelata A, et al. Electrocardiographic diagnosis of evolving acute myocardial infarction in the presence of left bundle-branch block. *N Engl J Med.* 1996;334(8):481-487.

12. Al-Faleh H, Fu Y, Wagner G, et al. Unraveling the spectrum of left bundle branch block in acute myocardial infarction: insights from the Assessment of the Safety and Efficacy of a New Thrombolytic (ASSENT 2 and 3) trials. *Am Heart J.* 2006;151(1):10-15.

13. McMahon R, Siow W, Bhindi R, et al. Left bundle branch block without concordant ST changes is rarely associated with acute coronary occlusion. *Int J Cardiol.* 2013;167(4):1339-1342. doi:10.1016/j.ijcard.2012.04.014

14. Tabas JA, Rodriguez RM, Seligman HK, et al. Electrocardiographic criteria for detecting acute myocardial infarction in patients with left bundle branch block: a meta-analysis. *Ann Emerg Med.* 2008;52(4):329-336.e1.

15. Smith SW, Dodd KW, Henry TD, et al. Diagnosis of ST-elevation myocardial infarction in the presence of left bundle branch block with the ST-elevation to S-wave ratio in a modified Sgarbossa rule. *Ann Emerg Med.* 2012;60(6):766-776.

16. Meyers HP, Limkakeng AT, Jaffa EJ, et al. Validation of the modified Sgarbossa criteria for acute coronary occlusion in the setting of left bundle branch block: a retrospective case-control study. *Am Heart J.* 2015;170(6):1255-1264.

17. Rajappan K. Permanent pacemaker implantation technique: part II. *Heart.* 2009;95(4):334-342.

18. Vassallo JA, Cassidy DM, Miller JM, et al. Left ventricular endocardial activation during right ventricular pacing: effect of underlying heart disease. *J Am Coll Cardiol.* 1986;7(6):1228-1233.

19. Sgarbossa EB, Pinski SL, Gates KB, et al. Early electrocardiographic diagnosis of acute myocardial infarction in the presence of ventricular paced rhythm. *Am J Cardiol.* 1996;77(5):423-424.

20. Caldera AE, Bryce M, Kotler M, et al. Angiographic significance of a discordant ST-segment elevation of ≥5 millimeters in patients with ventricular-paced rhythm and acute myocardial infarction. *Am J Cardiol.* 2002;90(11):1240-1243.

21. Freitas P, Santos MB, Faria M, et al. ECG evaluation in patients with pacemaker and suspected acute coronary syndrome: which score should we apply? *J Electrocardiol.* 2016;49(5):744-748.

22. Kligfield P, Gettes LS, Bailey JJ, et al. Recommendations for the standardization and interpretation of the electrocardiogram: Part I: The electrocardiogram and its technology: a scientific statement from the American Heart Association Electrocardiography and Arrhythmias Committee, Council on Clinical Cardiology; the American College of Cardiology Foundation; and the Heart Rhythm Society Endorsed by the International Society for Computerized Electrocardiology. *J Am Coll Cardiol.* 2007;49(10):1109-1127.

23. Kosuge M, Ebina T, Hibi K, et al. An early and simple predictor of severe left main and/or three-vessel disease in patients with non–ST-segment elevation acute coronary syndrome. *Am J Cardiol.* 2011;107(4):495-500.

24. Barrabés JA, Figueras J, Moure C, et al. Prognostic value of lead aVR in patients with a first non–ST-segment elevation acute myocardial infarction. *Circulation.* 2003;108(7):814-819.

25. Gorgels APM, Vos MA, Mulleneers R, et al. Value of the electrocardiogram in diagnosing the number of severely narrowed coronary arteries in rest angina pectoris. *Am J Cardiol.* 1993;72(14):999-1003.

26. Taglieri N, Saia F, Alessi L, et al. Diagnostic performance of standard electrocardiogram for prediction of infarct related artery and site of coronary occlusion in unselected STEMI patients undergoing primary percutaneous coronary intervention. *Eur Heart J Acute Cardiovasc Care.* 2014;3(4):326-339.

27. Kukla P, Kosior DA, Tomaszewski A, et al. Correlations between electrocardiogram and biomarkers in acute pulmonary embolism: analysis of ZATPOL-2 Registry. *Ann Noninvasive Electrocardiol.* 2017;22(4).

28. Kosuge M, Uchida K, Imoto K, et al. Prognostic value of ST-segment elevation in lead aVR in patients with type A acute aortic dissection. *J Am Coll Cardiol.* 2015;65(23):2570-2571.

29. Karabulut A, Cakmak M. Treatment strategies in the left main coronary artery disease associated with acute coronary syndromes. *J Saudi Heart Assoc.* 2015;27(4):272-276.

30. de Winter RJ, Verouden NJ, Wellens HJ, et al. A new ECG sign of proximal LAD occlusion. *N Engl J Med.* 2008;359(19):2071-2073.

31. Li RA, Leppo M, Miki T, et al. Molecular basis of electrocardiographic ST-segment elevation. *Circ Res.* 2000;87(10):837-839.

32. Verouden NJ, Koch KT, Peters RJ, et al. Persistent precordial "hyperacute" T-waves signify

proximal left anterior descending artery occlusion. *Heart*. 2009;95(20):1701-1706.
33. Goebel M, Bledsoe J, Orford JL, et al. A new ST-segment elevation myocardial infarction equivalent pattern? Prominent T wave and J-point depression in the precordial leads associated with ST-segment elevation in lead aVr. *Am J Emerg Med*. 2014;32(3):287.e5-e287.e8.
34. de Winter RW, Adams R, Verouden NJW. Precordial junctional ST-segment depression with tall symmetric T-waves signifying proximal LAD occlusion, case reports of STEMI equivalence. *J Electrocardiol*. 2016;49(1):76-80.
35. de Zwaan C, Bär FW, Wellens HJ. Characteristic electrocardiographic pattern indicating a critical stenosis high in left anterior descending coronary artery in patients admitted because of impending myocardial infarction. *Am Heart J*. 1982;103(4, Part 2):730-736.
36. Rhinehardt J, Brady WJ, Perron AD, et al. Electrocardiographic manifestations of Wellens' syndrome. *Am J Emerg Med*. 2002;20(7):638-643.
37. Smith SW, Whitwam W. Acute coronary syndromes. *Emerg Med Clin North Am*. 2006;24(1):53-89.
38. de Zwaan C, Bär FW, Janssen JHA, et al. Angiographic and clinical characteristics of patients with unstable angina showing an ECG pattern indicating critical narrowing of the proximal LAD coronary artery. *Am Heart J*. 1989;117(3):657-665.
39. van Bree MD, Roos YB, van der Bilt IA, et al. Prevalence and characterization of ECG abnormalities after intracerebral hemorrhage. *Neurocrit Care*. 2010;12(1):50-55.
40. Suzuki J, Watanabe F, Takenaka K, et al. New subtype of apical hypertrophic cardiomyopathy identified with nuclear magnetic resonance imaging as an underlying cause of markedly inverted T waves. *J Am Coll Cardiol*. 1993;22(4):1175-1181.
41. Dhawan SS. Pseudo-Wellens' syndrome after crack cocaine use. *Can J Cardiol*. 2008;24(5):404.
42. Hayden GE, Brady WJ, Perron AD, et al. Electrocardiographic T-wave inversion: differential diagnosis in the chest pain patient. *Am J Emerg Med*. 2002;20(3):252-262.

CHAPTER NINE

ACS Mimics Part I: Non-ACS Causes of ST-Segment Elevation

SEMHAR Z. TEWELDE AND **MAITE ANNA HUIS IN 'T VELD**

KEY POINTS

- Just as recognition of ST-segment elevation MI is critical for emergency physicians, distinguishing it from the most common mimics is essential.
- The presence of reciprocal ST-segment depression strongly favors true ST-segment elevation MI over ventricular aneurysm, pericarditis, and early repolarization.
- Pulmonary embolism can produce ST-segment elevation that mimics acute myocardial infarction.
- A short QTc in association with ST-segment elevation should suggest hypercalcemia.
- Peaked T waves in association with ST-segment elevation should suggest hyperkalemia.
- Acute MI is far more likely than pericarditis if any of the following is present:
  - Convex upward ST-segment elevation
  - ST-segment elevation in lead III that is greater than in lead II
  - ST-segment depression is present in any leads except aVR and V_1

Rapid recognition of STEMI is paramount to the initiation of lifesaving therapeutics such as emergent percutaneous coronary intervention and thrombolysis.[1,2] In the 2013 ACCF/AHA Guideline for the Management of STEMI, ST-segment elevation on the ECG indicative of STEMI is defined as new ST-segment elevation at the J point in at least two contiguous leads of 2 mm (0.2 mV) or more in men or 1.5 mm (0.15 mV) or more in women in leads V_2 and V_3 and/or of 1 mm (0.1 mV) or more in other contiguous chest leads or the limb leads, in the absence of left ventricular hypertrophy (LVH) and left bundle-branch block (LBBB).[2] In 2016, the European Society of Cardiology revised the age cutoff for ST-segment elevation in V_2 and V_3 for men: those younger then 40 years of age must have ST-segment elevation of 2.5 mm or more in two contiguous leads for the diagnosis of STEMI.[1]

A multitude of other ailments and pharmacologic agents can cause ST-segment elevation; it is therefore of utmost importance that emergency physicians are able to accurately identify electrocardiographic subtleties that differentiate acute MI from other mimics, thereby averting invasive and potentially harmful therapy in patients without need for them.[3] Discussed below are the most frequently encountered mimics of STEMI (Table 9.1) and nuances that aid in their identification.

LEFT VENTRICULAR HYPERTROPHY

Left ventricular hypertrophy causes changes in the ECG (Figure 9.1) due to altered repolarization through the hypertrophied myocardium.[4] These changes include both ST-segment and T-wave abnormalities; hence, LVH is one of the most, if not the most, challenging mimics of STEMI.[5] ST-segment elevation associated with LVH usually has a concave

TABLE 9.1. ST ELEVATION MIMICS mneminc for non-acute-MI causes of ST-segment elevation.

Shock (cardioversion/defibrillation)
Toxins (see Table 9.2)
Electrolytes (hyperkalemia, hypokalemia, hypercalcemia)
Left bundle-branch block/paced rhythm
Early repolarization syndrome
Ventricular hypertrophy, high left ventricular voltage
Aneurysm (left ventricular aneurysm)
Thailand/Laos (Brugada syndrome/arrhythmogenic cardiomyopathy)
Inflammation (pericarditis/myocarditis)
Osborn (hypothermia/acidosis)
Nonischemic/vasospasm (Prinzmetal angina)
Medications (see Table 9.2)
Injury (direct [eg, myocardial contusion])
Mechanical disorders
Cardiac (aortic dissection, coronary aneurysm, tumor)
Thoracic (pulmonary embolism, pneumothorax, pneumomediastinum)
Increased intracranial pressure and Intra-abdominal pressure
Cardiac preexcitation and demand ischemia
Wolff-Parkinson-White syndrome
Shock states (distributive/hemorrhagic/cardiogenic/obstructive)
Stress induced (takotsubo cardiomyopathy)

upwards contour and is generally limited to leads V_1 through V_3. ST-segment depression with T-wave inversion in leads I, aVL, II, and V_4 through V_6 can also be seen. ST-segment depression in LVH typically has a downsloping contour. Inverted T waves are typically asymmetric.

There is no general consensus on how to identify acute coronary syndrome (ACS) in patients with LVH. Both the European and the American guidelines for management of STEMI exclude LVH from interpretation of the ST-segment elevation. Neither document includes thresholds or criteria for the detection of ACS in patients with LVH.

Usual practice in the emergency department is to compare the current ECG with an old ECG, when available. Unfortunately, ECGs obtained from patients with LVH but without actual myocardial ischemia can show significant variation over time,

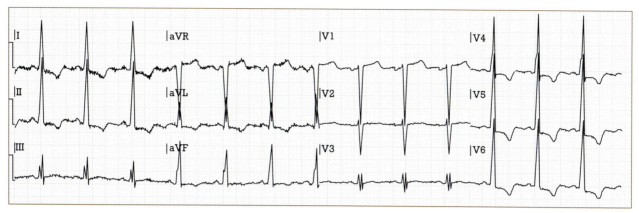

FIGURE 9.1. Left ventricular hypertrophy. ST-segment elevation in leads V_1 through V_2; downsloping ST-segment depression with inverted T waves in leads I, aVL, II, and V_4 through V_6; tall, slightly wide QRS complexes in leads I, aVL, II, and V_4 through V_6. Reproduced with permission from: Amal Mattu, MD, FACEP.

reducing the usual effectiveness of this practice.[5] In a retrospective analysis, Armstrong and colleagues reviewed ECGs from patients with LVH and ST-segment elevation in the anterior leads (V_1–V_3) exceeding 25% of the preceding R-S wave magnitude.[6] This finding increased specificity without compromising sensitivity for angiographic culprit lesions. To date, this criterion has not been validated and might be too insensitive for detection of ACS. Other criteria have been proposed, including evaluating the convexity of the ST-segment elevations; however, this is an imperfect marker because early ST-segment elevation in patients with ACS is often concave upwards and later transitions to a convex shape.[4]

Inverted T-wave symmetry has also been suggested as a marker of ACS, as inverted T waves typically found in LVH are asymmetric; however, this association has not been studied.[5] The current ACC/AHA STEMI guidelines do not include recommendations pertaining to the approach to identification of ACS based on electrocardiographic findings in patients with LVH.[2] The ESC guidelines recommend emergency echocardiography for patients with LVH and the possibility of ACS; however, it is important to note that the sensitivity for detection of segmental wall motion abnormalities in patients with LVH is decreased.[1] While we await future research on this topic, the best approach to patients with LVH and the suggestion of ACS consists of serial ECGs, comparison of new ECGs with previous ECGs, and echocardiographic evaluation with an understanding of its limitations.

LEFT VENTRICULAR ANEURYSM

Left ventricular aneurysm (LVA) is a localized area of dyskinetic, infarcted myocardium that bulges outward during both systole and diastole.[7] On the ECG (Figure 9.2), it persists as ST-segment elevation after acute MI, making it difficult to distinguish from a new ischemic event.[7] ST-segment elevation secondary to LVA frequently has a concave morphology, but it can also be convex.[8] The absence of reciprocal changes, the presence of Q waves, and the loss of R waves are all suggestive of LVA.[7,9] Small Q waves can develop within hours after infarction; therefore, the presence of Q waves alone should not be used to rule out acute MI.[7] Similarly, if ST-segment elevation is significant (>5 mm), suspicion should remain high for acute MI.

A recent validation study using two mathematical formulas demonstrated the ability to discriminate between acute MI and LVA with high sensitivity. Acute MI is prognostically more likely when:

- the T-wave amplitude divided by the QRS-wave amplitude in any single lead (V_1–V_4) is larger than 0.36 or
- the sum of T-wave amplitudes divided by the sum of QRS-wave amplitudes in leads V_1 through V_4 is more than 0.22.[10-12]

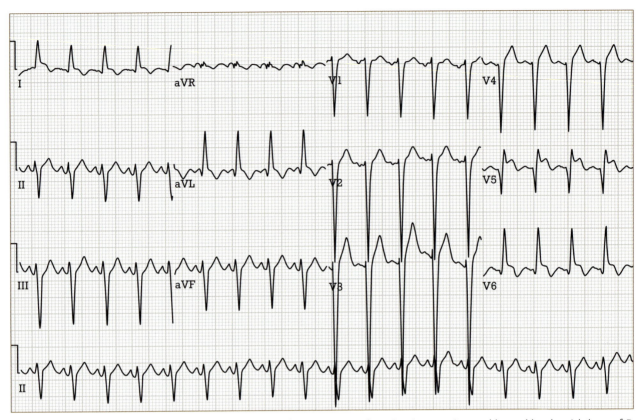

FIGURE 9.2. Left ventricular aneurysm. Pronounced ST-segment elevation in anterior and lateral leads with loss of R waves and significant Q waves. Note the absence of reciprocal ST-segment depression. Reproduced with permission from: Amal Mattu, MD, FACEP.

However, these formulas are cumbersome and unlikely to be of practical use in real-time emergency medicine practice.

PERICARDITIS

Between the visceral and parietal pericardium, a potential space exists where a small amount (<50 mL) of plasma ultrafiltrate naturally dwells. Inflammation of this space can lead to pericarditis. Pericarditis is diagnosed when at least two of four clinical criteria are met: typical chest pain (classically described as sharp, pleuritic, positional, radiating to the trapezius ridge), pericardial friction rub, typical ECG findings (widespread ST-segment elevation with PR-segment depression), and pericardial effusion. Electrocardiographic abnormalities (Figure 9.3) have long been known to occur with pericarditis and are seen in up to 90% of cases.[13] The culprit is circumferential irritation between the pericardial layers, so the ECG abnormalities are diffuse,[14] with the exception of leads V_1 and aVR, where ST-segment depression can be noted.[15]

The ST-segment elevation of pericarditis is best described as diffuse, concave upwards, transient, emerging over hours to days, and without concurrent reciprocal ST-segment depression outside of leads aVR and V_1. If ST-segment elevation is prominent (>10 mm in precordial leads, >5 mm in limb leads) or ST-segment depression is present in leads other than the aforementioned V_1 and aVR, the diagnosis of acute MI is more likely.[16] Likewise, the presence of Q waves, loss of R-wave progression, ST-segment elevation in lead III greater than in lead II, and prolongation of the QT interval all suggest acute MI.[13,17] Later in the course of pericarditis, the ST and PR segments normalize, but this is then followed by diffuse T-wave inversions that can develop and can last several weeks.[18] These changes are

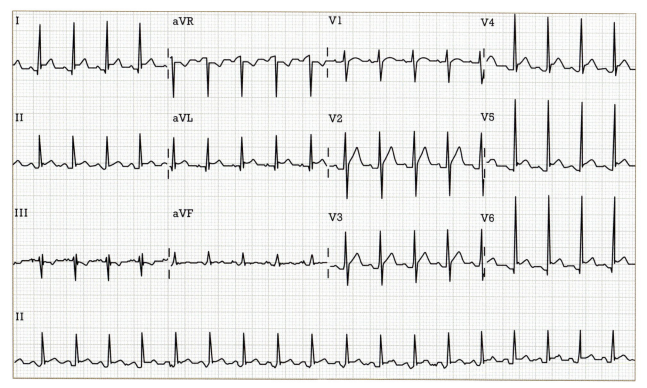

FIGURE 9.3. Acute pericarditis. Diffuse ST-segment elevation and PR depression. Note that the ST-segment elevation is concave upwards and there is no reciprocal ST-segment depression (excluding leads aVR and V₁).

followed by normalization back to baseline within several months. These four stages (diffuse ST-segment elevation, normalization, diffuse T-wave inversion, normalization) of electrocardiographic evolution can be appreciated in up to 50% of pericarditis cases.[19] PR depression is seen in pericarditis as well as other clinical scenarios, including normal variant and atrial infarction.[20] When it is diffuse and larger than 0.8 mm, PR depression is more specific for pericarditis.[21,22]

EARLY REPOLARIZATION

Early repolarization, also known as normal variant ST-segment elevation, is seen predominantly in young men. Once thought to be completely benign (hence, its former name, benign early repolarization), it is now known to confer some susceptibility to sudden cardiac death.[23] Early repolarization is recognized by 1) concave upward ST-segment elevation, 2) terminal QRS notching, and 3) large, somewhat asymmetric T waves (Figure 9.4). As with pericarditis, ST-segment depression outside of leads aVR and V₁ is typically absent. Unlike the diffuse changes typical of pericarditis, early repolarization abnormalities are more often limited to the precordial leads, although in a minority, both the precordium and limb leads are involved. The degree of ST-segment elevation then is larger in the precordium than in the limb leads. A highly sensitive (88%) and specific (90%) indicator in differentiating pericarditis from early repolarization is the ST/T ratio in lead V₆. A ratio of less than 0.25 suggests early repolarization, and a ratio above 0.25 suggests pericarditis or STEMI.[24] In contrast to the dynamic changes of acute MI, early repolarization abnormalities remain constant over protracted periods. Early repolarization also commonly manifests a notch or "fishhook" at the J point, especially in the lateral precordial leads (Figure 9.4). Another consideration is the magnitude of ST-segment elevation, which in early repolarization can be diminished by sympathetic stress (eg, elevated heart rate) and amplified by the reverse (eg, slow heart rate).

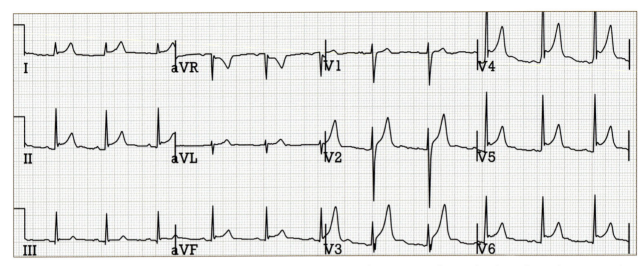

FIGURE 9.4. Early repolarization. Diffuse ST-segment elevation and J-point notching in leads V_4 through V_6. Note that the ST-segment elevation is concave upwards and there is no reciprocal ST-segment depression (excluding leads aVR and V_1).

In the setting of isolated precordial ST-segment elevation without any other abnormality, both early repolarization and anterior STEMI are possible. Several studies comparing patients with those two conditions have shown that using the QTc interval, QRS voltage in V_2, R-wave amplitude in V_4, and ST-segment elevation at 60 miliseconds after the J point in V_3 can, with great sensitivity and specificity, differentiate the two.[25,26] The following formula can be employed when anterior ST-segment elevation is present without another discernable abnormality:

$$[(0.052 \times QTc) - (0.151 \times V_2QRS) - (0.268 \times V_4R) + (1.062 \times V_3STE @ 60 \text{ milliseconds})].$$

Values higher than 18.2 are
highly predictive of acute MI.[25,26]

A less recognized normal variant that can mimic both STEMI and Wellens syndrome has been observed primarily in people of African or Caribbean descent. This variant is called the Afro-Caribbean pattern or the ST-segment elevation with negative T-wave variant (Figure 9.5). It produces precordial ST-segment elevation and terminal QRS (J point) notching similar to that of early repolarization, but it also has concomitant T-wave inversion in the precordial leads, making it hard to distinguish from acute MI. Obtaining an old ECG that reveals a similar pattern can confirm this presentation as a normal variant. Preservation of R-wave progression and lack of Q waves also aid in the diagnosis.[27,28]

BRUGADA SYNDROME

Another distinctive syndrome that often is mistaken for STEMI is the Brugada syndrome (Figure 9.6). Brugada syndrome is seen predominantly in male patients who typically present after syncope but are often asymptomatic at the time of medical evaluation. The findings of Brugada syndrome are more prominent during bradycardia and after sinus pauses, which might explain why the arrhythmias frequently occur during rest.[29]

Brugada syndrome is characterized by a complete or incomplete right bundle-branch block pattern in the right precordial leads (V_1–V_3) with concurrent ST-segment elevation. The QRS complex terminates in an inverted T wave. ST-segment elevation most often is a coved (convex upwards) pattern but could also be a "saddle," or concave upwards pattern.[30,31] Brugada syndrome is described in greater detail in Chapter 13.

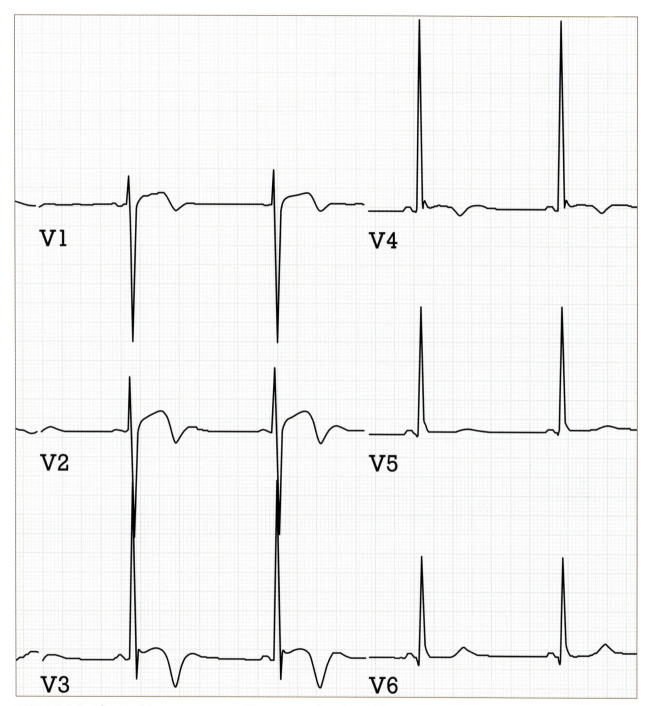

FIGURE 9.5. Afro-Caribbean pattern or ST-segment elevation with negative T-wave variant. Domed ST-segment elevation in the precordial leads followed by T-wave inversions. Reproduced with permission from: Amal Mattu, MD, FACEP.

LEFT BUNDLE-BRANCH BLOCK AND PACED RHYTHMS

The interpretation of LBBB on an ECG is challenging, as the altered ventricular depolarization produces both ST-segment elevation and depression. In a normal LBBB pattern, discordance exists between the ST segments and the main vector of the QRS complex (ie, in all of the leads); where the main

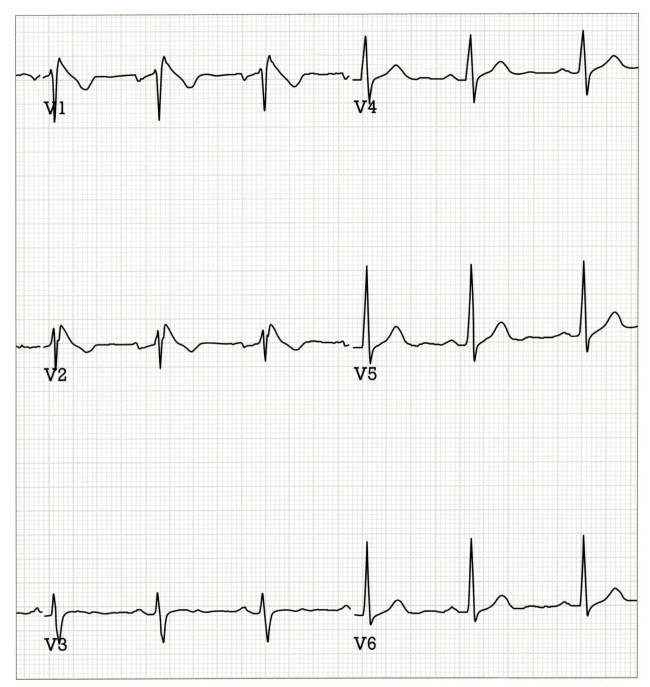

FIGURE 9.6. Brugada syndrome. Incomplete right bundle-branch block morphology with coved downsloping ST-segment elevation followed by T-wave inversions in the right precordial leads V_1 through V_2. Reproduced with permission from: Amal Mattu, MD, FACEP.

vector of the QRS points upwards (eg, the lateral leads), ST-segment depression is expected; and on the other hand, where the main vector of the QRS points downwards (eg, leads V_1–V_3), ST-segment elevation is expected. This is the normal pattern of an uncomplicated LBBB (Figure 9.7).

The challenge exists, then, in trying to distinguish whether the ST-segment abnormalities in the ECG of LBBB represent an acute coronary occlusion (ie, a "STEMI equivalent") or a normal pattern. Previous

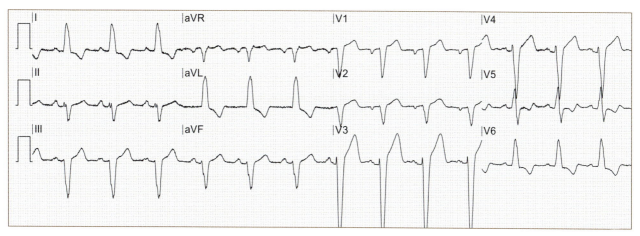

FIGURE 9.7. Uncomplicated LBBB. Note the presence of discordance between the QRS complexes and the ST segments, resulting in some leads with ST-segment elevation and some with ST-segment depression. Reproduced with permission from: Amal Mattu, MD, FACEP.

versions of STEMI guidelines included the presence of (suspected) new LBBB as a STEMI equivalent and therefore did not require evaluation of the ST segments.[32] However, recent studies have shown that the occurrence of new LBBB secondary to a large acute MI is rare in the absence of shock,[33,34] and therefore "STEMI equivalent" cannot be diagnosed purely on the basis of a new LBBB. Fortunately, criteria published in 1996, known as the Sgarbossa criteria,[35] have been found useful in distinguishing between STEMI equivalent versus uncomplicated LBBB. The 2013 ACC/AHA STEMI guidelines recommend the use of these Sgarbossa criteria to diagnose STEMI in patients with LBBB.[2] The criteria are:

- ST-segment elevation of at least 1 mm in the same direction as the main vector of the QRS complex ("concordant ST-segment elevation") in any lead,
- ST-segment depression of at least 1 mm in the same direction as the main vector of the QRS complex ("concordant ST-segment depression") in leads V_1 through V_3, and
- Excessively discordant ST-segment elevation, defined as 5 mm or more of ST-segment elevation when the main vector of the QRS is negative.

The Sgarbossa criteria have high specificity for the detection of acute MI, but low sensitivity.

A modification of the original criteria has been proposed to increase diagnostic utility. The third criterion was changed to a proportional criterion, in which the ratio of the ST segment to the S wave is greater than 0.25 in the presence of at least a 1-mm ST-segment elevation.[36] Early data show improved sensitivity and specificity for the modified Sgarbossa criteria, but further studies are required.[36,37] Other proposed features used to aid in the diagnosis of ACS on the ECG of patients with LBBB include convexity of the ST segment, T-wave concordance, and the presence of Q waves, yet none of these has proved to be predictive of ACS in patients with LBBB.[35,37] The diagnosis of acute MI in the presence of LBBB is described in Chapter 8.

Paced rhythms can produce discordant ST-segment changes similar to those of LBBB. The use of the Sgarbossa criteria has been proposed to distinguish acute coronary occlusion from the normal pacer pattern, but there are limited data to support this application.[38,39] The diagnosis of acute MI in the presence of pacers is also discussed in Chapter 8.

GLOBAL CARDIAC INJURY

Blunt cardiac injury and myocardial contusion can cause a wide variety of changes on the ECG. The abnormalities can be the result of direct myocardial cell damage but can also be the consequence

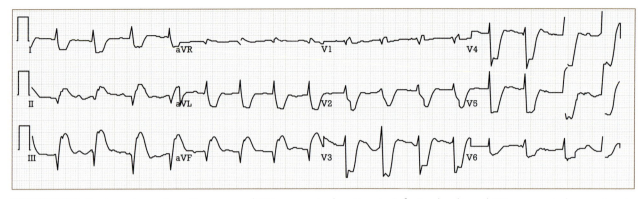

FIGURE 9.8. Postcardioversion. Pronounced ST-segment elevation in inferior leads and ST-segment depression in the anterolateral leads immediately after external cardioversion for ventricular fibrillation. The ST-segment changes gradually resolved after approximately 15 minutes. Reproduced with permission from: Amal Mattu, MD, FACEP.

of extracardiac factors such as hypoxia, anemia, electrolyte abnormalities, and changes in vagal or sympathetic tone.[40] The ECG changes include ST-segment elevation as well as ST-segment depression, Q waves, right bundle-branch block, LBBB, and arrhythmias.[40] The initial ECG can be normal; therefore, a repeat ECG is indicated if there is high clinical suspicion for myocardial injury. Right ventricular injury is known to cause subtle changes, and electrocardiographic deviations are often missed. Unfortunately, the addition of a right-sided ECG does not increase the likelihood of detecting blunt right ventricular injury.[41] No specific criteria to distinguish ST-segment elevation following blunt cardiac injury from that seen in acute MI have been defined. Serial cardiac marker measurements and echocardiography have been proposed to aid in the detection of blunt cardiac injury; however, abnormalities in either do not truly aid in the differentiation since abnormalities can be seen with acute MI as well.[42] If significant wall motion abnormalities are detected, angiography is indicated.[43]

Direct electrical current applied during cardioversion or defibrillation can also cause electrocardiographic variations. ST-segment elevation or depression can develop immediately after current has been applied (Figure 9.8).[44] ST-segment elevation can be either convex or concave in morphology and is most often seen in the anterior leads.[45] No specific treatment is indicated because there is no true myocardial injury and changes often resolve spontaneously within minutes to days.

EXTRACARDIAC CONSIDERATIONS

The ECG is vital in the evaluation of patients with altered mental status. It can aid in both diagnosis and management of those who are otherwise unable to provide an accurate history with regard to their medical condition or ingestions. Many disorders (electrolyte/metabolic derangements, hypoxia, intracranial pathology, hypothermia) and drugs (prescribed or illicit) can have cardiotoxic effects resulting in ST-segment elevation.

Pharmacologics

Many pharmacologic agents induce ST-segment elevation (Table 9.2), chief among them being sodium channel blockers. Inhibition of the fast Na+ channels results in QRS-complex widening that can easily be mistaken for ventricular tachycardia. In cases of severe toxicity, this widening can evolve to sine wave or asystole. One class of medications well known for this effect, in addition to its lethality, is tricyclic antidepressants (TCAs). Unlike other sodium channel blockers, TCAs at toxic levels produce rightward axis of the terminal 40 milliseconds of the QRS, which can be detected by a prominent S wave in lead I or aVL and a prominent R wave in lead aVR, with prolongation of all the intervals, especially the QRS and QT complex (Figure 9.9).

TABLE 9.2. Pharmacologic causes of ST-segment elevation.

Cardiac
- Beta blocker
- Calcium channel blocker
- Potassium channel blocker
- Sodium channel blocker

Chemotherapeutic
- Alkylating agent
- Anthracyclines
- Antimetabolite
- Microtubule targeting
- Monoclonal antibody

Psychotropic
- Anticonvulsant
- Antipsychotic
- Phenothiazine
- Selective serotonin inhibitor
- Tricyclic antidepressant

Toxic
- Amphetamine
- Carbon monoxide
- Cocaine
- Ethanol
- Gamma-hydroxybutyrate
- Hydrocarbons

Moreover, the risk of seizures and arrhythmias increases significantly when the QRS complex is larger than 100 milliseconds and larger than 160 milliseconds, respectively.[46]

Cocaine is a psychomotor stimulant that blocks the reuptake of dopamine, serotonin, and norepinephrine in addition to acting as a sodium channel blocker. At higher doses, it acts like a class IC antiarrhythmic, blocking both sodium and potassium channels, resulting in myocardial depression. Cocaine can produce myocardial dysfunction, atherosclerosis, and arrhythmia as well as precipitating coronary vasospasm with consequent ST-segment elevation.[47] Complications rarely occur more than 12 hours after arrival; however, when electrocardiographic changes are present, it is challenging to determine whether vasospasm or vessel thrombosis is causing flow limitation. If the changes persist, angiography is required.[48]

Spiked Helmet

A new cause of ST-segment elevation was identified recently: the spiked helmet sign. This electrocardiographic finding is seen primarily in critically ill patients and portends a poor prognosis.[49-51] The characteristic ST-segment elevation has an upward shift starting before the onset of the QRS complex, with a dome-and-spike pattern (Figure 9.10), described as having the appearance of a pickelhaube, the German military spiked helmet.[49] It is typically seen in the inferior or precordial leads.[52] The spiked helmet pattern in the limb leads appears to be associated with intraabdominal pathology, whereas the presence of the pattern in the precordial leads appears to be associated with intrathoracic pathology.[49-51] In either case, early recognition of the pattern should prompt immediate evaluation of an underlying, potentially deadly condition.

Electrolytes

Electrolytes have an poessential role in the depolarization and repolarization of the myocardial cell. Abnormalities in their levels are well known to cause electrocardiographic changes. Both hypercalcemia and hyperkalemia are known causes of ST-segment elevation. Hypercalcemia causes shortening of the QT interval and, at very high levels, induces ST-segment elevation resembling that of acute MI. It has been suggested that the QT interval becomes so short that the T waves are retracted within the ST segment, causing the appearance of ST-segment elevation (Figure 9.11).[53] The ST-segment elevations are most often seen in the anterior leads and

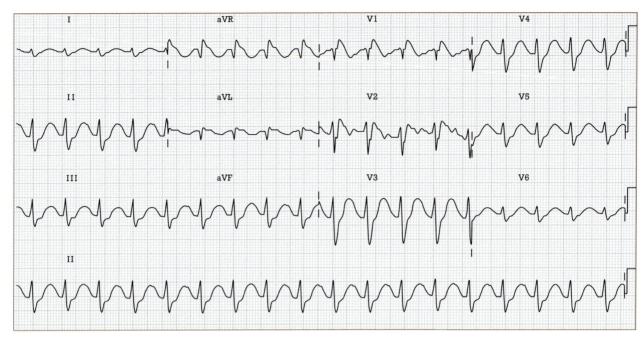

FIGURE 9.9. Tricyclic antidepressant overdose. Sinus tachycardia with right axis deviation, terminal R wave larger than 3 mm in aVR, prolonged QT interval, and an interventricular conduction delay.

can be accompanied by ST-segment depression, complicating differentiation from acute MI.[53,54] QT shortening is not typically seen in acute MI; in fact, it is quite the opposite—one should expect some degree of QT prolongation. This characteristic could aid in distinguishing between hypercalcemia and STEMI.

Hyperkalemia can cause a variety of electrocardiographic changes, which are usually progressive.[55] They progress from tall peaked T waves to intraventricular conduction delay and flattening followed by disappearance of the P wave. ST-segment elevation can be seen, most frequently in V_1 through V_2 and aVR (Figure 9.12). The ST-segment elevation is often downsloping, whereas the elevation seen in acute MI is frequently upsloping. Upsloping ST-segment depression is often seen in the inferior and especially in the lateral leads in hyperkalemia. These electrocardiographic changes resolve with treatment.

Pulmonary Pathology

Making the distinction between acute MI and pulmonary embolism (PE) can be very difficult based on clinical features alone. Unfortunately, the ECG differentiation can be equally difficult. Pulmonary embolism can lead to a wide variety of electrocardiographic manifestations. Most common, but nonspecific, is sinus tachycardia. More specific are the abnormalities associated with right heart strain—the $S_1Q_3T_3$ pattern, right axis deviation, complete or incomplete right bundle-branch block, and T-wave inversions. Concomitant inferior and right precordial T-wave inversions have a higher specificity for PE than for ACS. A recent retrospective study of hemodynamically unstable patients with PE found that three distinct and significant electrocardiographic patterns emerged during clinical deterioration:

- ST-segment elevation in leads V_1 through V_3/V_4,
- ST-segment elevation in lead aVR with concomitant ST-segment depression in leads I and V_4 through V_6 (Figure 9.13), and
- ST-segment elevation in leads III or V_1/V_2 with simultaneous ST-segment depression in leads V_4/V_5 through V_6.[56]

Other less commonly discussed pulmonary conditions that can also masquerade as acute MI are

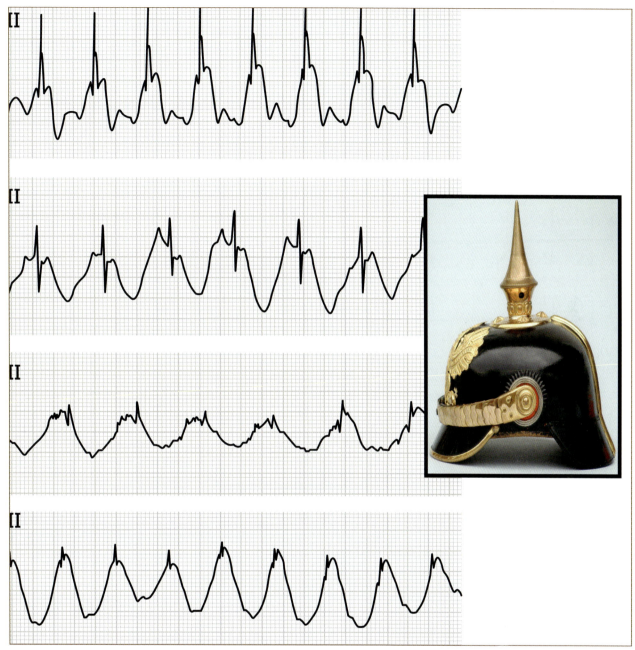

FIGURE 9.10. Spiked helmet sign. Spike and dome appearance resembling a German military helmet, pickelhaube. From: Littmann L, Monroe MH. The "spiked helmet" sign: a new electrocardiographic marker of critical illness and high risk of death. *Mayo Clin Proc.* 2011;86:1245-1246. Reproduced with permission from: Littmann L, Monroe MH. The "spiked helmet" sign: a new electromyographic marker of critical illness and high risk of death. *Mayo Clin Proc.* 2011;86:1245-1246. Copyright 2011 Elsevier Inc.

pneumothorax and pneumomediastinum. Cohort studies have shown that up to one-fourth of patients with pneumothorax have significant electrocardiographic changes (ST-segment elevation or depression) that resolve with treatment.[57] Similarly, pneumomediastinum has been associated with an assortment of electrocardiographic changes (T-wave inversion, low voltage, loss of R-wave progression,

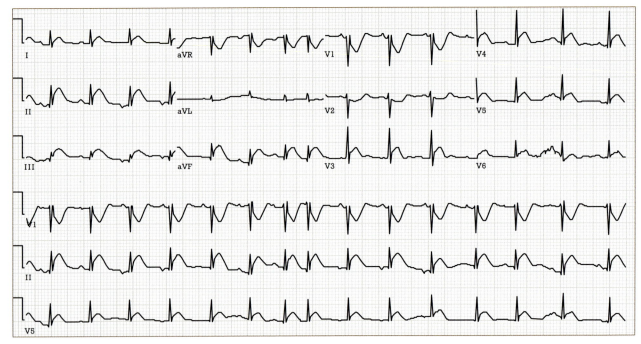

FIGURE 9.11. Hypercalcemia. ST-segment elevation in the inferior and anterolateral leads mimicking a large acute MI. Note the very short QT interval. Serum calcium concentration was 17 mg/dL.

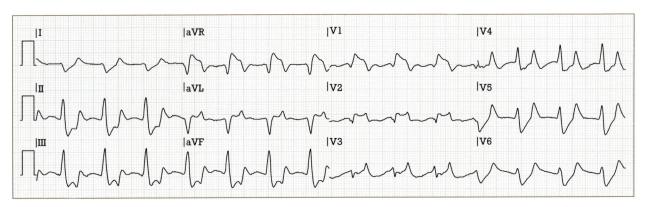

FIGURE 9.12. Hyperkalemia. Wide complex rhythm with ST-segment elevation in V_1, V_2, and aVR; peaked T waves; and ST-segment depression in the inferior-lateral leads. Reproduced with permission from: Amal Mattu, MD, FACEP.

and ST-segment elevation), none of which are from myocardial ischemia or injury but rather are attributed to cardiac displacement, vagal stimulation, ventricular enlargement, and mediastinal air.[58]

Elevated Intracranial Pressure

Increased intracranial pressure can lead to many electrocardiographic and rhythm abnormalities, including ST-segment elevation, ST-segment depression, QT prolongation, high-amplitude R waves, and most notably giant, cerebral T waves.[59,60] These changes occur within the first days after injury and resolve spontaneously, but they can sometimes persist for weeks.[61] Aside from clinical context, there are no criteria that can distinguish ST-segment elevation secondary to increased intracranial pressure from the elevation of acute MI.

Hypothermia

When the body temperature approaches 35°C (95°F), sinus bradycardia and diminished T-wave amplitude are common. With a further drop in

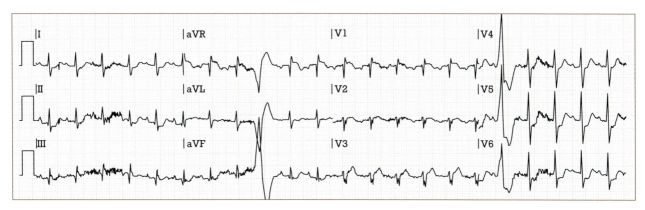

FIGURE 9.13. Pulmonary embolism mimicking acute MI. ST-segment elevation is present in leads V_1, V_2, and aVR, with ST-segment depression in inferior and lateral leads. Reproduced with permission from: Amal Mattu, MD, FACEP.

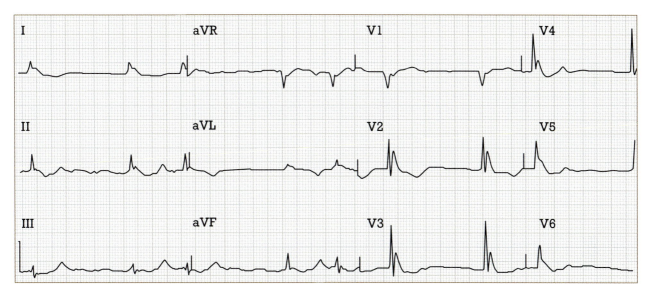

FIGURE 9.14. Hypothermia. Sinus bradycardia with prolongation of all intervals and the Osborn/J wave, a spiked deflection between the QRS and ST complex, produces the appearance of ST-segment elevation. Reproduced with permission from: Benjamin Lawner, DO.

temperature, this state is typically followed by prolongation of all the intervals (PR, QRS, and QT).[62] Below 32°C (90°F), Osborn waves (also known as J waves) become apparent (Figure 9.14). Once considered the hallmark of hypothermia, these waves are now known to be present in many other conditions[63-65] and are frequently mistaken for STEMI.[66,67] The electrocardiographic irregularities of hypothermia are not linked directly to temperature but are more likely linked to acidosis associated with the core temperature drop. Resolution of the acidosis while maintaining hypothermia has been shown to normalize the ECG.[68]

UNIQUE CONSIDERATIONS

When scrutinized, an ECG often proves vital in differentiating the clinical entities described in this chapter from acute MI; however, under certain clinical conditions, it is simply not possible to make the distinction. In these cases, the benefit of timely myocardial reperfusion and cardiovascular salvage far outweighs the possibility of a false-positive catheterization.

Stress-induced (takotsubo) cardiomyopathy is a self-resolving regional dysfunction of the left ventricular apex and midventricle, most commonly with relative hyperkinesis of the base. Its clinical presentation, electrocardiographic abnormalities, and biomarker rise make it nearly indistinguishable from acute MI. The largest cohort study conducted to date found that patients with takotsubo cardiomyopathy are more likely to have a normal axis with diffuse ST-segment elevation in the anterior-septal and lateral leads, given the extent of myocardium frequently involved, whereas ST-segment elevation in the inferior and right-sided precordial leads was rare. Stress-induced cardiomyopathy is a fairly new clinical entity with heterogeneous forms. Given our limited understanding of it, most patients in whom it is suspected will undergo coronary angiography and ventriculography to confirm the diagnosis.[69,70]

Myocarditis can produce a broad range of ECG abnormalities, from nonspecific ST-T wave abnormalities to ST-segment elevation with reciprocal depression mimicking that of acute MI. Cardiac biomarkers are typically elevated, further confounding the ability to make an easy distinction between myocarditis and STEMI. The diagnosis frequently is one of exclusion after negative catheterization.[71-73]

Prinzmetal angina or coronary vasospasm leads to transient ischemia and differs from STEMI in that there is no association with marked atherosclerosis; however, it is indistinguishable from STEMI on ECG. This variant affects younger people and women. Just as with all the other causes of vasospasm (cocaine, alcohol, cannabis, chemotherapeutics), if the spasm is not resolved, myocardial cell death can result, so intervention is essential.[74] Coronary vasospasm does not typically produce reciprocal ST-segment depression.

REFERENCES

1. Ibanez B, James S, Agewall S, Antunes MJ, et al. 2017 ESC guidelines for the management of acute myocardial infarction in patients presenting with ST-segment elevation: The Task Force for the management of acute myocardial infarction in patients presenting with ST-segment elevation of the European Society of Cardiology (ESC). *Eur Heart J.* 2017 Aug 26 [Epub ahead of print].
2. O'Gara PT, Kushner FG, Ascheim DD, et al. 2013 ACCF/AHA guideline for the management of st-elevation myocardial infarction: A report of the American College of Cardiology Foundation/American Heart Association Task Force on Practice Guidelines. *Circulation.* 2013;127:e362-425.
3. McCabe JM, Armstrong EJ, Kulkarni A, et al. Prevalence and factors associated with "false positive" ST-segment elevation myocardial infarction diagnoses at primary PCI-capable centers: a report from the Activate-SF registry. *Arch Intern Med.* 2012;172:864-871.
4. Brady WJ, Chan TC, Pollack M. Electrocardiographic manifestations: patterns that confound the EKG diagnosis of acute myocardial infarction-left bundle branch block, ventricular paced rhythm, and left ventricular hypertrophy. *J Emerg Med.* 2000;18:71-78.
5. Birnbaum Y, Alam M. LVH and the diagnosis of STEMI—how should we apply the current guidelines? *J Electrocardiol.* 2014;47:655-660.
6. Armstrong EJ, Kulkarni AR, Bhave PD, et al. Electrocardiographic criteria for ST-elevation myocardial infarction in patients with left ventricular hypertrophy. *Am J Cardiol.* 2012;110:977-983.
7. Engel J, Brady WJ, Mattu A, et al. Electrocardiographic ST segment elevation: left ventricular aneurysm. *Am J Emerg Med.* 2002;20:238-242.
8. Brady WJ, Syverud SA, Beagle C, et al. Electrocardiographic ST segment elevation: the diagnosis of AMI by morphologic analysis of the ST segment. *Acad Emerg Med.* 2001;8:961-967.
9. Rosenberg B, Messinger WJ. Electrocardiogram in ventricular aneurysm. *Am Heart J.* 1949;37:267-277.
10. Smith SW. T/QRS ratio best distinguishes ventricular aneurysm from anterior myocardial infarction. *Am J Emerg Med.* 2005;23:279-287.
11. Klein LR, Shroff GR, Beeman W, et al. Electrocardiographic criteria to differentiate acute anterior ST-elevation myocardial infarction from left ventricular aneurysm. *Am J Emerg Med.* 2015;33:786-790.
12. Ola O, Dumancas C, Mene-Afejuku TO, et al. Left ventricular aneurysm may not manifest as persistent ST elevation on electrocardiogram. *Am J Case Rep.* 2017;18:410-413.
13. Marinella MA. Electrocardiographic manifestations and differential diagnosis of acute pericarditis. *Am Fam Physician.* 1998;57:699-704.
14. Bonow R, Mann D, Libby P, Zipes D. *Braunwald's Heart Disease: A Textbook of Cardiovascular Medicine,* 9th ed. Philadelphia: Saunders; 2008.
15. Koos R, Schröder J, Kühl HP. Acute viral pericarditis without typical electrocardiographic changes assessed by cardiac magnetic resonance imaging. *Eur Heart J.* 2009;30:2844.

16. Surawicz B, Knilans TK, Chou TC. Chou's *Electrocardiography in Clinical Practice: Adult and Pediatric*. Philadelphia: Saunders; 2008.
17. *Imazio M,* Spodick DH, Brucato A, et al. Diagnostic issues in the clinical management of pericarditis. *Int J Clin Pract.* 2010;64:1384-1392.
18. Maisch B, Seferović PM, Ristić AD, et al. Guidelines on the diagnosis and management of pericardial diseases executive summary: The Task Force on the Diagnosis and Management of Pericardial Diseases of the European Society of Cardiology. *Eur Heart J.* 2004;25:587-610.
19. Spodick DH. Acute pericarditis: current concepts and practice. *JAMA.* 2003;289:1150-1153.
20. Shakir D, Arafa SO. Right atrial infarction, atrial arrhythmia and inferior myocardial infarction form a missed triad: a case report and review of the literature. *Can J Cardiol.* 2007;23:995-997.
21. Charles MA, Bensinger TA, Glasser SP. Atrial injury current in pericarditis. *Arch Intern Med.* 1973;131:657-662.
22. Spodick DH. Differential characteristics of the electrocardiogram in early repolarization and acute pericarditis. *N Engl J Med.* 1976;295:523-526.
23. Tikkanen JT, Wichmann V, Junttila MJ, et al. Association of early repolarization and sudden cardiac death during an acute coronary event. *Circ Arrhythm Electrophysiol.* 2012;5:714-718.
24. Ginzton LE, Laks MM. The differential diagnosis of acute pericarditis from the normal variant: new electrocardiographic criteria. *Circulation.* 1982;65:1004-1009.
25. Driver BE, Khalil A, Henry T, et al. A new 4-variable formula to differentiate normal variant ST segment elevation in V_2-V_4 (early repolarization) from subtle left anterior descending coronary occlusion - Adding QRS amplitude of V_2 improves the model. *J Electrocardiol.* 2017;50:561-569.
26. Smith SW, Khalil A, Henry TD, et al. Electrocardiographic differentiation of early repolarization from subtle anterior ST-segment elevation myocardial infarction. *Ann Emerg Med.* 2012;60:45-56.e2.
27. Drezner JA, et al. Electrocardiographic interpretation in athletes: the 'Seattle Criteria'. *Br J Sports Med.* 2013;47:122-124.
28. Roukoz H, Wang K. ST elevation and inverted T wave as another normal variant mimicking acute myocardial infarction: the prevalence, age, gender, and racial distribution. *Ann Noninvasive Electrocardiol.* 2011;16:64-69.
29. Antzelevitch C, Yan GX, Ackerman MJ, et al. J-wave syndromes expert consensus conference report: emerging concepts and gaps in knowledge. *J Arrhythm.* 2016;32:315-339.
30. Bayés de Luna A, Brugada J, Baranchuk A, et al. Current electrocardiographic criteria for diagnosis of Brugada pattern: a consensus report. *J Electrocardiol.* 2012;45:433-442.
31. de Luna AB, Garcia-Niebla J, Baranchuk A. New electrocardiographic features in Burgada syndrome. *Curr Cardiol Rev.* 2014;10:175-180.
32. Antman EM, Anbe DT, Armstrong PW, et al. ACC/AHA guidelines for the management of patients with ST-elevation myocardial infarction: a report of the American College of Cardiology/American Heart Association Task Force on Practice Guidelines (Committee to Revise the 1999 Guidelines for the Management of Patients With Acute Myocardial Infarction). *Circulation.* 2004;110:e82–e292.
33. Fahy GJ, Pinski SL, Miller DP, et al. Natural history of isolated bundle branch block. *Am J Cardiol.* 1996;77:1185-1190.
34. Jain S, Ting HT, Bell M, et al. Utility of left bundle branch block as a diagnostic criterion for acute myocardial infarction. *Am J Cardiol.* 2011;107:1111-1116.
35. Sgarbossa EB, Pinski SL, Barbagelata A, et al. Electrocardiographic diagnosis of evolving acute myocardial infarction in the presence of left bundle-branch block. GUSTO-1 (Global Utilization of Streptokinase and Tissue Plasminogen Activator for Occluded Coronary Arteries) Investigators. *N Engl J Med.* 1996;334:481-487.
36. Smith SW, Dodd KW, Henry TD, et al. Diagnosis of ST-elevation myocardial infarction in the presence of left bundle branch block with the ST-elevation to S-wave ratio in a modified Sgarbossa rule. *Ann Emerg Med.* 2012;60:766-776.
37. Meyers HP, Jaffa E, Smith SW, et al. Evaluation of T-wave morphology in patients with left bundle branch block and suspected acute coronary syndrome. *J Emerg Med.* 2016;51:229-237.
38. Sgarbossa EB, Pinski SL, Gates KB, et al. Early electrocardiographic diagnosis of acute myocardial infarction in the presence of ventricular paced rhythm. *Am J Cardiol.* 1996;77:423-424.
39. Maloy KR, Bhat R, Davis J, et al. Sgarbossa criteria are highly specific for acute myocardial infarction with pacemakers. *West J Emerg Med.* 2010;11:354-357.
40. Sybrandy KC, Cramer MJM, Burgersdijk C. Diagnosing cardiac contusion: old wisdom and new insights. *Heart.* 2003;89:485-489.
41. Walsh P, Marks G, Aranguri C, et al. Use of V4R in patients who sustain blunt chest trauma. *J Trauma.* 2001;51:60-63.

42. Clancy K, Velopulos C, Bilaniuk JW, et al. Eastern Association for the Surgery of Trauma screening for blunt cardiac injury: an Eastern Association for the Surgery of Trauma practice management guideline. *J Trauma Acute Care Surg*. 2012;73:S301-S306.
43. Alborzi Z, Zangouri V, Paydar S, et al. Diagnosing myocardial contusion after blunt chest trauma. *J Tehran Heart Cent*. 2016;11:49-54.
44. Eysmann SB, Marchlinski FE, Buxton AE, et al. Electrocardiographic changes after cardioversion of ventricular arrhythmias. *Circulation*. 1986;73:73-81.
45. Kok LC, Mitchell MA, Haines DE, et al. Transient ST elevation after transthoracic cardioversion in patients with hemodynamically unstable ventricular tachyarrhythmia. *Am J Cardiol*. 2000;85:878-881, A9.
46. Harrigan RA, Brady WJ. ECG abnormalities in tricyclic antidepressant ingestion. *Am J Emerg Med*. 1999;17:387-393.
47. McCord J, Jneid H, Hollander JE, et al. Management of cocaine-associated chest pain and myocardial infarction: a scientific statement from the American Heart Association Acute Cardiac Care Committee of the Council on Clinical Cardiology. *Circulation*. 2008;117:1897-1907.
48. Schwartz BG. Cardiovascular effects of cocaine. *Circulation*. 2010;122:2558-2569.
49. Littmann L, Monroe MH. The "spiked helmet" sign: a new electrocardiographic marker of critical illness and high risk of death. *Mayo Clin Proc*. 2011;86:1245-1246.
50. Tomcsányi J, Frész T, Bózsik B. ST elevation anterior "spiked helmet" sign. *Mayo Clin Proc*. 2012;87:309.
51. Agarwal A, Janz TG, Garikipati NV. Spiked helmet sign: an under-recognized electrocardiogram finding in critically ill patients. *Indian J Crit Care Med*. 2014;18:238-240.
52. Littmann L, Proctor P. Real time recognition of the electrocardiographic "spiked helmet" sign in a critically ill patient with pneumothorax. *Int J Cardiol*. 2014;173:e51-e52.
53. Littmann L, Taylor L 3rd, Brearley WD Jr. ST-segment elevation: a common finding in severe hypercalcemia. *J Electrocardiol*. 2007;40:60-62.
54. Durant E, Singh A. ST elevation due to hypercalcemia. *Am J Emerg Med*. 2017;35:1033.e3-1033.e6.
55. Sims DB, Sperling LS. ST-segment elevation resulting from hyperkalemia. *Circulation*. 2005;111:e295-e296.
56. Zhan ZQ, Wang CQ, Nikus KC, et al. Electrocardiogram patterns during hemodynamic instability in patients with acute pulmonary embolism. *Ann Noninvasive Electrocardiol*. 2014;19:543-551.
57. Senthilkumaran S, Meenakshisundaram R, Michaels AD, et al. Electrocardiographic changes in spontaneous pneumothorax. *Int J Cardiol*. 2011;153:78-80.
58. Brearley WD Jr, Taylor L 3rd, Haley MW, et al. Pneumomediastinum mimicking acute ST-segment elevation myocardial infarction. *Int J Cardiol*. 2007;117:e73-e75.
59. Chatterjee S. ECG changes in subarachnoid haemorrhage: a synopsis. *Neth Heart J*. 2011;19:31-34.
60. Takeuchi S, Nagatani K, Otani N, et al. Electrocardiograph abnormalities in intracerebral hemorrhage. *J Clin Neurosci*. 2015;22:1959-1962.
61. Gregory T. Cardiovascular complications of brain injury. *Contin Educ Anaesth Crit Care Pain*. 2012;12:67-71.
62. Aslam AF, Aslam AK, Vasavada BC, Khan IA. Hypothermia: evaluation, electrocardiographic manifestations, and management. *Am J Med*. 2006;119:297-301.
63. Douglas PS, Carmichael KA, Pavlsky PM. Extreme hypercalcemia and electrocardiographic changes. *Am J Cardiol*. 1984;54:674-675.
64. Sridharan MR, Horan LG. Electrocardiographic J wave of hypercalcemia. *Am J Cardiol*. 1984;54:672-673.
65. Gussak I, Bjerregaard P, Egan TM, et al. ECG phenomenon called the J wave: history, pathophysiology, and clinical significance. *J Electrocardiol*. 1995;28:49-58.
66. Glusman A, Hasan K, Roquin N. Contraindication to thrombolytic therapy in accidental hypothermia simulating acute myocardial infarction. *Int J Cardiol*. 1990;28:269-272.
67. Graham CA, McNaughton GW, Wyatt JP. The electrocardiogram in hypothermia. *Wilderness Environ Med*. 2001;12:232-235.
68. Edelman ER, Joynt K. J waves of Osborn revisited. *J Am Coll Cardiol*. 2010;55:2287.
69. Frangieh AH, Obeid S, Ghadri JR, et al. ECG criteria to differentiate between takotsubo (stress) cardiomyopathy and myocardial infarction. *J Am Heart Assoc*. 2016 Jun 13;5(6).
70. Templin C, Ghadri JR, Diekmann J, et al. Clinical features and outcomes of takotsubo (stress) cardiomyopathy. *N Engl J Med*. 2015;373:929-938.
71. Kindermann I, Barth C, Mahfoud F, et al. Update on myocarditis. *J Am Coll Cardiol*. 2012;59:779-792.
72. Sagar S, Liu PP, Cooper LT Jr. Myocarditis. *Lancet*. 2012;379:738-747.
73. Xu B, Michael Jelinek V, Hare JL, et al. Recurrent myocarditis—an important mimic of ischaemic myocardial infarction. *Heart Lung Circ*. 2013;22:517-522.
74. Slavich M, Patel RS. Coronary artery spasm: current knowledge and residual uncertainties. *Int J Cardiol Heart Vasc*. 2016;10:47-53.

CHAPTER TEN

ACS Mimics Part II: Non-ACS Causes of ST-Segment Depression and T-Wave Abnormalities

AMANDEEP SINGH

KEY FACTS

- Minor ST-T wave changes can signify myocardial ischemia/infarction or other important pathology.
- ST-segment depression is commonly seen with myocardial ischemia/infarction, digitalis effect, hypokalemia, intraventricular conduction disturbances, ventricular hypertrophy with strain, preexcitation, bundle-branch block, and ventricular rhythms.
- Diffuse ST-segment depression should generate consideration of diffuse myocardial ischemia, severe hypokalemia, or digitalis effect.
- Tall T waves are seen during the earliest stages of acute MI or with hyperkalemia.
- "Cerebral T waves," associated with central nervous system events or increased intracranial pressure, are deep, wide, and symmetrically inverted.
- T-wave inversions in both the anterior and inferior leads are suggestive of acute pulmonary embolism.
- Biphasic T waves that are initially positive and terminally negative can be seen with Wellens syndrome, pseudo-Wellens syndrome, benign T-wave inversion, and normal ST-T wave variation.

The ECG findings of ST-segment depression or T-wave abnormalities are commonly encountered in the emergency department. Heightened awareness of the various causes for these abnormalities and recognition of characteristic electrocardiographic patterns will allow the clinician to rapidly distinguish life-threatening disorders from benign pathologies.

ST-SEGMENT DEPRESSION

ST-segment deviation is measured at the end of the QRS complex (ie, the J point). There is debate about whether to reference this against the TP baseline or the end of the PR segment (ie, PQ junction), but either is acceptable.[1,2] The magnitude of ST-segment depression in relationship to the QRS complex amplitude, the morphology of the depressed ST segment (ie, upsloping, horizontal, downsloping), the focality of the ST-segment depression, and the reciprocality (ie, *reciprocal* to ST-segment elevation in anatomically opposite leads) can assist the provider in its correct interpretation. Common causes of ST-segment depression are listed in Table 10.1.

Physiologic J-Junctional Depression with Sinus Rhythm

During sinus rhythm, the normally inverted atrial repolarization wave (Ta wave) is masked by the QRS depolarization.[3] With tachycardia, subtle (<1 mm), upwardly coving ST-segment depression due to the Ta wave can be identified on the ECG. Notably, the PR segment is slightly depressed and has a slight downward cove to its shape. In this situation, the ST segment appears depressed relative to the TP segment, but not relative to the PR segment (Figure 10.1).

TABLE 10.1. Common causes of ST-segment depression.
Digitalis effect
Electrolyte and metabolic factors (eg, hypokalemia)
Myocardial ischemia/infarction
Physiologic J-junctional depression with sinus rhythm

Secondary ST-T wave repolarization abnormality
    Intraventricular conduction disturbance
    Preexcitation
    Ventricular hypertrophy, strain pattern
    Wide QRS-complex rhythm

Other: mitral valve prolapse, aortic dissection, pulmonary embolism, CNS event/increased ICP, hypothermia

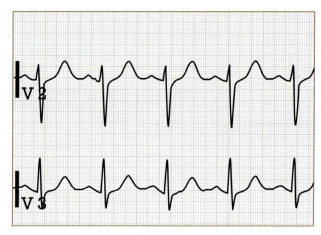

FIGURE 10.1. Physiologic J-junctional ST-segment depression. Note the upsloping ST-segment depression (usually 1 mm or less) associated with the downsloping PR segment and rapid heart rate of 145 beats/min.

Secondary ST-T Wave Repolarization Abnormality

Whereas primary ST-T wave repolarization abnormalities are a result of pathologic processes that affect ventricular repolarization in the presence of normal ventricular depolarization, secondary ST-T wave repolarization abnormalities are a result of an abnormal sequence to ventricular depolarization (eg, due to intraventricular conduction disturbance, ventricular hypertrophy with a strain pattern, preexcitation, or wide QRS-complex rhythms).[4] Secondary ST-T wave repolarization abnormalities share the following features:

- the morphology to the ST-segment depression is downsloping,
- the ST segment and T wave deviate together in the direction opposite (ie, discordant) to the corresponding QRS complex,
- there is asymmetry to the inverted T wave (slow downstroke followed by steep upstroke that often slightly overshoots the isoelectric baseline), and
- the ST-segment and T-wave abnormalities are generally static (ie, they do not change over the course of several hours, days, or weeks).

Ventricular hypertrophy is a compensatory mechanism in response to either pressure or volume overload. In the setting of left ventricular hypertrophy (LVH) primarily due to pressure overload (eg, systemic hypertension, aortic stenosis, coarctation of the aorta, or hypertrophic cardiomyopathy), secondary ST-T wave repolarization abnormalities have been described as a strain pattern.[5] With LVH primarily due to volume overload (eg, mitral regurgitation, aortic regurgitation, ventricular septal defect, peripheral arteriovenous shunt, anemia, or thyrotoxicosis), the increased voltages typical of LVH are present; however secondary ST-T wave repolarization abnormalities (ie, strain pattern) are not seen.[5] In LVH with strain, ST-segment depression, inverted asymmetrical T waves, and terminal T-wave overshoot (terminal positivity) are most prominent in leads with large R-wave voltage (typically left-sided leads—I, aVL, V_4 to V_5). Leads with deep S-wave voltage (typically right-sided leads—V_1 to V_2) will have some degree of ST-segment elevation with an upright T wave (Figure 10.2). In right ventricular hypertrophy with strain, T-wave inversion with

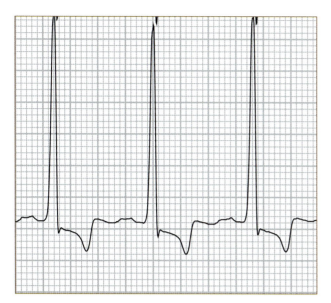

FIGURE 10.2. Left ventricular hypertrophy with strain. Note the depressed ST segment at the J point, with downsloping ST-segment depression into an inverted asymmetrical T wave. This slight positivity at the end of the T wave is termed terminal T-wave overshoot.

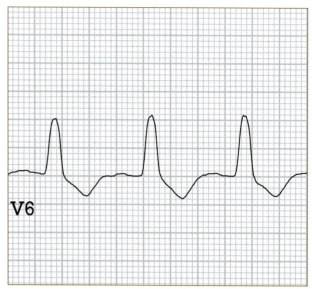

FIGURE 10.3. Left bundle-branch block with ST-T wave repolarization abnormality. Note the ST segment and T wave are discordant to the QRS vector.

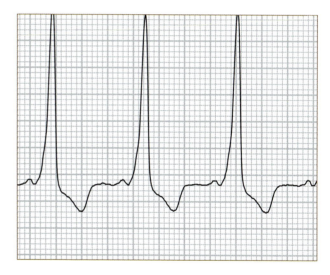

FIGURE 10.4. Preexcitation/Wolff-Parkinson-White syndrome. There is evidence of shortening to the PR segment, a delta wave at the onset of the QRS complex, and widening to the QRS complex. Secondary ST-T wave repolarization abnormalities are present with Wolff-Parkinson-White syndrome.

or without ST-segment depression can be seen in leads with abnormal R-wave voltage (typically V_1 to V_3). The degree of ST-segment depression and T-wave inversions is proportional to the amplitude or depth of the corresponding QRS complex—this sometimes gives the appearance that these ST-T wave repolarization abnormalities change over time.[6]

The electrocardiographic findings associated with intraventricular conduction disturbances[7] are discussed in Chapter 2. An example of the secondary ST-T wave repolarization abnormality seen with left bundle-branch block is shown in Figure 10.3.

Preexcitation (eg, Wolff-Parkinson-White syndrome)[8] can also cause a secondary ST-T wave repolarization abnormality (Figure 10.4) and is discussed further in Chapter 12.

Wide QRS-complex rhythms with secondary ST-T wave repolarization abnormalities include any supraventricular rhythm with aberrant condition, ventricular tachycardia, severe hyperkalemia, and overdoses involving medications that poison the sodium channels within the heart (eg, sodium channel blockers, digitalis).[9-11]

Digitalis Effect

At therapeutic levels, digitalis produces distinctive electrocardiographic changes, including mild PR prolongation, characteristic downsloping ST-segment depression, flattened, inverted, or positive biphasic T waves, prominent U waves, and shortening of the QT interval.[12,13] The morphology of the ST-segment/T wave has been described as "slurred," "sagging," or "scooped" and has been likened in appearance to the mustache of the famous Spanish surrealist artist Salvador Dali. The ST-segment changes are most often appreciated in the inferior and lateral leads. More on this is found in Chapter 17.

Electrolyte and Metabolic Factors

The electrocardiographic findings of hypokalemia are similar to those of digitalis effect (ie, diffuse, sagging ST-segment depression; flattened, inverted, or positive biphasic T waves; prominent U waves), except digitalis shortens the QT duration while hypokalemia prolongs the QT duration or more precisely the QU duration.[14,15] These findings can mimic diffuse subendocardial ischemia.[16] Similar to digitalis toxicity, severe hypokalemia can produce supraventricular rhythms with or without atrioventricular (AV) block or ventricular rhythms. Focal reciprocal ST-segment depression (ie, reciprocal to ST-segment elevation in anatomically opposite leads) has been noted in cases of hyperkalemia,[17,18] hypocalcemia,[19,20] and hypercalcemia.[21,22] Additionally, ST-segment depression or T-wave inversion can be seen with metabolic conditions resulting in hypothermia[23,24] or hypoglycemia[25] or with hyperventilation.[26,27] In general, the electrocardiographic findings in all of these conditions fluctuate with the severity of electrolyte, glucose, or respiratory abnormality. More on this in Chapter 15.

Other Conditions Associated with ST-Segment Depression

An assortment of other conditions can be associated with focal, focal reciprocal, or diffuse ST-segment depression. Focal ST-segment depression can be seen in mitral valve prolapse. The typical electrocardiographic findings of mitral valve prolapse include T-wave inversion with or without ST-segment depression in leads II, III, and aVF and occasionally extending to include lead I, aVL, V_5, and V_6, intraventricular conduction disturbances, and prolongation of the QT interval.[28,29] Additionally, notching or slurring at the J point has been reported to occur with greater frequency in patients with mitral valve prolapse.[30,31] Rarely, mitral valve prolapse can manifest as focal ST-segment elevation or diffuse subendocardial ischemia, although the practitioner should use extreme caution before attributing the finding to this diagnosis.[32,33] Focal reciprocal ST-segment depression can be seen with coronary vasospasm, coronary artery dissection, persistent ST-segment elevation after MI pattern, and rarely with acute localized pericarditis. Focal reciprocal ST-segment changes can also be seen with aortic dissection, pulmonary embolism, central nervous system (CNS) events or increased intracranial pressure (ICP), and hypothermia; however, all of these conditions can manifest an electrocardiographic pattern of diffuse subendocardial ischemia as well.

T-WAVE ABNORMALITIES

T-wave abnormalities commonly encountered on an ECG include the finding of nonspecific ST-T wave changes; tall T waves; flattened, inverted, or biphasic T waves; and T-wave notching.

Nonspecific ST-T Wave Changes

Nonspecific ST-T wave changes refer to the fact that the specificity of diagnosis resulting in the ST-T wave abnormalities can often be provided once the clinical circumstances in which the ECG was obtained are known.[34] Nonspecific ST-T wave changes have traditionally included minor ST-segment depression (Table 10.1) or elevation and flattened (Table 10.2), inverted (Table 10.3), or biphasic (Table 10.4) T waves. It is important to remember that in the

TABLE 10.2. Common causes of T-wave flattening.
Conditions resulting in low ECG voltage
Conditions resulting in nonspecific ST-T wave change
Myocardial ischemia/infarction
Pseudonormalization of the T wave

appropriate clinical setting, nonspecific ST-T wave changes can signify subtle myocardial ischemia/infarction or other important pathology.

Tall T Waves

Tall T waves are most commonly defined as those that are 5 mm or more in amplitude in the limb leads or 10 mm or more in amplitude in the precordial leads.[35] The most common causes of tall T waves are listed in Table 10.5. Tall T waves associated with myocardial ischemia/infarction include hyperacute T waves, de Winter T waves, and posterior reperfusion T waves (ie, Wellens pattern of the posterior wall).[36-39] In contrast to the broad-based, slightly asymmetric, and somewhat peaked T waves typically identified as the hyperacute T waves of MI, the tall T waves associated with hyperkalemia are characteristically narrow-based, symmetrical, and sharply peaked (Figures 10.5, 10.6).[40] Early repolarization can produce narrow- or wide-based, asymmetric, peaked, concordant T waves of large amplitude. These changes generally accompany other electrocardiographic signs of early repolarization, including widespread concave-up ST-segment elevation (most prominent in V_2 through V_5) and notching or slurring at the J point (fishhook morphology, best seen in lead V_4), and are absent reciprocal ST-segment depression (except in aVR).[41] Secondary ST-T wave repolarization abnormalities from left bundle-branch block[7] or LVH with strain,[5]

TABLE 10.3. Common causes of T-wave inversions.

Cardiac disease
    Cardiac memory
    Mitral valve prolapse
    Myocardial ischemia/infarction
    Myocarditis
    Pericarditis, subacute (stage III)

CNS event/increased ICP

Drugs: digitalis, sodium channel blockers (eg, tricyclic antidepressants)

Electrolyte and metabolic factors (eg, hypokalemia)

Normal variants

Pulmonary embolism

Secondary ST-T wave repolarization abnormalities
    Brugada pattern
    Cardiomyopathy (hypertrophic cardiomyopathy, apical-variant hypertrophy cardiomyopathy, arrhythmogenic right ventricular cardiomyopathy, dilated cardiomyopathy)
    Intraventricular conduction disturbance
    Preexcitation
    Ventricular hypertrophy, strain pattern
    Wide QRS complex rhythm

Other: pulmonary hypertension, pneumothorax, pneumonia, gastroenteritis, perforated ulcer, pancreatitis, acute cholecystitis, hypothyroidism

TABLE 10.4. Common causes of biphasic T waves.
Negative biphasic T wave
Physiologic T-wave inversion in athletes
Pseudo-Wellens pattern
ST-T normal variation
Wellens pattern
Positive biphasic T wave
Digitalis effect
Hypokalemia
LVH with strain
Posterior wall MI, acute

can produce tall T waves in the right precordial leads (V_1 to V_2) when deep S waves are present. In LVH without strain (eg, due to chronic volume overload), tall T waves can accompany tall R waves in the left-sided leads (I, aVL, V_4 to V_5). Other causes of tall T waves include:

- preexcitation,
- acute pericarditis,
- CNS event/increased ICP,
- mitral valve prolapse,
- hemopericardium,
- cor pulmonale,
- hyperthyroidism,
- exercise,
- anemia, and
- acidosis.[35]

T-Wave Flattening

The T wave is considered flat when its peak amplitude is between 1 mm and –1 mm in leads I, II, aVL (with an R wave taller than 3 mm), and V_4 to V_6.[4] Common causes of T-wave flattening are listed in Table 10.2. Pseudonormalization of the T wave occurs when an inverted T wave returns either to baseline or to an upright position. In the setting of angina, a symmetrically inverted or negative biphasic T wave can represent subcritical stenosis of a coronary artery (ie, Wellens pattern). A flattened or upright T wave in this setting is highly suggestive of acute coronary occlusion.[42,43] Other causes of T-wave flattening are conditions resulting in nonspecific ST-T wave changes (eg, hypokalemia) or low ECG voltage (eg, pericardial effusion, hypothyroidism).

T-Wave Inversions

T-wave inversions are graded according to their depth, symmetry, and location. Typical T-wave inversions are –1 mm to –5 mm in depth, deep T-wave inversions are –5 mm to –10 mm in depth, and giant T-wave inversions are greater than –10 mm

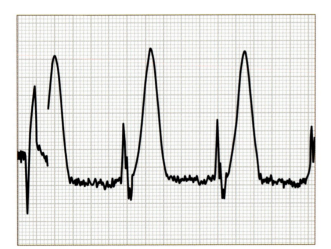

FIGURE 10.5. Hyperacute T wave. Note the broad base and somewhat peaked tall T waves.

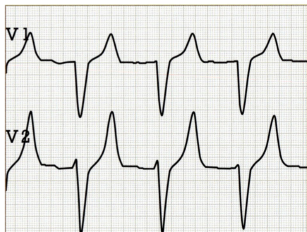

FIGURE 10.6. Hyperkalemia. Note the narrow based, symmetrical, sharply peaked tall T waves.

TABLE 10.5. Common causes of tall T waves.
Early repolarization
Hyperkalemia
Left bundle-branch block
LVH (with or without strain)
Myocardial ischemia/infarction

in depth.[4] T wave inversion symmetry occurs when the downstroke to the T-wave is a mirror image of the up-stroke. Global T-wave inversion is noted when there is diffuse T-wave inversion (or flattening in some leads) in all leads except lead aVR. Common causes of T-wave inversion are listed in Table 10.3.

NORMAL VARIANTS. In adults, the normal T wave is inverted in lead aVR; upright or inverted in leads aVF, aVL, III, and V_1 to V_2; and upright in leads I and II and in chest leads V_3 though V_6.[4] There are several normal variant electrocardiographic patterns that have characteristic ST-T wave changes with prominent T-wave inversions. The juvenile T-wave pattern is commonly seen in pediatric patients, is occasionally seen in young adults, and can be identified by asymmetrical T-wave inversions in leads V_1 through V_3.[4] Physiologic T-wave inversion in athletes is seen in healthy athletes, most commonly in black male athletes. It is characterized by dome-shaped, convex ST-segment elevation with T-wave inversion or negative biphasic T waves in leads V_1 through V_4.[44,45] ST-T normal variant has similar findings predominately in leads V_3 through V_6, sometimes extending to leads II, III, and aVF.[46]

CARDIAC DISEASE. Multiple nonischemic cardiac conditions can manifest as T-wave inversions, including subacute pericarditis, myocarditis, mitral valve prolapse, and cardiac memory. Stage III pericarditis (typically occurring several weeks after stage I pericarditis) is characterized by diffuse symmetrical T-wave inversions, without ST- or PR-segment deviation[47] (Figure 10.7). In contrast to pericarditis, the ECG does not have a major role in the diagnosis

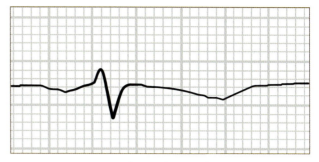

FIGURE 10.7. Pericarditis, subacute (stage III). Subacute pericarditis is characterized by T-wave inversions that can sometimes be difficult to distinguish from acute cardiac ischemia.

of myocarditis. Findings of myocarditis include nonspecific ST-T wave changes, T-wave inversions, intraventricular conduction disturbance, and prolongation of the QT interval.[48] Mitral valve prolapse manifests as T-wave inversions with or without ST-segment depression in the inferolateral leads.[28,29] Finally, the poorly understood phenomenon of cardiac memory can produce symmetrical T-wave inversions in the anterior leads mimicking Wellens pattern.[49,50] Cardiac memory can be seen following tachycardia (ie, posttachycardia T-wave pattern), electrical cardioversion or defibrillation, pacemaker device placement, electroshock therapy, or following intermittent episodes of left bundle-branch block or preexcitation.

SECONDARY ST-T WAVE REPOLARIZATION ABNORMALITIES. Secondary ST-T wave repolarization abnormalities accompany cases of intraventricular conduction disturbance, ventricular hypertrophy with strain, preexcitation, and wide QRS-complex rhythms. Repolarization abnormalities are also seen with Brugada syndrome and several cardiomyopathies. The electrocardiographic findings of Brugada syndrome are mainly localized to leads V_1 through V_3 and include initial ST-segment elevation of 2 mm or more, either slowly descending and concave in morphology terminating in a symmetrically inverted T wave or with "saddleback" morphology terminating in a positive or flat T wave.[51] T-wave changes can be found in:

- hypertrophic cardiomyopathy (ST-T wave repolarization abnormalities consistent with LVH with strain),
- apical-variant hypertrophic cardiomyopathy (deep or giant T-wave inversions in the precordial leads),
- dilated cardiomyopathy (ST-T wave repolarization abnormalities consistent with an incomplete or complete intraventricular conduction disturbance or ventricular hypertrophy with strain),
- arrhythmogenic right ventricular cardiomyopathy (T-wave inversions in V_1 through V_3 in the absence of juvenile T-wave inversion and right bundle-branch block; epsilon wave might be present, mild QRS widening of more than 110 milliseconds),
- peripartum cardiomyopathy (precordial T-wave inversion or flattening), and
- stress-induced cardiomyopathy (global or precordial, deep or giant T-wave inversion seen during the recovery phase following an episode of ST-segment elevation).[52]

DRUGS—DIGITALIS, SODIUM CHANNEL BLOCKERS. Digitalis use can result in characteristic downsloping ST-segment depression and T-wave inversion that is best appreciated in the inferolateral leads[7,8] (Figure 10.8). Sodium channel blocker medications when taken as an overdose can produce wide QRS complex tachycardias with secondary ST-T wave repolarization abnormalities.[10,11] More on this is found in Chapter 17.

ELECTROLYTE AND METABOLIC FACTORS. T-wave inversions can be seen with disorders resulting in depletion of the serum concentration of potassium, calcium, or magnesium or with disorders that result in hypoglycemia or hyperventilation. More on this is found in Chapter 15.

CENTRAL NERVOUS SYSTEM EVENTS AND INCREASED INTRACRANIAL PRESSURE. The term *cerebral T waves* is used to describe widespread, broad-based, deeply inverted T waves (deep or giant

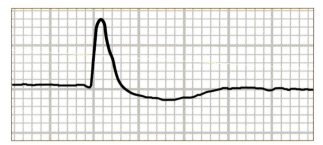

FIGURE 10.8. Digitalis effect. Note the characteristic "sagging" downsloped ST-segment depression.

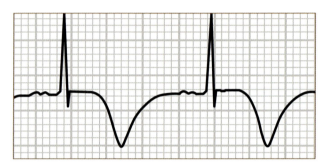

FIGURE 10.9. Central nervous system event/increased ICP. T-wave inversions due to CNS event/increased ICP are widespread, broad-based, and deeply inverted (deep or giant T waves) with a prolonged QT interval.

T waves) associated with CNS events and increased ICP[53] (Figure 10.9). These findings are accompanied by prolongation of the QT interval. Less commonly, tall T waves, prominent J waves, prominent U waves, focal ST-segment elevation with reciprocal ST-segment depression, or diffuse subendocardial ischemia patterns can be seen with intracranial pathology.[54] More on this is found in Chapter 16.

PULMONARY EMBOLISM. T-wave inversions associated with pulmonary embolism are most often seen in leads V_1 through V_4[55] (Figure 10.10). When combined with T-wave inversion in lead III (occasionally as part of the $S_1Q_3T_3$ pattern), the specificity for the diagnosis of pulmonary embolism is increased.[56] Additional electrocardiographic findings in pulmonary embolism can include sinus tachycardia, right axis deviation, right atrial enlargement, incomplete or complete right bundle-branch block, a Qr pattern in V_1, focal ST-segment elevation with reciprocal ST-segment depression, and diffuse subendocardial ischemia. More on this is found in Chapter 16.

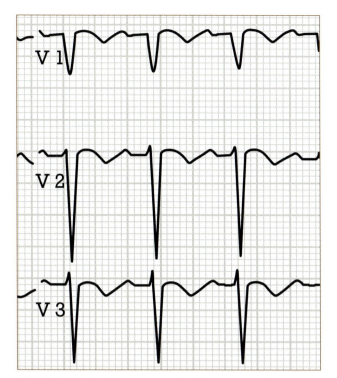

FIGURE 10.10. Pulmonary embolism. T-wave inversions associated with pulmonary embolism are most often seen in leads V_1 through V_4. When combined with T-wave inversion in lead III (occasionally as part of the $S_1Q_3T_3$ pattern), the diagnosis of pulmonary embolism becomes more likely.

BIPHASIC T WAVES

Biphasic T waves have both a positive and negative component to the T-wave complex and are classified based on the terminal component (Table 10.4). Whereas, *negative biphasic T waves* have an initial positive component followed by a negative component, *positive biphasic T waves* are identified by an initial negative component followed by a positive component. Common causes of negative biphasic T waves include Wellens syndrome (negative biphasic T waves in V_2 to V_3, underlying critical stenosis of the left anterior descending coronary artery), pseudo-Wellens syndrome (negative biphasic T waves in V_2 to V_3, occurring in the setting of nonobstructive coronary artery disease),[57-59] ST-T normal variation (negative biphasic T wave in V_3 through V_6, normal variant pattern),[44] and physiologic T-wave inversion in athletes (negative biphasic T wave in V_1 through V_4, normal variant pattern).[45,46] Common causes of positive biphasic T waves include moderate to severe hypokalemia, LVH with strain (due to slight terminal overshoot of the T wave in leads with large R-wave voltage), digitalis effect (positive biphasic T waves in leads with large R-wave voltage), and acute posterior wall MI (the T wave in leads V_1 through V_3 could be positive, negative, or positive biphasic in the setting of acute posterior wall MI).[60]

T-WAVE NOTCHING

A notch or split to the T wave resulting in two separate peaks has been termed bifid T waves (Table 10.6). Commonly, a superimposed P wave from prolonged first-degree AV block, nonconducted atrial premature contraction, or junctional rhythm with retrograde atrial conduction, or a prominent U wave from severe hypokalemia or severe hypocalcaemia can give the appearance of a bifid T wave.[61,62] Bifid T waves can be seen in pediatric patients as a normal variant, typically in leads V_2 and V_3,[63] with congenital or acquired causes of prolonged QT interval,[64,65] and with medications that block cardiac potassium channels.[66] Additionally, many of the etiologies that cause T-wave inversion or flattening can also cause T-wave notching.[67] A bifid or notched U wave can give the appearance of a double notch to the T wave.[68,69]

TABLE 10.6. Common causes of T-wave notching.

Drugs: potassium channel blockers (eg, quinidine)
Hypocalcemia
Hypokalemia
Junctional rhythm with retrograde atrial conduction
Nonconducted atrial premature contraction
Pediatric patients, normal finding
Prolonged first-degree AV block
Prolonged QT interval

REFERENCES

1. Wang K, Asinger RW, Marriott HJL. ST-segment elevation in conditions other than acute myocardial infarction. *N Engl J Med*. 2003;349:2128-2135.
2. Wang K, Asinger RW. Conditions associated with ST-segment elevation. *N Engl J Med*. 2004;350:1152-1155.
3. Holmqvist F, Carlson J, Platonov PG. Detailed ECG analysis of atrial repolarization in humans. *Ann Noninvasive Electrocardiol*. 2009;14:13-18.
4. Rautaharju PM, Surawicz B, Gettes LS. AHA/ACCF/HRS Recommendations for the standardization and interpretation of the electrocardiogram. Part IV: The ST segment, T and U waves, and the QT interval. *Circulation*. 2009;119:e241-e250.
5. Hancock EW, Deal BJ, Mirvis DM, et al. AHA/ACCF/HRS Recommendations for the standardization and interpretation of the electrocardiogram. Part V: Electrocardiogram changes associated with cardiac chamber hypertrophy. *Circulation*. 2009;119:e251-e261.
6. Shoenberger JM, Voskanian S, Johnson S, et al. Left ventricular hypertrophy may be transient in the emergency department. *West J Emerg Med*. 2009;10:140-143.
7. Garcia D, Mattu A, Holstege CP, Brady WJ. Intraventricular conduction abnormality—an electrocardiographic algorithm for rapid detection and diagnosis. *Am J Emerg Med*. 2009;27:492-502.
8. Mark DG, Brady WJ, Pines JM. Preexcitation syndromes: Diagnostic consideration in the ED. *Am J Emerg Med*. 2009;27:878-888.
9. Hollowell H, Mattu A, Perron AD, et al. Wide-complex tachycardia: beyond the traditional differential diagnosis of ventricular tachycardia vs supraventricular tachycardia with aberrant conduction. *Am J Emerg Med*. 2005;23:876-889.
10. Garmel GM. Wide complex tachycardias: Understanding this complex condition. Part 1 – Epidemiology and electrophysiology. *West J Emerg Med*. 2008;9:28-39.
11. Garmel GM. Wide complex tachycardias: Understanding this complex condition. Part 2 – Management, miscellaneous causes, and pitfalls. *West J Emerg Med*. 2008;9:97-103.
12. Holstege CP, Eldridge DL, Rowden AK. ECG manifestations – The poisoned patient. *Emerg Med Clin North Am*. 2006;24:159-177.
13. Ma G, Brady WJ, Pollack M, Chan TC. Electrocardiographic manifestations: digitalis toxicity. *J Emerg Med*. 2001;20:145-152.
14. Diercks DB, Shumaik GM, Harrigan RA, et al. Electrocardiographic manifestations: electrolyte abnormalities. *J Emerg Med*. 2004;27:153-160.
15. Webster A, Brady W, Morris F. Recognising signs of danger: ECG changes resulting from an abnormal serum potassium concentration. *Emerg Med J*. 2002;19:74-77.
16. Petrov DB, Sardovski SI, Milanova MH. Severe hypokalemia masquerading myocardial ischemia. *Cardiol Res*. 2012;3:236-238.
17. Wang K. "Pseudoinfarction" pattern due to hyperkalemia. *N Engl J Med*. 2004;351:593.
18. Bellazzini MA, Meyer T. Pseudo-myocardial infarction in diabetic ketoacidosis with hyperkalemia. *J Emerg Med*. 2010;39:e139-e141.
19. Ilveskoski E, Sclarovsky S, Nikus K. Severe hypocalcemia simulating ST-elevation myocardial infarction. *Am J Emerg Med*. 2012;30:256.e3-256.e6.
20. Gomez-Dominguez R, Hidalgo R, Garcia-Rubira JC. Severe hypocalcemia masquerading as acute coronary syndrome. *J Emerg Med*. 2013;45:715-717.
21. Chorin E, Rosso R, Viskin S. Electrocardiographic manifestations of calcium abnormalities. *Ann Noninvasive Electrocardiol*. 2016;21:7-9.
22. Durant E, Singh A. ST elevation due to hypercalcaemia. *Am J Emerg Med*. 2017;35:1033.e3-1033.e6.
23. Doshi HH, Giudici MC. The EKG in hypothermia and hyperthermia. *J Electrocardiol*. 2015;48:203-209.
24. Wang H, Hollingsworth J, Mahler S, Arnold T. Diffuse ST segment depression from hypothermia. *Int J Emerg Med*. 2010;3:451-454.
25. Sanon VP, Sanon S, Kanakia R, et al. Hypoglycemia from a cardiologist's perspective. *Clin Cardiol*. 2014;37:499-504.
26. Furberg C, Linderholm H. Effects of hyperventilation on ECG in patients with circulatory disturbances. *Acta Med Scand*. 1969;185:167-174.
27. Jacobs WF, Battle WE, Ronan JA. False-positive ST-T wave changes secondary to hyperventilation and exercise. A cineangiographic correlation. *Ann Intern Med*. 1974;81:479-482.
28. Meyers DG, Vallone NL, Engel TR. Repolarization abnormalities in mitral valve prolapse. *Am Heart J*. 1987;113:1414-1416.
29. Bhutto ZR, Barron JT, Liebson PR, et al. Electrocardiographic abnormalities in mitral valve prolapse. *Am J Cardiol*. 1992;70:265-266.
30. Alizadeh-Asl A. Reverse delta-wave as a possible sign in electrocardiography to diagnose mitral valve prolapse. *BMC Res Notes*. 2011;4:16.
31. Peighambari MM, Alizadehasal A, Totonchi Z. Electrocardiographic changes in mitral valve prolapse syndrome. *J Cardiovasc Thorac Res*. 2014:6:21-23.
32. Manenti V, Zuily S, Aliot E. Mitral valve prolapse

associated with electrocardiogram abnormalities mimicking acute coronary syndrome. *Arch Cardiovasc Dis.* 2013;106:340-341.
33. Floria M, Materiu M, Afrasanie VA, et al. Mitral valve prolapse mimicking an acute coronary syndrome. *Arch Clin Cases.* 2016;3;64-70.
34. Friedberg CK, Zager A. "Nonspecific" ST and T-wave changes. *Circulation.* 1961;23:655-661.
35. Somers MP, Brady WJ, Perron AD, Mattu A. The prominent T wave: electrocardiographic differential diagnosis. *Am J Emerg Med.* 2002;21:243-251.
36. Genzlinger MA, Eberhardt M. Analyzing prominent T waves and ST-segment abnormalities in acute myocardial infarction. *J Emerg Med.* 2012;43:e81-e85.
37. Zhong-qun Z, Nikus JC, Sclarvosky S. Prominent precordial T waves as a sign of acute anterior myocardial infarction: electrocardiographic and angiographic correlations. *J Electrocardiol.* 2011;44:533-537.
38. Verouden NJ, Koch KT, Peters RJ, et al. Persistent precordial "hyperacute" T waves signify proximal left anterior descending artery occlusion. *Heart.* 2009;95:1701-1706.
39. Driver BE, Shoff GR, Smith SW. Posterior reperfusion T-waves: Wellens' syndrome of the posterior wall. *Emerg Med J.* 2017;34:119-123.
40. Mattu A, Brady WJ, Robinson DA. Electrocardiographic manifestations of hyperkalemia. *Am J Emerg Med.* 2000;18:721-729.
41. Brady WJ, Chan TC. Electrocardiographic manifestations: benign early repolarization. *J Emerg Med.* 1999;17:473-478.
42. Ulucan C, Yavuzgil O, Kayikcioglu M, et al. Pseudonormalization: clinical, electrocardiographic, echocardiographic, and angiographic characteristics. *Anadolu Kardiyol Derg.* 2007;7 suppl 1:175-177.
43. Simon A, Robins LJH, Hooghoudt THE, et al. Pseudonormalisation of the T wave: old wine? *Neth Heart J.* 2007;15:257.259.
44. Papadakis M, Carre F, Kervio G, et al. The prevalence, distribution, and clinical outcomes of electrocardiographic repolarization patterns in male athletes of African/Afro-Caribbean origin. *Eur Heart J.* 2011;32:2304-2313.
45. Drezner JA, Fischbach P, Froelicher V, et al. Normal electrocardiographic findings: recognising physiologic adaptations in athletes. *Br J Sports Med.* 2013:47:125-136.
46. Roukoz H, Wang K. ST elevation and inverted T waves as another normal variant mimicking acute myocardial infarction: the prevalence, age, gender, and racial distributions. *Ann Noninvasive Electrocardiol.* 2011;16:64-69.
47. Imazio M, Gaita F. Diagnosis and treatment of pericarditis. *Heart.* 2015;101:1159-1168.
48. Kindermann I, Barth C, Mahfoud F, et al. Update on myocarditis. *J Am Coll Cardiol.* 2012;59:779-792.
49. Kershaw MA, Rogers FJ. Intermittent left bundle-branch block: an overlooked cause of electrocardiographic changes that mimic high-grade stenosis of the left anterior descending artery. *J Am Osteopath Assoc.* 2014;114:868-873.
50. Oliveira M, Azevedo O, Calvo L, et al. Cardiac memory, an underdiagnosed condition. *Int J Cardiovasc Sci.* 2017;30:359-362.
51. De Luna AB, Brugada J, Baranchuk A, et al. Current electrocardiographic criteria for diagnosis of Brugada pattern: a consensus report. *J Electrocardiol.* 2012;45:433-442.
52. Maron BJ, Towbin JA, Thiene G, et al. Contemporary definitions and classification of the cardiomyopathies. *Circulation.* 2006;113:1807-1816.
53. Catanzaro JN, Meraj PM, Zheng S, et al. Electrocardiographic T-wave changes underlying acute cardiac and cerebral events. *Am J Emerg Med.* 2008;28:716-720.
54. Levis JT. ECG diagnosis: deep T wave inversions associated with intracranial hemorrhage. *Perm J.* 2017;21:16-049.
55. Digby GC, Kukla P, Zhan ZQ, et al. The value of electrocardiographic abnormalities in the prognosis of pulmonary embolism: a consensus paper. *Ann Noninvasive Electrocardiol.* 2015;20:207-223.
56. Witting MD, Mattu A, Rogers R, Halvorson C. Simultaneous T-wave inversions in anterior and inferior leads: an uncommon sign of pulmonary embolism. *J Emerg Med.* 2012;43:228-235.
57. Langston W, Pollack M. Pseudo-Wellens syndrome in a cocaine user. *Am J Emerg Med.* 2006;24:122-129.
58. Batra R, Mishra A, Ng K. Pseudo-Wellens syndrome – A case report. *Kardiol Pol.* 2008;66:340-342.
59. Ferreras ML, Das A, Okwuosa T. Pseudo-Wellens syndrome after heavy marijuana use. *Cleve Clin J Med.* 2017;84:590-591.
60. Brady WJ, Erling B, Pollack M, Chan TC. Electrocardiographic manifestations: acute posterior wall myocardial infarction. *J Emerg Med.* 2001;20:391-401.
61. Aizawa Y, Tanaka T, Fukuda K, Funazaki T. Notch on the T wave. *Intern Med.* 2011;50:1353.
62. Glancy DL, Diwan PM. ECG of the month: ECG in a 30-year-old woman. *J La State Med Soc.* 2015;167:140-141.
63. Calabro MP, Barberia I, La Mazza A, et al. Bifid T waves in leads V_2 and V_3 in children: a normal variant. *Ital J Pediatr.* 2009;35:17.

64. Lehmann MH, Suzuki F, Fromm BS, et al. T-wave "humps" as a potential electrocardiographic marker of the long QT syndrome. *J Am Coll Cardiol*. 1994;24:746-754.
65. Klimusina J, Menafoglio A. A dangerous "notch". *Cardiovasc Med*. 2012;15:208-210.
66. Galeotti L, van Dam PM, Johannesen L, et al. Computer simulation to investigate the causes of T-wave notching. *J Electrocardiol*. 2015;48:927-932.
67. Dressler W, Roesler H, Lackner H. The significance of notched upright T waves. *Br Heart J*. 1951;13:496-502.
68. Ker J. The double U wave – Should the electrocardiogram be interpreted echocardiographically? *Clin Med Insights: Cardiol*. 2010;4:77-83.
69. Ariyarajah V, Khadem A, Spodick DH. Can U waves be "notched"? *Ann Noninvasive Electrocardiol*. 2008;13:426-428.

CHAPTER ELEVEN

Pericarditis, Myocarditis, and Pericardial Effusions

MICHAEL C. BOND AND LEEN ALBLAIHED

KEY POINTS

Acute Pericarditis

- PR-segment depression is the first electrocardiographic change noted in acute pericarditis.
- PR-segment depression by itself is *not pathognomonic* of acute pericarditis. It is nonspecific and unreliable.
- The combination of PR-segment depression with ST-segment elevation is highly specific for acute pericarditis.
- PR-segment elevation in aVR is suggestive of, but *not pathognomonic* of, acute pericarditis. It can be found in the setting of an MI as well.
- ST-segment elevation should be concave upward. ST-segment elevation that is convex upward (tombstone shaped) or horizontal is highly suggestive of cardiac ischemia or acute MI.
- ST-segment elevation should never be present in aVR.
- ST-segment depression can be found in leads aVR and V1. In any other lead, it suggests cardiac ischemia.
- ST-segment elevation in lead III greater than that found in lead II suggests cardiac ischemia.
- Simultaneous ST-segment elevation and T-wave changes suggest ischemia.
- New Q waves are indicative of acute coronary syndrome and will not be seen on the ECGs of patients with pericarditis.

Myocarditis

- Although the ECG has specific findings that can be diagnostic for pericarditis, this is not the case with myocarditis.
- Sinus tachycardia is by far the most common arrhythmia.
- Nonspecific ST-T-wave changes are the most common abnormality noted.
- PR-segment depression is common with myopericarditis.
- Evolving Q waves suggest MI.
- Echocardiography is often needed to differentiate myocarditis from MI when ST-segment elevations and depressions are present.

Pericardial Effusion/Tamponade

- Electrical alternans occurs in the minority of patients with pericardial effusion/tamponade, so its absence should not be used to rule out the diagnosis.
- Low voltage is common but nonspecific for large pericardial effusions.
- The presence of tachycardia plus *new* low voltage on the ECG, compared with a previous ECG, is highly specific for large pericardial effusions.
- Pericardial tamponade is a clinical or echocardiographic diagnosis and should not be ruled in or ruled out based on the ECG.

PERICARDITIS

Approximately 5% of patients presenting to an emergency department with nonischemic chest pain are diagnosed with acute pericarditis.[1] Reaching this diagnosis requires that the physician combine skills in interpreting the ECG with an understanding of the clinical presentation. The common causes of pericarditis are listed in Table 11.1,[2] and its common signs and symptoms are presented in Table 11.2. Most patients with pericarditis have chest pain and ST-segment elevation on their ECGs. The major challenge is to differentiate pericarditis from acute MI because, if an incorrect diagnosis of MI is made, a patient with pericarditis will likely be given thrombolytics or anticoagulants, leading to hemorrhagic pericardial effusion or tamponade.

In addition to the history and physical examination, an echocardiogram can aid in the diagnosis of pericarditis. Pericardial effusion (generally mild) is found in about 60% of patients with pericarditis.[3] Saricam and Saglam showed that echocardiography has a sensitivity of 81% and a specificity of 65.6% in detecting pericardial effusion in patients with pericarditis. They described "the echo probe sign" (pain in the fifth left intercostal space induced by pressure from the echocardiographic probe, analogous to Murphy sign in acute cholecystitis), which had a sensitivity of 90% and a specificity of 86.7% with a positive predictive rate of 88.3% in identifying pericardial effusion.[4]

A sound understanding of the electrocardiographic changes associated with pericarditis is critical to reduce the chance of misdiagnosis. The classic changes associated with pericarditis are diffuse ST-segment elevation and PR-segment depression. Unfortunately, it is uncommon to see them, and PR-segment depression is nonspecific and unreliable. These changes are caused by inflammation of the pericardium, extending to the epicardial layer. Inflammation of the ventricles results in ST-segment elevation, while PR-segment depression represents subepicardial injury to the atrium.[2] Since the pericardium covers most of the heart (a small portion of the left atrium is outside the pericardium), the ST-segment elevation should be diffuse and without reciprocal changes. However, pericarditis can occur in a more localized fashion (eg, after open heart surgery), resulting in ST-segment elevation in only a few leads and, rarely, reciprocal changes. In such localized cases, an echocardiogram is often necessary to definitively distinguish between pericarditis and acute myocardial ischemia/infarction. Echocardiographic clues to pericarditis include absence of wall motion abnormalities (their presence is typical of acute myocardial ischemia/infarction) and sometimes the presence of pericardial effusion. Serial measurements of cardiac enzyme concentrations and serial ECGs are also helpful in distinguishing between these two diagnoses.

Figure 11.1 demonstrates the electrocardiographic areas of interest when evaluating patients for pericarditis: the PR segment, the ST segment, and the TP segment. The TP segment, the isoelectric point on the ECG, is the portion used as the baseline of the ECG and the area of reference when judging the PR and ST segments for elevation or depression.

PR-segment depression is the first electrocardiographic sign of acute pericarditis and is often noted prior to ST-segment elevation.[5] It tends to be greatest in the inferior leads (II, aVF) and lateral precordial leads (V_4 through V_6). PR-segment depression is not seen in leads aVR or V_1. Although PR-segment depression is commonly taught as a classic finding in all types of pericarditis, it is most commonly found in cases of *viral* pericarditis, and its presence is often transient. It has also been seen in takotsubo cardiomyopathy, so it is not specific for pericarditis.[6] PR-segment elevation of more than 0.5 mm in aVR is suggestive of, but not specific for, pericarditis, and it can be seen in patients with MIs, so it should not be relied on for the diagnosis. PR-segment elevation can also be seen in lead V_1.[7] In other leads, it suggests atrial infarction, a relatively rare entity.

The ST-segment elevation should be upwardly concave (analogous to a cup holding water). Additionally, it should not follow any specific arterial distribution (ie, it should be diffuse). Common exceptions occur in patients with postoperative pericarditis and those with pericardial adhesions from previous surgery or

TABLE 11.1. Causes of pericarditis.	
Drugs	**Neoplastic**
Hydralazine	Primary
Methyldopa	Mesothelioma
Penicillin	Sarcoma
Procainamide	Metastatic
Infectious	Breast
Bacterial	Lung
Haemophilus	Lymphoma
Meningococcus	**Rheumatologic**
Pneumococcus	Ankylosis spondylitis
Salmonella	Dermatomyositis
Staphylococcus	Lupus
Syphilis	Polyarteritis nodosa
Tuberculosis	Rheumatoid arthritis
Viral	Sarcoidosis
Coxsackievirus	Scleroderma
Echovirus	Vasculitis
Epstein-Barr virus	**Other**
HIV	Aortic dissection
Mumps	Cardiac surgery
Parasites and fungi	Chest trauma
Amebiasis	Dressler syndrome
Aspergillosis	MI
Blastomycosis	Myxedema
Coccidioidomycosis	Radiation therapy
Echinococcosis	Uremia
Histoplasmosis	**Pregnancy**
Rickettsia	**Idiopathic**

injury. They can have pericarditis localized to specific regions of the heart, resulting in ST-segment elevation limited to fewer leads. If the ST segment plateaus (becomes horizontal) or is convex upward (tombstone shaped), one must consider myocardial ischemia as the cause, as these findings essentially exclude pericarditis.[2] The ST-segment elevation is usually less than 5 mm in amplitude and tends to be

TABLE 11.2. Signs and symptoms of pericarditis.
Signs
Tachycardia
Three-phase pericardial friction rub (rare to hear all three phases)
Symptoms
Chest pain: can be positional (worse supine, better when sitting up) or pleuritic and often is felt along the trapezius ridge
Low-grade fever
Nonproductive cough
Shortness of breath

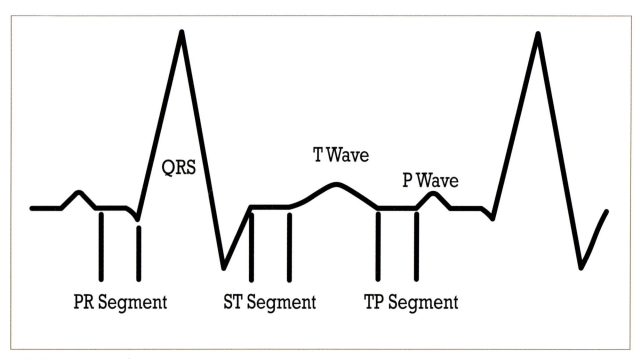

FIGURE 11.1. ECG reference.

greatest in leads II and V_5 because the ST-segment axis is typically leftward/anterior/inferior (over the left ventricle).[8] ST-segment elevation in lead II usually exceeds the ST-segment elevation in lead III. If the reverse is true, cardiac ischemia should be strongly suspected. The ST-segment elevation tends to decrease across the precordial leads .[9] A final clue suggestive of acute pericarditis is based on a comparison of the height of the ST-segment elevation and the height of the T wave in lead V_6. Both should be measured from the isoelectric point, the TP segment, in millimeters. An ST:T ratio of more than 0.25 in V_6 suggests acute pericarditis and has the greatest diagnostic accuracy in differentiating between pericarditis and early repolarization.[8,10]

ST-segment depression is commonly seen in lead aVR, but ST-segment elevation should *never* be found in that lead in patients with acute pericarditis.

ST-segment elevation in lead aVR is worrisome for underlying ischemia. ST-segment depression in any leads other than aVR and V_1, especially aVL, suggests acute myocardial ischemia or infarction until proved otherwise.[11,12] The electrocardiographic findings of acute pericarditis are summarized in Table 11.3.

Spodick described the electrocardiographic changes of pericarditis as occurring in four stages (Table 11.4).[13,14] Untreated patients tend to progress through them. Today, except for patients with purulent pericarditis, it is rare to see patients beyond stage 1.[15] Most patients are seen and treated promptly during that initial stage, so they never progress through the remaining stages. If the electrocardiographic findings of stages 2 through 4 do occur, they will be found in the same leads in which the stage 1 changes occur.

A Spodick sign is seen in approximately 80% of patients with acute pericarditis. It is the downsloping of the TP segment seen most prominently in lead II and the lateral pericardial leads.[9] This sign itself is not specific, but when seen with PR depression, it is highly suggestive of that condition.[16]

T-wave flattening, T-wave inversion, and notched T waves have all been described in patients who evolve through the later stages of pericarditis. These changes *never* occur in pericarditis until after the ST-segment elevation has resolved. Simultaneous T-wave inversion with ST-segment elevation should always be considered cardiac ischemia until proved otherwise.[17] The QRS complex and QT interval can also help differentiate acute MI from pericarditis. Rossello and colleagues observed that acute myocardial ischemia also caused QRS widening and QT interval shortening in leads with ST-segment elevation.[18] This finding was not seen in patients with pericarditis. Chhabra and Spodick speculated that the QRS widening and QT interval might be related to the fact that these patients are often seen earlier in their disease, so the changes could be a hypersympathetic response to the acute MI.[19]

Arrhythmias are uncommon in patients with uncomplicated pericarditis. Sinus tachycardia and supraventricular arrhythmias are uncommon, except in the presence of pericardial effusion or myocarditis. Imazio and associates reported the incidence of new-onset atrial fibrillation (AF) and flutter in patients with acute pericarditis to be only 4%.[20] However, Chhabra and colleagues countered Imazio's findings by stating that pericarditis might

TABLE 11.3. Common electrocardiographic findings in acute pericarditis.	
PR-segment depression	Usually early finding and transient
	Depression >0.8 mm is specific but not sensitive
	Greatest in leads II, aVF, V_4 through V_6
ST-segment elevation	Upwardly concave
	Diffuse
	Does not correspond to any coronary artery distribution
	Usually <5 mm compared with the PR segment and tends to be greatest in leads II and V_5
	An ST/T ratio >0.25 in V_6 suggests acute pericarditis
	Never found in aVR
	ST-segment elevation in lead II is generally greater than the ST-segment elevation in lead III
ST-segment depression	Commonly found in aVR and V_1

ELECTROCARDIOGRAPHY IN EMERGENCY, ACUTE, AND CRITICAL CARE

TABLE 11.4. Stages of pericarditis.	
Stage 1	Diffuse concave-upward ST-segment elevation with concordance of T waves
	PR-segment depression, generally present in the same leads as those with ST-segment elevation; most prominent in *viral* pericarditis
	ST-segment depression in aVR and V_1 is common
	Absence of reciprocal ST-segment depression in any other leads
Stage 2	ST segments return to baseline; T-wave flattening
Stage 3	T-wave inversion, primarily in leads in which prior ST-segment elevation occurred
Stage 4	Gradual resolution of T-wave inversion and return to baseline ECG

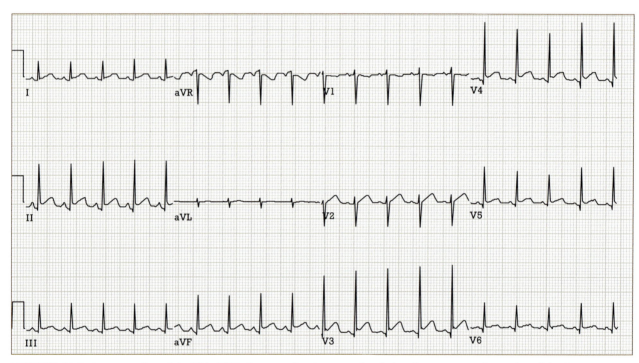

FIGURE 11.2. Acute pericarditis. This ECG shows a classic example of the changes seen in pericarditis. PR segments are depressed and slope downward compared with the TP segment in several leads; there is diffuse concave-upward ST-segment elevation in multiple leads. PR-segment elevation in lead aVR is present and is suggestive, though not diagnostic, of acute pericarditis. The PR- and ST-segment changes are more pronounced in lead II compared with lead III, another finding typical of acute pericarditis. A Spodick sign is also noted, with downward sloping of the TP segment. Reproduced with permission from: Amal Mattu, MD, FACEP.

unmask AF in a patient with prior asymptomatic paroxysmal AF or simply reflect the presence of prior underlying risk factors for AF such as left atrial enlargement or left ventricular systolic or diastolic dysfunction.[21] In patients with pericarditis, the detection of AF is more likely in those of advanced age with hypertension, an enlarged left atrium, and left ventricular dysfunction.[22] Intraventricular conduction delays are most often found in myocarditis and should not occur if the inflammation is limited to the pericardium.[23]

Figure 11.2 shows the typical ECG of a patient with acute pericarditis. Diffuse ST-segment elevation is present in all leads except aVR, aVL, and V_1,

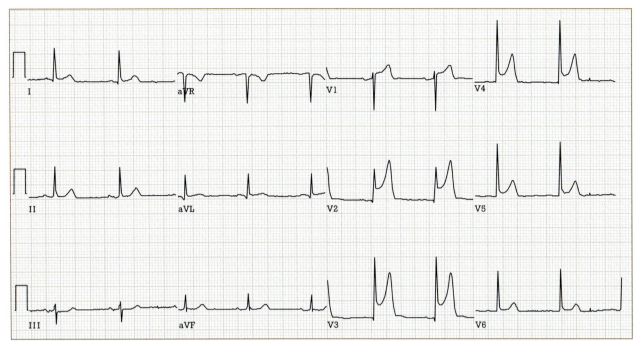

FIGURE 11.3. Localized pericarditis. ST-segment elevation is localized to the anterior leads. The patient developed chest pain two days after cardiac surgery. Echocardiography and serial cardiac biomarker testing were used to confirm the diagnosis. Note the absence of PR-segment depression. PR-segment depression is present primarily in patients with viral causes of acute pericarditis. Reproduced with permission from: Amal Mattu, MD, FACEP.

and the magnitude of the ST-segment elevation in lead II is greater than in lead III. The PR segments slope downward and are depressed compared with the TP segment. PR elevation is present in lead aVR. Spodick sign is also prominent in lead II, with downsloping of the TP segment. Finally, ST-segment depressions are generally found only in lead aVR.

Figure 11.3 demonstrates localized pericarditis in a patient who had recent cardiac surgery. The distinction between pericarditis versus acute myocardial ischemia is more difficult here because of the absence of diffuse ST-segment elevation and PR depression. Echocardiography and cardiac biomarker testing were necessary to confirm the diagnosis of postoperative pericarditis.

Figure 11.4 is the ECG of a patient with an acute anterolateral wall MI that was misdiagnosed as pericarditis. This ECG shows ST-segment elevation in limb leads I and aVL and precordial leads V_2 through V_6. PR-segment elevation is present in lead aVR, *suggestive* of acute pericarditis. The most important finding, however, is the presence of reciprocal ST-segment depression in leads II, III, and aVF. This change alone should rule out acute pericarditis. PR elevation in aVR has been seen on approximately 80% of ECGs from patients with pericarditis, but it can be seen in acute MI and cannot be considered pathognomonic for pericarditis.[7,24]

Figure 11.5 is an ECG from a patient who was misdiagnosed with pericarditis because of the presence of PR-segment depression in multiple leads. Concurrent ST-segment elevation is absent, but ST-segment depression is present in the inferior leads, confirming that this patient has acute cardiac ischemia. Any ST-segment depression in leads other than aVR and V_1 must be diagnosed as acute cardiac ischemia.

The following questions constitute an approach to reading an ECG from a patient suspected of having pericarditis. If any of the following are noted, it should be assumed that the patient has myocardial ischemia until proved otherwise:

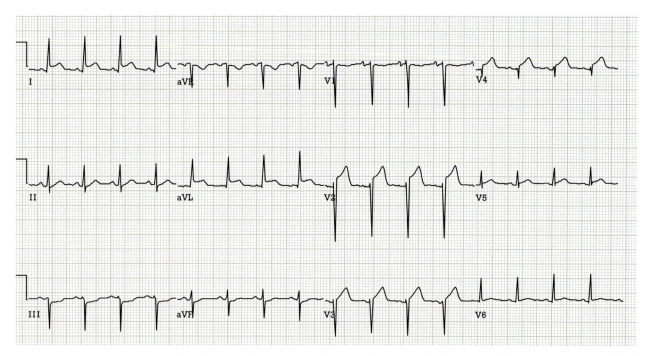

FIGURE 11.4. Acute myocardial infarction. ST-segment elevation is present in the precordial leads (V_2 through V_6) and limb leads I and aVL. The ST-segment depression in leads II, III, and aVF represents reciprocal changes, essentially ruling out acute pericarditis. Note the presence of PR-segment elevation in lead aVR, a finding often misinterpreted as being pathognomonic of acute pericarditis. Reproduced with permission from: Amal Mattu, MD, FACEP.

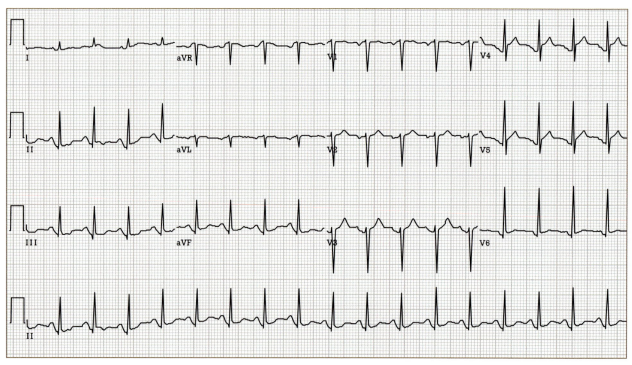

FIGURE 11.5. Acute cardiac ischemia. This ECG was misinterpreted as acute pericarditis because of the presence of PR-segment depression in multiple leads and the presence of PR segment elevation in lead aVR. The physician was misled into thinking that ST-segment elevation was present because he used the PR segment as the baseline. By using the TP segment as the baseline instead, one can easily see that ST-segment elevation is not present. In fact, ST-segment depression is present in leads II, III, and aVF, a finding that excludes the diagnosis of acute pericarditis. Reproduced with permission from: Amal Mattu, MD, FACEP.

- Is any ST-segment depression present (excluding leads V₁ and aVR)?
- Is ST-segment elevation present in lead aVR?
- Is the ST-segment elevation in lead III greater than in lead II?
- Are any of the ST segments convex upward (are they tombstone shaped)?
- Do you see any *new* Q waves?
- Are any T-wave flattening, T-wave inversion, or notched T waves present at the same time as ST-segment elevation?

MYOCARDITIS

Myocarditis is an inflammatory process involving the entire myocardium. The causes of pericarditis and myocarditis are very similar; however, myocarditis is also commonly associated with Kawasaki disease, the peripartum state, and cardiac transplant rejection. In the Myocarditis Treatment Trial,[25] 89% of patients reported having a viral-like prodrome and 50% of patients reported having a recent upper respiratory or gastrointestinal infection. Table 11.5 lists symptoms and signs commonly found in patients with myocarditis.[26]

Patients with myocarditis often present with chest pain and shortness of breath, and they can have an ECG that demonstrates ST-segment elevation or depression, suggesting acute myocardial ischemia.[27] These "pseudoischemia" patterns can be very difficult to differentiate from true myocardial ischemia or infarction on a single ECG. ST- and T-wave changes that occur with myocarditis do not tend to evolve over the course of hours, as they do with acute myocardial ischemia/infarction, so serial electrocardiographic testing to evaluate for developing reciprocal ST-segment depression or developing infarction Q waves is helpful. However, there are no reliable criteria that make a clear distinction between myocarditis and myocardial ischemia on a single initial ECG. Further complicating the distinction between myocarditis and myocardial ischemia is the frequent presence of elevated cardiac biomarkers early on in both conditions. Echocardiography is often needed to make the diagnosis. Diffuse wall motion abnormalities, often with global hypokinesis, are found in myocarditis, whereas regional wall motion abnormalities are found in patients with MI.

It is rare to find a patient with myocarditis who has a completely normal ECG. Although the ECG has specific findings that can be diagnostic for pericarditis, this is not the case with myocarditis. Many types of patterns have been reported in these patients (Table 11.6), but no changes are highly *specific* for myocarditis. Sinus tachycardia is the most common arrhythmia; other tachyarrhythmias are common as well. Diffuse nonspecific T-wave inversions tend to be the most common abnormality.[23,26,28-30] Atrioventricular blocks and ST abnormalities are common during the first month of symptoms, whereas left bundle-branch blocks, AF, and left ventricular hypertrophy are more common in late

TABLE 11.5. Signs and symptoms of myocarditis.

Signs
Cardiac gallop (S₃, S₄, or both)
Displaced point of maximal impulse (due to cardiomegaly)
Hypotension or cardiogenic shock
Rales
Pedal edema
Tachycardia

Symptoms
Chest pain: can be positional, pleuritic, or substernal pressure
Cough
Dizziness
Fever
Myalgia
Shortness of breath (orthopnea, dyspnea on exertion, paroxysmal nocturnal dyspnea)
Syncope
Weakness

TABLE 11.6. Common electrocardiographic findings in myocarditis.
Incomplete AV and intraventricular blocks are most common; complete AV block is less common.
Left and right bundle-branch block
Low voltage QRS complexes can be present.
PR-segment depression (if myopericarditis is present)
Prolonged QT interval
Sinus tachycardia
ST-segment elevation or depression (often misdiagnosed as acute cardiac ischemia/infarction)
Supraventricular or ventricular arrhythmias
T-wave inversions

disease.[31] The electrocardiographic abnormalities of myocarditis are often transient (eg, there should be no residual Q waves) and tend to resolve as the underlying condition resolves.

Figure 11.6 is an ECG from a patient with myocarditis, showing the most common arrhythmia, sinus tachycardia. The patient was a young man who presented with a low-grade fever, tachycardia out of proportion to the fever, and mild evidence of heart failure—the classic presentation of acute myocarditis. The clinical presentation and the ECG prompted additional cardiac evaluation to secure the proper diagnosis.

Figure 11.7 is an ECG from an older patient who presented after a syncopal episode; she has third-degree atrioventricular heart block, which was initially presumed to be caused by coronary artery disease. An echocardiogram demonstrating diffuse hypokinesis and new heart failure prompted an extensive workup, resulting in a final diagnosis of myocarditis induced by Lyme disease.

PERICARDIAL EFFUSION AND CARDIAC TAMPONADE

The diagnosis of pericardial effusion and cardiac tamponade is difficult to make based on physical examination. Pulsus paradoxus is only 77% sensitive in patients with cardiac tamponade, and the Beck

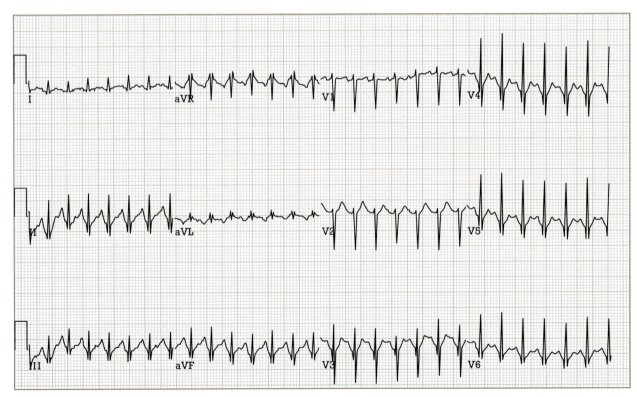

FIGURE 11.6. Acute myocarditis. Extreme sinus tachycardia. Reproduced with permission from: Amal Mattu, MD, FACEP.

triad of hypotension, elevated central venous pressure, and quiet heart sounds is seen so infrequently that its absence does not rule out the diagnosis. Because the physical examination is so unreliable, ancillary testing is usually needed to secure the diagnosis of pericardial effusion or cardiac tamponade. Echocardiography is the diagnostic test of choice to visualize the presence of pericardial effusion and to evaluate for evidence of pericardial tamponade. Tamponade is diagnosed when pericardial fluid pressure causes right atrial or right ventricular collapse, most commonly during diastole. Right heart catheterization can also accurately diagnose pericardial tamponade when the right atrial, right ventricular diastolic, pulmonary arterial diastolic, and pulmonary capillary wedge pressures are nearly equal (within 5 mm Hg). However, right heart catheterization does not diagnose pericardial effusions that are not causing tamponade.[32]

Echocardiography and right heart catheterization are often not available in the emergency department. Consequently, physicians should be familiar with the electrocardiographic findings that suggest large pericardial effusions. The triad of electrical alternans, low QRS voltage, and PR-segment depression is often taught as classic for the diagnosis, but a recent review found that, although the specificity was very good (89% to 100%), the sensitivity of this triad was poor (1% to 17%) in diagnosing pericardial effusions and cardiac tamponade.[33] The primary limitation of this triad is that it assumes that the pericardial effusion is caused by viral pericarditis. Other causes of pericardial effusion are not reliably associated with PR-segment depression. The presence of electrical alternans is also less common than most clinicians believe, with a sensitivity of approximately 30% in patients with pericardial effusions.[34]

The most common abnormalities found in patients with large pericardial effusions are sinus tachycardia and low voltage on the ECG. Both findings are present in well over 50% of patients.[34] The definition of low QRS voltage varies among authors. A sensitive method of defining it is as follows: when the total amplitude of the QRS complexes in leads I, II, and III adds up to less than 15 mm *or* when the total amplitude of the QRS complexes in leads V_1, V_2,

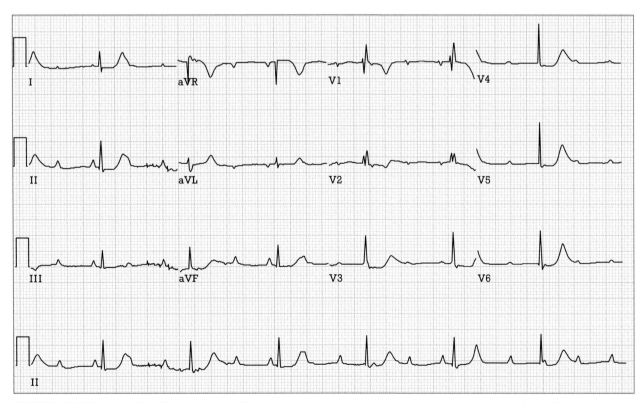

FIGURE 11.7. Myocarditis. Sinus tachycardia is present with a new incomplete right bundle-branch block and complete heart block. The patient was found to have Lyme disease. Reproduced with permission from: Amal Mattu, MD, FACEP.

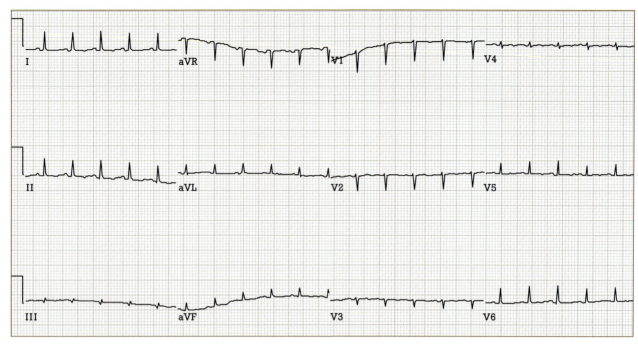

FIGURE 11.8. Large pericardial effusion. The combination of tachycardia plus low voltage (a new finding in this patient) is highly suggestive of the diagnosis. Low voltage in this patient is diagnosed based on the QRS amplitudes in leads V_1 through V_3. Reproduced with permission from: Amal Mattu, MD, FACEP.

and V_3 adds up to less than 30 mm, then low voltage is diagnosed (Figure 11.8). A more specific definition of low voltage requires the QRS complex amplitudes in *each* of the limb leads to be less than 5 mm *or* the QRS complex amplitudes in *each* of the precordial leads to be less than 10 mm. The sensitive definition is often preferred by emergency physicians, including the authors, whereas the specific definition is commonly preferred by cardiologists.

Low voltage is found not only in patients with pericardial effusions but also in those with amyloidosis, sarcoidosis, myxedema, chronic obstructive pulmonary disease, pleural effusion, obesity, anasarca, and pneumothorax and after open heart surgery. As a result, the specificity of low voltage *alone* for large pericardial effusions is low. However, when the low voltage is new compared with recent ECGs and concurrently associated with sinus tachycardia, the specificity for large pericardial effusions is better than 80%.[34]

Electrical alternans is a cyclic beat-to-beat variation in the amplitude or axis of the electrical complexes on the ECG. It can be caused by the heart swinging within the pericardial sac, as seen in patients with pericardial effusion. Numerous other potential causes (eg, MI, cardiomyopathy, supraventricular and ventricular tachycardias, hypothermia, AF, and electrolyte disturbances) have been described as well.[34-39] The most common type of electrical alternans involves the QRS complex (Figure 11.9). Electrical alternans involving the P wave or the T wave is also well described, though it is much less common. Patients with large pericardial effusions can demonstrate *total* electrical alternans, in which cyclic beat-to-beat variations in the P-wave, QRS, and T-wave axes all occur together. Total electrical alternans is more than 90% specific for large pericardial effusions,[34] but it is a rare finding. In patients with large pericardial effusions, the sensitivity of electrical alternans is only 30%. However, when it occurs in combination with low voltage and tachycardia, it is almost pathognomonic for a large pericardial effusion. PR-segment depression can also occur in patients with large pericardial effusions, especially when the effusion is caused by viral pericarditis, malignancy, or connective tissue disorders.[40]

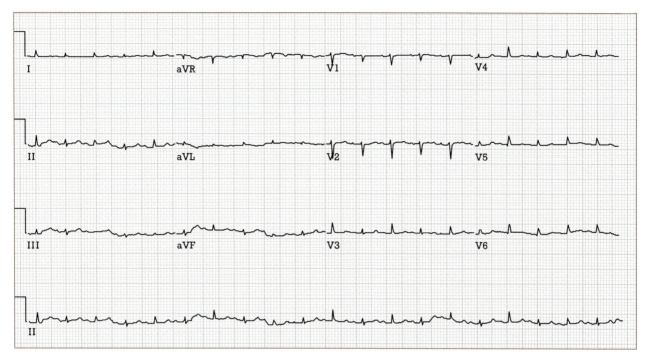

FIGURE 11.9. Large pericardial effusion. The classic triad of sinus tachycardia, low voltage, and electrical alternans (best seen in precordial leads) is present. The patient also had hypotension and echocardiographic evidence of pericardial tamponade. Reproduced with permission from: Amal Mattu, MD, FACEP.

Pericardial tamponade induces no specific electrocardiographic changes other than those already described for pericardial effusion; however, it is common to see tachycardia as the heart tries to compensate for the diminished cardiac output. Table 11.7 summarizes the typical electrocardiographic findings in patients with large pericardial effusions and tamponade. A detailed clinical examination and judicious use of ancillary tests will assist the clinician in making the correct diagnosis.

TABLE 11.7. Electrocardiographic findings in pericardial effusion and tamponade.

Electrical alternans
Low voltage
Nonspecific T-wave abnormalities
PR-segment depression, especially if precipitated by acute pericarditis; can be transient
Sinus tachycardia

REFERENCES

1. LeWinter MM. Clinical practice. Acute pericarditis. *N Engl J Med.* 2014;371(25):2410-2416.
2. Marinella MA. Electrocardiographic manifestations and differential diagnosis of acute pericarditis. *Am Fam Physician.* 1998;57(4):699-704.
3. Adler Y, Charron P, Imazio M, et al. 2015 ESC Guidelines for the diagnosis and management of pericardial diseases: The Task Force for the Diagnosis and Management of Pericardial Diseases of the European Society of Cardiology (ESC): Endorsed by: The European Association for Cardio-Thoracic Surgery (EACTS). *Eur Heart J.* 2015;36(42):2921-2964.
4. Saricam E, Saglam Y. A handy echocardiographic marker in acute pericarditis: echo probe sign. *Am J Emerg Med.* 2016;34(9):1883-1884.
5. Baljepally R, Spodick DH. PR-segment deviation as the initial electrocardiographic response in acute pericarditis. *Am J Cardiol.* 1998;81(12):1505-1506.
6. Extramiana F. ST segment elevation: a common ECG sign for different diseases and different mechanism. *J Electrocardiol.* 2013;46(2):90-91.

7. Pericarditis and myocarditis. In: Smith SW, Zvosec Dl, Sharkey SW, Henry TD, eds. *ECG in Acute MI: An Evidence-Based Manual on Reperfusion Therapy*. Philadelphia, PA: Lippincott Williams & Wilkins; 2002.
8. Imazio M, Gaita F. Diagnosis and treatment of pericarditis. *Heart*. 2015;101(14):1159-1168.
9. Spodick DH. Electrocardiogram in acute pericarditis: distributions of morphologic and axial changes by stages. *Am J Cardiol*. 1974;33(4):470-474.
10. Ginzton LE, Laks MM. The differential diagnosis of acute pericarditis from the normal variant: new electrocardiographic criteria. *Circulation*. 1982;65(5):1004-1009.
11. Bischof JE, Worrall C, Thompson P, et al. ST depression in lead aVL differentiates inferior ST-elevation myocardial infarction from pericarditis. *Am J Emerg Med*. 2016;34(2):149-154.
12. Celik T, Ozturk C, Balta S, et al. The role of combined electrocardiogram criteria in differential diagnosis of acute pericarditis: PR segment and QT interval. *Am J Emerg Med*. 2016;34(7):1309.
13. Spodick DH. Diagnostic electrocardiographic sequences in acute pericarditis: significance of PR segment and PR vector changes. *Circulation*. 1973;48(3):575-580.
14. Spodick DH. Pericardial diseases. In: Braunwald E LP, ed. *Heart Disease*, 6th ed. Philadelphia, PA: Saunders; 2001:1823-1866.
15. Spodick DH. Acute pericarditis: current concepts and practice. *JAMA*. 2003;289(9):1150-1153.
16. Chaubey VK, Chhabra L. Spodick's sign: a helpful electrocardiographic clue to the diagnosis of acute pericarditis. *Perm J*. 2014;18(1):e122.
17. Lee PT, See CK, Chiam PT, Lim ST. Electrocardiographic changes in acute perimyocarditis. *Singapore Med J*. 2015;56(1):e1-3.
18. Rossello X, Wiegerinck RF, Alguersuari J, et al. New electrocardiographic criteria to differentiate acute pericarditis and myocardial infarction. *Am J Med*. 2014;127(3):233-239.
19. Chhabra L, Spodick DH. Electrocardiography in pericarditis and ST-elevation myocardial infarction: timing of observation is critical. *Am J Med*. 2014;127(5):e17.
20. Imazio M, Lazaros G, Picardi E, et al. Incidence and prognostic significance of new onset atrial fibrillation/flutter in acute pericarditis. *Heart*. 2015;101(18):1463-1467.
21. Chhabra L, Bhattad VB, Sareen P, et al. Atrial fibrillation in acute pericarditis: an overblown association. *Heart*. 2015;101(18):1518.
22. Mayosi BM. Pericarditis-associated atrial fibrillation. *Heart*. 2015;101(18):1439-1440.
23. Demangone D. ECG manifestations: noncoronary heart disease. *Emerg Med Clin North Am*. 2006;24(1):113-131.
24. Saricam E, Saglam Y. Potentially missed acute pericarditis: atypical pericarditis. *Am J Emerg Med*. 2016;34(12):2451-2453.
25. Mason JW, O'Connell JB, Herskowitz A, et al. A clinical trial of immunosuppressive therapy for myocarditis. The Myocarditis Treatment Trial Investigators. *N Engl J Med*. 1995;333(5):269-275.
26. Brady WJ, Ferguson JD, Ullman EA, et al. Myocarditis: emergency department recognition and management. *Emerg Med Clin North Am*. 2004;22(4):865-885.
27. Punja M, Mark DG, McCoy JV, et al. Electrocardiographic manifestations of cardiac infectious-inflammatory disorders. *Am J Emerg Med*. 2010;28(3):364-377.
28. Ander D, Heilpern K. Myocarditis. In: Chat T, Brady W, Harrigan R, eds. *ECG in Emergency Medicine and Acute Care*. St Louis, MO: Mosby-Year Book; 2004:204-206.
29. Oakley CM. Myocarditis, pericarditis and other pericardial diseases. *Heart*. 2000;84(4):449-454.
30. Durani Y, Egan M, Baffa J, et al. Pediatric myocarditis: presenting clinical characteristics. *Am J Emerg Med*. 2009;27(8):942-947.
31. Morgera T, Di Lenarda A, Dreas L, et al. Electrocardiography of myocarditis revisited: clinical and prognostic significance of electrocardiographic changes. *Am Heart J*. 1992;124(2):455-467.
32. Scarpinato L. Pericardial effusion and cardiac tamponade diagnostic methods. Where are we headed? *Chest*. 1996;110(2):308-310.
33. Eisenberg MJ, de Romeral LM, Heidenreich PA, et al. The diagnosis of pericardial effusion and cardiac tamponade by 12-lead ECG. A technology assessment. *Chest*. 1996;110(2):318-324.
34. Surawicz B, Knilans T. *Chou's Electrocardiography in Clinical Practice*, 5th ed. Philadelphia, PA: WB Saunders; 2001.
35. Cheng TC. Electrical alternans: an association with coronary artery spasm. *Arch Intern Med*. 1983;143(5):1052-1053.
36. Crosson JE, Dunnigan A. Propranolol induced electrical and mechanical alternans in orthodromic reciprocating tachycardia. *Pacing Clin Electrophysiol*. 1993;16(3 Pt 1):496-500.
37. Konno T, Araki T, Soma R, et al. Electrical and mechanical alternans during percutaneous transluminal coronary angioplasty in a patient with acute myocardial infarction--a case report. *Angiology*. 2004;55(5):569-571.

38. Lau TK, Civitello AB, Hemandez A, Coulter SA. Cardiac tamponade and electrical alternans. *Tex Heart Inst J.* 2002;29(1):66-67.
39. Wasir HS, Mohan JC. Exercise induced QRS, ST, T electrical alternans in a normal person. *Indian Heart J.* 1987;39(1):69-70.
40. Kudo Y, Yamasaki F, Doi T, et al. Clinical significance of low voltage in asymptomatic patients with pericardial effusion free of heart disease. *Chest.* 2003;124(6):2064-2067.

CHAPTER TWELVE

Preexcitation and Accessory Pathway Syndromes

STEPHEN Y. LIANG AND ALI FARZAD

KEY POINTS

- Preexcitation and accessory pathway syndromes result from abnormal connections between atrial and ventricular myocardial tissues, which circumvent usual conduction and predispose patients to development of tachyarrhythmias.
- The most common accessory pathway syndrome is Wolff-Parkinson-White (WPW) syndrome, a congenital condition associated with episodes of supraventricular tachyarrhythmia and the electrocardiographic pattern of preexcitation.
- The classic electrocardiographic pattern of WPW syndrome consists of a short PR interval and a prolonged QRS interval (with characteristic slurring of the QRS complex, also called the delta wave).
- Patients with accessory pathway syndromes are at risk for development of reentrant tachycardia circuits or preexcited tachycardia in the setting of atrial flutter or atrial fibrillation. This can result in extreme tachycardia with heart rates that can approach 250 to 300 beats/min.
- All wide complex, irregular tachycardias in patients with WPW syndrome require special clinical considerations, as pharmacologic atrioventricular nodal blockade (eg, as induced by amiodarone) is contraindicated and can result in ventricular fibrillation.

In the normal heart, electrical impulses generated in the sinoatrial node pass through the atrioventricular (AV) node, where the impulse is slowed before conduction through the His-Purkinje system to the ventricular myocardium. The PR interval represents the time from onset of atrial depolarization to onset of ventricular depolarization and depicts the entirety of the AV conduction system.

Preexcitation refers to activation of the ventricular myocardium by a supraventricular impulse earlier than would occur by the normal pathway through the AV node. This early activation occurs via an additional or accessory pathway that connects the atria and ventricles, bypassing the AV node. Preexcitation typically manifests a short PR interval.

The Wolff-Parkinson-White (WPW) syndrome[1] is the most common accessory pathway syndrome. It consists of the electrocardiographic triad of short PR interval, slightly prolonged QRS complex, and a characteristic slurring of the upstroke of the QRS complex, referred to as the delta wave. Patients with WPW are prone to developing episodic paroxysmal supraventricular tachycardia and, less commonly, atrial fibrillation. Accessory pathways have several possible types of anatomic substrate and can conduct impulses in one or both directions. The direction of conduction affects the appearance of the EGG in sinus rhythm and during tachyarrhythmias.

ANATOMIC SUBSTRATE

Anomalous bundles of conducting tissue that bypass all or part of the normal AV conduction system form the anatomic substrate for preexcitation.[2] Several types of accessory pathways exist. An AV bypass tract, or Kent bundle, is the most common type, directly connecting atrial and ventricular myocardium, circumventing the AV node and the His-Purkinje system altogether. Concurrent activation of the ventricular myocardium via this AV bypass tract as well as via the normal AV conduction pathway creates the characteristic QRS complex, or fusion beat, of the WPW pattern and syndrome (Figure 12.1).

James fibers (intranodal or atrionodal tracts) are associated with the Lown-Ganong-Levine (LGL) syndrome, a rare accessory pathway syndrome. Mahaim fibers have AV node-like properties and connect the atrium (atriofascicular or Brechenmacher tract) to the right ventricle through a Purkinje-like network. All of these pathways are congenital, resulting from incomplete separation of the atria and ventricles.

ASSOCIATED ABNORMALITIES AND EPIDEMIOLOGY

The WPW pattern is present in 0.1% to 0.3% of the general population.[3,4] Men are affected twice as often as women. The incidence of the other types of preexcitation is much lower. Substantially less than 50% of patients with the WPW pattern become symptomatic (reported numbers vary).[5,6]

Although most patients with the WPW pattern have no associated organic heart disease, a variety of conditions is associated with it, including Ebstein anomaly, hypertrophic cardiomyopathy, mitral valve prolapse, tricuspid atresia, endocardial

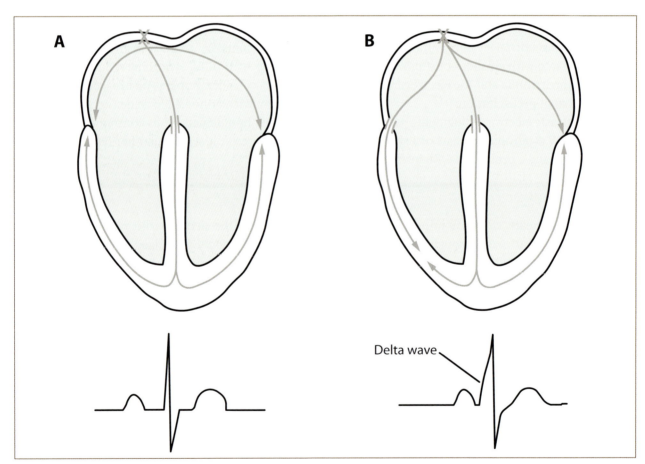

FIGURE 12.1. Relationship between an anatomic Kent bundle and physiologic preexcitation of the ventricular myocardium (top) and the typical ECG changes of ventricular preexcitation (bottom). **A.** Normal conduction. **B.** Abnormal conduction. Adapted with permission from: Wagner GS, Waugh RA, Ramo BW. *Cardiac Arrhythmias*. New York, NY: Churchill Livingstone; 1983:13. Copyright 1983 Churchill Livingstone.

fibroelastosis, rheumatic heart disease, and hyperthyroidism. A familial component is suggested by an increased prevalence among first-degree relatives. With coexistent age-related conditions such as coronary or hypertensive heart disease, the WPW pattern is an unrelated finding.

THE ELECTROCARDIOGRAPHIC PATTERN

The classic electrocardiographic pattern of WPW syndrome (Figure 12.2) consists of four elements:

- a PR interval less than 120 milliseconds with a normal P wave,
- initial slurring of the QRS complex (delta wave),
- a wide QRS complex with a duration of 110 milliseconds or more, and
- discordant ST-segment and T-wave changes.

Because the supraventricular impulse bypasses the AV node (avoiding the associated delay), the onset of ventricular activation occurs earlier than expected and the preexcited PR interval is shortened. In most cases, the PR interval is less than 110 milliseconds.[7] Unless there is coexistent atrial pathology, the P-wave morphology is normal. Direct depolarization of nonspecialized ventricular myocardium (which conducts at a slower rate than the His-Purkinje system) at the site of bypass tract insertion generates an initial slurring of the QRS complex (the delta wave). Delta waves are not seen with non-WPW types of preexcitation in which the accessory pathways terminate in the conducting system or within the ventricular myocardium close to the conducting system.

In the presence of a bypass tract, supraventricular impulses might be conducted only through the AV node, only through the bypass tract (full preexcitation), or simultaneously through both

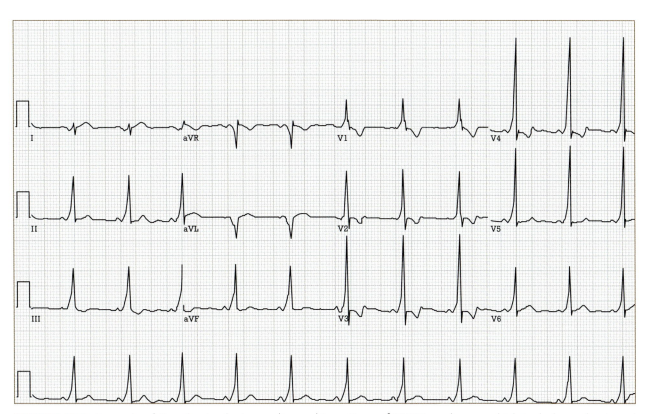

FIGURE 12.2. Example of the classic electrocardiographic pattern of WPW syndrome, which includes a shortened PR interval (<120 milliseconds) with a normal P wave, initial slurring of the QRS complex (delta wave), wide QRS complex with a duration of 110 milliseconds or more, and discordant ST-segment and T-wave abnormalities.

the AV node and bypass tract, causing a variety of fusion complexes. Electrocardiographic findings are determined by the relative timing and direction of impulse flow. With increasing relative contribution of conduction through the bypass tract, the PR interval shortens, the delta wave becomes more prominent, and the QRS complex widens. Conversely, with increasing relative contribution of conduction through the AV node, the PR interval lengthens, the delta wave becomes less prominent, and the QRS complex shortens.[8] However, it is important to remember that the ECG is normal in many patients with WPW syndrome.

Several other factors influence the degree of PR-interval shortening and QRS-interval widening—the site of origin of the atrial impulse, interatrial conduction time, atrial refractoriness, and the conduction properties of both the accessory pathway and the normal pathway (AV node/His-Purkinje system). The autonomic nervous system affects the conduction properties of both pathways. During sinus tachycardia, when sympathetic tone is increased and vagal tone is decreased, preexcitation can be less apparent.

Secondary repolarization abnormalities (ST-segment and T-wave changes) occur in patients with the WPW pattern as a consequence of the altered sequence of ventricular activation. Similar to the repolarization changes of ventricular hypertrophy or bundle-branch block, the direction of the ST segment and T wave is discordant with or in opposition to the direction of the delta wave and the main QRS complex.

RELATED ELECTROCARDIOGRAPHIC PHENOMENA

Concealed Accessory Pathway

Although accessory pathways usually conduct in both directions, most tracts are capable of only retrograde conduction. Because these concealed accessory pathways do not preexcite the ventricles, the ECG during sinus rhythm is normal. Concealed bypass tracts can serve as a conduit in the retrograde direction in an AV reentrant circuit and thus are associated with reentrant arrhythmias.

Lown-Ganong-Levine Syndrome

Lown-Ganong-Levine syndrome is a rare accessory pathway syndrome characterized by a short PR interval (≤120 milliseconds), a normal QRS complex without a delta wave, and paroxysmal tachycardia. Data from electrophysiologic studies have cast doubt on the existence of this syndrome as a distinct entity, revealing that the short PR interval of the LGL syndrome is on the end of the spectrum of normal variants and that most patients with LGL syndrome have another cause for paroxysmal tachycardia, usually AV nodal reentrant tachycardia or a concealed accessory pathway.

Intermittent Preexcitation and Preexcitation Alternans

In most patients with the WPW pattern, electrocardiographic changes appear intermittently. The change from the preexcitation pattern to a normal conduction pattern (and back again) can occur in the same continuous tracing (Figure 12.3). It occurs in the absence of any appreciable change in heart rate and is usually associated with an accessory pathway with a relatively long antegrade refractory period. In preexcitation alternans, the preexcitation pattern alternates with a normal conduction pattern (Figure 12.4).

Concertina Effect

The degree of preexcitation can show a cyclic pattern, with progressive shortening of the PR interval and corresponding widening of the QRS complex over several cycles, followed by a gradual decrease in the degree of preexcitation over several cycles, despite a constant heart rate. The P end of the QRS interval remains constant. This "concertina effect" produces a characteristic electrocardiographic pattern (Figure 12.5).

Type A and Type B WPW Syndrome

A left-sided accessory pathway produces a QRS complex that is mostly positive in lead V_1 (type A), and a right-sided accessory pathway produces a QRS complex that is mostly negative (type B). Type A is more common. This classification scheme is

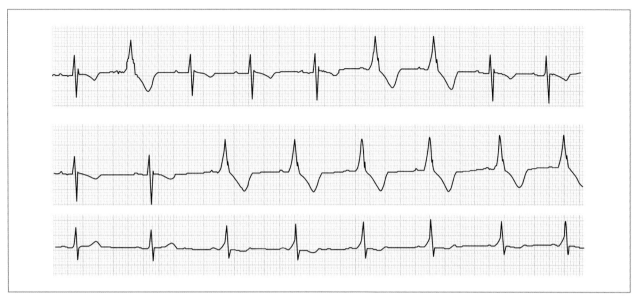

FIGURE 12.3. Intermittent WPW syndrome. The top tracing shows intermittent preexcitation mimicking frequent premature ventricular contractions. The middle tracing shows intermittent preexcitation from same patient simulating accelerated idioventricular rhythm. The bottom tracing was taken simultaneously with tracing B with a different lead reveals a short PR interval with delta wave and confirms intermittent preexcitation. Reproduced with permission from: Wang K, Asinger R, Hodges M. Electrocardiograms of Wolff-Parkinson-White syndrome simulating other conditions. *Am Heart J.* 1996;132:152-155. Copyright 1996 Elsevier Inc.

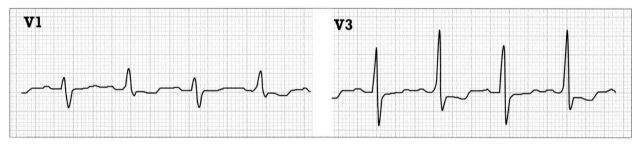

FIGURE 12.4. Preexcitation in alternate beats simulating electrical alternans. Reproduced with permission from: Wang K, Asinger R, Hodges M. Electrocardiograms of Wolff-Parkinson-White syndrome simulating other conditions. *Am Heart J.* 1996;132:152-155. Copyright 1996 Elsevier Inc.

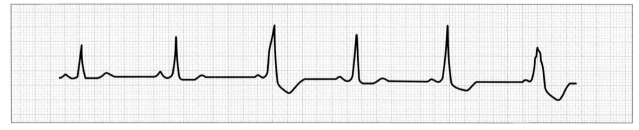

FIGURE 12.5. ECG lead II of a patient with intermittent WPW preexcitation demonstrates a "concertina" effect, in which increasing preexcitation shortens the PR interval and lengthens the QRS complex, with the interval from P to the end of QRS remaining constant. This tracing also is an example of secondary T-wave changes, with the T wave becoming more negative as the QRS duration increases. Of the six consecutive complexes, the first is conducted through the AV node alone and the sixth presumably through the accessory pathway alone (fully preexcited), whereas the second, fourth, fifth, and third complexes show increasing degrees of fusion between the AV nodal and accessory pathway conduction. Reproduced with permission from: Ventricular preexcitation (Wolff-Parkinson White syndrome and its variants). In: Surawicz B, Knilans TK, eds. *Chou's Electrocardiography in Clinical Practice.* 2007; 5e:463. Copyright 2007 Elsevier Inc.

of no significant clinical importance in the emergency setting and is considered outdated by most electrophysiologists.

Pseudoinfarction Pattern and the Diagnosis of MI in the Presence of the WPW Pattern

When the delta wave is negative, it can resemble an abnormal Q wave associated with MI.[9] Negative delta waves in the right precordial leads can create a pseudoinfarction pattern, suggesting anterior MI; a negative delta wave in lead aVL can mimic lateral MI; and negative delta waves in leads II, III, and aVF can resemble inferior MI. An upright delta wave in lead V_1 can look like a posterior MI or right bundle-branch block (Figure 12.6).

Abnormal Q waves of true MI are frequently obscured by the preexcitation pattern. Secondary repolarization abnormalities are common in WPW syndrome and can mimic acute ischemic changes. In patients with the WPW pattern, the ST segment should be either isoelectric or depressed in leads with an upright QRS complex; ST-segment elevation is usually indicative of acute injury (Figure 12.7).

CLINICAL SIGNIFICANCE

Tachyarrhythmias

The most important clinical features of the accessory pathway syndromes are their association with and propensity for tachyarrhythmias. Accessory pathways are capable of rapid conduction and recovery and can, in rare cases, lead to atrial flutter with 1:1 conduction to the ventricles (300 bpm). Atrial fibrillation can be conducted even more rapidly, with possible degeneration into ventricular fibrillation. Standard pharmacologic management of certain tachyarrhythmias administered inappropriately in this setting can have dire consequences. An understanding of the mechanisms of tachyarrhythmias associated with accessory pathways is fundamental to proper management.

Paroxysmal supraventricular tachycardia is the most common rhythm in symptomatic patients with WPW syndrome, occurring in 70% to 80%. Atrioventricular reentrant (or reciprocating) tachycardia (AVRT) and atrioventricular nodal reentrant tachycardia are the two most common forms of paroxysmal supraventricular tachycardia. Atrial fibrillation is less common, being detected in 10% to 30% of patients.[10]

Mechanisms of tachyarrhythmias associated with accessory pathway syndromes can be classified into two groups:

- tachycardias requiring an accessory pathway for initiation and maintenance (eg, AVRT) and
- tachycardias in which the accessory pathway might act only as a "facilitator," providing a rapid route of conduction (eg, atrial fibrillation and atrial flutter).

Tachycardias Requiring an Accessory Pathway for Initiation and Maintenance

The accessory path(s), together with the normal AV conduction system, atrial myocardium, and ventricular myocardium, form a reentrant pathway that produces and sustains the tachycardia. Differences in conduction time and refractoriness between the bypass tract and the normal AV conduction system permit a properly timed premature impulse (premature atrial contraction, premature junctional complex, or premature ventricular contraction) to initiate reentry and establish a circus movement.

Two forms of conduction can occur in this type of tachyarrhythmia: orthodromic AVRT and antidromic AVRT (Figure 12.8). In orthodromic AVRT, anterograde conduction (toward the ventricle) occurs through the normal AV conduction system, and retrograde conduction (toward the atrium) occurs through the accessory pathway. The ventricle is activated via the normal pathway, and there is no degree of ventricular preexcitation; the QRS complex is narrow, and a delta wave is absent (Figure 12.9). However, in the presence of a preexisting or rate-related bundle-branch block, the QRS complex can be wide in orthodromic AVRT. The tachycardia is rapid (150–250 bpm). P waves can be found within the ST-T-wave segment.

Less commonly, the anterograde limb is the accessory pathway and the retrograde limb is the normal AV conduction system (antidromic AVRT); the QRS complex is wide (Figure 12.10). Retrograde P waves are usually obscured by the wide preexcited QRS complex and ST-T-wave segment but sometimes can be identified within the ST-T-wave segment.

Tachycardias in Which the Accessory Pathway Facilitates Rapid Transmission

In some types of tachycardias associated with accessory pathway syndromes, the bypass tract is

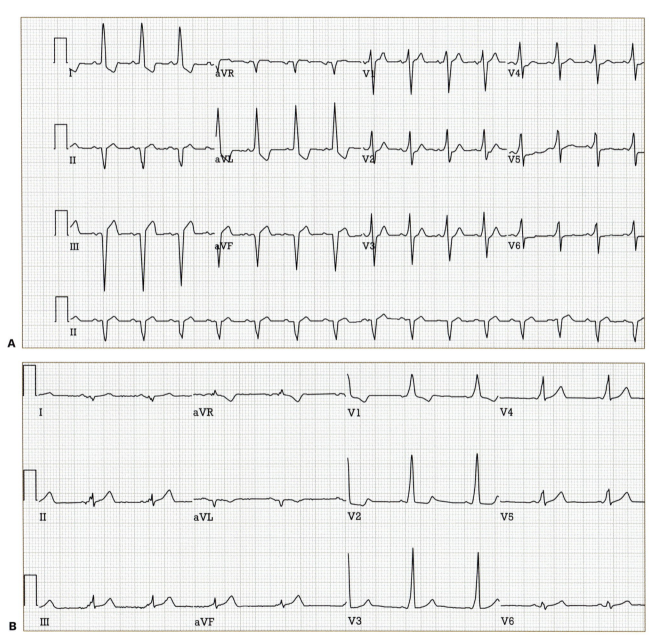

FIGURE 12.6. Pseudoinfarction patterns in WPW syndrome. **A.** Negative delta waves and QRS complexes in leads II, III, and aVF resemble large Q waves, suggesting prior inferior MI. **B.** Upright delta waves and monophasic R waves in leads V1 through V2 suggest prior posterior MI. Reproduced with permission from: Amal Mattu, MD, FACEP.

not required for initiation and maintenance of the arrhythmia but can "facilitate" rapid transmission of impulses to the ventricles. This group includes atrial fibrillation and atrial flutter.

Atrial fibrillation occurs in 10% to 30% of individuals with the WPW syndrome. Coexistent structural heart disease (a common cause of atrial fibrillation in patients without accessory pathways) is uncommon in the WPW syndrome and cannot explain the high frequency of atrial fibrillation. Fibrillation is often preceded by AVRT in these patients.

Atrial fibrillation originates in the atria, independent of the accessory pathway. Atrial impulses can be conducted down both the normal AV conduction system and the accessory pathway. The accessory pathway can function as a route for rapid conduction of atrial impulses to the ventricles, producing wide QRS complexes with rapid ventricular rates (Figures 12.11, 12.12). The irregularity of the ventricular response helps differentiate atrial fibrillation in WPW syndrome from ventricular tachycardia.

When the ventricular rate exceeds 200 beats/min, however, the irregularity of atrial fibrillation can become less apparent. Failure to appreciate the irregularity and consequent misdiagnosis of the rhythm as supraventricular tachycardia or ventricular tachycardia can be disastrous. Typical treatment of supraventricular tachycardia is with AV nodal blockers, and treatment of ventricular tachycardia is commonly performed with amiodarone. Unfortunately, treatment of atrial fibrillation with rapid ventricular response rates in WPW syndrome with either AV nodal blockers or amiodarone can cause degeneration of the rhythm into ventricular fibrillation.[11-14]

Atrial flutter results from an atrial reentrant circuit, independent of the accessory pathway. Atrial impulses are conducted to the ventricles through the accessory pathway, causing wide QRS complexes. The conduction ratio can be 2:1 or 1:1. The regular rhythm and wide QRS complexes can mimic ventricular tachycardia.

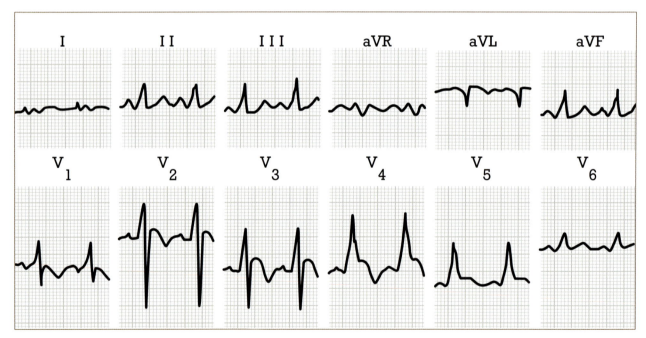

FIGURE 12.7. Acute MI in the presence of a WPW pattern in a 49-year-old man with the typical symptoms and enzyme changes of acute MI. The tracing shows a WPW pattern. The presence of acute injury is indicated by the ST-segment elevation in leads V_3 through V_5. In uncomplicated cases of WPW pattern, the ST segment is either isoelectric or depressed in leads with an essentially upright QRS complex. Reproduced with permission from: Ventricular preexcitation (Wolff-Parkinson White syndrome and its variants). In: Surawicz B, Knilans TK, eds. *Chou's Electrocardiography in Clinical Practice.* 2007; 5e: 487. Copyright 2007 Elsevier Inc.

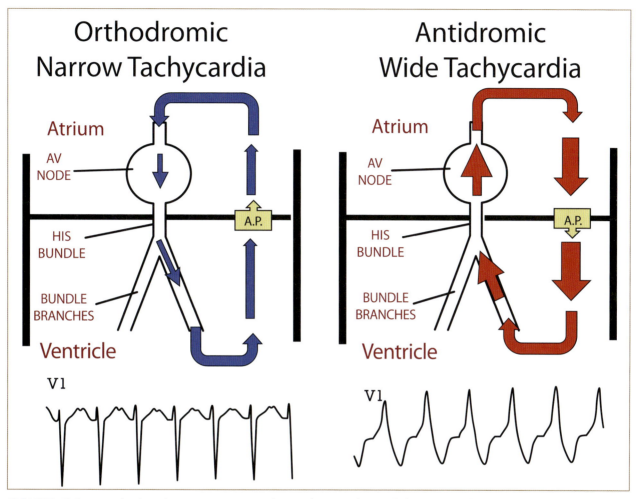

FIGURE 12.8. In orthodromic AVRT, anterograde conduction (toward the ventricle) occurs through the normal AV conduction system and results in a narrow complex tachycardia. Conversely, antidromic AVRT occurs during retrograde conduction (toward the atrium) through the accessory pathway and results in a wide complex tachycardia. (A.P. is accessory pathway.)

ACKNOWLEDGMENT

The authors acknowledge the significant contributions of Edward B. Bolgiano, MD, to this chapter in the first edition.

REFERENCES

1. Wolff L, Parkinson J, White PD. Bundle-branch block with short PR interval in healthy young people prone to paroxysmal tachycardia. *Am Heart J.* 1930;5:685-704.
2. Becker AE, Anderson RH, Durrer D, et al. The anatomic substrates of Wolff-Parkinson-White syndrome: a clinicopathologic correlation in seven patients. *Circulation.* 1978;57:870-879.
3. Chung KY, Walsh TJ, Massie E. Wolff-Parkinson-White syndrome. *Am Heart J.* 1965;69:116-133.
4. Krahn AD, Manfreda J, Tate RB, et al. The natural history of electrocardiographic preexcitation in men: the Manitoba follow-up study. *Ann Intern Med.* 1992;116:456-460.
5. Fitzsimmons PJ, McWhirter PD, Peterson DW, et al. The natural history of Wolff-Parkinson-White syndrome in 228 military aviators: a long-term followup of 22 years. *Am Heart J.* 2001;142:530-536.
6. Munger TM, Packer DL, Hammill SC, et al. A population study of the natural history of Wolff-Parkinson-White syndrome in Olmstead County, Minnesota, 1953 to 1989. *Circulation.* 1993;87:866-873.
7. Gallagher JJ, Pritchett ELC, Sealy WC, et al. The

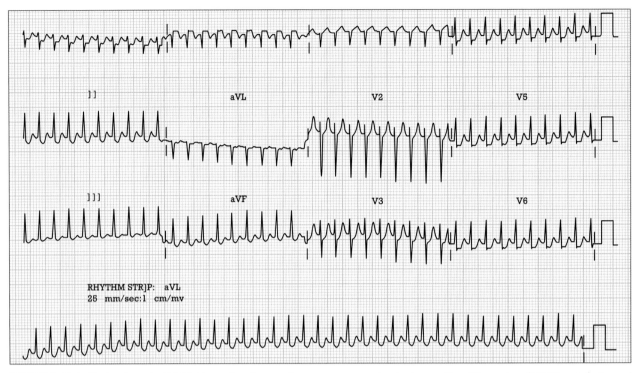

FIGURE 12.9. Orthodromic AVRT. Example of a regular narrow complex tachycardia with a rate of 225 beats/min and no discernible P waves. Orthodromic (anterograde) conduction results in a narrow complex tachycardia. Reproduced with permission from: Edward Burns, MD, and the Life in the Fastlane ECG Library, https://lifeinthefastlane.com/ecg-library/preexcitation-syndromes.

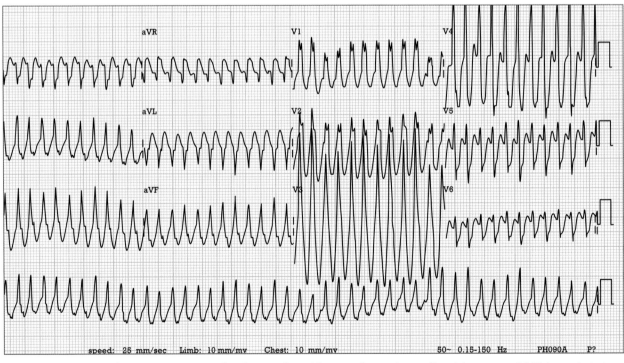

FIGURE 12.10. Antidromic AVRT. Example of a regular wide complex tachycardia with a rate of 280 beats/min in a 5-year-old boy with WPW syndrome. Antidromic (retrograde) conduction results in a wide complex tachycardia. Reproduced with permission from: Edward Burns, MD, and the Life in the Fastlane ECG Library, https://lifeinthefastlane.com/ecg-library/preexcitation-syndromes.

PREEXCITATION AND ACCESSORY PATHWAY SYNDROMES

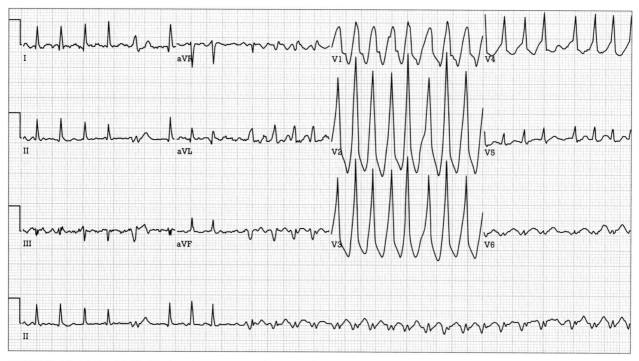

FIGURE 12.11. Atrial fibrillation in WPW syndrome. The rhythm is irregularly irregular, and rates in some areas approach 250 to 300 beats/min. Note the changing morphologies of the QRS complexes. Reproduced with permission from: Amal Mattu, MD, FACEP.

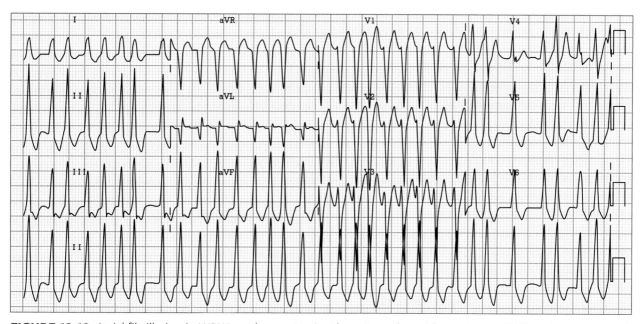

FIGURE 12.12. Atrial fibrillation in WPW syndrome. Notice the extremely rapid rate (up to 300 bpm in some areas) with frequent variation of QRS complex morphology. Reproduced with permission from: Edward Burns, MD, and the Life in the Fastlane ECG Library, https://lifeinthefastlane.com/ecg-library/preexcitation-syndromes.

preexcitation syndromes. *Prog Cardiovasc Dis.* 1978; 20:285-327.
8. Wellens HJJ, Atie J, Penn OC, et al. Diagnosis and treatment of patients with accessory pathways. *Cardiol Clin.* 1990;8:503-521.
9. Wang K, Asinger R, Hodges M. Electrocardiograms of Wolff-Parkinson-White syndrome simulating other conditions. *Am Heart J.* 1996;132:152-155.
10. Yee R, Klein GJ, Sharma AD, et al. Tachycardia associated with accessory atrioventricular pathways. In: Zipes DP, Jalife J, eds. *Cardiac Electrophysiology.* Philadelphia, PA: WB Saunders; 1990.
11. McGovern B, Garan H, Ruskin JN. Precipitation of ventricular fibrillation by verapamil in patients with Wolff-Parkinson-White syndrome. *Ann Intern Med.* 1986;104:791-794.
12. Page RL, Joglar JA, Caldwell MA, et al. 2015 ACC/AHA/HRS Guideline for the management of adult patients with supraventricular tachycardia: a report of the American College of Cardiology/American Heart Association Task Force on Clinical Practice Guidelines and the Heart Rhythm Society. *Circulation.* 2016;133:e506-e574.
13. Nebojša M, Dragan S, Nebojša A, et al. Lethal outcome after intravenous administration of amiodarone in patient with atrial fibrillation and ventricular preexcitation. *J Cardiovasc Electrophysiol.* 2011;22:1077-1078.
14. January CT, Wann LS, Alpert JS, et al. 2014 AHA/ACC/HRS Guideline for the Management of Patients With Atrial Fibrillation: Executive Summary: A Report of the American College of Cardiology/American Heart Association Task Force on Practice Guidelines and the Heart Rhythm Society. *J Am Coll Cardiol.* 2014;64:e1-e76.

CHAPTER THIRTEEN

Inherited Syndromes of Sudden Cardiac Death

BENJAMIN S. ABELLA AND JAYARAM CHELLURI

KEY POINTS

Brugada Syndrome
- ST-segment elevation with downsloping morphology is observed in leads V_1 and V_2 with no reciprocal ST-segment depression and is often followed by an inverted T wave.
- Sodium channel blockers and vagotonic agents can unmask concealed electrocardiographic manifestations of Brugada syndrome.

Hypertrophic Cardiomyopathy
- Patients can exhibit findings of left ventricular hypertrophy, including left-axis deviation, increased QRS voltage, and T-wave changes consistent with a "strain pattern," which tend to be pronounced in the precordial leads.
- Septal hypertrophy is often reflected as abnormal Q waves, which can mimic MI (infarction-related Q waves are wider).

Arrhythmogenic Right Ventricular Cardiomyopathy
- The ECG often indicates progressive deterioration of cardiac function, which is one of the key indicators of this condition.
- Epsilon waves, small-amplitude waves that immediately follow the QRS complex, are specific findings in the condition and likely reflect delayed right ventricular conduction.
- Hallmarks of this condition are T-wave inversions in V_1 through V_3 in the absence of complete right bundle-branch block as well as selective prolongation of the QRS complex in V_1 through V_3 compared with V_6.

Long QT Syndrome
- A QTc interval of more than 440 milliseconds (using the Bazett formula) is observed.
- Lead II is generally regarded as the best single lead for measuring the QT interval.
- Torsades de pointes variant of ventricular tachycardia suggests underlying long QT syndrome.

Sudden cardiac death (SCD) is most commonly seen in the setting of ischemic heart disease, in which patients suffer the acute onset of a lethal rhythm in response to new ischemia or as a result of a myocardial injury from an old ischemic event. This common scenario is a widespread cause of mortality in the developed world, leading to more than 250,000 deaths in the United States per year.[1] Despite recent advances in cardiopulmonary resuscitation and defibrillation techniques, survival rates remain poor, and survivors often suffer long-term morbidity, including neurologic disability. It is therefore important to identify patients at risk for SCD whenever possible.

A variety of inherited conditions predispose people to SCD in the absence of ischemic heart disease; these conditions include Brugada syndrome, hypertrophic cardiomyopathy (HCM), arrhythmogenic right ventricular cardiomyopathy (ARVC), and long QT syndrome (LQTS). Individuals with these genetic conditions might remain asymptomatic and never suffer a cardiac event, or they might suffer SCD at a young age. Genetic predisposition to SCD has received some notoriety in recent years, since several prominent athletes have died from undiagnosed cardiac conditions that predisposed them to it. This chapter describes the clinical aspects and electrocardiographic findings associated with these syndromes (Table 13.1).

BRUGADA SYNDROME

Brugada syndrome is an inherited arrhythmogenic disease characterized by a right bundle-branch–like pattern on the ECG, associated with ST-segment elevation in leads V_1 and V_2. V_3 is no longer considered part of the diagnostic criteria, according to the expert consensus statement issued conjointly by three medical societies in 2013.[2] The ST segment is typically downsloping and often followed by an inverted T wave. This pattern has been associated with a high incidence of sudden death among previously healthy individuals, particularly Asian men.[3] Brugada syndrome is believed to be responsible for 4% to 12% of all cases of nonischemic SCD and for approximately 20% of sudden deaths in people with structurally normal hearts. It has been shown to be identical to the disorder known as sudden unexplained nocturnal death syndrome.[4]

People with Brugada syndrome are predisposed to episodes of ventricular tachycardia, usually polymorphic in nature. If the arrhythmia terminates spontaneously, the patient is likely to present with complaints of palpitations or syncope. Conversely, if the arrhythmia is prolonged, the result is SCD. Patients who present initially with aborted sudden death are at the highest risk for recurrence, whereas patients presenting with syncope and individuals who are asymptomatic when found coincidentally to have ECGs consistent with Brugada syndrome are at lower risk for SCD.[5] Intravenous administration of a class 1C antiarrhythmic (eg, flecainide or propafenone) has adverse cardiovascular effects in most patients with the syndrome.

The typical age at the time of diagnosis is in the fourth or fifth decade of life, although the original report by Brugada described adolescents with the condition.[6] Bradycardia resulting from altered autonomic balance or other factors can contribute to initiation of the arrhythmia.[7,8] In most cases, malignant arrhythmias occur during sleep. It is believed that circadian variations in sympathovagal balance, hormonal fluctuation, and other metabolic factors contribute to this pattern.[9,10]

Genetic predisposition to Brugada syndrome is most commonly a result of autosomal dominant mutations in the cardiac sodium channel gene, classically *SCN5A*. However, only 18% to 30% of patients with clinically diagnosed Brugada syndrome are found to have these genetic mutations, suggesting the possible involvement of other genes as well. In fact, recent research has elucidated at least 19 genotypes.[11] The high incidence of ventricular arrhythmias is associated with mutation of the sodium channel, which shortens the cardiac action potential, making cardiac tissue vulnerable to reentry circuits.

Noninvasive methods of risk stratification involve detection of spontaneous changes in the ST segment on the ECG combined with a history of syncopal episodes or a family history consistent with SCD.[2] The three electrocardiographic patterns associated with Brugada syndrome are described in Table 13.2. All of them have findings suggestive of right bundle-branch block (RBBB) or incomplete RBBB, with ST-segment elevations in V_1 through V_3 (Figure 13.1); most often, an incomplete RBBB is noted. ST-segment depression is usually not observed. Additionally, there is often slight prolongation of the PR interval. Given the dynamic nature and day-to-day variation of ECGs, signal-averaged electrocardiographic techniques are useful to more accurately determine whether a patient exhibits Brugada syndrome. Other conditions that can mimic the precordial ST-segment elevation seen in Brugada syndrome can be divided into acute (ie, infectious or metabolic disorders) and persistent (ie, RBBB or left ventricular hypertrophy) conditions.

Under the 2013 update of the multisociety, expert consensus statement, diagnostic criteria are based solely on the ECG (see Figure 13.2).[2] The diagnosis is based on the presence of type 1 morphology in V_1

TABLE 13.1. Congenital arrhythmic syndromes.				
SYNDROME	**ECG FINDINGS**	**SYMPTOMS, DIAGNOSIS**	**GENETIC FACTORS**	**TREATMENT**
Arrhythmogenic right ventricular cardiomyopathy	Epsilon waves in any of leads V_1 through V_3, and inverted T waves in each of leads V_1 through V_3	Should be considered in young patients presenting with syncope, VT, or cardiac arrest and in adults with acute heart failure	Autosomal dominant disorder	Implantable defibrillator
Brugada	Incomplete or complete RBBB pattern with ST-segment elevation in leads V_1 and V_2	Syncope • 2 mm or larger ST-segment elevation of type 1 morphology in V_1 or V_2, either spontaneous or elicited by drug challenge with Class I antiarrhythmic drugs • Conversion of ST-segment elevation of type 2 or 3 morphology in V_1 and V_2 to type 1 under provocative testing by Class I antiarrhythmic drugs	Autosomal dominant, incomplete penetrance; 12 genotypes causing a decrease in inward sodium or calcium currents and increase in potassium outward current[2]	Implantable defibrillator
Hypertrophic cardiomyopathy	Findings consistent with left ventricular hypertrophy; deep narrow Q waves in inferior or lateral leads	Syncope, chest pain, sudden death	12 genes identified; most common genetic autosomal dominant cardiovascular disease	Beta blockers or calcium channel blockers, surgical intervention
Long QT	Prolonged QTc interval	Syncope, sudden death; commonly presents in young children and adolescents. Many patients are asymptomatic until the onset of their first cardiac arrest.	Mutations in *KCNQ1* and *KCNQ2* are responsible for this version of the syndrome, which is accompanied by deafness.	Beta blockers

TABLE 13.2. Types of Brugada syndrome by electrocardiographic analysis.

TYPE	DESCRIPTION
1	ST-segment elevation is triangular ("coved" or "convex upward" pattern) and the T waves can be inverted in leads V_1 to V_3
2	Downward displacement of the ST segment lies between the two elevations of the segment in leads V_1 to V_3 ("concave upward") but does not reach the baseline
3	Downward displacement of the ST segment lies between the two elevations of the segment in leads V_1 to V_3, and the middle part of the ST segment touches the baseline

or V_2, observed either spontaneously or in response to provocative testing with a class I antiarrhythmic agent. The diagnosis can also be made in patients with type 2 or 3 morphology in V_1 or V_2 who convert to type 1 morphology under provocative testing. This approach departs from previous guidelines that included electrocardiographic criteria for V_3 and clinical findings.[2] Clinical criteria (ie, a family history of SCD, syncope/nocturnal agonal respiration) remain important factors in risk stratification.

Placement of the right precordial leads in a more rostral position (up to the second intercostal space) can increase the sensitivity of the ECG for detecting the Brugada phenotype in some patients, both in the presence and absence of drugs used to unmask it. Sodium channel blockers and vagotonic agents may be used to unmask concealed electrocardiographic manifestations of Brugada syndrome.[12,13] Potent sodium channel blockade, achieved with type 1C antiarrhythmic agents, can provoke the syndrome's characteristic changes.[14] Patients should be monitored with continuous electrocardiographic recording while the drugs are being administered; administration should be terminated when the diagnostic arrhythmia is observed. Such testing should be reserved for experienced electrophysiologists.

S-wave duration of more than 80 milliseconds in V_1 or ST-segment elevation of 80 milliseconds or more in V_2 measured from the J point is thought to be indicative of high risk for ventricular arrhythmias in patients with Brugada syndrome (these parameters are not part of the consensus statement).[15] Proper treatment strategies are urgently needed to treat symptomatic patients at high risk of sudden death.

Despite a growing body of knowledge regarding this condition, clinical management of Brugada syndrome is limited by the lack of pharmacologic therapies. At the Second Consensus Conference on Brugada syndrome,[7] it was recommended that symptomatic individuals be offered implantable cardiac defibrillators (ICDs), and this recommendation remains in the latest guidelines. The mortality rate associated with Brugada syndrome from the time of first clinical manifestation is 10% per year. Medical therapy has not been demonstrated to improve outcome; ICD placement is the only proven effective strategy.[2]

HYPERTROPHIC CARDIOMYOPATHY

Hypertrophic cardiomyopathy, a genetic disorder caused by an autosomal dominant mutation in 1 of at least 12 genes, is the most common cause of SCD in the young.[16] Some HCM patients present for the first time as cardiac arrest victims; others present with episodes of syncope and angina pectoris.[17] Patients with HCM can experience SCD at any time. Exertional activity is a trigger for arrhythmia in some individuals; fright, anger, and other extreme, sudden emotions spark arrhythmia in others. In fact, the concept of adrenergically related syncope is more appropriate than exertional syncope.

Hypertrophic cardiomyopathy is characterized by hypertrophy of the left ventricle in the absence of another cardiac or systemic disease capable of producing hypertrophy of this magnitude. In most patients, HCM goes clinically unrecognized.[16] The

INHERITED SYNDROMES OF SUDDEN CARDIAC DEATH

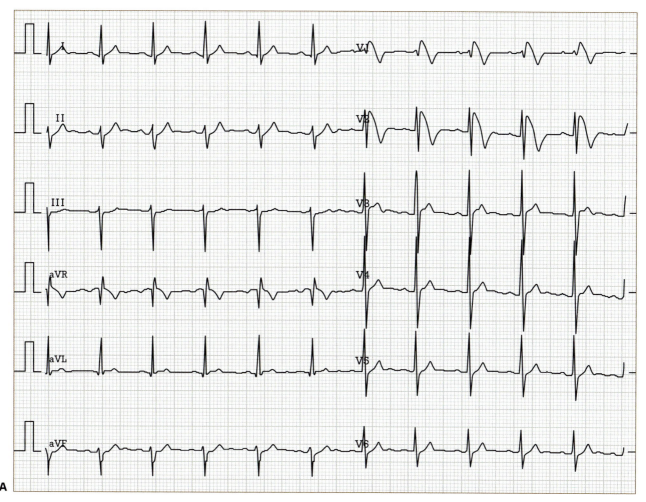

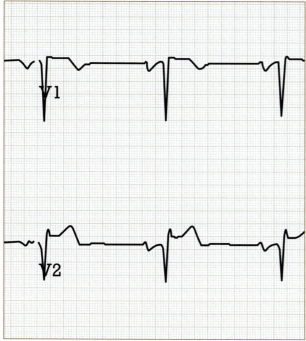

FIGURE 13.1. ECGs from patients with Brugada syndrome. **A.** The ST segments in lead V_1 demonstrate a "coved" or "convex upward" pattern, commonly referred to as the Brugada type I pattern. **B.** The ECG demonstrates an incomplete RBBB pattern with ST-segment elevation. Lead V_2 especially demonstrates the Brugada type II pattern with convex-upward ST-segment elevation. Reproduced image 13.1B with permission from: Amal Mattu, MD, FACEP.

low rate of diagnosis is partially attributed to the fact that most patients are asymptomatic until the condition manifests as SCD.

The diagnosis of HCM can be entertained on the basis of typical clinical, echocardiographic, hemodynamic, and electrocardiographic features. Individuals with HCM can express a variety of symptoms, including angina-type chest pain and symptoms of heart failure. Additionally, HCM patients often experience exertional angina, despite the absence of coronary artery disease.[18]

Pathophysiologic changes that coincide with the clinical symptoms include left ventricular (LV) diastolic dysfunction, impaired coronary reserve, myocardial ischemia, and supraventricular or ventricular tachyarrhythmias.[19] Left ventricular hypertrophy is commonly asymmetric, with disproportionate thickening of the intraventricular septum.[20] In a minority of HCM patients, progression to dilated cardiomyopathy can occur, characterized by thinning of the ventricular wall and LV dysfunction.[21] Another histopathologic feature of HCM is small vessel disease, or arterial dysplasia, characterized by narrowing of the intramural coronary arterioles secondary to wall thickening from increased intimal and medial collagen deposition. Consequent tissue death leads to myocardial scarring and fibrosis, which exacerbate transition from the compensated HCM phase to the decompensated, dilated phase.[22]

Although the 12-lead ECG can suggest the diagnosis, HCM is usually diagnosed based on the results of electrocardiography and Doppler echocardiography. The latter technique is recognized as generally being more reliable, providing detailed information regarding the distribution and severity of hypertrophy and LV size and function.[19] Other methods that are helpful in confirming a diagnosis of HCM or identifying individuals at high risk for sudden death include exercise testing and ambulatory Holter monitoring; a history of cardiac events in other family members contributes to the diagnosis.[19]

The ECG can demonstrate findings suggestive of the diagnosis, but, more commonly, it is normal (in 5% to 10% of HCM patients) or exhibits LV hypertrophy (Figure 13.2). In these presentations, the diagnosis is quite challenging and is most often not established at that time. Other electrocardiographic findings include those noted in Table 13.3.[23]

Q waves seen in HCM caused by septal hypertrophy are most commonly reflected in the lateral leads (a very specific finding); they are less commonly observed in the inferior leads or they might not be present at all (Figure 13.2A, 13.2B). They can mimic Q waves seen in MI. Myocardial infarction is associated with Q waves that are at least 0.04 seconds wide (1 mm), whereas the Q waves of HCM tend to be deep but very narrow. It is important to note that recent guidelines have reclassified several previously diagnostic electrocardiographic criteria as nonpathologic, normal changes of the athletic heart. These include left atrial enlargement or left-axis deviation in isolation, T-wave inversion confined to leads V_1 through V_4 and preceded by J-point elevation in athletes of African origin, and Q waves larger than 3 to 4 mm (Table 13.3).[23]

Symptomatic HCM patients *should* receive negative inotropic agents, including beta blockers, verapamil, or disopyramide, to reduce the exercise gradient. For patients who are unresponsive to pharmacologic treatment or who have symptoms of significant heart failure, relief should be targeted at the obstruction and mitral regurgitation. The "gold standard" intervention is ventricular septal myectomy. An alternative is percutaneous alcohol septal ablation, but it is thought to be less effective and carries greater risk of morbidity over time from intramyocardial scarring. Alcohol ablation is generally recommended for elderly patients and for those vehemently against surgery.[2]

TABLE 13.3. Electrocardiographic findings suggestive of hypertrophic cardiomyopathy.

Large amplitude QRS complexes
Tall R-wave in leads V1 and V2
Deep narrow Q waves, most commonly in lateral leads
Nonspecific intraventricular conduction delay (QRS >/= 100 ms)

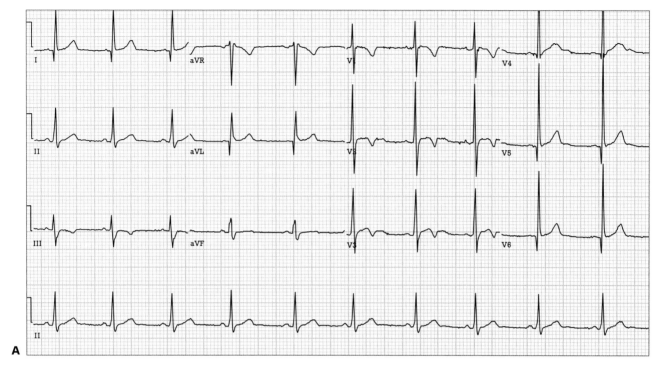

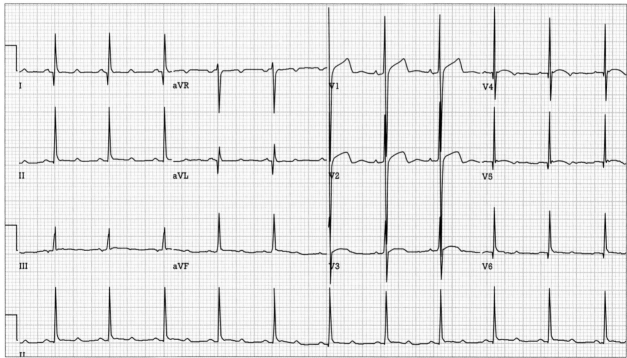

FIGURE 13.2. ECG from a patient with hypertrophic cardiomyopathy. **A.** The ECG demonstrates the classic findings of HCM: large-amplitude QRS complexes and deep narrow Q waves in all lateral leads (I, aVL, V_5, V_6). **B.** The ECG demonstrates large-amplitude QRS complexes and deep narrow Q waves limited to lateral leads I and aVL. Reproduced with permission from: Amal Mattu, MD, FACEP.

ARRHYTHMOGENIC RIGHT VENTRICULAR CARDIOMYOPATHY

Arrhythmogenic right ventricular cardiomyopathy is a genetic cardiomyopathy characterized by ventricular arrhythmias and structural abnormalities of the right ventricle. It is believed to be responsible for up to 20% of SCD in young people. Histologically, ARVC is typified by the gradual replacement of myocytes with adipose and fibrous tissue. Originally localized to right ventricular (RV) involvement, it is now recognized that ARVC can progress to diffuse RV and LV involvement, resulting in biventricular heart failure (now simply referred to as arrhythmogenic cardiomyopathy). If the process progresses to this extreme, ARVC is difficult to distinguish from dilated cardiomyopathy.[24] The regions of the right ventricle most frequently affected are the RV inflow area, the apex, and the infundibulum.

Arrhythmogenic right ventricular cardiomyopathy is typically inherited as an autosomal dominant trait with variable penetrance and incomplete expression. The prevalence of ARVC in the general population is approximately 1 in 1,000 to 5,000, but the disease is often not recognized because of the difficulty of diagnosis.[24] The condition should be considered in young patients presenting with syncope, ventricular tachycardia, and cardiac arrest and in select adult patients with idiopathic acute heart failure. Diagnostic criteria are listed in Table 13.4 and are considered positive if two major criteria, one major and two minor criteria, or four minor criteria are met.[24]

Patients with ARVC who demonstrate functional and structural worsening of RV performance are at high risk for SCD. Progressive deterioration of cardiac function is one of the key indicators for diagnosing this condition, and the ECG often evolves concomitantly with these functional changes. The isolated patches of fibro-fatty tissue found in ARVC generate macro-reentry electrical circuits and form the arrhythmogenic substrate for the malignant cardiac arrhythmias responsible for sudden death. Because these arrhythmias are typically induced by adrenergic stimulation such as physical exercise, it is recommended that young subjects with this condition be prohibited from vigorous athletic competition, even after their condition is treated, for example, with an ICD.

Electrocardiographic findings in ARVC include T-wave inversions in V_1 through V_3 in the absence of complete RBBB (Figure 13.3). However, RBBB occurs in up to 15% of cases. Selective prolongation of the QRS complex in V_1 through V_3 compared with V_6 is another hallmark of ARVC. Unfortunately, these findings, while seen in ARVC, are by no means diagnostic in and of themselves. Epsilon waves, small-amplitude waves that immediately follow the QRS complex, are a specific finding in the condition and likely reflect delayed right ventricular conduction. Sometimes biatrial enlargement is discerned, with biphasic or notched P waves in V_1. When arrhythmia occurs in ARVC, it is typically monomorphic ventricular tachycardia, which is rarely initiated by complexes of different configurations, suggesting the tachycardia originates from a single focus.[24]

Patients with ARVC can develop isolated right heart failure or biventricular failure, which typically presents during the fourth and fifth decades of life. Arrhythmogenic RV cardiomyopathy is one of the few myocardial diseases that causes RV heart failure without pulmonary hypertension. Rather, the mechanisms of RV failure are dilation, thinning of the wall, and progressive loss of contractile function because of myocardial atrophy. Arrhythmogenic RV cardiomyopathy can also involve the left ventricle, resulting in mild decreases in its function. Left ventricular failure is uncommon; when it does occur, it is commonly misdiagnosed as idiopathic or viral dilated cardiomyopathy.

If noninvasive testing suggests ARVC, invasive testing with an RV angiogram, biopsy, and electrophysiology study are recommended. Endomyocardial biopsy can eliminate the possibility of other conditions that mimic ARVD such as myocarditis involving the right ventricle.[25] However, diagnosis by endomyocardial biopsy is difficult because the disease is segmental and because the target of biopsy, the interventricular septum, is often spared as the disease progresses.

Once the diagnosis of ARVC is established, the main treatment decision involves whether to implant

TABLE 13.4. Criteria for diagnosis of arrhythmogenic right ventricular cardiomyopathy.		
	MAJOR CRITERIA	**MINOR CRITERIA**
Global or regional dysfunction and structural alterations	Two-dimensional echocardiography: regional RV akinesia, dyskinesia, or aneurysm + severe dilation/reduced ejection fraction Magnetic resonance imaging: regional RV akinesia or dyskinesia or dyssynchronous RV contraction + severe dilation/reduced ejection fraction RV angiography: RV akinesia, dyskinesia, or aneurysm	Two-dimensional echocardiography: regional RV akinesia, dyskinesia + mild dilation/reduced ejection fraction Magnetic resonance imaging: regional RV akinesia or dyskinesia or dyssynchronous RV contraction + mild dilation/reduced ejection fraction
Tissue characterization of wall	Degree of fibrofatty replacement of the myocardium and residual myocyte percentage on endomyocardial biopsy	
Repolarization abnormalities	Inverted T waves in right precordial leads (V_1, V_2, and V_3) Patients older than 14 years; in absence of RBBB	Inverted T waves in right precordial leads (V_1 and V_2) (patients older than 14 years; in absence of RBBB) or in V_4 through V_6 or Inverted T waves in right precordial leads (V_1 through V_4) (patients older than 14 years; in the presence of RBBB)
Depolarization/ conduction abnormalities	Epsilon waves in right precordial leads (V_1, V_2, and/or V_3)	Various criteria depending on QRS duration
Arrhythmias	Nonsustained or sustained ventricular tachycardia of LBBB with superior axis	Nonsustained or sustained ventricular tachycardia of RV outflow configuration, LBBB morphology with inferior axis or of unknown axis
Family history	AVRC in first-degree relative meeting task force criteria Genetic identification of pathogenic mutation	History of AVRC in first-degree relative unable to formally meet task force criteria History of premature sudden death at <35 years old in first-degree family member AVRC pathologically confirmed in second-degree family member

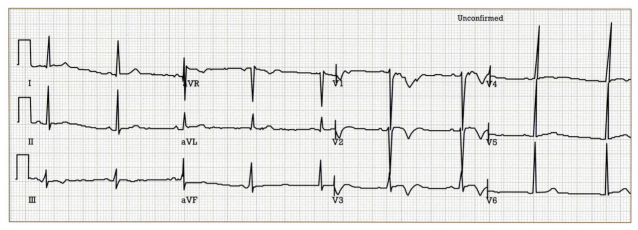

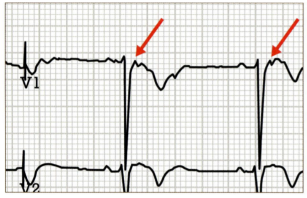

FIGURE 13.3. ECG from a patient with arrhythmogenic right ventricular cardiomyopathy. In the enlargement, the arrows indicate the epsilon waves following the QRS complexes in lead V_1. Reproduced with permission from: Moshe Simons, MD.

an ICD or to administer pharmacologic treatment, depending on risk stratification. Implantation of ICDs is generally recommended for patients who have experienced syncope or cardiac arrest or sustained ventricular arrhythmias and for patients with overt evidence of AVRC, particularly if the electrophysiology study is abnormal or if there is a family history of sudden death. Defibrillator implantation poses risks to these patients: the thinned and weakened RV myocardial wall could be penetrated and the device could fail to adequately sense arrhythmias because of the sclerotic nature of the right ventricle.

LONG QT SYNDROME

Prolongation of the QT interval (measured from the beginning of the Q wave to the end of the T wave) is associated with a higher risk of mortality from sudden cardiac arrest.[26] Congenital LQTS is a clinical disorder characterized by prolongation of the QT interval (Figure 13.4) and the occurrence of sudden death or of life-threatening arrhythmias caused by torsades de pointes ventricular tachycardia.[27] A variety of hereditary mutations in genes encoding for myocardial membrane channels is believed to be the source of the QT-interval prolongation. Two hereditary variants exist: one is associated with deafness (Jervell and Lange-Nielsen syndrome), and the other is not (Romano-Ward syndrome). The most common mutation implicated in LQTS is associated with a higher risk of cardiac events in boys until puberty and in women during adulthood.[28]

In addition to the congenital variants of LQTS, QT-interval prolongation can be related to entities other than genetic (Table 13.5).[29] They include an adverse event related to a medication, electrolyte abnormalities (particularly hypokalemia and hypomagnesemia), and other cardiac and systemic issues (eg, acute coronary syndrome and central nervous system hemorrhage). It is thought that, in situations involving medication or electrolytes, a less dominant gene for QT-interval prolongation likely exists; in these scenarios, exposure to the medication or electrolyte deficiency produces the QT-interval prolongation.

Long QT syndrome often clinically manifests in otherwise healthy young individuals, mostly children and adolescents, when they are under physical or emotional stress. The arrhythmia-induced loss of

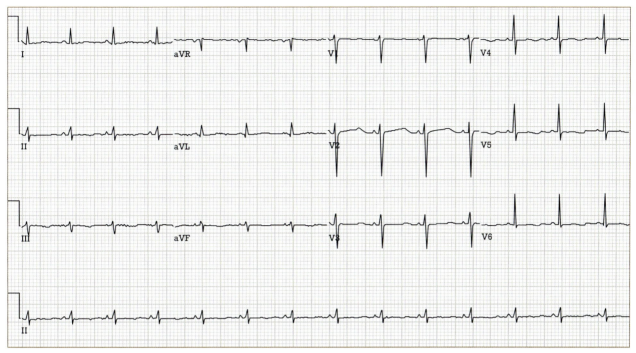

FIGURE 13.4. ECG from a patient with long QT syndrome. Reproduced with permission from: Amal Mattu, MD, FACEP.

TABLE 13.5. Nongenetic causes of QTc prolongation.
Acute cardiac ischemia
Electrolyte disorders: hypokalemia, hypomagnesemia, hypocalcemia
Elevated intracranial pressure
Hypothermia
Sodium channel and potassium efflux blocking agents

consciousness might be misdiagnosed as epileptic convulsions.[30] The disease also dramatically manifests as syncopal episodes, which often result in cardiac arrest. When diagnosed, however, LQTS can be treated effectively and cardiac arrest can be averted.

A widely accepted method for correcting the QT interval for rate is the Bazett formula[31]:

$$QTc = QT/\sqrt{R\text{-}R} \text{ interval}$$

A corrected QT interval (QTc) longer than 440 milliseconds is considered prolonged.[32] However, a minority of patients with LQTS have a QTc less than the 440 millisecond cutoff on their initial ECG. The greatest risk of development of torsades de pointes is believed to occur when the QTc exceeds 500 milliseconds. It is recommended that multiple ECGs be obtained if LQTS is suspected from the family history or clinical presentation.[32] Lead II is generally regarded as the best single lead for measuring the QT interval because the end of the T wave is usually discrete, and the QT interval obtained from this lead is usually well correlated with the maximal QT measured from the remainder of the ECG. Other diagnostic features on the ECG include notched T waves in several leads and a tendency toward bradycardia. Finally, torsades de pointes is suggestive of underlying LQTS (Table 13.6). Criteria based on 2011 guidelines also include findings of genetic mutations.[33]

Therapies for the management of LQTS, in order of increasing severity of the condition, are administration of beta blockers, cardiac pacing, left cardiac sympathetic denervation, and finally, for the most severe cases, implantation of an ICD. Cardiac pacing might be beneficial for high-risk LQTS patients by preventing pauses; however, it should always be used in conjunction with beta blockers and should never be considered a sole treatment for LQTS, especially because pacemaker problems attributed to T-wave sensing and rate adjusting are relatively common.[34]

Recent developments have made gene-specific therapies for LQTS treatment increasingly viable. The genotype is generally identified after beta-blocker therapy has started. An experienced cardiologist should be able to predict the genotype based on the clinical history, the circumstances associated with the cardiac events, and sometimes according to the T-wave morphology on the ECG; nevertheless, confirmation must be sought from the molecular laboratory.

REFERENCES

1. Benjamin EJ, Blaha MJ, Chiuve SE, et al. Heart disease and stroke statistics—2017 update: a report from the American Heart Association. *Circulation*. 2017;135(10):e146-e603. http://doi.org/10.1161/CIR.0000000000000485
2. Priori SG, Wilde AA, Horie M, et al. HRS/EHRA/APHRS Expert Consensus Statement on the Diagnosis and Management of Patients with Inherited Primary Arrhythmia Syndromes: document endorsed by HRS, EHRA, and APHRS in May 2013 and by ACCF, AHA, PACES, and AEPC in June 2013. *Heart Rhythm*. 2013;10(12):1932-1963. http://doi.org/10.1016/j.hrthm.2013.05.014
3. Fernández-Falgueras A, Sarquella-Brugada G, Brugada J, et al. Cardiac channelopathies and sudden death: recent clinical and genetic advances. *Biology*.

TABLE 13.6. Long QT syndrome diagnostic criteria.[28]

ELECTROCARDIOGRAPHIC FINDING		POINTS
QTc interval	≥480 ms	3
	460–470 ms	2
	450 ms	1
Torsades de pointes		2
T-wave alternans		1
Notched T wave in three leads		1
Low heart rate for age (bradycardia)		0.5
Clinical history	Syncope with stress	2
	Syncope without stress	1
	Congenital deafness	0.5
Family history	Family members with definite LQTS	1
	Unexplained sudden cardiac death among immediate family members younger than 30 years	0.5

A total point score of 2 or 3 suggests intermediate probability of LQTS, requiring serial ECG measurements. If the score is higher than 3.5 points, the probability of LQTS is high. Reproduced with permission from: Schwartz PJ, Moss AJ, Vincent GM, Crampton RS. Diagnostic criteria for the long QT syndrome: an update. *Circulation*. 1993;88 (2):782-784. Copyright 1993 Wolters Kluwer Health, Inc.

2017;6(1):7-21. http://doi.org/10.3390/biology6010007

4. Vatta M, Dumaine R, Varghese G, et al. Genetic and biophysical basis of sudden unexplained nocturnal death syndrome (SUNDS), a disease allelic to Brugada syndrome. *Hum Mol Genet*. 2002;11(3):337-345.

5. Brugada P, Brugada R, Mont L, et al. Natural history of Brugada syndrome: the prognostic value of programmed electrical stimulation of the heart. *J Cardiovasc Electrophysiol*. 2003;14(5):455-457.

6. Brugada P, Brugada J. Right bundle branch block, persistent ST segment elevation and sudden cardiac death: A distinct clinical and electrocardiographic syndrome: A multicenter report. *J Am Coll Cardiol*. 1992;20:1391–1396.

7. Antzelevitch C, Brugada P, Borggrefe M, et al. Brugada syndrome: report of the Second Consensus Conference. *Circulation*. 2005;111:659-670.

8. Kasanuki H, Onishi S, Ohtuka M, et al. Idiopathic ventricular fibrillation induced with vagal activity in patients without obvious heart disease. *Circulation*. 1997;95:2277-2285.

9. Nogami A, Nakao M, Kubota S, et al. Enhancement of J-ST-segment elevation by the glucose and insulin test in Brugada syndrome. *Pacing Clin Electrophysiol*. 2003;26(1 Pt 2):332-337.

10. Nishizaki M, Sakurada H, Ashikaga T, et al. Effects of glucose-induced insulin secretion on ST segment elevation in the Brugada syndrome. *J Cardiovasc Electrophysiol*. 2003;14(3):243-249.

11. Antzelevitch C, Patocskai B. Brugada syndrome: clinical, genetic, molecular, cellular, and ionic aspects. *Curr Probl Cardiol*. 2016;41(1):7–57. http://doi.org/10.1016/j.cpcardiol.2015.06.002

12. Brugada P, Brugada J, Brugada R. Arrhythmia induction by antiarrhythmia drugs. *Pacing Clin Electrophysiol*. 2000;23(3):291-292.

13. Brugada R, Brugada J, Antzelevitch C, et al. Sodium channel blockers identify risk for sudden death in patients with ST-segment elevation and right bundle branch block but structurally normal hearts. *Circulation*. 2000;101:501-515.

14. Antzelevitch C, Olivia A. Amplification of spatial dispersion of repolarization underlies sudden cardiac death associated with catecholaminergic polymorphic VT, long QT, short QT and Brugada syndromes. *J Intern Med*. 2006;259:48-58.

15. Atarashi H, Ogawa S, for the Idiopathic Ventricular Fibrillation Investigators. New ECG criteria for high-risk Brugada syndrome. *Circulation*. 2003;67:8-10.

16. Poliac L, Barron M, Maron B. Hypertrophic cardiomyopathy. *Anesthesiology*. 2006;104:183-192.

17. Wigle E, Rakowski H, Kimball B, et al. Hypertrophic cardiomyopathy: clinical spectrum and treatment. *Circulation*. 1995;92:1680-1692.

18. Yoshida N, Ikeda H, Wada T, et al. Exercise-induced abnormal blood pressure responses are related to subendocardial ischemia in hypertrophic cardiomyopathy. *J Am Coll Cardiol*. 1998;32:1938-1942.

19. Doolan A, Nguyen L, Semsarian C. Hypertrophic cardiomyopathy from "heart tumor" to a complex molecular genetic disorder. *Heart Lung Circ*. 2004;13(1):15-25.

20. Davies MJ, McKenna WJ. Hypertrophic cardiomyopathy: pathology and pathogenesis. *Histopathology*. 1995;26:493-500.

21. Biagini E, Coccolo F, Ferlito M, et al. Dilated-hypokinetic evolution of hypertrophic cardiomyopathy. *J Am Coll Cardiol*. 2005;46(8):1543-1550.

22. Hatcher CJ, Basson CT. Taking a bite out of hypertrophic cardiomyopathy: soy diet and disease. *J Clin Invest*. 2006;116(1):16-19.

23. Zorzi A, Calore C, Vio R, et al. Accuracy of the ECG for differential diagnosis between hypertrophic cardiomyopathy and athlete's heart: comparison between the European Society of Cardiology (2010) and International (2017) criteria. *Br J Sports Med*. 2017 Jul 12 [Epub ahead of print].

24. Corrado D, Basso C, Judge DP. Cardiomyopathy compendium: arrhythmogenic cardiomyopathy. *Circ Res*. 2017;121:784-802. http://doi.org/10.1161/CIRCRESAHA.117.309345

25. Chimenti C, Pieroni M, Maseri A, et al. Histologic findings in patients with clinical and instrumental diagnosis of sporadic arrhythmogenic right ventricular dysplasia. *J Am Coll Cardiol*. 2004;43(12):2305-2313.

26. Dekker J, Crow R, Hannan PJ, et al. Heart rate-corrected QT interval prolongation predicts risk of coronary heart disease in black and white middle-aged men and women. *J Am Coll Cardiol*. 2004;43:565-571.

27. Schwartz P. The congenital long QT syndromes from genotype to phenotype: clinical implications. *J Intern Med*. 2006;259:39-47.

28. Zareba W, Moss A, Locati EH, et al. Modulating effects of age and gender on the clinical course of long QT syndrome by genotype. *J Am Coll Cardiol*. 2003;42:103-109.

29. Schwartz PJ, Moss AJ, Vincent GM, Crampton RS. Diagnostic criteria for the long QT syndrome: an update. *Circulation*. 1993;88(2):782-784.

30. Schwartz P, Zaza A, Locati E, et al. Stress and sudden death: the case of the long QT syndrome. *Circulation.* 1991;83(4 suppl):II71-II80.
31. Bazett H. An analysis of the time-relations of electrocardiograms. *Heart.* 1920;7:353-370.
32. Chiang C, Roden DM. The long QT syndromes: genetic basis and clinical implications. *J Am Coll Cardiol.* 2000;36(1):1-12.
33. Ackerman MJ, Priori SG, Willems S, et al. HRS/EHRA expert consensus statement on the state of genetic testing for the channelopathies and cardiomyopathies: this document was developed as a partnership between the Heart Rhythm Society (HRS) and the European Heart Rhythm Association (EHRA). *Europace.* 2011;13(8):1077-1109. http://doi.org/10.1093/europace/eur245
34. Eldar M, Griffin J, Van Hare GF, et al. Combined use of beta-adrenergic blocking agents and long-term cardiac pacing for patients with the long QT syndrome. *J Am Coll Cardiol.* 1992;20(4):830-837.

CHAPTER FOURTEEN

Pacemakers and Pacemaker Dysfunction

ELIZABETH KWAN

KEY POINTS

- The most common reason for apparent pacemaker dysfunction is pseudomalfunction (ie appropriate function that is misinterpreted).
- The pacemaker and myocardium form a closed circuit. Problems at any part of the circuit may cause malfunction. Emergency evaluation should include workup of problems at both pacemaker (formal interrogation) and the myocardium.
- Slow ventricular rates in patients with pacemakers can be due to pseudomalfunction or by failure at any part of the circuit.
- Rapid ventricular rates in patients with pacemakers are most commonly caused by a rapid intrinsic heart rate. Pacemaker arrhythmias (eg, pacemaker-mediated tachycardia) do not exceed a programmed maximum rate and will terminate with the use of a magnet. True pacemaker failure such as runaway pacemaker is exceedingly rare.

As cardiac device technology has evolved, the range of indications for the use of these devices has increased as has the complexity of the devices and their programming. Pacemakers provide atrial or ventricular pacing to prevent symptomatic bradycardia. Implantable cardioverter-defibrillators (ICDs) can provide cardioversion and defibrillation to prevent sudden cardiac death from ventricular tachyarrhythmias as well as provide antitachycardia and bradycardia pacing functions. Biventricular pacemakers, known as cardiac resynchronization therapy (CRT) devices, coordinate the action of right and left ventricles for patients with severely reduced systolic function and prolonged QRS duration. Cardiac resynchronization therapy devices typically include a defibrillator (CRT-D) because these patients are at high risk for ventricular tachyarrhythmias.[1]

Advances in technology have made cardiac devices more reliable but also more challenging for the nonsubspecialist to understand. Unexpected or unusual ECG findings are far more frequently a pseudomalfunction, that is, the failure to understand appropriate programming and function, rather than actual pacemaker malfunction. Typical categories of pacemaker malfunction—undersensing, oversensing, failure to capture, and failure to pace—can be more useful to an electrophysiologist programming a pacemaker than to an emergency physician. Disruption of the closed circuit formed by the pacemaker and the myocardium affects both pacing and sensing and can manifest itself as *any* of these categories of malfunction.

Emergency physicians should prioritize rapid identification of life-threatening and reversible causes of the potential pacemaker malfunction. Causes of disruptions of the circuit at the myocardium include:

- hyperkalemia,
- myocardial ischemia and infarction,
- hypoxia,
- hypercarbia, and
- medications.

Any severe metabolic derangements can alter the pacing threshold or change the ability to sense intrinsic signal.

Formal device interrogation can be critical. It provides information about remaining battery life, programming, lead integrity, and a record of all sensed and paced events. Dangerous pacemaker malfunction might not otherwise be evident during an emergency evaluation. Workup of other serious causes of a patient's presentation, however, should never be delayed while awaiting interrogation.

This chapter will present a review of pacemaker function, nomenclature, and programming. It will also provide a systematic approach to the evaluation of a paced ECG, with a differential diagnosis that includes both pacemaker malfunction and pseudomalfunction.

INDICATIONS FOR PACEMAKER PLACEMENT

Consensus guidelines for pacemaker placement are established by the American College of Cardiology, the American Heart Association, and the Heart Rhythm Society (ACC/AHA/HRS).[2] Pacemakers are placed most often for symptomatic bradycardia from sinus node dysfunction or atrioventricular block. Select

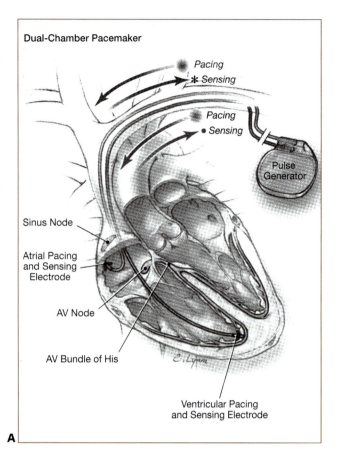

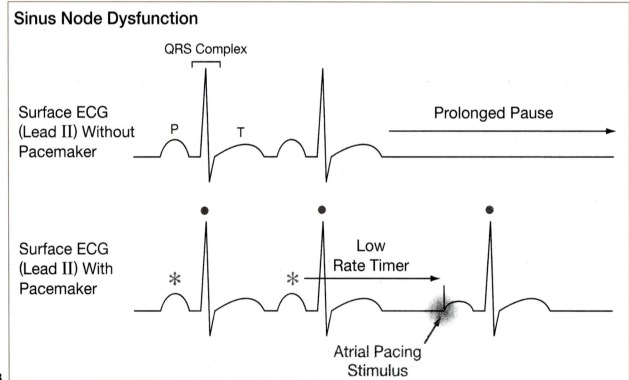

patients with recurrent neurocardiogenic syncope or supraventricular tachycardia failing medications and ablation may also be paced. Biventricular pacemakers improve cardiac function, quality of life, and survival in some patients with advanced heart failure.[3]

PACEMAKER PARTS AND FUNCTION

A pacemaker has three main functions:

- to create electrical impulses to pace the myocardium,
- to sense intrinsic cardiac signal and respond by pacing or inhibiting pacing, and
- to store diagnostic information.

Pacemakers consist of two main parts, a pulse generator and the lead or leads. The generator consists of a battery and circuitry to interpret sensor information and create pacing stimuli. The generator is usually palpable in a subcutaneous pocket in the upper anterior chest. Circuitry within the generator carries out programming. The leads are wires

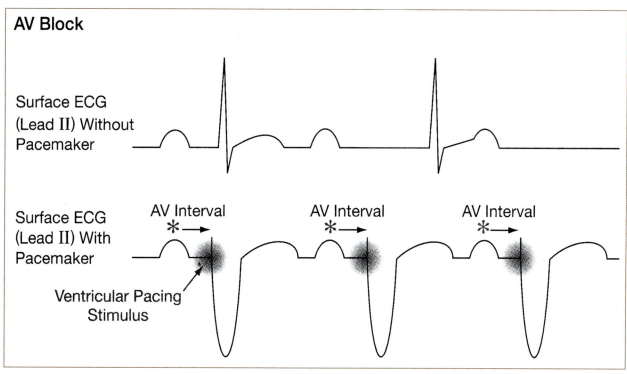

C

FIGURE 14.1. Dual-chamber pacing function. **A** (previous page). Schematic of a dual-chamber pacemaker. The atrial and ventricular leads run from the implanted generator through the subclavian or cephalic vein and enter the appropriate chambers through the superior vena cava. Leads transmit electrical impulses to the myocardium (pacing) and detect electrical cardiac activity (sensing). **B** (previous page). This initial tracing from a patient with sinus node dysfunction shows sinus p waves with normal conduction resulting in intrinsic ventricular activity. After the second complex, ventricular activity is absent due to failure of the sinus node. In the second tracing, a dual-chamber pacemaker has been implanted. Sinus p waves with normal AV conduction result in intrinsic ventricular activity and both are sensed, appropriately suppressing pacemaker function. A pause in atrial activity exceeds the lower rate timer and results in an atrial pacing stimulus. This conducts appropriately through the AV node and generates intrinsic ventricular depolarization, which is sensed and suppresses ventricular pacing. **C.** (above). This initial tracing from a patient with complete AV nodal block shows an atrial rate that is unrelated to the junctional escape rate that generates ventricular activity. In the second tracing, a dual-chamber pacemaker has been implanted. The intrinsic atrial activity is sensed, and a paced ventricular impulse is delivered after a programmed AV delay expires without sensed ventricular activity. No atrial pacing is occurring in this example. Reproduced with permission from: Kusumoto FM, Goldschlager N. Device therapy for cardiac arrhythmias. *JAMA*. 2002;287:1848-1852. Copyright 2002 American Medical Association. All rights reserved.

connected to the generator that deliver electrical impulses to and from the myocardium (Figure 14.1)

The pacemaker forms a closed circuit with myocardial tissue to carry out pacing and sensing functions. The circuit *must remain a closed loop* for appropriate function. A change in integrity or resistance at any part of the circuit can affect both pacing and sensing. These changes include battery depletion; damaged circuitry; lead fracture or disconnection from the generator or myocardium; lead insulation breaks; and changes to the tissue interface due to fibrosis, inflammation, metabolic changes, or ischemia.

With unipolar leads, the negative electrode is at the end of the wire and the positive electrode is the metal pacemaker generator casing. This generates a large, visible pacer artifact ("spike") on the surface ECG. Bipolar leads, which are now far more common, are less likely to stimulate other body tissue or to oversense (mistake other electrical activity as cardiac impulses). With bipolar leads, the negative electrode is at the tip of the lead and the positive electrode forms a ring just proximal to the tip. Because the electrodes are very close together, the area of current flow is smaller, resulting in smaller, less visible electrocardiographic artifacts (Figure 14.2).

Leads are generally guided fluoroscopically from the left subclavian vein into position in the right heart. They may be fixed passively into the trabeculae of the myocardium or fixed using screws. Right heart leads are *endocardial*. The atrial lead is in the right atrial appendage. The right ventricular lead can be at the apex, right ventricular outflow tract, or interventricular septum. In biventricular pacing, a third lead that coordinates pacing of right and left ventricles is passed through veins to the *epicardial* surface of the heart into the coronary sinus.

PACEMAKER NOMENCLATURE

The North American Society for Pacing and Electrophysiology (NASPE) uses a five-letter pacemaker code that has been adopted throughout the industry (Table 14.1). The combination of these letters describes the pacemaker mode or function. The first three letters are the ones most commonly used.

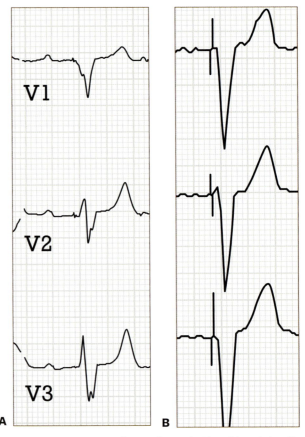

FIGURE 14.2. A. Leads V_1 through V_3 with minimally evident ventricular pacing spike from a pacer with bipolar leads. **B.** Leads V_1 through V_3 with a clearly evident ventricular pacing spike from a pacer with a unipolar lead.

The first letter designates the chamber(s) paced. Chambers are designated as atrial (A), ventricular (V), both atrial and ventricular (D or dual), or none (O). The second letter designates the chamber(s) in which intrinsic impulses are sensed. These are designated as atrial (A), ventricular (V), both atrial and ventricular (D or dual), or none (O). The third letter designates how the pacemaker responds to sensed intrinsic electrical activity. A sensed event might inhibit (I) the pacemaker, trigger (T) a response, both inhibit and trigger (D), or cause no response (O) from the pacemaker generator.

Of all new pacemaker implantations in 2009, 82% were DDD pacemakers (Figure 14.3), compared to single chamber VVI (14%) and AAI (1%) pacemakers.[4] Although patients with sinus dysfunction

PACEMAKERS AND PACEMAKER DYSFUNCTION

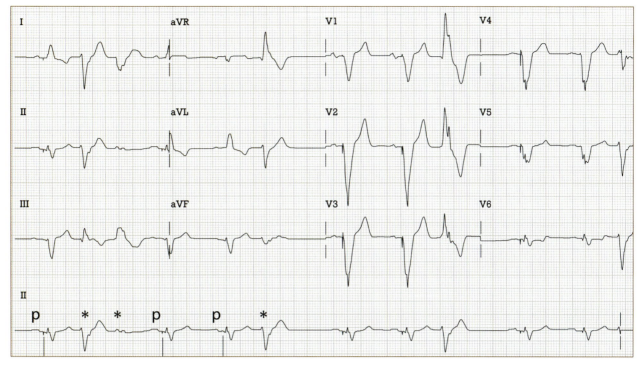

FIGURE 14.3. DDD pacemaker with ventricular ectopy. Ventricular pacing as well as dual-chamber sensing are demonstrated on this ECG. Intrinsic sinus p waves (*p*) are sensed, suppressing atrial pacing. A paced ventricular impulse is delivered in response to the sensed p wave after a programmed AV interval expires without intrinsic ventricular response (*bar*). A premature ventricular beat (*star*) is sensed and appropriately suppresses both atrial and ventricular pacing. A subsequent sinus p wave occurs before the pacemaker fires at its lower rate limit, again triggering a ventricular pacing impulse after the appropriate AV delay. Note that the amplitude of the pacer spike from the bipolar ventricular lead is small and is best seen in leads V_2 through V_4. Although pacing spikes are absent in two of the paced complexes, these have the same QRS morphology as the other paced complexes and can be assumed to be paced. Reproduced with permission from: Jeffrey A. Tabas, MD, FACEP.

TABLE 14.1. North American Society for Pacing and Electrophysiology pacemaker codes.

POSITION	I	II	III	IV	V
INTERPRETATION	CHAMBER(S) PACED	CHAMBER(S) SENSED	RESPONSE TO SENSING	RATE RESPONSIVENESS	MULTICHAMBER PACING
Variable	o	o	o	o	o
	A	A	T	R	A
	V	V	I		V
	D (A + V)	D (A + V)	D (T + I)		D (A + V)

A = atria, D = dual, I = inhibited, o = none, R = rate responsiveness, T = triggered, V = ventricle

but intact atrioventricular (AV) conduction only require AAI pacing, they often get a dual chamber pacemaker because of the risk of developing subsequent AV conduction problems. As indications for biventricular pacemakers expand, they are becoming more common, representing 10% of pacemakers placed from 2007 to 2013.[1]

The fourth letter refers to whether the pacemaker is rate responsive, a function that matches rate to estimated metabolic demands (R) or if this feature is absent or turned off (O). The fifth letter now designates multiple-chamber pacing. Currently only biventricular pacing is available, but nomenclature allows for atrial (A), ventricular (V), both atrial and ventricular (D or dual), or none (O). The fifth letter previously designated whether the device had an ICD function.

PACEMAKER TIMING CYCLE

Programmed intervals determine when a pacemaker will pace (Tables 14.2, 14.3). In the most common mode, DDD, the timing cycle starts with either an intrinsic or paced atrial depolarization. This starts the AV interval, the actual time from *atrial to ventricular* depolarization. The AV interval is analogous to the PR interval. A programmed AV delay is analogous to the longest AV interval the pacemaker will wait for an intrinsic impulse before initiating a paced ventricular impulse. If an intrinsic QRS occurs within the programmed AV delay, the pacemaker is inhibited. Note that "inhibition" refers to lack of impulse generation by the pacemaker. Although a paced depolarization makes the myocardium temporarily refractory to further impulses, pacemakers do not directly inhibit intrinsic cardiac activity. Ventricular depolarization starts the ventricular-atrial interval, the time from *ventricular to atrial* depolarization. A programmed atrial escape interval is the programmed interval the pacemaker will wait for an intrinsic p wave before initiating a paced atrial impulse.[5] The *lower* ventricular rate limit allowed before initiation of pacing is determined by two programmed intervals—the AV delay plus the atrial escape interval.

The pacemaker's *upper* rate limit is determined by the *minimum* time before the pacemaker triggers the next AV interval. This period of time that the pacemaker will not trigger the next AV interval, the total atrial refractory period, is composed of two intervals, the AV interval (actual time between p and QRS waves) and a programmed postventricular-atrial refractory period that follows the QRS wave. The beginning of this refractory period is a brief blanking period, during which the pacemaker

TABLE 14.2. Programmed pacemaker intervals.	
AV interval	*Actual* time between p and QRS waves regardless of trigger
AV delay	Programmed maximum time pacemaker waits for QRS before pacing the ventricle
Ventricular-atrial interval	*Actual* time between QRS and p waves regardless of trigger
Atrial escape interval	Programmed maximum time pacemaker waits for p wave before pacing the atrium

TABLE 14.3. Pacemaker lower and upper rate limits.	
Pacemaker lower rate limit	Determined by two programmed intervals, the AV delay and the atrial escape interval
Pacemaker upper rate limit	Determined by an actual time, the AV interval, plus a programmed postventricular-atrial refractory period

will neither sense nor record any impulses, preventing the misinterpretation of the pacemaker's own impulse as an intrinsic depolarization. During the rest of the refractory period, the pacemaker senses and records the impulse, but it will not alter the timing cycle.[5] The patient's actual heart rate could exceed the upper rate limit because the pacemaker cannot inhibit intrinsic activity.

Consider a patient with a pacemaker in DDD mode and a programmed upper rate limit of 120 beats/min. This patient develops atrial fibrillation with an atrial rate of 150 beats/min. If AV conduction is *intact* and there is rapid ventricular response, the pacemaker will be fully inhibited. The total atrial refractory period, which determines the soonest the pacemaker restarts a timing cycle, has an upper rate limit of 120 beats/min. The ECG will show an irregular rate of 150 beats/min without pacemaker artifacts. If AV conduction is *absent* and the ventricular response *must* be paced, the pacemaker will be refractory to any intrinsic p waves that occur within the total atrial refractory period. In other words, the pacemaker will not trigger a ventricular response to intrinsic p waves when the atrial rate exceeds the upper rate limit. The ECG will show an irregular rate that does not exceed 120 beats/min and some nonconducted p waves (Figure 14.4).

COMMON PROGRAMMING FEATURES

Under perfect conditions, a pacemaker would identify intrinsic electrical impulses with perfect sensitivity and specificity and approximate a patient's normal physiology, matching pacemaker rate to metabolic demands and minimizing unnecessary pacing and the deleterious effects of pacing. Programming features target these goals. An understanding of some of these programming features can help identify pseudomalfunctions.

Optimizing Safety: Preventing Crosstalk

Pacemakers must distinguish intrinsic depolarizations from other electrical signals and correctly identify the chamber of origin to safely inhibit or pace. Bipolar leads have greatly reduced oversensing from noncardiac sources, so programming focuses on intracardiac signals. A pacing stimulus from one chamber misinterpreted as an intrinsic depolarization in the other is called crosstalk. If an atrial pacing signal is misinterpreted as intrinsic ventricular depolarization, ventricular pacing is inappropriately inhibited indefinitely, leading to asystole.[5]

BLANKING PERIOD AFTER PACING. To prevent crosstalk, pacemakers have a brief blanking period in all chambers immediately after each pacing stimulus. During the blanking period, the pacemaker does not sense or record intrinsic electrical activity. An intrinsic depolarization can occur immediately after a pacing impulse and go undetected.

VENTRICULAR SAFETY PACING. Ventricular safety pacing is additional protection against crosstalk and protection from ventricular tachyarrhythmias initiated by the R-on-T phenomenon. After each pacing stimulus and blanking period, the pacemaker has a crosstalk sensing window. If any ventricular activity is sensed within the crosstalk window, the pacemaker initiates a ventricular impulse early. If the signal sensed in the ventricle was a misinterpreted atrial pacing event, the early ventricular safety pacing prevents inappropriate inhibition of the pacemaker. If the sensed signal in the crosstalk window is an intrinsic premature ventricular contraction (PVC), the early ventricular pacing artifact prevents pacing during the vulnerable part of the T wave that could precipitate ventricular tachyarrhythmias. Suspect ventricular safety pacing when you see a ventricular pacing artifact soon after either an atrial pacer artifact or a PVC that lands when you would expect an atrial pacing artifact.[6] If ventricular safety pacing follows a PVC, the myocardium will be refractory, so the ECG will show a pacing stimulus without an additional QRS.

Physiologic Pacing

MATCHING METABOLIC DEMANDS: RATE RESPONSIVENESS. Rate-responsive pacemakers estimate metabolic demands by using one or more

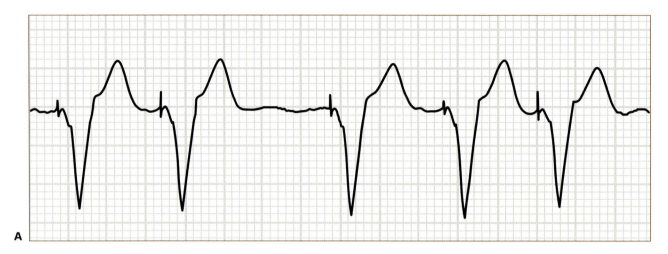
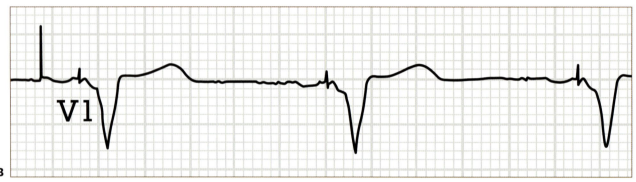

FIGURE 14.4. Rapid paced ventricular rate in a patient with a DDD pacemaker caused by atrial fibrillation. **A.** Recording of the presenting rhythm (lead V_1) in a patient with rapid (100 beats/min) irregular pacemaker discharges and ventricular capture. This is most likely the result of atrial fibrillation waves sensed by the atrial lead, resulting in delivery of a paced ventricular impulse after expiration of the programmed AV interval. This leads to rapid ventricular response with rates as fast as the upper rate limit of the pacemaker. The shortest R-R interval in this strip is at a rate of 115 beats/min. There are no discernible P waves, and there is a ventricular complex that might represent a fusion complex between a conducted atrial and a generated ventricular impulse. **B.** Recording from the same patient after he spontaneously reverted to sinus rhythm. Sensed atrial sinus beats trigger ventricular pacing with appropriate capture. The pacemaker was subsequently reprogrammed to decrease the maximum ventricular pacing rate. Some devices use internal logic that will analyze and detect atrial fibrillation, thus avoiding excessively rapid ventricular responses. Reproduced with permission from: Steven A. Pace, MD.

sensors. Two common methods use an accelerometer to detect motion or changes in chest wall bioelectric impedance as measures of minute ventilation. The pacemaker interprets an increase in motion or minute ventilation as increased activity and increases the pacemaker rate to accommodate exercise, an important feature for active patients. Rate responsiveness is turned off when a magnet is placed, and the pacemaker is made asynchronous.[7]

MINIMIZING RIGHT VENTRICULAR PACING. Right ventricular (RV) pacing depolarizes the myocardium from the right ventricle to the septum and then to the left ventricle, simulating a left bundle-branch block on the ECG. Pacing from the right ventricle has been shown to cause altered left ventricular (LV) perfusion, dyssynchrony between the left atrium and ventricle, and adverse remodeling.[8,9] Pacing that maintains AV synchrony such as AAI mode (when AV conduction is intact) can decrease these long-term deleterious effects, especially in patients with reduced ejection fraction, and can also reduce the incidence of atrial fibrillation and stroke.[10] Keeping AV synchrony produces a better ejection fraction by preserving "atrial kick." Patients with preexisting LV dysfunction are at highest risk for the deleterious effects of long-term pacing from an RV lead.[11]

Pacemaker syndrome is caused by adverse hemodynamic effects of AV asynchrony. Although the pacemaker is functioning as programmed, patients can have anxiety, dizziness, fatigue, dyspnea, or pulsations in the neck. Nonspecific symptoms require that other life-threatening causes of these symptoms such as sepsis or ischemia be excluded. The diagnosis of pacemaker syndrome is usually made by the cardiologist after comprehensive echocardiography and a full evaluation of the pacemaker.

Atrioventricular asynchrony leads to decreased LV filling and cardiac output. Elevated atrial pressures can initiate a vagal reflex causing syncope and near syncope. High wedge pressure can cause dyspnea. Patients with retrograde one-to-one ventricular to atrial conduction are more symptomatic, but pacemaker syndrome can occur in the absence of retrograde conduction.[12,13]

The adverse effects on LV function increase with the frequency and duration of RV pacing.[10] Advances in pacemaker technology allow minimizing RV pacing when possible through automatic mode switching and allowing slow native rates. These measures preserve AV synchrony, minimizing the long-term harm.

AUTOMATIC MODE SWITCH. An automatic mode switch allows a pacemaker to be in AAI mode whenever AV conduction is intact. If AV conduction is not detected, the pacemaker will automatically switch to DDD mode. The device periodically switches back to AAI mode to check for intrinsic AV conduction.[14] The automatic mode switch also protects against fast atrial rates. If an atrial tachycardia is detected, the pacemaker can switch from a DDD mode, which will track an intrinsic atrial rhythm up to the programmed maximum rate indefinitely, to VVI or DDI or DVI mode to stop the triggering of ventricular pacing by atrial impulses. When the intrinsic atrial rate falls below a programmed threshold, the pacemaker will switch back to DDD mode.[6]

REST, SLEEP, AND HYSTERESIS MODES. The heart benefits from a naturally decreased heart rate during sleep. Experimental data on patients with DDD pacemakers show that systolic and diastolic function decline without this rest.[11] Pacemakers have programming to mimic this phenomenon, allowing rates slower than the lower rate limit.

St. Jude pacemakers offer a rest mode that is 10 to 20 beats lower than the lower rate limit if patient activity decreases below a preset threshold for 15 to 20 minutes. Activity is measured with the same accelerometer as the rate-response feature. Medtronic sleep mode decreases the paced rate during specific hours of the day. Because neither rest nor sleep mode relies on sensing intrinsic rhythm, these features will *not* be turned off by magnet application.[15]

Boston Scientific pacemakers have a *hysteresis* (from the Greek work for "late") function. The pacemaker can have a programmed lower rate limit of 60 beats/min when pacing but a hysteresis rate of 50 beats/min. The pacemaker will allow the intrinsic rate to fall as low as 50 beats/min before it starts pacing at a rate of 60 beats/min. Because this feature relies on sensing intrinsic rate, turning off sensing with magnet application *will* turn off hysteresis.[15]

Approach to Potential Pacemaker Dysfunction

An emergency department workup of potential pacemaker dysfunction includes careful consideration of etiologies not related to the device, as well as of pacemaker complications not related to malfunction. Pacemaker patients are generally older and can have multiple comorbidities. Symptoms from pacemaker malfunction or complications can also be intermittent, mild, or nonspecific, not immediately implicating the pacemaker.

As usual, first determine if the patient is stable or unstable by assessing airway, breathing, and circulation. Patients should be placed on a cardiac monitor with secure intravenous access. Have a low threshold for placing defibrillator pads in case the patient needs transcutaneous pacing, cardioversion, or defibrillation.

A transvenous pacemaker can be placed for patients with unstable bradycardia without a reversible cause if the permanent pacemaker is nonfunctional. However, risks and benefits compared to medical management and transcutaneous pacing must be carefully considered, ideally with a cardiologist's input. If the patient is unstable, is it because of the rhythm? Are there reversible causes of bradycardia, such as oversensing, medication, or hyperkalemia? In those cases, focus on reversal; do not delay treatment by doing a procedure. Placing a transvenous pacemaker with a nonfunctional permanent pacemaker in place bears the additional risks of disturbing a thrombus, introducing a device infection, or complicating its replacement.

Any defect in the circuit can cause dysfunction, so both the pacemaker and the myocardium must be evaluated. Formal interrogation is critical to evaluate the pacemaker. Workup of other emergent conditions at the myocardium or other etiologies for the patient's presentation, however, should not be delayed while awaiting interrogation. Emergent processes affecting the circuit at the myocardium include severe metabolic abnormalities, sepsis, ischemia, and inflammation.

Pacemaker Interrogation

Pacemakers store a record of each sensed and paced event, which allows determination of undersensing and oversensing, as well as information such as range of heart rate, percentage of time pacing, arrhythmia logs, and any ICD discharges. Pacemaker interrogation also evaluates battery life and lead integrity. The device interrogation by the manufacturer representative or cardiology technician is a critical part of the emergency evaluation of a patient presenting with symptoms that might be attributed to the pacemaker. Manufacturers can arrange interrogations through their 24-hour phone lines (Table 14.4). In some cases, the interrogator, in consultation with the patient's cardiologist, is able to identify problems and reprogram the device to avoid an admission.

TABLE 14.4. Cardiac rhythm management device manufacturer phone numbers.

MANUFACTURER	TELEPHONE NUMBER
Biotronik	1-800-547-0394
Boston Scientific (Guidant)	1-800-CARDIAC 1-800-227-3422
Medtronic	1-800-MEDTRONIC 1-800-633-8766
Sorin GP (ELA Medical)	1-800-352-6466
St. Jude	1-800-PACEICD 1-800-722-3774

Identifying the Patient's Device

The patient might know the device or manufacturer's name or have a wallet card from the manufacturer. The patient's medical record, including outside facility records, might have device information. Even without these sources, you can likely identify the device by calling manufacturers. Each of the five main manufacturers of cardiac rhythm management devices (CRMDs) have a 24-hour phone line that can find a patient within their database and arrange interrogations.[16] Finally, a chest radiograph can reveal the number and appearance of leads and the appearance of the generator. When ordering a chest radiograph to identify a device, be explicit in your request and ask for an overpenetrated view of the device itself. This view can also help you identify the device by its manufacturer-specific radiopaque alphanumeric code.

Paced ECG Appearance

Small pacer artifacts of bipolar leads might not be visible in every lead. The typical paced QRS complex of a dual chamber pacemaker with a lead in the right ventricle shows a left bundle-branch block (LBBB) pattern. A right bundle-branch block (RBBB) pattern is normal in 17% of patients due to variations in lead placement.[17] Patients with biventricular pacing can show an RBBB pattern since lead position is variable.

Patients with CRT devices are usually paced continuously for the improved ejection fraction from the coordination of both ventricles. A biventricular paced ECG will usually show an atrial and two, closely spaced, RV and LV pacing stimuli. The coordinated RV and LV depolarizations result in a hybrid QRS that is usually narrower than that found in RV pacing. Lead positions are variable in CRT, resulting in variable ECG morphology. Figure 14.5 shows the ECG of a patient with severe heart failure in atrial fibrillation with a rate of 58 beats/min and an LBBB pattern with a QRS duration of 194 milliseconds and the same patient after CRT. The QRS has narrowed to 168 milliseconds, and the LBBB pattern is no longer present.

If the axis of the pacer artifact and QRS complex in a dual-chamber pacemaker has changed compared to an old ECG, it suggests lead migration or perforation through the myocardium. In a biventricular pacemaker, a change in axis could mean one ventricular lead is not functioning. Figure 14.6 shows the baseline of a patient on CRT and the acute change when the RV lead was dislodged.

Magnet Exam

- Turns off sensing to diagnose and treat oversensing,
- Terminates pacemaker arrhythmias that are due to sensing, and
- Can indicate battery depletion.

A standard doughnut-shaped magnet is made for CRMDs, but a generic magnet will also work. The magnet opens a reed switch that turns off the sensing circuit. This initiates asynchronous pacing at a programmed rate that varies by manufacturer. Figure 14.7 shows the effect of magnet placement. If a slow rate is caused by oversensing, placement of the magnet resolves the bradycardia. If the heart rate remains slow or if long pauses continue after the magnet is placed, it suggests a component of the system (generator, battery, or leads) has failed. Rarely, if the heart rate remains slow, the device may be programmed to ignore the magnet, or the pacemaker could be in a sleep mode based on time of day or rest mode based on activity level.[15]

If the magnet exam identifies oversensing as the cause of failure to pace, the magnet can be taped in place to continue pacing until the device can be reprogrammed. If the effect is intermittent, make sure the magnet is directly over the pacemaker generator. If the patient is obese or the generator is behind the pectoral muscle, two magnets might be needed. The magnet's effects stop once the magnet is removed.

The magnet exam is considered safe enough to be done routinely at a device clinic and even remotely from home. However, symptomatic emergency patients are an undifferentiated population whose risk is not quantified. Pacemakers at the *very* end of their battery life also have an unpredictable response to a magnet. In addition, asynchronous pacing during the magnet exam can theoretically precipitate ventricular tachyarrhythmias via the R-on-T phenomenon. Therefore, have defibrillator pads in place before performing the magnet exam.

- If asynchronous pacing triggers ventricular tachycardia (VT) or ventricular fibrillation (VF), you will be prepared to cardiovert or defibrillate.
- If the bradycardic patient becomes unstable, you will be prepared for transcutaneous pacing.
- The magnet turns off the ICD function. Patients requiring ICDs are at high risk for ventricular tachyarrhythmias.

APPROACH TO PACEMAKER ECG WITH HEART RATE TOO FAST

A systematic approach to the paced ECG is essential to determine whether there is malfunction. The first priority when interpreting a paced ECG is identifying any emergent condition that needs immediate action:

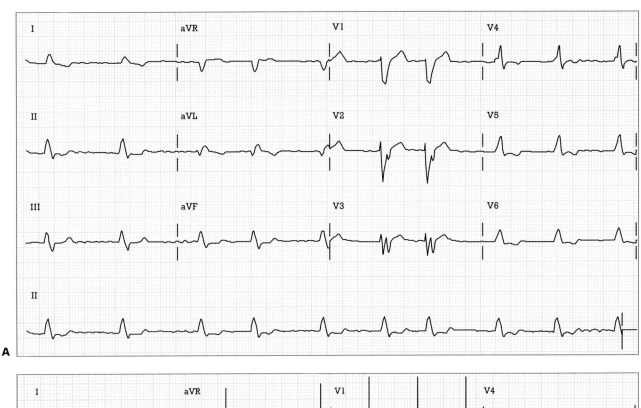

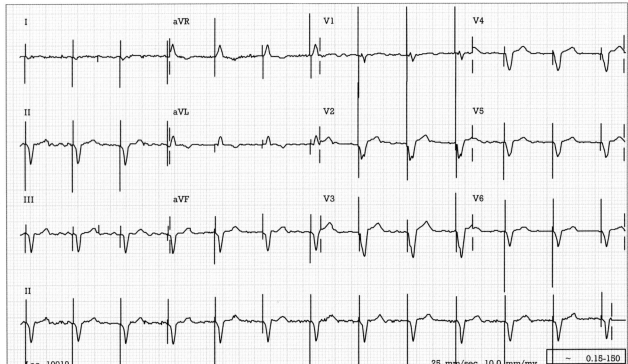

FIGURE 14.5. Biventricular pacing or cardiac resynchronization therapy (CRT). **A.** The ECG of a patient with symptoms of severe heart failure—atrial fibrillation at a rate of 58 beats/min and left bundle-branch block with a QRS duration of 194 milliseconds. **B.** The ECG of the same patient after CRT. A ventricular pacer spike represents simultaneous impulse delivery from right and left ventricular leads. The QRS is narrowed to 168 milliseconds, and the left bundle-branch pattern is no longer present. Reproduced with permission from: Nora Goldschlager, MD.

ischemia, hyperkalemia, or an unstable bradycardia or tachycardia. Do not delay workup or treatment of emergent conditions while awaiting pacemaker interrogation or the interpretation of a paced rhythm.

If the rate is too fast (Figure 14.8), determine:

- whether the ventricular rate exceeds the programmed upper rate limit. If not, then determine
- whether a magnet exam resolves the fast rate.

When the Ventricular Rate Exceeds the Programmed Upper Rate Limit

Although you might not know the programmed upper rate limit, it is generally no more than 75% to 85% of the patient's maximum predicted heart rate (220 bpm minus age). For an 80-year-old patient, the maximum predicted heart rate is 140. A reasonable upper rate limit should be no more than 85% of 140, or 120 beats/min.

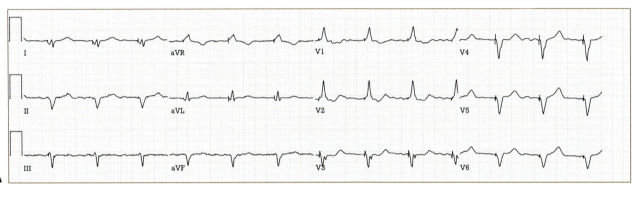
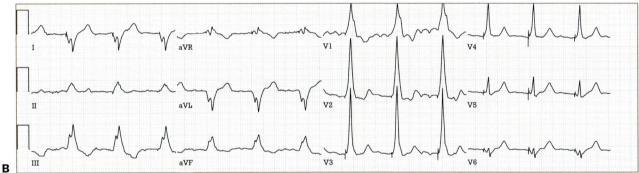

FIGURE 14.6. ECG from a patient with CRT before (**A**) and after (**B**) the right ventricular lead is dislodged. Note the changed axis and wider QRS.

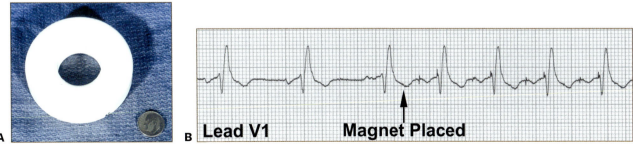

FIGURE 14.7. Magnet application. **A.** A magnet. **B.** Lead V₁ reveals a normal sinus rhythm with right bundle-branch block. Placement of a magnet over the pacemaker reveals AV sequential pacing with 100% capture at 100 beats/min.

When the ventricular rate exceeds the programmed upper rate limit, the differential is relatively narrow—either pseudomalfunction or true generator failure, which is extremely rare.

PSEUDOMALFUNCTION CAUSED BY FAST INTRINSIC VENTRICULAR RATES. Tachycardia in a patient with a pacemaker is often due to fast intrinsic rates. Remember that the pacemaker

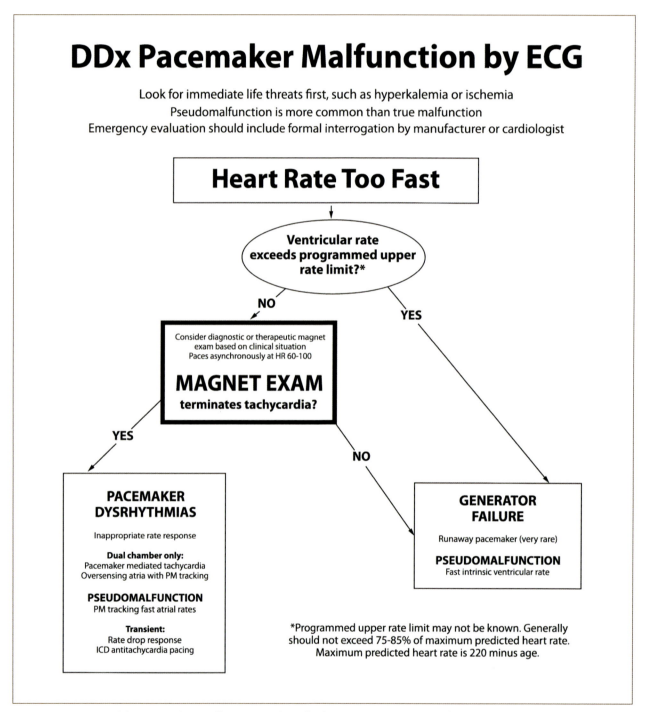

FIGURE 14.8. Possible pacemaker malfunctions when the heart rate appears too fast.

cannot directly inhibit the heart. Always consider fast intrinsic rates, especially when the rate exceeds a reasonable programmed upper rate limit. Consider potential underlying causes of tachycardia such as pain, dehydration, and sepsis. An intrinsic rhythm such as ventricular tachycardia or supraventricular tachycardia with intact AV conduction could be fully inhibiting the pacemaker. A lead dislodged from the endocardium can precipitate intermittent VT just as a free wire might during central line placement.

RUNAWAY PACEMAKER. Runaway pacemaker is a true pulse generator failure. It has become exceedingly rare after improvements in pacemaker technology such as hermetic sealing of the generator. Runaway pacemaker can cause dramatically rapid rates. Impulses in runaway pacemaker are from a failing generator, so they might not meet the capture threshold to trigger ventricular depolarization. The actual heart rate varies, and the patient could even be bradycardic. Frequent pacing stimuli increase the risk of an R-on-T phenomenon inducing VT or VF. Magnet application has no effect on runaway pacemaker since this is not a problem of sensing.[18] Treatment requires emergent pacemaker reprogramming or, if this fails, disconnecting the leads in the pacemaker pocket.[6,18]

When the Ventricular Rate is Fast but Does Not Exceed the Programmed Upper Rate Limit, Consider Performing a Magnet Exam

If the fast rate is intrinsic (ie, physiologically appropriate for a clinical situation such as dehydration or sepsis) asynchronous pacing will not resolve the tachycardia.

If the magnet exam terminates the tachycardia, the differential includes inappropriate rate response, pacemaker-mediated tachycardia, oversensing, and pseudomalfunction.

INAPPROPRIATE RATE RESPONSIVENESS (SENSOR-DRIVEN TACHYCARDIA). Rate-responsive pacemakers use one or more sensors to estimate metabolic demands and determine when to increase heart rate. Common methods include an accelerometer to measure movement and chest wall and electrical impedance to measure minute ventilation. The accelerometer can misinterpret movement of the generator by arm, shoulder, or muscle tremor. Bioelectrical impedance of the chest wall varies by respiratory rate and volume. A current created between the generator casing and one of the leads is used to measure impedance and estimate minute ventilation. Hyperventilation, fever, and cautery use near the pacemaker can change impedance and inappropriately trigger rate-responsive pacemakers to increase the heart rate.

Common cardiac monitors also use impedance to measure respiratory rate and detect when a lead has become detached. Multiple case reports of monitors triggering pacemaker rate response have been reported. Because this is a rare and inconsistent malfunction, many clinicians might not consider it. The resulting wide complex tachycardia can be mistaken for VT.[19,20] Taking the patient off the monitor restored normal pacing rate within two minutes in one case report.[21] To test for this interference, turn off the monitor and check the heart rate by pulse or bedside ultrasound. Placing the patient on a portable monitor defibrillator or ECG machine might also resolve the sensor-driven tachycardia, although these devices also use impedance to detect lead connection to the patient. Rate responsiveness is also turned off when a magnet is placed. Beware that asynchronous pacing of an intrinsic T wave could precipitate VF.[22,23]

PACEMAKER-MEDIATED TACHYCARDIA. Pacemaker-mediated tachycardia is only seen in dual-chamber pacemakers. Retrograde conduction through the AV node of a paced ventricular signal (crosstalk) or a paced ventricular impulse causes the pacemaker to oversense the atrium. This triggers another ventricular pacing stimulus and forms a reentrant loop. Because pacemaker-mediated tachycardia will not exceed the upper rate limit, patients are usually stable. Treatment requires interrupting the loop. This can be done by Valsalva maneuver, a medication that blocks the AV node, or by turning off sensing with a magnet (Figure 14.9).

OVERSENSING ATRIAL SIGNALS. Atrial oversensing can cause fast rates if the pacemaker triggers the ventricle. For example, if the R wave is misinterpreted as an additional intrinsic atrial signal and the pacemaker paces the ventricle for each atrial signal, the pacemaker rate will be twice the true atrial rate.

PSEUDOMALFUNCTION: TRACKING FAST INTRINSIC ATRIAL RATES. If AV conduction is not intact, and the pacemaker triggers the ventricle in response to fast atrial rates, the heart rate will not exceed the programmed upper rate limit. If the atrial rate exceeds the programmed maximum tracking rate, the AV interval will progressively increase, and eventually a p wave will occur in the pacemaker refractory period and not be conducted. The ECG will show a pacemaker Wenckebach pattern. As the atrial rate increases further, and the P-to-P interval becomes shorter than the total atrial refractory period, the ECG will show a 2-to-1 AV block.

PSEUDOMALFUNCTION: RATE-DROP RESPONSE. Programmed rate-drop response for patients with recurrent vasovagal syncope can be mistaken for malfunction. With rate-drop response, the pacemaker will respond to a sudden drop in intrinsic rate by pacing for 1 to 2 minutes at 100 to 120 beats/min, or at 70% to 80% of the maximum tracking rate. This has been shown to significantly reduce episodes of syncope.[24]

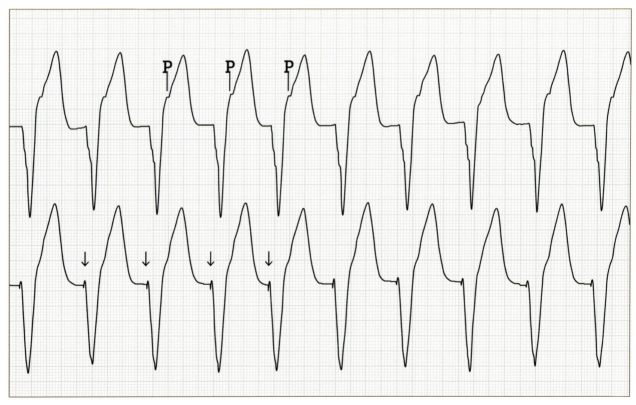

FIGURE 14.9. Rapid paced ventricular rate caused by pacemaker tachycardia. Tracing from leads V_2 and V_3 of a patient with a DDD pacer and pacemaker-mediated tachycardia at the upper rate limit of 100 beats/min. The pacer spikes from the bipolar leads are barely seen in lead V_3 (*arrow*). The retrograde P wave (*p*) that is perpetuating the tachycardia is seen buried in the ventricular complex. The patient's pacemaker was reprogrammed to prevent this problem. Reproduced with permission from: Nora Goldschlager, MD.

PSEUDOMALFUNCTION: ANTITACHYCARDIA PACING BY ICD. Although discussion of ICDs is outside the scope of this chapter, antitachycardia pacing of a pacemaker ICD can also cause transient fast rates. When the ICD identifies VT or VF, it uses a programmed algorithm to terminate the arrhythmias. For VT, the pacemaker will initiate one or more trials of antitachycardia pacing, 6 to 10 paced impulses at a rate close to the VT rate. This will terminate VT quickly and painlessly in up to 89% of cases at VT rates of 188 to 250 beats/min, preventing painful shocks.[25,26]

APPROACH TO PACEMAKER ECG WITH HEART RATE TOO SLOW OR NORMAL

If the rate is normal or too slow, determine:

- whether there is pacemaker artifact,
- if there is no paced artifact, whether the magnet exam resolves the slow rate,
- whether each pacemaker artifact is followed by a p or QRS wave, and
- whether each intrinsic p or QRS wave inhibits the pacemaker (Figure 14.10).

When the Ventricular Rate is Normal or Too Slow and There is No Visible Pacemaker Artifact, Consider Performing a Magnet Exam

In a stable patient with no visible pacemaker artifacts, consider small artifacts or an intrinsic rate above the threshold set for the pacemaker to trigger. Programming features to minimize RV pacing such as hysteresis, rest, or sleep mode allow rates lower than a pacemaker's lower rate limit.

When Magnet Application Results in Pacing as Expected at a Ventricular Rate of 60 to 100 beats/min

If this occurs, then the magnet can be taped to the chest until programming can be changed. The differential diagnosis includes pseudomalfunction and oversensing.

The most common reason for failure to pace is ventricular oversensing, when the pacemaker is inappropriately inhibited by misinterpreted signals, most often intracardiac signals (Figure 14.11).

OVERSENSING INTRACARDIAC SIGNALS. Intrinsic P or T waves or crosstalk from the pacer's own signal, when misinterpreted as ventricular depolarization, inhibits the pacemaker, resulting in slow ventricular rates. Tall T waves, especially in hyperkalemia or LV hypertrophy, are a common cause of oversensing the ventricle.[6]

Oversensing a pacemaker's atrial signal as intrinsic ventricular depolarization, a form of crosstalk, inappropriately inhibits ventricular pacing and ultimately leads to asystole. Brief blanking periods immediately after pacing, during which no sensing occurs, and ventricular safety pacing during a crosstalk window are meant to prevent crosstalk.

Note that oversensing the *atria* can cause inappropriate *fast* rates when an atrial signal triggers pacing of the ventricle. If an R wave is oversensed as an atrial signal, the ventricle will be paced for both the P and R wave, doubling the rate.

OVERSENSING NONCARDIAC SIGNALS. Myopotentials from the chest wall or diaphragm and electromagnetic interference (EMI) can be oversensed as ventricular signal and result in pacemaker inhibition. Sources of EMI within the hospital include electrocautery close to the generator, magnetic resonance imaging, defibrillation or cardioversion, radiofrequency ablation, ionizing radiation, and dental composite curing.[27] Battery powered single-use cautery devices used in the emergency department are unlikely to cause pacemaker malfunction.[14]

Outside of the medical environment, EMI is very unlikely to affect pacemakers. Nonmedical sources of EMI include airport metal detectors, cosmetic lasers, retail antitheft sensors, and cellular phones. Patients are nevertheless advised to avoid keeping a cellular phone over the pacemaker pocket or lingering near antitheft sensors in stores.[27]

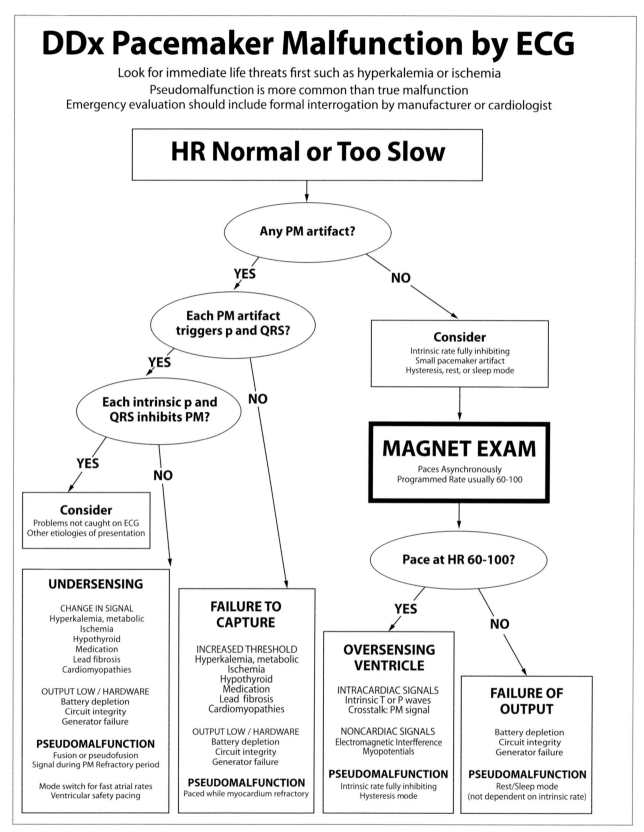

FIGURE 14.10. Possible pacemaker malfunctions when the heart rate is normal or too slow.

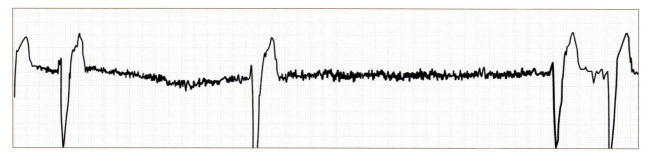

FIGURE 14.11. Oversensing. Tracing reveals background artifact that is sensed inappropriately, thereby suppressing pacemaker impulses. Occasional intrinsic ventricular complexes are seen. Reproduced with permission from: Nora Goldschlager, MD.

When Magnet Application Does Not Result in Pacing as Expected at a Ventricular Rate of 60 to 100 beats/min

When a pacemaker fails to deliver a pacing stimulus after a pause that exceeds the programmed AV delay, it is called failure to pace. Continuous failure to pace can be life threatening for a pacemaker-dependent patient. Life-threatening but reversible causes such as hyperkalemia, medication overdose, and ischemia must be worked up immediately. Be prepared to use transcutaneous or transvenous pacing if the patient is unstable. Failure to pace is most commonly caused by oversensing but can also be caused by failure of output. The magnet exam, performed in collaboration with a cardiologist, distinguishes these two mechanisms.

FAILURE OF OUTPUT. Failure of output can originate from problems in any component of the pacemaker hardware or discontinuity of the circuit the pacemaker makes with the myocardium. The circuit must be closed and intact to move current. If a lead becomes disconnected from the generator or myocardium or is fractured or damaged, the device might be unable to pace.

Batteries commonly used in pacemakers can last 5 to 10 years, depending on the proportion of time paced, impedance from leads and myocardium, and the programmed output. Battery depletion can cause failure to pace, sense, or capture. Elective replacement indicators of battery depletion vary by manufacturer. It can be an incremental slowing of the rate or a lower paced rate on magnet exam. These signs indicate approximately 3 months of remaining life. At the very end of battery life, pacemaker behavior can be unpredictable, including its behavior on magnet exam.[18]

PSEUDOMALFUNCTIONS. Rest and sleep modes that do not rely on sensing will not be resolved by the magnet exam. Examples include programming decreased rates by time of day.

When Pacemaker Artifact is Visible but Each Pacemaker Artifact Fails to Initiate a P or QRS

In this case, there is failure to capture or pseudomalfunction.

FAILURE TO CAPTURE. Capture is the depolarization of the myocardium after a pacemaker stimulus (Figure 14.12). Failure to capture is detected when a ventricular pacemaker impulse fails to generate a QRS complex at a time when the myocardium is *not* refractory. This can be caused by inadequate output delivered to the myocardium or by an increased threshold required due to conditions at the tissue interface (Table 14.5).

FAILURE TO CAPTURE DUE TO INCREASED THRESHOLD. Hyperkalemia and ischemia are common and immediately life-threatening causes of increased capture threshold. Any critically ill patient with a pacemaker can develop failure to capture. Severe metabolic abnormalities such as acidosis, alkalosis, hyperglycemia, hypercarbia, and hypoxemia, as well as multiple medications, can alter pacing thresholds. Fibrosis and inflammation at the tissue interface in the weeks following implantation or from cardiomyopathies can also increase the capture threshold.[18]

TABLE 14.5. Factors that can change capture thresholds.[18]

Drugs that increase or decrease pacing thresholds

Increase threshold
- Dofetilide class III
- Flecainide class IC
- Mineralocorticoids
- Propafenone class IC
- Sotalol class III

Possibly increase threshold
- Beta-adrenergic blockers class II
- Ibutilide class III
- Lidocaine class IB
- Procainamide class IA
- Quinidine class IA

Decrease threshold
- Atropine
- Epinephrine
- Glucocorticoids
- Isoproterenol

Metabolic factors that increase capture thresholds
- Acidosis
- Alkalosis
- Hypercarbia
- Hyperkalemia
- Hypoxemia
- Myxedema
- Severe hyperglycemia

FAILURE TO CAPTURE DUE TO OUTPUT LOW HARDWARE FAILURE. Decreased current delivered to the heart can be enough to cause a pacemaker artifact but could fail to depolarize the myocardium. Factors that could lead to inadequate output delivered from generator to the myocardium include any condition that changes the integrity of the closed circuit: battery depletion; lead insulation breaks; lead fracture, dislodgement, or disconnection; perforation, and generator failure.

PSEUDOMALFUNCTION. When the myocardium is paced while refractory, the pacemaker artifact will not be followed by a QRS complex. The pacemaker artifact might have followed a PVC.

When Pacemaker Artifact is Visible but Intrinsic Atrial or Ventricular Activity Fails to Appropriately Inhibit Pacemaker Output

In this case, there is undersensing or pseudomalfunction.

UNDERSENSING. Failure to sense is a result of the inability of the pacemaker to sense the intrinsic cardiac activity. It is recognized by noting pacemaker spikes on the ECG despite the patient's intrinsic cardiac rate being higher than the pacemaker's programmed rate (Figure 14.13). Patients might present with weakness, lightheadedness, and syncope because of alterations in rhythm due to competition with the native cardiac rhythm.

UNDERSENSING DUE TO CHANGE IN SIGNAL. Causes of undersensing include conditions that alter the myocardial signal and overlap with the causes of failure to capture. These include metabolic derangements, new bundle-branch blocks, fibrosis of the leads, myocardial ischemia, and cardiomyopathies.

UNDERSENSING DUE TO OUTPUT LOW AND HARDWARE FAILURE. Any change in the integrity of the circuit can cause undersensing, just as it causes any of the other categories of malfunction discussed so far. The circuit is affected by poor electrode position, lead dislodgement, reed switch malfunction, breaks in the lead insulation, battery failure, and inappropriate programming of the sensitivity of the pulse generator. Low-amplitude QRS complexes or broad QRS complexes with a low slow rate, as in a bundle-branch block, might also be responsible for pacemaker sensing problems.[18]

PSEUDOMALFUNCTION. *Fusion beats and pseudofusion beats* reflect the normal delay required for sensing and inhibition.

An intrinsic signal can occur within the pacemaker's refractory period. During the blanking period immediately after pacing, no sensing or recording occurs and intrinsic beats will be ignored. During the pacemaker refractory period, intrinsic signals are sensed and recorded but do not alter the pacemaker timing cycle.

Ventricular safety pacing appears as a pacemaker artifact closely following a PVC that occurs within the crosstalk window.

Automatic mode switch for fast atrial rates can cause a dual-chamber pacemaker to change to asynchronous pacing and appear to undersense the atria.

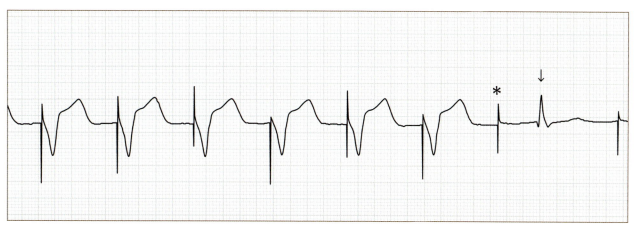

FIGURE 14.12. Failure of ventricular capture. The rhythm strip from lead V₁ shows normal paced ventricular complexes at a rate of 80 beats/min until a paced impulse (*star*), which fails to capture, is recorded. A junctional escape beat (*arrow*) follows the delay in ventricular activity. Reproduced with permission from: Nora Goldschlager, MD.

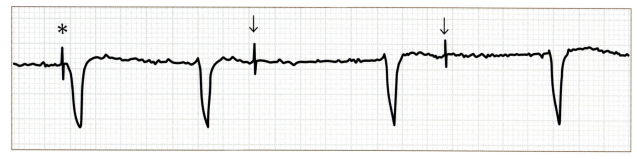

FIGURE 14.13. Undersensing (failure to sense). This rhythm strip from lead V1 shows pacemaker impulses at a fixed rate of 60 beats/min despite intrinsic ventricular activity. Normal sensing would detect intrinsic ventricular activity that occurs before expiration of the lower rate limit and suppress impulse delivery. The first paced impulse results in capture (*star*) while subsequent paced impulses that occur during the refractory period of conducted ventricular beats fail to capture (*arrows*). This is an example of magnet application to a VVI pacemaker in a patient with underlying atrial fibrillation. Reproduced with permission from: Steven A. Pace, MD.

When Pacemaker Malfunction Is Suspected but No Abnormality Is Detected on ECG

Always consider other etiologies not related to the pacemaker as well as pacemaker malfunction not caught while in the emergency department. Evaluation of potential pacemaker malfunction must include interrogation by the manufacturer or a cardiologist.

Even if emergency evaluation and interrogation are unremarkable, patients could have symptoms from AV asynchrony, known as pacemaker syndrome. This diagnosis is made by the cardiologist after comprehensive echocardiography and pacemaker evaluation.

REFERENCES

1. Gupta N, Kiley ML, Anthony F, et al. Multi-center, community-based cardiac implantable electronic devices registry: population, device utilization, and outcomes. *J Am Heart Assoc.* 2016;5(3):e002798.
2. Epstein AE, DiMarco JP, Ellenbogen KA, et al. ACC/AHA/HRS 2008 guidelines for device-based therapy of cardiac rhythm abnormalities. *J Am Coll Cardiol.* 2008;51(21):e62. Available online at: http://www.sciencedirect.com/science/article/pii/S0735109708007122. Accessed June 14, 2018. doi: 10.1016/j.jacc.2008.02.032
3. Talwar S, Saxon LA. Clinical trials of cardiac resynchronization therapy: pacemakers and defibrillators. In: Ellenbogen KA, Kay GN, Lau C, Wilkoff BL, eds. *Clinical Cardiac Pacing, Defibrillation and Resynchronization Therapy.* 4th ed. Philadelphia, PA: W.B. Saunders; 2011:279-299.
4. Greenspon AJ, Patel JD, Lau E, et al. Trends in permanent pacemaker implantation in the United States from 1993 to 2009: increasing complexity of patients and procedures. *J Am Coll Cardiol.* 2012;60(16):1540-1545.
5. Kirk M. Basic principles of pacing. In: Chow AWC, Buxton AE, eds. *Implantable Cardiac Pacemakers and Defibrillators: All You Wanted to Know.* Hoboken, NJ: Blackwell Publishing Ltd; 2007:1-28. http://dx.doi.org/10.1002/9780470750537.ch1
6. Kaszala K. Evaluation, troubleshooting, and management of pacing system malfunctions. In: Ellenbogen KA, Kaszala K, eds. *Cardiac Pacing and ICDs.* Hoboken, NJ: John Wiley & Sons, Ltd; 2014:272-322. http://dx.doi.org/10.1002/9781118459553.ch7
7. Lau C, Siu C, Tse H. Implantable sensors for rate adaptation and hemodynamic monitoring. In: Ellenbogen KA, Kay GN, Lau C, Wilkoff BL, eds. *Clinical Cardiac Pacing, Defibrillation and Resynchronization Therapy.* 4th ed. Philadelphia, PA: W.B. Saunders; 2011:144-174.
8. Beck H, Curtis AB. Right ventricular versus biventricular pacing for heart failure and atrioventricular block. *Curr Heart Fail Rep.* 2016;13(5):230-236.
9. Sweeney MO, Prinzen FW. A new paradigm for physiologic ventricular pacing. *J Am Coll Cardiol.* 2006;47(2):282-288. http://www.sciencedirect.com/science/article/pii/S0735109705025842. doi: 10.1016/j.jacc.2005.09.029
10. Healey JS, Toff WD, Lamas GA, et al. Cardiovascular outcomes with atrial-based pacing compared with ventricular pacing. *Circulation.* 2006;114(1):11.
11. Prinzen FW, Strik M, Regoli F, Auricchio A. Basic physiology and hemodynamics of cardiac pacing. In: Ellenbogen KA, Kay GN, Lau C, Wilkoff BL, eds. *Clinical Cardiac Pacing, Defibrillation and Resynchronization Therapy.* 4th ed. Philadelphia: W.B. Saunders; 2011:203-233.
12. Link MS, Hellkamp AS, Estes NA 3rd, et al. High incidence of pacemaker syndrome in patients with sinus node dysfunction treated with ventricular-based pacing in the Mode Selection Trial (MOST). *J Am Coll Cardiol.* 2004;43(11):2066-2071.
13. Martindale J, deSouza IS. Managing pacemaker-related complications and malfunctions in the emergency department. *Emerg Med Pract.* 2014;16(9):2.
14. Venkatachalam KL. Common pitfalls in interpreting pacemaker electrocardiograms in the emergency department. *J Electrocardiol.* 2011;44(6):616-621.
15. Streckenbach SC. Intraoperative pacemaker rate changes associated with the rest mode. *Anesthesiology.* 2008;109(6):1137-1139.
16. Jacob S, Shahzad MA, Maheshwari R, et al. Cardiac rhythm device identification algorithm using X-rays: CaRDIA-X. *Heart Rhythm.* 2011;8(6):915-922.
17. Refaat MM, Hashash JG, Shalaby AA. Late perforation by cardiac implantable electronic device leads: clinical presentation, diagnostic clues, and management. *Clin Cardiol.* 2010;33(8):466-475.
18. Love CJ. 29 - pacemaker troubleshooting and follow-up. In: Ellenbogen KA, Kay GN, Lau C, Wilkoff BL, eds. *Clinical Cardiac Pacing, Defibrillation and Resynchronization Therapy.* 4th ed. Philadelphia, PA: W.B. Saunders; 2011:844-888.
19. Lau W, Corcoran SJ, Mond HG. Pacemaker tachycardia in a minute ventilation rate-adaptive pacemaker induced by electrocardiographic monitoring. *Pacing Clin Electrophysiol.* 2006;29(4):438-440.

20. Southorn PA, Kamath GS, Vasdev GM, Hayes DL. Monitoring equipment induced tachycardia in patients with minute ventilation rate-responsive pacemakers. *Br J Anaesth*. 2000;84(4):508-509.
21. Houtman S, Rinia M, Kalkman C. Monitor-induced tachycardia in a patient with a rate-responsive pacemaker. *Anaesthesia*. 2006;61(4):399-401. Available at: http://dx.doi.org/10.1111/j.1365-2044.2006.04540.x. Accessed June 14, 2018. doi: 10.1111/j.1365-2044.2006.04540.x
22. Van Rooden CJ, Molhoek SG, Rosendaal FR, et al. Incidence and risk factors of early venous thrombosis associated with permanent pacemaker leads. *J Cardiovasc Electrophysiol*. 2004;15(11):1258-1262.
23. Polyzos KA, Konstantelias AA, Falagas ME. Risk factors for cardiac implantable electronic device infection: a systematic review and meta-analysis. *Europace*. 2015;17(5):767-777.
24. Berecki-Gisolf J, Sheldon RS. Pacing in neurally mediated syncope syndromes. In: Ellenbogen KA, Kay GN, Lau C, Wilkoff BL, eds. *Clinical Cardiac Pacing, Defibrillation and Resynchronization Therapy*. 4th ed. Philadelphia, PA: W.B. Saunders; 2011:361-373.
25. Iftikhar S, Mattu A, Brady W. ED evaluation and management of implantable cardiac defibrillator electrical shocks. *Am J Emerg Med*. 2016;34(6):1140-1147.
26. Epstein AE, Riley MP. Troubleshooting of implantable cardioverter-defibrillators. In: Ellenbogen KA, Kay GN, Lau C, Wilkoff BL, eds. *Clinical Cardiac Pacing, Defibrillation and Resynchronization Therapy*. 4th ed. Philadelphia, PA: W.B. Saunders; 2011:889-910.
27. Kaszala K, Nazarian S, Halperin H. Electromagnetic interference and CIEDs. In: Ellenbogen KA, Kay GN, Lau C, Wilkoff BL, eds. *Clinical Cardiac Pacing, Defibrillation and Resynchronization Therapy*. 4th ed. Philadelphia, PA: W.B. Saunders; 2011:1004-1027.

CHAPTER FIFTEEN

Metabolic Abnormalities: Effects of Electrolyte Imbalances and Thyroid Disorders on the ECG

MALKEET GUPTA AND FREDRICK M. ABRAHAMIAN

KEY POINTS

- The electrocardiographic findings of hyperkalemia do not reliably follow a progressive pattern. Any suggestive changes should be considered indications of hyperkalemia until proved otherwise.
- Consider hyperkalemia in the setting of bradycardia with diminished or absent P waves.
- In hypokalemia, the U-wave amplitude exceeds the T-wave amplitude in several leads.
- The prolonged QT and biphasic T waves associated with hypokalemia are actually inverted T waves fused with prominent U waves.
- Although hypercalcemia shortens the QTc, severe hypercalcemia can lengthen the T-wave duration and "normalize" the overall QTc interval.
- Atrial fibrillation is a common electrocardiographic finding of hyperthyroidism, but more than 99% of patients with atrial fibrillation do not have hyperthyroidism.

ELECTROLYTE IMBALANCES

Hyperkalemia

The ECG can provide clues to the presence of hyperkalemia (Table 15.1). Although the likelihood of an abnormal ECG increases as the serum potassium level increases, "classic" electrocardiographic changes can be seen at even modest elevations. The electrocardiographic findings of hyperkalemia described below might be as much associated with the rate or acuity of elevation as with a given potassium level.[1]

MILD HYPERKALEMIA (K+=5.5–6.5 MEQ/L). T-wave changes caused by shortened repolarization are often the initial electrocardiographic finding of mild hyperkalemia.[1] The normal T wave is asymmetric with a gradual ascent followed by steep descent, and its normal amplitude is less than 6 mm in the limb leads and 10 mm or less in the precordial leads. The T wave associated with hyperkalemia is symmetric and has an amplitude of more than 6 mm in the limb leads and more than 10 mm in the precordial leads. Additionally, the duration of the T wave narrows, shortening the QT interval (Figure 15.1).

Note that a peaked T wave is not diagnostic of hyperkalemia—this pattern can also be seen in healthy individuals as well as in people with acute MI, hypermagnesemia, left ventricular hypertrophy, left bundle-branch block, and intracranial hemorrhage. Some of these conditions will have additional suggestive electrocardiographic findings not found in hyperkalemia. For example, the T waves associated with acute MI often have a prolonged duration with a long QT interval. Additionally, the T-wave changes are found in the leads associated with the area of infarction, whereas in hyperkalemia, the changes are more diffuse.

MODERATE HYPERKALEMIA (K+=6.5–8 MEQ/L). As serum potassium levels increase,

TABLE 15.1. Electrocardiographic findings in potassium abnormalities.	
HYPERKALEMIA	**HYPOKALEMIA**
Peaked symmetric T waves	T-wave flattening
Flattened P wave	Prominent P waves
Widened QRS	Prominent U waves
Conduction blocks	Inverted T- and U-wave fusion
ST-segment elevation or depression	ST-segment depression, ST-segment elevation in aVR
Bradycardias	
Atrial or ventricular tachycardias	
Sine wave	

additional changes occur on the ECG: widening of the QRS complex, ST-segment elevation or depression, and P-wave changes (seen with K+ >7 mEq/L) (Figures 15.1, 15.2). Changes in the P wave include a decrease in amplitude (ie, a "flat" appearance), an increase in duration (resulting in PR interval prolongation), and absence of the wave altogether, which is frequently seen with a serum potassium level above 8 mEq/L.

ST-segment elevation related to hyperkalemia, which becomes more common at higher potassium levels, can be diffuse or more localized, resembling that associated with acute MI.[2,3] Most commonly the ST-segment elevation occurs in leads V_1 to V_2 and aVR. Unlike the typical plateau or upsloping ST segment associated with acute MI, the ST-segment elevation in hyperkalemia often displays a downsloping appearance. Concurrent ST-segment depression is common in some leads as well. The ST segments returns to baseline with treatment.[4]

SEVERE HYPERKALEMIA (K+ >8 MEQ/L). As the QRS complex widens, it gradually merges with the T wave, resulting in the classic sine wave pattern (Figure 15.3). There is a proportional correlation between the duration of the QRS complex and the plasma potassium concentration. Arrhythmias and conduction disturbances seen with hyperkalemia can include bradycardia, any type of block (eg, atrioventricular [AV] blocks, fascicular blocks, or bundle-branch blocks), ventricular tachycardia, ventricular fibrillation, idioventricular rhythm, and asystole. The QRS axis also commonly shifts, especially in a rightward direction as a result of an intraventricular conduction delay.[5]

CAVEATS. Although the electrocardiographic changes of hyperkalemia are often described as occurring in the order presented above, the findings at any given level can vary. Conditions that can blunt electrocardiographic responses to hyperkalemia include:

- alkalosis,
- hypernatremia,
- hypercalcemia, and
- hypothermia.[6]

Finally, hyperkalemic patients who have underlying renal insufficiency, especially those with end-stage renal disease undergoing hemodialysis, with even profoundly elevated potassium levels, might not demonstrate significant electrocardiographic changes.[7,8] Hence, any changes suggestive of hyperkalemia warrant clinical attention.

Hypokalemia

Hypokalemia is defined as a serum potassium level below 3.5 mEq/L. The likelihood of an abnormal ECG increases when the serum potassium level falls below 2.7 mEq/L. Hypokalemia prolongs repolarization; as

METABOLIC ABNORMALITIES

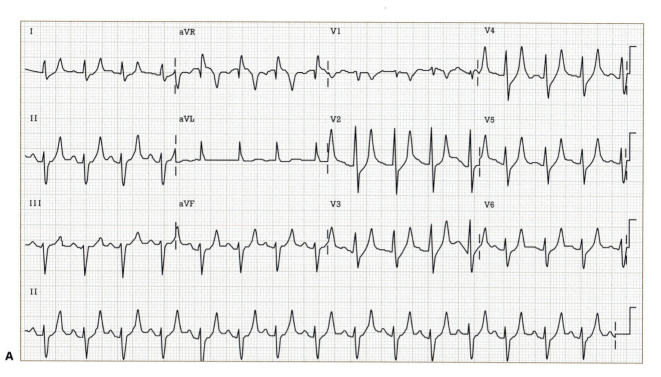

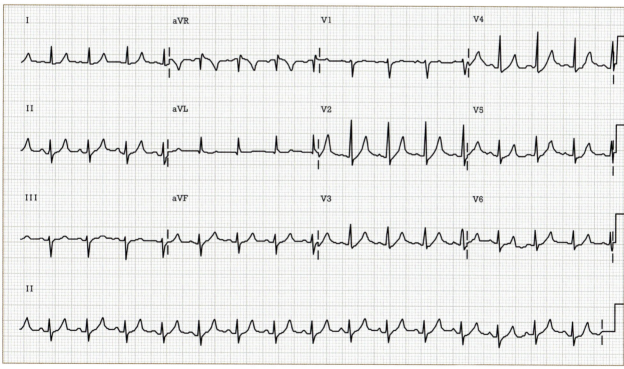

FIGURE 15.1. A. Hyperkalemia (serum K+ = 8.1 mEq/L). Note the diffuse, tall, peaked, narrow-based T waves. In addition, there are associated ST-segment depressions in leads V_2 through V_5 and widened QRS complexes. **B.** Repeat ECG after partial treatment of hyperkalemia. Note the normalization of QRS complexes and improvement of ST-segment depression in the precordial leads. The T waves are less peaked and smaller. They are more asymmetric and have an initial slow ascent followed by a steep descent.

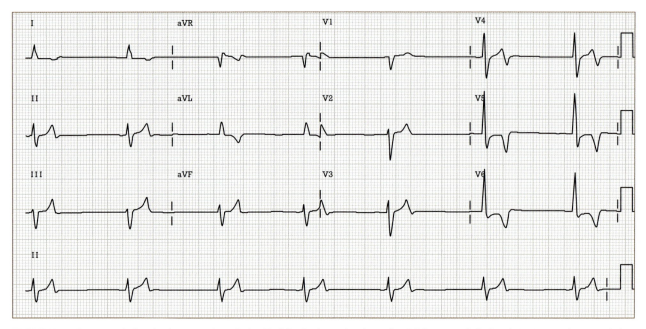

FIGURE 15.2. Hyperkalemia (serum K+ = 8.4 mEq/L). A closer look at the ECG, especially leads II, V_2, and V_3, and the rhythm strip, reveals diminished and flattened P waves, which are frequently seen with a serum potassium level above 8 mEq/L. Note the ST-segment depression and T-wave inversion in leads V_5 and V_6. Bradycardia is also present. These changes reverted to normal with treatment of the hyperkalemia.

a result, its earliest clues include changes in the ST segment, T wave, and U wave (Table 15.1).

ST segments are often depressed in hypokalemia, although ST-segment elevation can be seen in lead aVR. The T waves can either have a decrease in amplitude (flattening) or be inverted. Finally, prominent U waves can occur (best seen in leads V_2 to V_4) (Figure 15.4). Normally, the T and U waves are separated and resemble a "camel's hump." However, in advanced stages of hypokalemia, the inverted T waves and prominent U waves fuse, making it impossible to accurately measure the QT interval. Some authors have stated that hypokalemia causes a prolonged QT interval, but it is frequently the QU interval that they are reporting. Fusion of the inverted T wave and prominent U wave can mimic a biphasic T wave in the mid-precordial leads.

Other electrocardiographic changes seen in advanced hypokalemia include increased amplitude and duration of the P wave (ie, a prominent P wave) and QRS complex and slight or moderate prolongation of the PR interval. Arrhythmias and conduction disturbances associated with hypokalemia can include:

- any type of block,
- premature atrial or ventricular complexes,
- ventricular tachycardia,
- torsades de pointes, and
- ventricular fibrillation.

Conditions other than hypokalemia associated with a prominent U wave include:

- hypomagnesemia,
- hypercalcemia,
- bradyarrhythmias,
- hypothermia,
- left ventricular hypertrophy,
- drugs (eg, digitalis, quinidine, amiodarone, isoproterenol),
- organic heart disease, and
- intracranial pathology (eg, hemorrhage or cerebrovascular accident).

In these conditions, the normal T/U-wave amplitude ratio is usually not altered, with the

T wave being significantly larger than the U wave. However, in severe hypokalemia, the U-wave amplitude might exceed the T-wave amplitude in several leads.

Hypercalcemia

Hypercalcemia is defined as an ionized calcium level of more than 5.3 mEq/L. Electrocardiographic abnormalities associated with hypercalcemia are

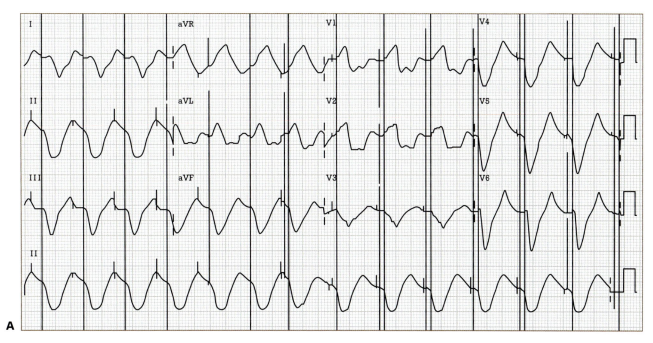

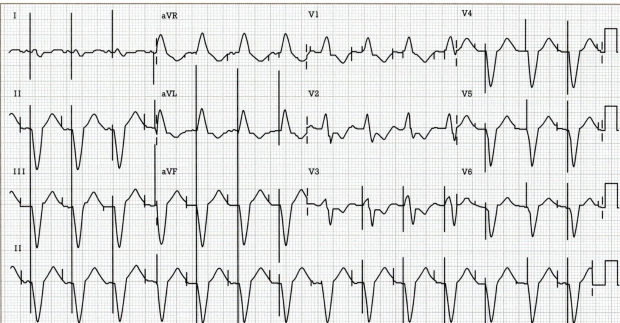

FIGURE 15.3. A. Severe hyperkalemia (serum K+ = 8.7 mEq/L) in the setting of atrial and ventricular pacing. The ECG demonstrates a near sine-wave pattern associated with severe hyperkalemia, in which the QRS complex widens and merges with the T wave. Although ventricular pacing is expected to widen the QRS complex, the observed widening is much greater than expected for a typical paced ventricular complex. **B.** Repeat ECG after aggressive treatment of hyperkalemia. The observed wide QRS complexes are more typical of those associated with ventricular pacing.

caused by elevations in the concentration of ionized, not total (protein-bound plus ionized), calcium.

Calcium primarily affects the plateau section (phase 2) of the cardiac muscle action potential curve, which determines the duration of the ST segment of the ECG. Hypercalcemia shortens the ST segment (ie, shortens the duration of phase 2) and therefore shortens the overall duration of the QTc interval. In extreme cases, the T wave can begin at the terminal end of the QRS complex. Although the QTc is inversely proportional to the degree of hypercalcemia, this relationship is not strongly correlated. Many other factors also affect the length of the QTc interval, including age, sex, and medications.[9]

Severe hypercalcemia can also lengthen the T-wave duration; as a result, the overall QTc interval can appear normal even though the ST segment is shortened.[10] Hypercalcemia usually has no effect on the morphology of the P or T wave. It might cause an increase in the amplitude of the U wave and slight prolongation of the QRS interval duration. A few case reports have demonstrated that hypercalcemia can cause Osborne J waves (similar to those seen in patients with hypothermia) as well as ST-segment elevation that mimics an acute MI.[11,12]

Hypercalcemia does not commonly result in cardiac arrhythmias, although sinus bradycardia and ventricular fibrillation have been reported.[13,14]

Hypocalcemia

Hypocalcemia is defined as an ionized calcium level below 4.5 mEq/L. It primarily prolongs the length of the ST segment (ie, prolongs the duration of phase 2) without affecting the duration of the T wave (Figure 15.5). Hypothermia is the only other condition that can have this effect on the ECG.[15]

The duration of the ST segment is inversely

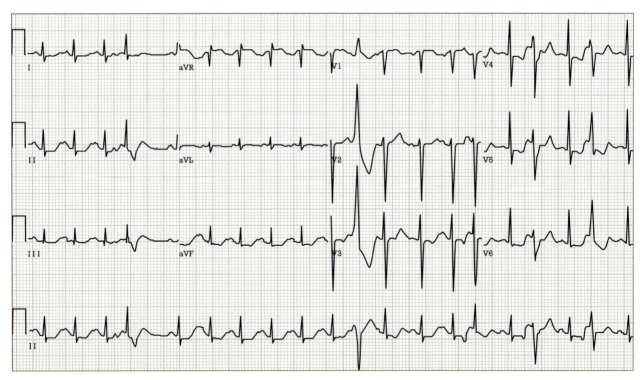

FIGURE 15.4. Hypokalemia (serum K+ = 2.1 mEq/L). Note the diffuse ST-segment depression with ST-segment elevation in lead aVR, decrease in T-wave amplitude, and prominent U waves (best seen in leads II and aVF). In hypokalemia, the U-wave amplitude often exceeds the T-wave amplitude. Because of the close proximity of the T and U waves, the QT interval is difficult to measure accurately. Premature ventricular complexes, likely induced by hypokalemia, are also seen. Reproduced with permission from: Amal Mattu, MD, FACEP.

associated with the plasma calcium concentration. As a result of ST-segment prolongation, the QTc interval is also prolonged, but rarely more than 140% of normal. A prolonged QTc is the most common and earliest finding of hypocalcemia. If the QTc interval exceeds 140% of normal, this suggests that the U wave has been integrated into the T wave and the QU segment is being measured. Prolongation of the QTc interval can result in torsades de pointes, but this is less commonly observed than the association of torsades de pointes with hypokalemia or hypomagnesemia.

The T-wave morphology is usually not affected because calcium has no effect on phase 3 of the action potential. However, occasionally, flat, low, or sharply inverted T waves can be seen in leads with upright QRS complexes. This is likely secondary to an alteration in the sequence of repolarization. The P-wave morphology, PR interval, and QRS complex are usually not affected by hypocalcemia. ST-segment elevation mimicking MI has also been reported with hypocalcemia.[16]

Magnesium

Alterations in magnesium levels within the range encountered in clinical settings do not result in specific electrocardiographic abnormalities, and changes in isolation from other significant electrolyte abnormalities are limited to case reports. Electrocardiographic changes and cardiac arrhythmias have been described with isolated hypomagnesemia but, again, only as case reports. Hypermagnesemia can depress AV and intraventricular conduction but at levels higher than those associated with respiratory arrest.

THYROID DISORDERS

Hyperthyroidism

The cardiovascular system is exquisitely sensitive to circulating thyroid hormones. These hormones act by multiple direct and indirect mechanisms to alter hemodynamics, causing a variety of electrocardiographic changes. Hyperthyroidism is considered a state of adrenergic hyperactivity; as a consequence,

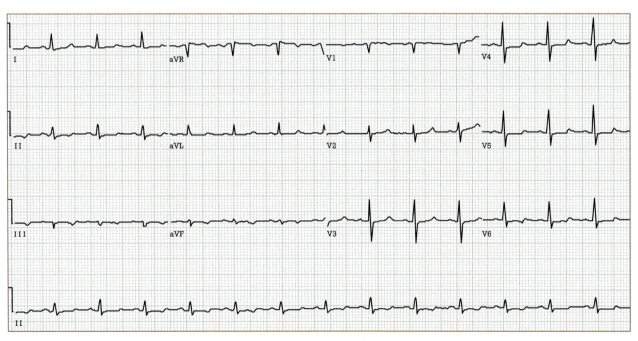

FIGURE 15.5. Hypocalcemia (ionized serum calcium = 3.3 mEq/L). The QT interval is prolonged, with QT/QTc of 430/530 milliseconds, respectively. Note the prolonged ST segment with a normal T-wave duration. Most other causes of QT prolongation cause prolongation of the T wave rather than the ST segment. Hypothermia is the only other exception. Reproduced with permission from: Amal Mattu, MD, FACEP.

sinus tachycardia is the most commonly observed electrocardiographic abnormality, occurring in nearly half of patients with hyperthyroidism. In a study of 880 patients, resting tachycardia was second only to goiter as the most common finding of hyperthyroidism, although the frequency of tachycardia decreases with advancing age.[17]

Atrial fibrillation is the second most common rhythm observed in patients with hyperthyroidism.[18,19] The risk of atrial fibrillation increases after age 55 years. Despite the relatively common association of hyperthyroidism with atrial fibrillation, a large study determined that less than 1% of patients with atrial fibrillation had hyperthyroidism as their inciting event.[20] Atrial flutter, paroxysmal supraventricular tachycardia, and ventricular arrhythmias are all uncommon in patients with hyperthyroidism.

A variety of other less commonly observed electrocardiographic abnormalities has been reported with hyperthyroidism. In one study, intraventricular conduction delays occurred in 13% of 466 patients with hyperthyroidism but without associated heart conditions or other cause of the delay. The most common intraventricular conduction abnormalities were incomplete right bundle-branch block and left anterior fascicular block.[21] First-degree AV block is more common than second- or third-degree AV block in patients with hyperthyroidism. Occasionally, PR prolongation precedes atrial fibrillation. Additional nonspecific ST-segment and T-wave changes are seen in up to 25% of patients with hyperthyroidism. These changes vary daily and, unlike the changes of pericarditis or myocarditis, are short-lived and transient.

Hypothyroidism

Hypothyroidism leads to a slowing of the metabolic rate and contractility of the myocardium; hence, sinus bradycardia is common in patients with untreated hypothyroidism. Additional electrocardiographic changes associated with hypothyroidism include low-voltage QRS complexes, T-wave changes (eg, low-amplitude "flattened" T waves or deeply inverted T waves), low P-wave amplitude, and a prolonged QT interval. Because of low T-wave amplitude, the QT interval is often hard to measure accurately. A prolonged QT interval can predispose patients to ventricular arrhythmias such as torsades de pointes.[22,23] Compared with the general population, patients with hypothyroidism have a higher incidence of AV block (eg, first-degree AV block) and intraventricular conduction disturbances.

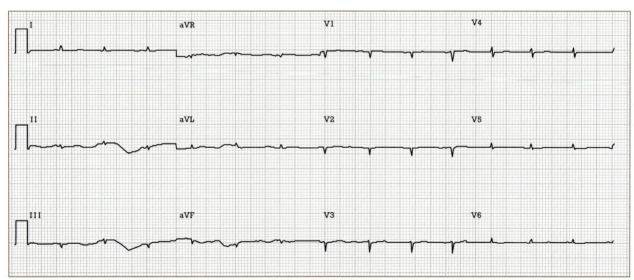

FIGURE 15.6. Low-voltage ECG, defined when the entire QRS complex (R+S) amplitudes in each of the limb leads is 5 mm or less when the entire QRS complex amplitudes in each of the precordial leads is less than 10 mm. This patient's presentation was concerning for myxedema, and the diagnosis was confirmed on thyroid function testing. Reproduced with permission from: Zachary Dezman, MD.

Low-voltage QRS complexes are defined when the entire QRS complex (R+S) amplitude in the limb leads is 5 mm or less or when the entire QRS complex amplitude in each of the precordial leads is less than 10 mm (Figure 15.6). The prevalence of pericardial effusions among patients with hypothyroidism is variable, ranging from 3% of those with subclinical hypothyroidism to 80% of those with myxedematous states.[24-27] The presence of pericardial effusions can contribute to the appearance of low QRS voltage; however, hypothyroidism rarely produces large pericardial effusions. In one study of patients with large pericardial effusions, only 1.5% of the effusions were attributed to hypothyroidism.[28]

REFERENCES

1. Mattu A, Brady WJ, Robinson DA. Electrocardiographic manifestations of hyperkalemia. *Am J Emerg Med*. 2000;18:721-729.
2. Chawla KK, Cruz J, Kramer NE, et al. Electrocardiographic changes simulating acute myocardial infarction caused by hyperkalemia: report of a patient with normal coronary arteriograms. *Am Heart J*. 1978;95:637-640.
3. Simon BC. Pseudomyocardial infarction and hyperkalemia: a case report and subject review. *J Emerg Med*. 1988;6:511-515.
4. Wang K, Asinger RW, Marriott HJ. ST-segment elevation in conditions other than acute myocardial infarction. *N Engl J Med*. 2003;349:2128-2135.
5. Ewy GA, Karliner J, Bedynek JL Jr. Electrocardiographic QRS axis shift as a manifestation of hyperkalemia. *JAMA*. 1971;215:429-432.
6. Mattu A, Brady WJ, Perron AD. Electrocardiographic manifestations of hypothermia. *Am J Emerg Med*. 2002;20:314-326.
7. Aslam S, Friedman EA, Ifudu O. Electrocardiography is unreliable in detecting potentially lethal hyperkalaemia in haemodialysis patients. *Nephrol Dial Transplant*. 2002;17:1639-1642.
8. Szerlip HM, Weiss J, Singer I. Profound hyperkalemia without electrocardiographic manifestations. *Am J Kidney Dis*. 1986;7:461-465.
9. Wald DA. ECG manifestations of selected metabolic and endocrine disorders. *Emerg Med Clin North Am*. 2006;24:145-157.
10. Lind L, Ljunghall S. Serum calcium and the ECG in patients with primary hyperparathyroidism. *J Electrocardiol*. 1994;27:99-103.
11. Otero J, Lenihan DJ. The "normothermic" Osborn wave induced by severe hypercalcemia. *Tex Heart Inst J*. 2000;27:316-317.
12. Turhan S, Kilickap M, Kilinc S. ST segment elevation mimicking acute myocardial infarction in hypercalcaemia. *Heart*. 2005;91:999.
13. Kiewiet RM, Ponssen HH, Janssens EN, et al. Ventricular fibrillation in hypercalcaemic crisis due to primary hyperparathyroidism. *Neth J Med*. 2004;62:94-96.
14. Ziegler R. Hypercalcemic crisis. *J Am Soc Nephrol*. 2001;12(suppl 17):S3-S9.
15. Diercks DB, Shumaik GM, Harrigan RA, et al. Electrocardiographic manifestations: electrolyte abnormalities. *J Emerg Med*. 2004;27:153-160.
16. Lehmann G, Deisenhofer I, Ndrepepa G, et al. ECG changes in a 25-year-old woman with hypocalcemia due to hypoparathyroidism: hypocalcemia mimicking acute myocardial infarction. *Chest*. 2000;118:260-262.
17. Nordyke RA, Gilbert FI Jr, Harada AS. Graves' disease: influence of age on clinical findings. *Arch Intern Med*. 1988;148:626-631.
18. Fadel BM, Ellahham S, Ringel MD, et al. Hyperthyroid heart disease. *Clin Cardiol*. 2000;23:402-408.
19. Osman F, Gammage MD, Sheppard MC, et al. Clinical review 142: cardiac dysrhythmias and thyroid dysfunction: the hidden menace? *J Clin Endocrinol Metab*. 2002;87:963-967.
20. Krahn AD, Klein GJ, Kerr CR, et al. How useful is thyroid function testing in patients with recent-onset atrial fibrillation? The Canadian Registry of Atrial Fibrillation Investigators. *Arch Intern Med*. 1996;156:2221-2224.
21. Staffurth JS, Gibberd MC, Hilton PJ. Atrial fibrillation in thyrotoxicosis treated with radioiodine. *Postgrad Med J*. 1965;41:663-671.
22. Klein I, Ojamaa K. Thyroid hormone and the cardiovascular system. *N Engl J Med*. 2001;344:501-509.
23. Kumar A, Bhandari AK, Rahimtoola SH. Torsade de pointes and marked QT prolongation in association with hypothyroidism. *Ann Intern Med*. 1987;106:712-713.
24. Chou SL, Chern CH, How CK, et al. A rare case of massive pericardial effusion secondary to hypothyroidism. *J Emerg Med*. 2005;28:293-296.
25. Casale PN, Devereux RB, Kligfield P, et al. Pericardial effusion: relation of clinical echocardiographic and electrocardiographic findings. *J Electrocardiol*. 1984;17:115-121.
26. Eisenberg MJ, de Romeral LM, Heidenreich PA, et al. The diagnosis of pericardial effusion and cardiac tamponade by 12-lead ECG: a technology assessment. *Chest*. 1996;110:318-324.

27. Habashy AG, Mittal A, Ravichandran N, et al. The electrocardiogram in large pericardial effusion: the forgotten "P" wave and the influence of tamponade, size, etiology, and pericardial thickness on QRS voltage. *Angiology*. 2004;55:303-307.

28. Sagristà-Sauleda J, Mercé J, Permanyer-Miralda G, Soler-Soler J. Clinical clues to the causes of large pericardial effusions. *Am J Med*. 2000;109(2):95-101.

CHAPTER SIXTEEN

The ECG in Selected Noncardiac Conditions

TARLAN HEDAYATI

KEY POINTS

Hypothermia
- Shivering artifact can be seen on the ECG in hypothermic patients at temperatures above 32°C (89.6°F).
- The most common rhythm in hypothermia is atrial fibrillation with a slow ventricular response.
- Specific morphologies such as the Osborn wave and Brugada pattern are common in severely hypothermic patients.

Pulmonary Embolism
- Patients with pulmonary embolism (PE) frequently present with normal sinus rhythm.
- The $S_1Q_3T_3$ pattern traditionally associated with PE is an unreliable finding that can neither confirm nor exclude the presence of PE.
- Several morphologic patterns seen in association with PE, including right axis deviation, right bundle-branch block, ST-segment depression, ST-segment elevation, and anterior T-wave inversion, could be electrocardiographic reflections of reversible right heart strain, but their absence is not sufficient to rule out the diagnosis.

Thoracic Aortic Dissection
- Rarely, dissection presents with ST-segment elevation. In these cases, further tests must be done to clarify the pathology. ST-segment elevation could represent primary MI or dissection with secondary involvement of the coronary ostia. Proper treatment depends on making this determination correctly.

Pneumothorax
- Pneumothorax induces electrocardiographic findings and thus can mimic other life-threatening conditions such as PE and MI.

Chronic Obstructive Pulmonary Disease
- Some abnormalities seen with COPD such as an increase in the P-wave amplitude can be transient during acute exacerbations and can resolve with treatment.
- Tachyarrhythmias are common in COPD patients. They can be related to the underlying disease, to cardiac ischemia, or to the effects of medications.

Central Nervous System Events
- QT-interval prolongation and abnormalities of the ST segment and T wave can mimic those associated with acute coronary syndrome. In some cases, this can create sufficient clinical uncertainty to warrant further and more definitive investigation to rule out a simultaneous cardiac process.

Electrical Injuries
- Patients with electrocardiographic abnormalities following exposure to an electrical current that has crossed through the thorax should receive continuous monitoring.

Although the electrocardiographic changes associated with noncardiac conditions are usually neither sensitive nor specific, emergency physicians must know how to recognize them and assess their life-threatening potential. Failure to appreciate that a single electrocardiographic appearance can represent two or more very different diagnoses can lead to inappropriate and dangerous management decisions. This chapter outlines electrocardiographic findings associated with several life-threatening noncardiac conditions. Emphasis is placed on the differential diagnosis of certain patterns and the role of the ECG in emergency decision making.

HYPOTHERMIA

Hypothermia, defined as a core body temperature below 35°C (95°F), has been linked to both benign and fatal pacemaker abnormalities, conduction delays, and cardiac arrhythmias. The common electrocardiographic findings associated with hypothermia are summarized in Table 16.1.

The initial finding is a tremor artifact of the baseline caused by shivering. Below 32°C (89.6°F), the body is often no longer able to generate heat by shivering, so the baseline frequently returns to normal, a finding associated with poorer outcome.[1] At a body temperature around 35°C (95°F), the first nonartifact electrocardiographic abnormalities are progressive sinus bradycardia and decreased T-wave voltage.[2] Atrial fibrillation with a slow ventricular response is the most common arrhythmia associated with hypothermia, occurring in 50% to 60% of patients. Other ectopic rhythms such as atrial flutter, atrioventricular (AV) junctional rhythm, premature ventricular contractions, ventricular tachycardia, and ventricular fibrillation are also seen but with far less frequency. With progressive hypothermia, all the intervals—R-R, PR, QRS, and QT—become prolonged. When temperatures fall below 29.4°C (85°F), the progressive QRS widening can degenerate to ventricular fibrillation and, with further hypothermia, asystole.[2] The vast majority of arrhythmias associated with hypothermia are reversible with rewarming, although several days to months can be required for normal sinus rhythm to return.[3,4]

TABLE 16.1. Electrocardiographic findings in hypothermia.

Artifact	Shivering artifact
Rhythm	Asystole
	Atrial fibrillation with slow ventricular response
	Junctional rhythms
	PR, QRS, QT, and R-R interval prolongation
	Sinus bradycardia
	Ventricular fibrillation
	Ventricular premature complexes
	Ventricular tachycardia
Morphology	Brugada syndrome–like morphology
	Decreased T-wave voltage
	Osborn J wave

The Osborn wave (also called a J wave, camel-hump wave, late delta wave, and hypothermic wave) was first described by Grosse-Brockhoff and Schoedel in 1943 and later named by Dr. John Osborn in 1953, based on ECGs obtained from hypothermic dogs. Osborn described the finding as a convex deflection between the QRS complex and the beginning of the ST segment, so close to the QRS complex that it produces a "hump" in the terminal portion of the QRS. This reversible finding, best seen in the inferior and lateral precordial leads, is detectable in 80% of patients with a core temperature below 30°C (86°F).[5] The J wave increases in amplitude as the temperature falls, eventually leading to T-wave inversion in the same leads. Although it is highly sensitive and specific for hypothermia, it is not entirely pathognomonic; Osborn waves are sometimes seen in patients with intracranial hemorrhage, cardiac ischemia, and hypercalcemia and as a normal variant.[4,6] As the J wave increases in amplitude, the terminal portion

THE ECG IN SELECTED NONCARDIAC CONDITIONS

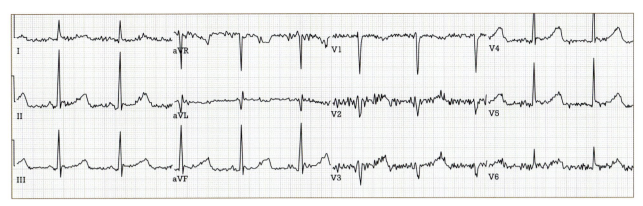

FIGURE 16.1. Hypothermia. This is the initial ECG of a 59-year-old man with unknown medical history who was "found down." His rectal temperature when he reached the emergency department was 33°C (91.4°F). The ECG is notable for shivering artifact. The regularity of the ventricular response (QRS complexes) helps to differentiate this baseline pattern from atrial fibrillation, which is also common in hypothermia. The ventricular rate of 63 is common in hypothermia. Osborn J waves can be seen in the terminal QRS, particularly in leads II, III, aVF, V_4, and V_5.

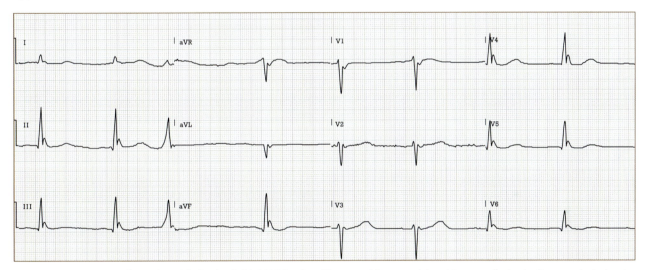

FIGURE 16.2. Hypothermia. This is the initial ECG of a 62-year-old man with a history of alcoholism and cirrhosis, brought in by paramedics for evaluation of altered mental status after being found outside. His initial rectal temperature was 30°C (86°F). The ECG demonstrates atrial fibrillation with slow ventricular response and Osborn waves.

of the QRS complex rises and can be mistaken for a bundle-branch block, ST-segment elevation pattern, or Brugada syndrome.[5,7]

The Brugada pattern is defined as ST-segment elevation in leads V_1 through V_3 and a right bundle-branch block (RBBB) without the usual terminal S waves laterally; it has been linked to sudden cardiac death in young patients. Severely hypothermic patients have exhibited this phenomenon.[7,8] The best ways to differentiate a true Brugada syndrome from a hypothermic mimic are to note the presence of Osborn waves and watch for the reversibility of findings with rewarming. Figure 16.1 shows an ECG of a hypothermic patient, demonstrating both shivering artifact and Osborn waves. Figure 16.2 demonstrates an ECG of a hypothermic patient whose initial core body temperature was measured at 30°C (86° F). The ECG is notable for a junctional rhythm, long QT interval, and a pronounced Osborn wave, enlarged in Figure 16.3.

PULMONARY EMBOLISM

Pulmonary embolism (PE) continues to be one of the most underdiagnosed fatal diseases in emergency

ELECTROCARDIOGRAPHY IN EMERGENCY, ACUTE, AND CRITICAL CARE

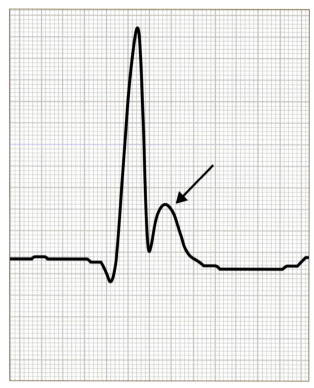

FIGURE 16.3. Hypothermia. Osborn J wave, magnified.

TABLE 16.2. Electrocardiographic findings associated with pulmonary embolism.

Rhythm	Normal sinus rhythm
	Sinus tachycardia
Morphology	Complete or incomplete RBBB
	Dominant R wave in aVR
	P pulmonale (P-wave amplitude >2.5 mm in lead II)
	PR-segment displacement
	qR or QR in V_1
	Rightward shift of QRS axis
	S_1Q_3 or $S_1Q_3T_3$
	Slurred S in V_1 or V_2
	ST-segment depression
	ST-segment elevation in III, aVR, or V_1
	T-wave inversions (V_1 through V_4 most commonly, less often in III and aVF)

medicine. Unfortunately, the electrocardiographic abnormalities associated with PE can be subtle and nonspecific. Because many patients with PE present to an emergency department with complaints of chest pain or dyspnea, an ECG is usually obtained on arrival. The principal role of this initial ECG is to identify other cardiac abnormalities such as acute infarction, ischemia, pericarditis, and life-threatening arrhythmias. Several electrocardiographic findings associated with PE (Table 16.2) have been described, as well as their possible association with PE size, severity of RV outflow obstruction, and value in predicting clinical deterioration.[9]

Multiple investigations focused on the emergency department population have demonstrated that the most common electrocardiographic pattern in patients with acute submassive PE (ie, PE without circulatory collapse) is normal sinus rhythm. Sinus tachycardia, frequently thought to be near universal in cases of PE, is actually less than universal but is still one of the most common electrocardiographic abnormalities in the setting of PE. Atrial fibrillation and flutter can also be seen.[10-12]

Morphologic changes associated with PE include a slurred S wave in V_1 or V_2, decreased QRS voltage, complete or incomplete RBBB, PR-segment displacement, and dominant R wave in aVR.[10] The findings of prominent S waves in lead I and Q waves in lead III, each of amplitude exceeding 1.5 mm, with T-wave inversions present in lead III (the so-called $S_1Q_3T_3$ pattern) were first reported by McGinn and White in the 1930s in a series of seven patients with acute cor pulmonale caused by PE. These patients had severe embolic obstruction and massive PE.[13,14] Since then, this finding has become closely linked with PE in the minds of most clinicians. However, more recent studies have called this association into question. The incidence of the $S_1Q_3T_3$ pattern ranges widely in different series (from <10% to 60%) and depends on the nature of patient selection in each study. Some data suggest that the $S_1Q_3T_3$ pattern might be equally prevalent in certain patients without PE.[12,15,16] Confounding the utility of the $S_1Q_3T_3$ pattern is that a Q wave and inverted T wave in lead III are occasional normal variants. Furthermore, there is no agreed on definition of how large the S wave in lead I should be before concern for PE should arise. However, an S wave in lead I that approaches the size or exceeds the size of the R wave (producing a rightward axis) should always be considered abnormal and, in the right clinical setting, should prompt strong consideration of PE.

Large PEs can elevate pulmonary artery, RV, and right atrial (RA) pressures, leading to varying degrees of RV obstruction, RV strain, RV dysfunction, and ischemic patterns on the ECG (Figures 16.4, 16.5). P pulmonale and peaked P waves in leads II, III, or aVF are signs of increased RA pressure or RA enlargement. Because this combination has been reported equally in patients with both massive and submassive PE, it has little value, as an isolated finding, in predicting the size of the embolus.[13,17]

Incomplete or complete RBBB has been reported in the setting of PE associated with RV strain. The reported incidence of RBBB varies widely, from 6% to 67%.[15] Dynamic monitoring in an intensive care setting has shown that in PE patients with both an $S_1Q_3T_3$ pattern and RBBB, the $S_1Q_3T_3$ pattern often temporally precedes development of RBBB.[12] The presence of incomplete RBBB has also been associated with elevated mean pulmonary artery pressure and RV end-diastolic pressure.[13] Right bundle-branch block and $S_1Q_3T_3$-type patterns have been associated with an elevated risk of RV dysfunction in patients with acute PE (3.9- and 5.7-fold, respectively).[19] However, the strength of the apparent correlation between RBBB and PE should not be overstated. In one large study that prospectively followed 212 patients receiving diagnostic imaging for suspected PE, incomplete RBBB and sinus tachycardia were significantly more frequent in the group with negative imaging results.[18]

Petruzzelli and colleagues.[10] found that, although ST-segment depression was common in patients both with and without a final diagnosis of PE, it resolved in those ultimately diagnosed with PE as

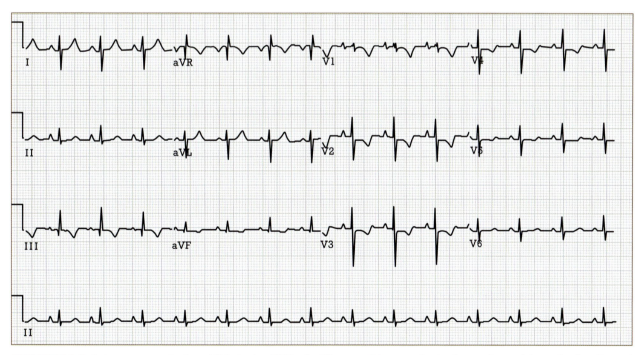

FIGURE 16.4. Pulmonary embolism. This is the ECG of a 33-year-old man who had experienced 1 week of unilateral leg swelling and now had acute onset of chest pain and dyspnea. On arrival, he was hypotensive and tachycardic. A bedside echocardiogram demonstrated RV dilation. The ECG demonstrates several features associated with PE, including the $S_1Q_3T_3$ pattern, ST-segment elevation in aVR, incomplete RBBB pattern, and T-wave inversions in inferior and anteroseptal leads. Reproduced with permission from: Amal Mattu, MD, FACEP.

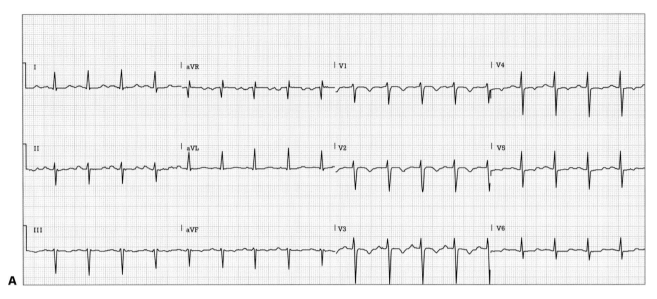

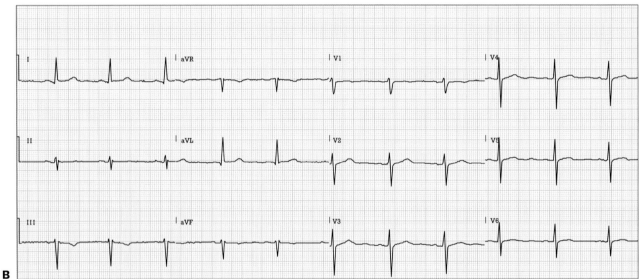

FIGURE 16.5. Pulmonary embolism. This series of ECGs was obtained from a 62-year-old patient who presented to the emergency department after experiencing 1 day of chest pain and shortness of breath. Bedside echocardiogram demonstrated RV dilatation. **A.** The patient's ECG on emergency department arrival. **B.** The same patient's ECG 3 months later, after PE resolution.

they recovered.[10] ST-segment depression in the setting of PE is also associated with elevated RV end-diastolic pressure.[13] Further, the presence of inverted T waves in leads V_1 through V_4 correlates with the severity of the PE.[10,13,20] In patients who receive fibrinolytic therapy for treatment of massive PE, normalization of the T wave was accelerated compared with nonfibrinolyzed patients.[20] Thus, several patterns, including RBBB, ST-segment depression, and anterior T-wave inversion, in patients with PE could all be a reflection of reversible right heart strain. T-wave inversions can occur simultaneously in the anterior leads as well as in the inferior leads, especially leads III and aVF. T-wave inversions and ST changes can be easily mistaken for cardiac ischemia, leading to an incorrect workup and disposition. Figure 16.4 demonstrates electrocardiographic findings in a patient with massive PE before and after receiving fibrinolysis in the emergency department.

Although various electrocardiographic abnormalities have been linked to the presence and size of PE, the ECG, by itself, cannot provide a definitive diagnosis. Knowledge of the electrocardiographic abnormalities associated with PE, however, could prompt the emergency physician to initiate further investigations to pursue this diagnosis. In certain circumstances, it can also lead to initiation of empiric therapy that might otherwise be withheld until more definitive study results become available.

THORACIC AORTIC DISSECTION

Thoracic aortic dissections are classified based on anatomic location and time from onset. The Stanford classification divides dissections based on the location of the intimal tear. Dissections in the ascending aorta are Stanford type A and represent approximately 62% of all dissections; those occurring distal to the left subclavian artery are classified as Stanford type B and make up the remaining 38%. Within 14 days after the onset of dissection, morbidity and mortality are high. For this reason, dissection is considered acute within this period. Patients who survive the initial 2 weeks carry a diagnosis of chronic dissection.[21]

Ninety-five percent of patients diagnosed with acute thoracic dissection present with chest pain.[22] The most critical diagnosis to differentiate from aortic dissection is acute MI, specifically STEMI, because fibrinolytic or anticoagulation therapy can be cataclysmic for a patient with dissection. However, these conditions can exist contemporaneously; a dissection can progress proximally to involve the coronary ostia, causing acute occlusion in the proximal coronary artery by an intimal flap or hematoma.[23] Dissections can also extend into the atrial septum and AV conduction system, resulting in heart block.[24]

A 12-year study of 89 patients diagnosed with acute aortic dissection in Japan demonstrated that 40% of all patients with dissection had an acute electrocardiographic abnormality on presentation, defined as a new shift in the ST segment larger than 0.1 mm in any lead or a change in the polarity or morphology of the T wave. Left ventricular hypertrophy, bundle-branch blocks, and abnormal Q waves were considered chronic changes and were seen in 30% of all patients, most commonly in type B dissections. Acute changes occurred in 55% of patients with type A dissection but only 22% with type B. These changes consisted most often of 0.1-mm ST-segment depression.[23]

Also in that study, patients with type A dissection and acute electrocardiographic changes had a higher incidence of shock, cardiac tamponade, and hypotension. Four of the 89 patients demonstrated ST-segment elevation on the ECG (three in the inferior leads). Four patients in the study group were found to have type A dissections; one was treated with a fibrinolytic for an incorrect diagnosis of acute MI, resulting in death secondary to cardiac tamponade. With respect to arrhythmias, atrial and ventricular premature beats as well as AV blocks were recorded, but in only a few patients.[23]

The International Registry of Acute Aortic Dissections is a repository of data about patients with aortic dissections from 30 referral centers in 11 countries. The registry has been enrolling patients since 1996 and has accumulated data on more than 5,000 patients to date. Among the initial 464 patients enrolled and followed in the registry, 69% demonstrated some abnormality on their ECGs. The most common was nonspecific ST-T wave changes (41%), followed by left ventricular hypertrophy (26%), ischemic patterns (15%), and infarction patterns (11%).[22]

Emergency physicians must consider aortic dissection in the differential diagnosis of any patient presenting to the emergency department with acute chest pain. Fortunately, the predominant electrocardiographic findings of aortic dissection rarely mimic those of STEMI, lessening the likelihood of unintended administration of fibrinolytic therapy (Table 16.3). Nevertheless, because most patients with dissection present with either normal, nonspecific, or frankly ischemic electrocardiographic changes, differentiation of dissection from the more common acute coronary syndromes remains difficult on the basis of the ECG alone. Therefore, imaging studies must be considered, especially when elements of the history and physical examination suggest the

TABLE 16.3. Electrocardiographic findings associated with thoracic aortic dissection.	
Rhythm	Atrial and ventricular premature beats
	AV block
	Sinus tachycardia
Morphology	Ischemic or infarction patterns
	Left ventricular hypertrophy
	Nonspecific ST-segment changes
	ST-segment elevation (uncommon)

possibility of dissection or when anticoagulation is being considered.

PNEUMOTHORAX

Pneumothorax is defined as the presence of air in the pleural space, resulting in partial or total collapse of the affected lung. Data from intensive care units have shown that electrocardiographic changes often precede clinical signs and symptoms of pneumothorax.[25] Like the signs and symptoms of pneumothorax itself, the associated electrocardiographic changes depend on the size of the collapse, the presence or absence of tension, and whether the pneumothorax is right or left sided. Because most of these patients present with chest pain and dyspnea, an ECG is typically part of the initial evaluation. The electrocardiographic findings associated with pneumothorax are summarized in Table 16.4.

The mechanisms proposed for induction of electrocardiographic abnormalities in pneumothorax include cardiac rotation or displacement, air within the thoracic cavity, acute RV dilation or overload, and interposition of air or lung tissue between the electrodes and cardiac muscle.[25,26]

One of the largest series looking at patients with right-sided pneumothoraces comes from a tuberculosis treatment study performed prior to the availability of effective antimicrobial therapy. In that era, creation of an artificial pneumothorax was an important therapeutic modality in tuberculosis. A meta-analysis examining 82 patients with such iatrogenic right pneumothoraces found that more than one-third of them had an S wave in lead I and right axis deviation.[28] In addition, case reports of the $S_1Q_3T_3$ pattern typically associated with pulmonary embolism have described the same pattern in patients with pneumothoraces, even very small (10%) ones.[28,29] Thus, careful examination of the chest radiograph from a patient with right axis deviation on the ECG can obviate the need for further diagnostic evaluation if a pneumothorax is found. Diagnostic certainty is enhanced with resolution of the axis changes following reexpansion of the affected lung.[28,29] Electrocardiographic abnormalities consistent with acute MI are rarely present in patients with right-sided pneumothorax. Reports of patients with changes mimicking both posterior MI (prominent R-wave voltage with associated loss of S-wave voltage in lead V_2) as well as anterior wall MI (ST-segment elevation and T-wave inversion in leads V_1 through V_3)[30,31] underscore the importance of the initial radiograph. Moreover, if the patient's clinical presentation is more suggestive of a pneumothorax than MI, more definitive imaging, including emergent computed tomography of the chest, could be appropriate before specific therapy for MI is initiated. After lung reexpansion, the ECG should revert to normal.[31]

TABLE 16.4. Electrocardiographic findings associated with pneumothorax.	
Left sided	Decreased QRS voltage
	Electrical alternans
	Poor R-wave progression
	Sinus tachycardia
	T-wave inversion in precordial leads
Right sided	Anterior or posterior MI pattern (rare)
	Decreased QRS voltage
	Sinus tachycardia
	S wave in V_1
	$S_1Q_3T_3$ pattern

Electrocardiographic changes associated with left-sided pneumothoraces have been widely reported. In one series, all patients with left-sided pneumothorax demonstrated decreased QRS amplitude, and approximately half had right axis deviation.[30] Other common findings associated with left-sided pneumothorax include poor R-wave progression and T-wave inversion.[26,27] One case report described phasic voltage variations in the ECG that depended on respiration, a finding common in pericardial effusions and tamponade. These variations disappeared after tube thoracostomy.[32] Another case report detailed the uncommon findings of PR-segment elevation in the inferior leads (II, III, and aVF) and PR-segment depression in lead aVR in a patient with 100% left tension pneumothorax.[33] These changes also resolved after chest tube placement.

Although pneumothorax is not a diagnosis made based on the ECG, its ability to cause certain electrocardiographic changes and mimic other life-threatening processes is significant. If emergent decompression becomes necessary, a repeat ECG is essential to ensure that the signs that could indicate other conditions have resolved.

CHRONIC OBSTRUCTIVE PULMONARY DISEASE

Chronic obstructive pulmonary disease is characterized by progressive inflammation and obstruction of the airways. Because of the ensuing hyperinflation, the diaphragm occupies a lower, stiffer position and the heart is forced into a more vertical position, with a clockwise rotation along its longitudinal axis. This results in a rightward shift of the P and QRS axes in the frontal plane and a posterior displacement of the QRS vector in the horizontal plane. It also produces a larger P-wave amplitude in the inferior leads and a smaller QRS amplitude in the limb leads. The hyperinflated lungs also add to the relatively low QRS voltage seen in COPD patients. As the disease advances, chronic hypoxia leads to pulmonary arterial vasoconstriction, increased pulmonary artery pressure, and right heart strain. This right heart strain eventually results in RV hypertrophy, dilation, and failure, known as cor pulmonale. Pulmonary hypertension is a poor prognostic indicator in COPD patients.[34] The electrocardiographic findings associated with COPD are summarized in Table 16.5.

In 1959, Spodick[35] described verticalization of the frontal P-wave axis in patients with diffuse lung disease. Normally, this axis varies between +45° and +64°. A rightward shift in the P axis to +70° to +90°, most easily recognized as a negative P wave in lead aVL, was found in 83% of the 79 consecutive patients in Spodick's series. P-axis verticalization has a sensitivity of 89% and specificity of 96% in COPD.[36] Subsequent studies demonstrated a relationship between increasing verticality of the P axis and the degree of airway obstruction. P pulmonale, defined as tall and peaked P waves greater than 2.5 mm in the inferior leads, is typically associated with right heart strain or enlargement. This finding has been reported in up to 25% of COPD patients, typically those with moderately severe to severe disease (Figure 16.6).[37]

P-wave abnormalities can be dynamic and reversible during an acute COPD exacerbation. Asad and colleagues[38] compared the initial emergency department ECGs of 50 patients with acute COPD exacerbations with subsequent posttreatment ECGs from the inpatient unit. Ninety-six percent of patients who initially had a P-wave amplitude larger than

TABLE 16.5. Electrocardiographic findings associated with chronic obstructive pulmonary disease.

Rhythm	Atrial fibrillation
	Multifocal atrial tachycardia
	Sinus tachycardia
Morphology	Decreased QRS amplitude
	Poor R-wave progression
	P pulmonale
	P-wave axis >90°
	QRS axis >90° (right axis deviation)
	Q waves anterolaterally
	$S_1S_2S_3$ pattern

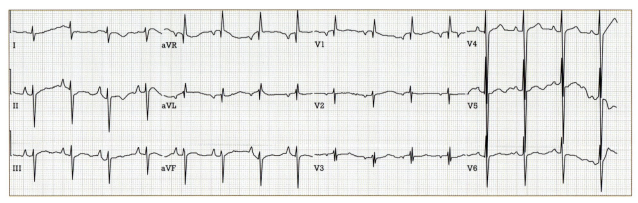

FIGURE 16.6. Chronic obstructive pulmonary disease. This is the ECG of a 53-year-old patient with a history of COPD, admitted for an acute exacerbation. The tracing demonstrates extreme right axis deviation, P pulmonale, as well as verticalization of the P-wave axis, which can be identified by the inverted P wave in lead aVL. These findings have been associated with moderate to severe COPD.

1.5 mm in leads II and aVF demonstrated a significant decrease in P-wave amplitude 24 hours after initiation of treatment. One patient whose P-wave amplitude had decreased with treatment in the emergency department developed a second COPD exacerbation on the ward; the repeat ECG demonstrated an increase in P-wave amplitude in association with the repeat exacerbation. This lability in the P-wave amplitude can provide a fast, noninvasive method of evaluating the presence, degree, and resolution of acute right heart strain in the setting of COPD exacerbations.

Electrocardiographic findings associated with COPD also have prognostic value, mostly related to the degree of pulmonary hypertension and RV strain.[39] In one study, COPD patients who demonstrated either a P-wave axis greater than 90° or an $S_1S_2S_3$ pattern (seen in up to 25% of patients) had a 3-year survival rate of 44%. If both signs were present, the 3-year survival rate dropped to 14%.[40] Another study found that COPD patients demonstrating a P-wave amplitude of more than 2 mm had a 4-year survival rate of 42%.[41] This seems logical in that more electrocardiographic findings of pulmonary hypertension and right heart strain means the disease process is more severe and thus the mortality rate is higher.

QRS abnormalities in association with COPD have also been reported. In addition to a decreased QRS amplitude, indeterminate or right axis deviation of more than 60° in the frontal plane has been described in about 60% of patients.[42] The 4-year survival rate for COPD patients with QRS axis deviation between +90° and +180° was 37% in one study.[41] Poor R-wave progression with Q waves from lead V_1 to the lateral leads occurs in almost 10% of COPD patients. Partial or complete normalization of this finding can sometimes be achieved by simply shifting the chest leads one interspace inferiorly on the chest wall, mimicking the new position of the heart caused by the diaphragmatic changes described above.

The most common arrhythmias associated with COPD are supraventricular in origin: sinus tachycardia, multifocal atrial tachycardia, and atrial fibrillation. These arrhythmias tend to be transient, occur in association with acute exacerbations, and typically resolve with treatment. Premature ventricular contractions and nonsustained ventricular tachycardia in patients with COPD and respiratory failure have been reported, but they are uncommon.[43]

Although the abnormalities and arrhythmias described above are typical in patients with COPD, these patients often present with comorbid conditions, acute and chronic, that also influence the ECG. In particular, manifestations of ischemic heart disease can be superimposed on or obscured by these changes. For emergency physicians, the presence of underlying ischemia is a constant consideration, and changes consistent with both ischemia and pulmonary disease should be treated as being of cardiac origin, especially if they do not resolve with appropriate treatment aimed at the pulmonary disease. In addition, medications used for treatment such as beta-adrenergic agents and theophylline result in specific electrocardiographic changes and arrhythmias. These must also be considered.

CENTRAL NERVOUS SYSTEM EVENTS

Many reports have documented electrocardiographic changes associated with acute neurologic events. Such abnormalities have been described consistently for a wide variety of neurologic conditions, including stroke,[44–48] increased intracranial pressure,[45] and epilepsy.[50–55]

From the emergency physician's point of view, it is important to understand the acute changes that occur with central nervous system events because they must be differentiated from those that can reflect a primary cardiac process. This is especially true when the clinical picture is ambiguous. For example, a stroke could be secondary to an aortic dissection, diminished cardiac output during an acute coronary syndrome, or an embolism from a mural thrombus complicating MI. Therapy directed at a primary cardiac process (eg, heparin for myocardial ischemia) can be dangerous in a patient in whom electrocardiographic changes were merely a reflection of a stroke. In some cases, this critical distinction can be made only with the assistance of further testing, typically imaging with computed tomography or magnetic resonance.

A relationship between stroke and the electrocardiographic tracing has been recognized for many decades. Because large numbers of patients who suffer stroke have coexisting disease that affects their baseline ECG, it has been very difficult to study this relationship. However, in the case of subarachnoid hemorrhage (SAH), in which electrocardiographic changes are often dramatic, the relationship is much more clearly understood, in part because the younger population affected by SAH is less likely to have underlying cardiac disease. The electrocardiographic changes associated with SAH (Table 16.6) likely result from increased activity along the neurohumoral axis, specifically a surge in sympathetic output and circulating catecholamines. This results in a number of cardiovascular effects, including increased myocardial oxygen demand, increased afterload, and possibly coronary vasospasm. Several studies have documented specific evidence of myocardial dysfunction such as wall motion abnormalities on echocardiography. In a minority of cases, increases in serum biomarkers demonstrate actual myocardial necrosis.[44]

The electrocardiographic changes of SAH often mimic those of primary cardiac processes such as coronary ischemia and thus can cause confusion in emergency department management. The most prominent electrocardiographic finding associated with SAH is the appearance of deep, inverted T waves (Figure 16.7). These were first described by Byer in 1947 and subsequently by many other authors.[44] In the largest series reported, involving 406 patients with SAH, 32% had abnormalities of the T wave.[48] It was inverted and large (>5 mm) in 2.5% of patients, negative with a more modest amplitude in another 15%, and notched in another 8%. Other abnormalities of repolarization are even more common such as the presence of U waves and prolongation of the

TABLE 16.6. Electrocardiographic findings associated with subarachnoid hemorrhage.

Rhythm	Atrial fibrillation
	AV block
	Paroxysmal supraventricular tachycardia
	Sinus bradycardia
	Sinus tachycardia
	Ventricular fibrillation
	Ventricular tachycardia
Morphology	Pathologic Q waves
	Prominent U waves
	QT prolongation
	ST-segment depression
	ST-segment elevation
	T-wave inversion

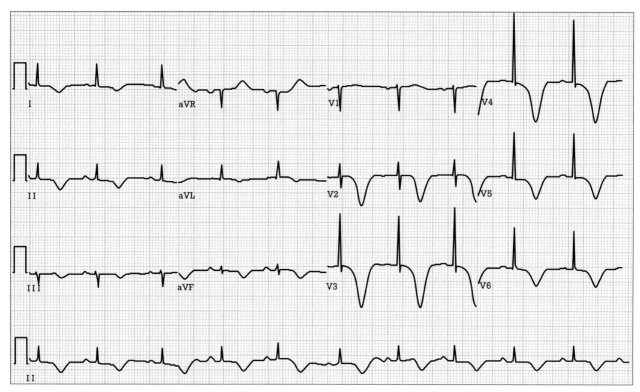

FIGURE 16.7. Subarachnoid hemorrhage. This is the ECG of a patient who presented with an acute headache that was followed by a decreased level of consciousness. The patient had a large intracranial hemorrhage. The ECG demonstrates the classic appearance of large T-wave inversions, which most commonly manifest in the precordial leads and are typically associated with a prolonged QT interval. Reproduced with permission from: Amal Mattu, MD, FACEP.

QT interval. In a study by Rudehill et al,[48] 47% of patients presented with U waves larger than 1 mm, and 24% presented with a QTc of more than 440 milliseconds. These patients are at risk of torsades de pointes.[56,57]

Although abnormalities of the ST segment are less common in SAH, they can create an even greater dilemma in the management of patients in whom a primary cardiac event appears possible. Fortunately, in SAH, ST-segment depression is more common than ST-segment elevation, so therapies most perilous to patients with intracranial hemorrhage such as administration of fibrinolytic agents are less likely to be considered. The use of antiplatelet and anticoagulant agents commonly employed in the management of non-ST–segment elevation acute coronary syndrome (ACS) could be equally devastating to a patient with SAH. Rudehill et al[48] found that ST-segment depression occurred in 15% of patients with SAH but none of the patients in this series had ST-segment elevation. In another series involving 100 patients with SAH, only 3% had ST-segment depression.

Q waves have also been reported in patients with SAH (in 3% of patients in the largest series); their presence can further complicate its differentiation from ACS. The ST-segment and Q-wave changes that mimic ACS can persist for weeks, but they do eventually resolve.[58] Because the published data in case series on cardiac biomarkers are not necessarily paired with electrocardiographic changes, it is difficult to conclude how many of these patients actually suffer myocardial damage as a secondary process to SAH. In one study, ST-segment deviation in patients with SAH did not correlate with elevation of the cardiac troponin I concentration.[45]

Although normal sinus rhythm is the most common rhythm seen in patients with SAH, a variety of bradyarrhythmias and tachyarrhythmias has been described, dating back to the observations of Harvey Cushing at the turn of the last century. The more commonly reported arrhythmias are supraventricular tachycardia, sinus bradycardia (likely caused by increased intracranial pressure), AV blocks, and premature beats, both atrial and ventricular.[44,45,47,48,59]

Only in the minority of cases is a normal ECG obtained from a patient with SAH even when patients with a history of cardiovascular disease are excluded.[48] The literature is subject to spectrum bias toward patients with more severe cases of SAH (ie, those who are diagnosed on presentation and admitted). In recent years, the literature on SAH has focused on "sentinel leaks," small warning bleeds that frequently precede a more catastrophic SAH. It is not known whether the incidence of electrocardiographic changes is different in this patient population, but it is likely to be much lower.

Increased intracranial pressure is associated with sinus bradycardia. It is part of the reflex described by Cushing, which also includes an increase in systolic blood pressure. Other electrocardiographic abnormalities described in association with increased intracranial pressure include many of those described with SAH. Because only limited data are available, it can be difficult to distinguish the changes specific to each.[49]

Several clinicians have investigated the electrocardiographic changes related to epilepsy—during seizures themselves and during the postictal period. Much of this research is aimed at uncovering the underlying mechanism of sudden unexpected death in epilepsy (the sudden death rate among people with epilepsy is many times higher than the death rate in the general population[50-55]). Although many of the arrhythmias described during seizures are likely related to respiratory compromise, neurohumoral influences and antiepileptic drugs also influence the ECG and are partly responsible for QT-interval and ST-segment changes.

SELECTED GASTROINTESTINAL DISORDERS

Gastrointestinal disorders often present with symptoms typical of ACS such as chest pain and

TABLE 16.7. Electrocardiographic findings associated with selected gastrointestinal disorders.

Cholecystitis	
Rhythm	Sinus tachycardia
Morphology	Brugada-type pattern
	ST-segment elevation
Gastric dilation and intestinal obstruction	
Morphology	ST-segment elevation
	T-wave inversion
Pancreatitis	
Rhythm	Sinus tachycardia
Morphology	Intraventricular conduction delays and bundle-branch blocks
	ST-segment elevation
	T-wave inversion

epigastric pain. Multiple case reports and studies have described the various electrocardiographic findings associated with these disease processes (Table 16.7). Clinically, the ECG is not helpful in the diagnosis of these disorders, but the electrocardiographic abnormalities associated with them can create uncertainty and result in further cardiac investigations.

Patients with pancreatitis (inflammation of the pancreas and surrounding tissues) typically present with upper abdominal pain that can radiate to the midback. They generally appear in distress and can present with tachycardia because of pain, fever, or shock. Electrolyte abnormalities such as hypocalcemia, hypomagnesemia, hyperkalemia, and hypokalemia are common in pancreatitis and, if they are severe enough, lead to electrocardiographic abnormalities. Several case reports have described ST-segment elevation "pseudoinfarction" patterns, T-wave inversions, intraventricular conduction delays, and bundle-branch blocks in these patients.[60-62] Unfortunately, no large studies have investigated electrocardiographic abnormalities in patients with pancreatitis and normal electrolyte levels. Investigators have also been unable to link serum pancreatic amylase or lipase levels with the prevalence of electrocardiographic abnormalities in patients with pancreatitis.[63]

Case reports have described gastric dilation and intestinal obstruction causing ST-segment elevation in the inferior or anterior leads and T-wave inversions in the lateral leads. In all cases, prompt resolution of the abnormalities was achieved with nasogastric decompression.[64-66]

Finally, acute cholecystitis, or inflammation of the gallbladder, has also been associated with electrocardiographic abnormalities, including ST-segment elevation patterns[67] and Brugada-type patterns.[68] The obvious risk to patients with acute cholecystitis and with these patterns on the ECG is a delay in definitive surgical treatment while a cardiology workup and clearance are pursued. However, although emergency physicians should be aware of these pseudoinfarction patterns, pursuit of a life-threatening cardiovascular cause of such abnormalities is essential.

ELECTRICAL INJURIES

Electrical injuries are categorized as alternating current (AC) or direct current (DC) injury and as high-voltage (>1,000 V) or low-voltage exposure. Residential AC emits 120 to 220 volts, and high-tension power lines can generate well over 100,000 volts of AC. Lightning injuries represent very brief high-voltage DC exposure. Cardiac injury is caused by passage of the exogenous electrical current across the heart, disrupting normal cardiac electrical pathways. The thermal and ischemic injuries produced by electrical current also contribute to arrhythmias and electrocardiographic abnormalities following electrical injuries (Table 16.8).

Immediate lethality is the result of asystole or ventricular fibrillation, the most common causes of death after exposure to electrical current. Lethal domestic AC injury typically results in ventricular fibrillation, whereas lightning strikes produce asystolic arrests.[69] As many as half of all surviving victims of electrical injuries have some electrocardiographic abnormality. Electrocardiographic findings following lightning injuries appear to be related to the type of strike. A direct cloud-to-victim strike can result in life-threatening pericardial effusions and QTc prolongation. A "side-splash" (lightning that hits an object and then the victim secondarily) results in sinus tachycardia and nonspecific ST-T wave changes. A third type of lightning strike is a current that enters the ground and then spreads to the victim; these patients typically have sinus tachycardia or nonspecific ST-T wave changes as well.[70] Other abnormalities and arrhythmias described after electrical injuries include ST-segment elevation, bundle-branch blocks, sick sinus syndrome, supraventricular arrhythmias, ventricular extrasystole, and ventricular tachycardia.[71-73]

Patients with documented arrhythmias in the field or an abnormal ECG on emergency department presentation should be admitted to a monitored setting. Patients with chest pain, loss of consciousness, exposure to high voltage, or a history of cardiac disease should also be admitted for cardiac monitoring.

TABLE 16.8. Electrocardiographic findings associated with electrical injuries.

Rhythm	Sick sinus syndrome
	Supraventricular arrhythmias
	Ventricular extrasystole
	Ventricular tachycardia
Morphology	Bundle-branch blocks
	Nonspecific ST-T changes
	QT prolongation
	ST-segment elevation

REFERENCES

1. Graham CA, McNaughton GW, Wyatt JP. The electrocardiogram in hypothermia. *Wilderness Environ Med.* 2001;12(4):232-235.
2. Mustafa S, Shaikh N, Gowda RM, et al. Electrocardiographic features of hypothermia. *Cardiology.* 2005;103(3):118-119.

3. Vassallo SU, Delaney KA, Hoffman RS, et al. A prospective evaluation of the electrocardiographic manifestations of hypothermia. *Acad Emerg Med.* 1999;6(11):1121-1126.
4. Aslam AF, Aslam AK, Vasavada BC, et al. Hypothermia: evaluation, electrocardiographic manifestations, and management. *Am J Med.* 2006;119(4):297-301.
5. Nolan J, Soar J. Images in resuscitation: the ECG in hypothermia. *Resuscitation.* 2005;64(2):133-134.
6. Mattu A, Brady WJ, Perron AD. Electrocardiographic manifestations of hypothermia. *Am J Emerg Med.* 2002;20(4):314-326.
7. Noda T, Shimizu W, Tanaka K, et al. Prominent J wave and ST segment elevation: serial electrocardiographic changes in accidental hypothermia. *J Cardiovasc Electrophysiol.* 2003;14(2):223.
8. Ansari E, Cook JR. Profound hypothermia mimicking a Brugada type ECG. *J Electrocardiol.* 2003;36(3):257-260.
9. Sheng FQ, Xu R, Xia JD, et al. ECG patterns indicate severity of acute pulmonary embolism: insights from serial ECG changes in a patient treated with thrombolysis. *J Emerg Med.* 2017;52(6):e251-e253.
10. Petruzzelli S, Palla A, Pieraccini F, et al. Routine electrocardiography in screening for pulmonary embolism. *Respiration.* 1986;50(4):233-243.
11. Richman PB, Loutfi H, Lester SJ, et al. Electrocardiographic findings in emergency department patients with pulmonary embolism. *J Emerg Med.* 2004;27(2):121-126.
12. Petrov DB. Appearance of right bundle-branch block in electrocardiograms of patients with pulmonary embolism as a marker for obstruction of the main pulmonary trunk. *J Electrocardiol.* 2001;34(3):185-188.
13. Stein PD, Dalen JE, McIntyre KM, et al. The electrocardiogram in acute pulmonary embolism. *Prog Cardiovasc Dis.* 1975;17(4):247-257.
14. McIntyre KM, Sasahara AA, Littmann D. Relation of the electrocardiogram to hemodynamic alterations in pulmonary embolism. *Am J Cardiol.* 1972;30(3):205-210.
15. Chan TC, Vilke GM, Pollack M, et al. Electrocardiographic manifestations: pulmonary embolism. *J Emerg Med.* 2001;21(3):263-270.
16. Ahonen A. Electrocardiographic changes in massive pulmonary embolism. I. Analysis of the changes in P wave and QRS complex. *Acta Med Scand.* 1977;201(6):539-542.
17. Ahonen A. Electrocardiographic changes in massive pulmonary embolism. II. Analysis of the changes in ST segment and T wave. *Acta Med Scand.* 1977;201(6):543-545.
18. Rodger M, Makropoulos D, Turek M, et al. Diagnostic value of the electrocardiogram in suspected pulmonary embolism. *Am J Cardiol.* 2000;86(7):807-809, A810.
19. Keller K, Beule J, Balzer JO, et al. Right bundle branch block and S_IQ_{III}-type patterns for risk stratification in acute pulmonary embolism. *J Electrocardiol.* 2016(49):512-518.
20. Ferrari E, Imbert A, Chevalier T, et al. The ECG in pulmonary embolism: predictive value of negative T waves in precordial leads—80 case reports. *Chest.* 1997;111(3):537-543.
21. Khan IA, Nair CK. Clinical, diagnostic, and management perspectives of aortic dissection. *Chest.* 2002;122(1):311-328.
22. Hagan PG, Nienaber CA, Isselbacher EM, et al. The International Registry of Acute Aortic Dissection (IRAD): new insights into an old disease. *JAMA.* 2000;283(7):897-903.
23. Hirata K, Kyushima M, Asato H. Electrocardiographic abnormalities in patients with acute aortic dissection. *Am J Cardiol.* 1995;76(16):1207-1212.
24. Jessen ME, Horn VP, Weaver DE, et al. Successful surgical repair of aortic dissection presenting with complete heart block [abstract]. *Ann Thorac Surg.* 1996;62(4):1202-1203.
25. Ti LK, Lee TL. The electrocardiogram complements a chest radiograph for the early detection of pneumothorax in post-coronary artery bypass grafting patients. *J Cardiothorac Vasc Anesth.* 1998;12(6):679-683.
26. Raev D. A case of spontaneous left-sided pneumothorax with ECG changes resembling acute myocardial infarction. *Int J Cardiol.* 1996;56(2):197-199.
27. Ortega-Carnicer J, Ruiz-Lorenzo F, Zarca MA, et al. Electrocardiographic changes in occult pneumothorax. *Resuscitation* 2002;52(3):306-307.
28. Goddard R, Scofield RH. Right pneumothorax with the $S_1Q_3T_3$ electrocardiogram pattern usually associated with pulmonary embolus. *Am J Emerg Med.* 1997;15(3):310-312.
29. Summers RS. The electrocardiogram as a diagnostic aid in pneumothorax. *Chest.* 1973;63(1):127-128.
30. Alikhan M, Biddison JH. Electrocardiographic changes with right-sided pneumothorax. *South Med J.* 1998;91(7):677-680.
31. Maheshwari M, Mittal SR. Right-sided pneumothorax simulating anterior wall myocardial infarction. *Indian Heart J.* 2004;56(1):73.
32. Kozelj M, Rakovec P, Sok M. Unusual ECG variations in left-sided pneumothorax. *J Electrocardiol.* 1997;30(2):109-111.
33. Strizik B, Forman R. New ECG changes associated with a tension pneumothorax: a case report. *Chest.* 1999;115(6):1742-1744.

34. Hurdman J, Condliffe R, Elliot CA, et al. Pulmonary hypertension in COPD: results from the ASPIRE registry. *Eur Respir J.* 2013(41):1292-1301.
35. Spodick DH. Electrocardiographic studies in pulmonary disease. I. Electrocardiographic abnormalities in diffuse lung disease. *Circulation.* 1959;20:1067-1072.
36. Baljepally R, Spodick DH. Electrocardiographic screening for emphysema: the frontal plane P axis. *Clin Cardiol.* 1999;22(3):226-228.
37. Ikeda K, Kubota I, Takahashi K, et al. P-wave changes in obstructive and restrictive lung diseases. *J Electrocardiol.* 1985;18 (3):233-238.
38. Asad N, Johnson VM, Spodick DH. Acute right atrial strain: regression in normal as well as abnormal P-wave amplitudes with treatment of obstructive pulmonary disease. *Chest.* 2003;124(2):560-564.
39. Alkukhun L, Baumgartner M, Budev M, et al. Electrocardiographic differences between COPD patients evaluated for lung transplantation with and without pulmonary hypertension. *COPD.* 2014;11(6):670-680.
40. Incalzi RA, Fuso L, De Rosa M, et al. Electrocardiographic signs of chronic cor pulmonale: a negative prognostic finding in chronic obstructive pulmonary disease. *Circulation.* 1999;99(12):1600-1605.
41. Kok-Jensen A. Simple electrocardiographic features of importance for prognosis in severe chronic bronchial obstruction. *Scand J Respir Dis.* 1975;56(5):273-284.
42. Kilcoyne MM, Davis AL, Ferrer MI. A dynamic electrocardiographic concept useful in the diagnosis of cor pulmonale: result of a survey of 200 patients with chronic obstructive pulmonary disease. *Circulation.* 1970;42(5):903-924.
43. Incalzi RA, Pistelli R, Fuso L, et al. Cardiac arrhythmias and left ventricular function in respiratory failure from chronic obstructive pulmonary disease. *Chest.* 1990;97(5):1092-1097.
44. Davis TP, Alexander J, Lesch M. Electrocardiographic changes associated with acute cerebrovascular disease: a clinical review. *Prog Cardiovasc Dis.* 1993;36(3):245-260.
45. Sommargren CE, Zaroff JG, Banki N, et al. Electrocardiographic repolarization abnormalities in subarachnoid hemorrhage. *J Electrocardiol.* 2002;35(suppl):257-262.
46. Oppenheimer SM. Neurogenic cardiac effects of cerebrovascular disease. *Curr Opin Neurol.* 1994;7(1):20-24.
47. Andreoli A, di Pasquale G, Pinelli G, et al. Subarachnoid hemorrhage: frequency and severity of cardiac arrhythmias: a survey of 70 cases studied in the acute phase. *Stroke.* 1987;18(3):558-564.
48. Rudehill A, Olsson GL, Sundqvist K, et al. ECG abnormalities in patients with subarachnoid haemorrhage and intracranial tumours. *J Neurol Neurosurg Psychiatry.* 1987;50(10):1375-1381.
49. Jachuck SJ, Ramani PS, Clark F, et al. Electrocardiographic abnormalities associated with raised intracranial pressure. *Br Med J.* 1975;1(5952):242-244.
50. Opherk C, Coromilas J, Hirsch LJ. Heart rate and EKG changes in 102 seizures: analysis of influencing factors. *Epilepsy Res.* 2002;52(2):117-127.
51. Oppenheimer SM, Cechetto DF, Hachinski VC. Cerebrogenic cardiac arrhythmias. Cerebral electrocardiographic influences and their role in sudden death. *Arch Neurol.* 1990;47(5):513-519.
52. Kandler L, Fiedler A, Scheer K, et al. Early post-convulsive prolongation of QT time in children. *Acta Paediatr.* 2005;94(9):1243-1247.
53. Zijlmans M, Flanagan D, Gotman J. Heart rate changes and ECG abnormalities during epileptic seizures: prevalence and definition of an objective clinical sign. *Epilepsia.* 2002;43(8):847-854.
54. Tigaran S, Molgaard H, Dam M. Atrio-ventricular block: a possible explanation of sudden unexpected death in epilepsy. *Acta Neurol Scand.* 2002;106(4):229-233.
55. Tigaran S. Cardiac abnormalities in patients with refractory epilepsy. *Acta Neurol Scand.* 2002;177(suppl):9-32.
56. Di Pasquale G, Andreoli A, Lusa AM, et al. Cardiologic complications of subarachnoid hemorrhage. *J Neurosurg Sci.* 1998;42(1 suppl 1):33-36.
57. Di Pasquale G, Pinelli G, Andreoli A, et al. Torsade de pointes and ventricular flutter-fibrillation following spontaneous cerebral subarachnoid hemorrhage. *Int J Cardiol.* 1988;18(2):163-172.
58. Brouwers PJ, Wijdicks EF, Hasan D, et al. Serial electrocardiographic recording in aneurysmal subarachnoid hemorrhage. *Stroke.* 1989;20(9):1162-1167.
59. Weidler DJ. Myocardial damage and cardiac arrhythmias after intracranial hemorrhage: a critical review. *Stroke.* 1974;5(6):759-764.
60. Albrecht CA, Laws FA. ST segment elevation pattern of acute myocardial infarction induced by acute pancreatitis. *Cardiol Rev.* 2003;11(3):147-151.
61. Hung SC, Chiang CE, Chen JD, et al. Images in cardiovascular medicine: pseudo-myocardial infarction. *Circulation.* 2000;101(25):2989-2990.
62. Pezzilli R, Barakat B, Billi P, et al. Electrocardiographic abnormalities in acute pancreatitis. *Eur J Emerg Med.* 1999;6(1):27-29.
63. Rubio-Tapia A, Garcia-Leiva J, Asensio-Lafuente E, et al. Electrocardiographic abnormalities in patients with acute pancreatitis. *J Clin Gastroenterol.* 2005;39(9):815-818.

64. Frais MA, Rodgers K. Dramatic electrocardiographic T-wave changes associated with gastric dilatation. *Chest.* 1990;98(2):489-490.
65. Asada S, Kawasaki T, Taniguchi T, et al. A case of ST-segment elevation provoked by distended stomach conduit. *Int J Cardiol.* 2006;109(3):411-413.
66. Mixon TA, Houck PD. Intestinal obstruction mimicking acute myocardial infarction. *Tex Heart Inst J.* 2003;30(2):155-157.
67. Ryan ET, Pak PH, DeSanctis RW. Myocardial infarction mimicked by acute cholecystitis. *Ann Intern Med.* 1992;116(3):218-220.
68. Furuhashi M, Uno K, Satoh S, et al. Right bundle branch block and coved-type ST-segment elevation mimicked by acute cholecystitis. *Circ J.* 2003;67(9):802-804.
69. Carleton SC. Cardiac problems associated with electrical injury. *Cardiol Clin.* 1995;13(2):263-266.
70. Lichtenberg R, Dries D, Ward K, et al. Cardiovascular effects of lightning strikes. *J Am Coll Cardiol.* 1993;21(2):531-536.
71. Blackwell N, Hayllar J. A three year prospective audit of 212 presentations to the emergency department after electrical injury with a management protocol. *Postgrad Med J.* 2002;78(919):283-285.
72. Kose S, Iyisoy A, Kursaklioglu H, et al. Electrical injury as a possible cause of sick sinus syndrome. *J Korean Med Sci.* 2003;18(1):114-115.
73. Varol E, Ozaydin M, Altinbas A, et al. Low-tension electrical injury as a cause of atrial fibrillation: a case report. *Tex Heart Inst J.* 2004;31(2):186-187.

CHAPTER SEVENTEEN

The ECG and the Poisoned Patient

SUZANNE DOYON

KEY POINTS

- Sodium channel blocker overdoses are associated with prolongation of the QRS, prominent R wave in aVR, and occasionally a Brugada pattern.
- Some patients with sodium channel blocker overdoses who experience QRS prolongation of more than 120 milliseconds are more likely to experience seizures, coma, malignant tachyarrhythmias, and death.
- Potassium channel blocker overdoses are associated with QTc prolongation.
- Sodium-potassium-pump (Na/K ATPase) inhibitor overdoses can present with either bradyarrhythmias or tachyarrhythmias.
- Digitalis effect is not synonymous with digitalis toxicity, although they can co-occur.

Emergency physicians routinely evaluate ECGs in poisoned patients. Adverse cardiovascular events are encountered in 9% of all overdose cases and in up to 16% of patients hospitalized with drug overdoses; drug overdoses are a leading cause of death.[1-3] In this chapter, drugs have been divided into six main groups based on the main electrocardiographic manifestations.[4,5]

SODIUM CHANNEL BLOCKER TOXICITY

Propagation of the cardiomyocyte action potential is mediated by voltage-gated sodium channels (Na_v).[6] Under normal physiologic conditions, activation of these channels leads to a rapid increase in sodium entry and a steep upward slope of phase 0 of the action potential in cardiomyocytes.

The Na_v blocker group of agents is diverse (Table 17.1). In many instances, the Na_v blocking properties are essential to the pharmacologic effect of the drug and, therefore, the toxicity represents an extension of the pharmacologic effect of the medication (eg, procainamide, flecainide, etc.). In other instances, the Na_v blocking properties are secondary to the pharmacologic effect of the drug (eg, cyclic antidepressants, chloroquine, etc.). Amitriptyline is a very potent Na_v blocker, although almost all cyclic antidepressants can block Na_v. Grayanotoxins (rhododendron plant, mad honey disease) are naturally occurring Na_v blockers. Regardless of the agent, the effect of blocking myocardial Na_v results in one or more of the following electrocardiographic findings:

- intraventricular conduction defects,
- ventricular arrhythmias, and, occasionally,
- bradyarrhythmias.

INTRAVENTRICULAR CONDUCTION

Voltage-gated sodium channel blockers will slow phase 0 of the action potential, decreasing propagation of the action potential resulting in slowing of intraventricular conduction. Clinically, this is manifest by prolongation of the QRS complex to 100 milliseconds (or more) and morphological changes in the QRS appearance in aVR. The right bundle is more susceptible to this effect because it is longer and thinner than the left.[7] A rightward axis deviation of the terminal 40 milliseconds of the frontal plane QRS axis in aVR is associated with the presence of

TABLE 17.1. Common sodium channel blockers.

Amantadine	
Anesthetic agents	Bupivacaine
Antidepressant agents	Amitriptyline, amoxapine, citalopram, desipramine, doxepin, imipramine, maprotiline, nortriptyline, paroxetine, venlafaxine
Antiepileptic agents	Carbamazepine, lamotrigine, lacosamide
Antimalarial agents	Chloroquine, hydroxychloroquine, quinine
Antipsychotic agents	Mesoridazine, thioridazine, loxapine, quetiapine
Beta blockers	Propranolol, acebutolol, betaxolol, oxprenolol
Calcium channel blockers	Diltiazem, verapamil
Class Ia antiarrhythmic agents	Procainamide, quinidine, disopyramide
Class Ic antiarrhythmic agents	Encainide, flecainide, propafenone
Diphenhydramine	
Orphenadrine	
Propoxyphene	

a tricyclic antidepressant.[8] The axis of the frontal plane of the terminal 40 milliseconds is not easily measured on a regular ECG. An abnormal axis can be inferred by observing the QRS pattern in leads I and aVR; an S wave in lead I and R wave in aVR signify a rightward axis deviation (Figures 17.1, 17.2).

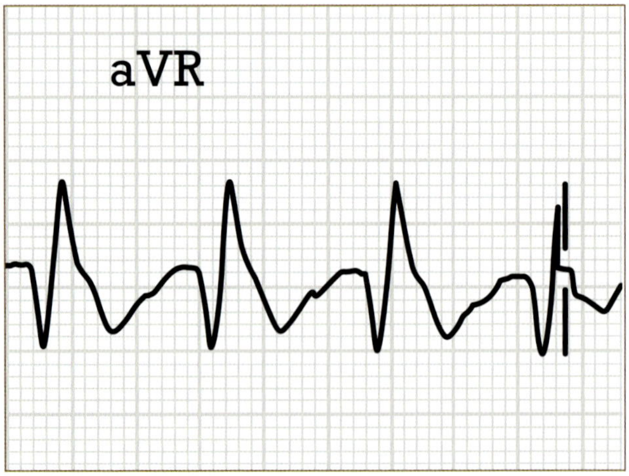

In the general overdose population, the positive and negative predictive values of the combination of these electrocardiographic findings are 66% and 100%, respectively.[8] In a prospective study of a group of cyclic antidepressant overdose patients, the amplitude of the terminal R wave and the R/S ratio in lead aVR were statistically significantly greater in patients with severe cyclic antidepressant

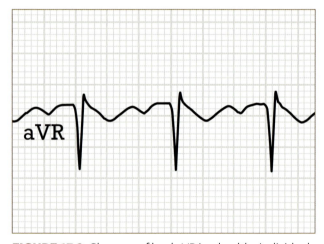

FIGURE 17.1. Close-up of lead aVR in a tricyclic antidepressant overdose with QRS 140 milliseconds. Axis of terminal 40 milliseconds of QRS in aVR is deviated rightward.

FIGURE 17.2. Close-up of lead aVR in a healthy individual.

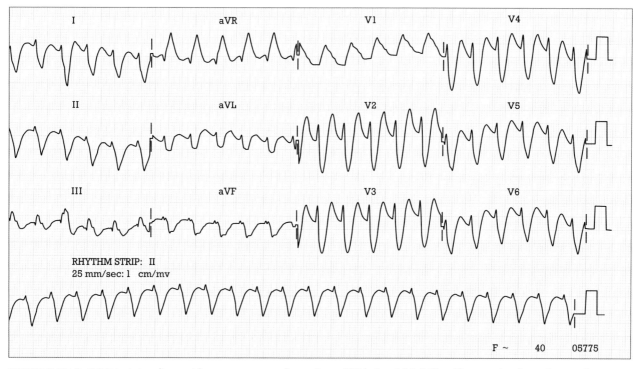

FIGURE 17.3. ECG in tricyclic antidepressant overdose. Rate 130/min, QRS 240 milliseconds, deep S wave in I, R_{aVR} greater than 3 mm in amplitude, and rightward axis deviation.

poisoning.[9] Of note, the presence of QRS interval prolongation, the Brugada pattern, or an R_{aVR} greater than 3 mm in amplitude is superior to the urine toxicology screen at detecting the presence of a cyclic antidepressant.[10] Occasionally a right bundle-branch block (RBBB) pattern is detected along with the electrocardiographic findings described previously (Figures 17.3, 17.4).

The Brugada syndrome is a cardiac disorder associated with a genetic defect in the alpha subunit of the Na_V causing dysfunction. The myocardium remains structurally normal.[11] The Brugada syndrome is associated with an increased incidence of sudden death. The Brugada electrocardiographic pattern is defined by RBBB and ST-segment elevation in V_1 through V_3. Voltage-gated sodium channel blockers can both unmask and produce this pattern. In a large case series, 15% to 17% of overdose patients with cyclic antidepressants met the criteria for Brugada pattern on ECG.[12,13] The mortality rate was 6.7% among patients with Brugada pattern and 2.4% if the Brugada pattern was absent.[13] The Brugada pattern has been detected following overdoses of other Na_V blockers: diphenhydramine, cocaine, procainamide, flecainide, and encainide.[13-16]

In some cases, the Na_V blockade is so profound that both the right and left bundles are affected, resulting in a dangerously lengthened QRS where supraventricular and ventricular rhythms become indistinguishable from each other.[7] The development of a sine wave is possible (Figure 17.5).

In a large case series, a QRS of 120 milliseconds or more was associated with a 33% incidence of seizures, and a QRS of 160 milliseconds or more was associated with a 50% incidence of ventricular arrhythmias.[17] Other studies confirmed that QRS prolongation (>100 milliseconds) is associated with an increased risk of coma, seizures, and ventricular arrhythmias.[18] Furthermore, a terminal R_{aVR} wave of 3 mm or greater and an R/S ratio of 0.7 or more is associated with an increased incidence of seizures and arrhythmias.[9,19] Conversely, absence of QRS prolongation or R_{aVR} after 6 hours' observation is associated with absence of seizures and arrhythmias.[17,18,20] The differential diagnosis of QRS prolongation includes

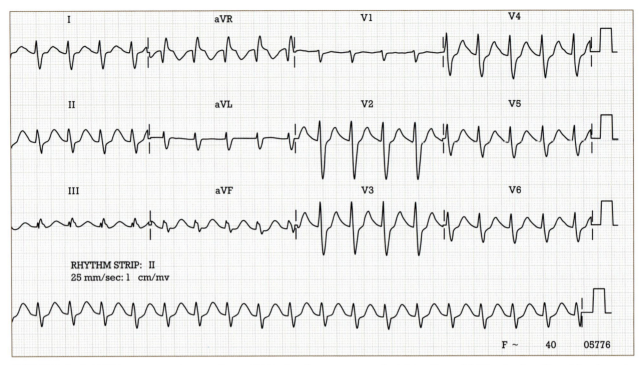

FIGURE 17.4. ECG in same patient as figure 17.3 after intravenous administration of 100 mL of sodium bicarbonate 8.4%. Rate 110/min, QRS 160 milliseconds, lessened S wave in I, lessened amplitude of R_{aVR}.

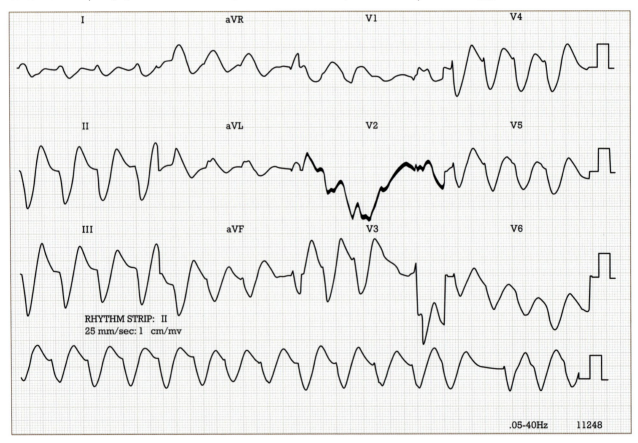

FIGURE 17.5. ECG in tricyclic antidepressant overdose. Rate 90/min, QRS 280 milliseconds, R_{aVR} greater than 3 mm in amplitude. Sine wave pattern in aVR and other leads. This sine wave pattern can be found in severe hyperkalemia as well.

bundle-branch blocks (particularly RBBB and left anterior fascicular block), pacemaker rhythms, ventricular premature beats, Wolff-Parkinson-White syndrome, electrolyte disorders, and left ventricular hypertrophy.

Ventricular Arrhythmias

The Na_v blockers can prolong intraventricular conduction to the extent that unidirectional blocks and reentrant circuits develop resulting in ventricular tachycardia. The ventricular tachycardia can deteriorate into ventricular fibrillation.

Bradyarrhythmias

The Na_v blockers can depress automaticity and cause sinus bradycardia, escape junctional rhythms, or ventricular rhythms, and even asystole in large overdoses (Table 17.2). The naturally occurring grayanotoxins are good examples.[21] The mechanism by which grayanotoxins and other Na_v blockers inhibit automaticity is unclear but could be related to depression of slope of phase 4 of the action potential. Importantly, many Na_v blockers are anticholinergic or sympathomimetic and associated with tachycardia (Table 17.3).

The presence of a wide QRS *and* bradycardia is an ominous sign and signifies a profound degree of Na_v blockade. The patient with the ECG shown in Figure 17.5 died from profound hypotension and poor perfusion a few hours after the ECG was obtained.

POTASSIUM RECTIFIER CURRENT INHIBITION

Potassium channels encoded by the hERG genes are responsible for the rectifier potassium current (I_{Kr}) and repolarization of the action potential. Blockade of these channels causes QT prolongation.[22] The channel's central cavity is surrounded by four deep hydrophobic pockets, which explains its sensitivity to many drugs.[23]

The I_{Kr} inhibitor group is larger and more diverse than the sodium channel blocker group. It includes antiarrhythmics, antipsychotics, methadone, loperamide, arsenic trioxide, and certain metals.[24-29] Since 2005, the US Food and Drug Administration has recommended both "non-clinical cardiac safety study" and "thorough QT study" of all new human pharmaceuticals.[27] It is estimated that 3% of all noncardiac medications are associated with I_{Kr} inhibition.[26] Importantly, the *S*(+) enantiomer of methadone inhibits I_{Kr}, whereas the *R*(-) enantiomer has little to no effect on the I_{Kr} but has most of the opioid agonist effects.[29] Table 17.4 lists common I_{Kr} inhibitors. A registry of pharmaceuticals that inhibit I_{Kr} is maintained

TABLE 17.2. Substances that cause bradycardia.

Antiarrhythmic agents	Procainamide, disopyramide, quinidine, sotalol
Alpha-adrenergic agonists	Clonidine, tizanidine, guanfacine, dexmedetomidine, oxymetazoline, naphazoline, tetrahydrozoline
Beta blockers	All
Calcium channel blockers	Verapamil, diltiazem, nifedipine to a lesser extent
Carbamate insecticides	Carbaryl, aldicarb, carbofuran
Ciguatera	
Digitalis glycosides	Digoxin
Opioids	
Organophosphate insecticides	Malathion
Sedative-hypnotic agents	Benzodiazepines, barbiturates, baclofen, zolpidem, others

by www.crediblemeds.org. This website is up-to-date, user friendly, and highly recommended. It does not include nonpharmaceuticals like barium, cesium, liquid protein diets, and organophosphates.

Blockade of the I_{Kr} prolongs the cardiac cycle and lengthens the QT interval. It also delays repolarization and decreases the difference in potential across the myocardial membrane. This less-than expected difference in potential can result in activation of the inward current (early afterdepolarization), which can trigger another action potential. Therefore, I_{Kr} inhibition is associated with QT prolongation (Figure 17.6). As the heart rate increases, the QT interval usually shortens. Multiple formulas may be used to correct the QT interval when tachycardia is present. The Bazett formula is most commonly used.[30,31]

The upper limit of the average normal QTc duration is 440 milliseconds in men and 460 milliseconds in women (Figure 17.6). The differential diagnosis of long QT syndrome includes hypokalemia, hypomagnesemia, hypocalcemia, hypothyroidism, cerebrovascular accident, myocardial infarction, and hypothermia.

Inhibition of I_{Kr} can result in activation of the inward current (early afterdepolarization) which can trigger another action potential. These I_{Kr}-triggered action potentials can deteriorate into reentrant circuits and result in polymorphic ventricular tachycardia (torsades de pointes) (Figures 17.6, 17.7). The risk of torsades de pointes increases

TABLE 17.3. Substances that cause tachycardia.	
Amphetamines	Ephedrine, pseudoephedrine, epinephrine, methylphenidate, methamphetamine
Anticholinergic agents	Atropine, scopolamine, benztropine, cyclobenzaprine, others
Antihistamines	Diphenhydramine, chlorpheniramine, meclizine, others
Antipsychotic agents	Haloperidol, risperidone, olanzapine, others
Arsenic (acute)	
Carbamates	Aldicarb, benfuracarb, carbaryl, carbofuran, methomyl, oxamyl
Carbon monoxide	
Cocaine	
Cyclic antidepressant agents	Amitriptyline, nortriptyline, imipramine, desipramine
Disulfiram-ethanol	
Iron	
Methylxanthines	Theophylline, caffeine
Monoamine oxidase inhibitors	Phenelzine, isocarboxazid, moclobemide, selegiline, rasagiline, tranylcypromine, procarbazine
Organophosphates	Chlorpyrifos, diazinon, dichlorvos, malathion, parathion
Phencyclidine	
Sedative-hypnotic agents	Benzodiazepines, barbiturates, glutethimide, zolpidem and others, etchlorvynol
Thyroxine	

at increasing QTc durations but can occur at any degree of prolongation. Drug-induced QT prolongation seems independent of dose and serum concentrations.[25,32] Concomitant treatment with more than one QT-prolonging drug can severely affect the QTc and be proarrhythmic.[33] Risks of torsades de pointes include QTc greater than 500 milliseconds or QTc change from baseline of more than 60 milliseconds, bradycardia, female sex, advanced age, diuretic use, hypokalemia, hypomagnesemia, hypocalcemia, and use of sympathomimetic agents.[23,34]

Some authors suggest the "QT dispersion" is a better predictor of torsades de pointes than a QT interval of more than 500 milliseconds. QT dispersion refers to the difference between the shortest and the longest QT interval on the 12-lead ECG and is a marker for conduction instability. The risk of torsades de pointes is greatest if the QT dispersion exceeds 100 milliseconds.[35]

SODIUM-POTASSIUM PUMP INHIBITION

Inhibitors of the Na-K ATPase pump are a much smaller group of substances. Digoxin is the best known of these agents, but many naturally occurring toxins figure prominently in this group (Table 17.5). This group will be referred generally as cardiac glycosides.

Cardiac glycosides inhibit the outward movement of sodium and inward movement of potassium. This

TABLE 17.4. Common Ikr inhibitors.

Antidepressants	Amitriptyline, amoxapine, citalopram, desipramine, doxepin, imipramine, nortriptyline, maprotiline, venlafaxine
Antihistamines	Loratadine, diphenhydramine
Antimalarials	Chloroquine, hydroxychloroquine, quinine
Antipsychotics	Chlorpromazine, droperidol, haloperidol, mesoridazine, thioridazine, pimozide, quetiapine, risperidone, ziprasidone
Arsenic trioxide	
Barium	
Bepridil	
Cisapride	
Class Ia antiarrhythmics	Quinidine, procainamide, disopyramide
Class Ic antiarrhythmics	Encainide, flecainide, moricizine, propafenone
Class III antiarrhythmics	Amiodarone, dofetilide, ibutilide, sotalol
Fluoroquinolones	Ciprofloxacin, gatifloxacin, levofloxacin, moxifloxacin, sparfloxacin
Halofantrine	
Lithium (possibly)	
Macrolides	Clarithromycin, erythromycin
Opioids	Methadone, levomethadyl acetate, loperamide
Pentamidine	
Tacrolimus	

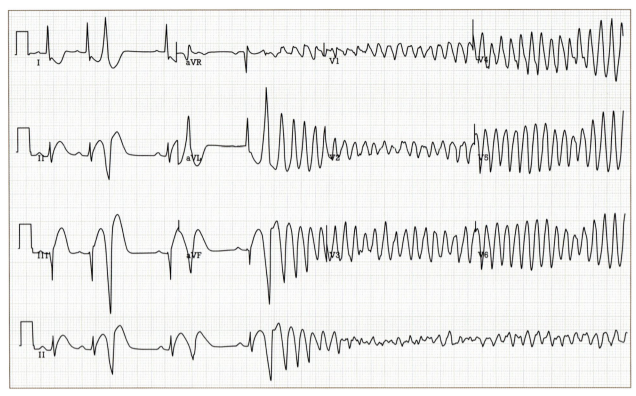

FIGURE 17.6. ECG in a loperamide overdose. QTc greater than 600 milliseconds. R-on-T phenomenon triggering torsades de pointes (ie, polymorphic ventricular tachycardia).

results in an increase in extracellular potassium and an increase in intracellular sodium. The increase in intracellular sodium activates the sodium-calcium exchange pump and results in the increase in intracellular calcium, which, in turn, stimulates myosin activity and exerts a positive inotropic effect. Cardiac glycosides also depress atrioventricular (AV) nodal conduction. Therapeutically, cardiac glycosides are used to increase inotropy and slow AV nodal conduction.

Digitalis Effect

Cardiac glycosides have been associated with several electrocardiographic changes. These changes can occur at therapeutic digoxin concentrations and when concentrations are in the toxic range. At therapeutic concentrations, T waves can be inverted or flattened and can be coupled with a scooping ST segment (Figures 17.8, 17.9). These findings are particularly evident in precordial leads with tall R waves and can be confused with diffuse ischemic disease, left ventricular strain, combined anterior-inferior infarction, subendocardial infarction, and hypokalemia. Other electrocardiographic changes associated with therapeutic concentrations include QT shortening resulting from rapid ventricular repolarization and PR interval prolongation resulting from increased vagal tone.

TABLE 17.5. Sodium-potassium pump inhibitors.
Bufadienolides
Digoxin and digitoxin
Foxglove
Lily-of-the-valley
Oleander
Red squill

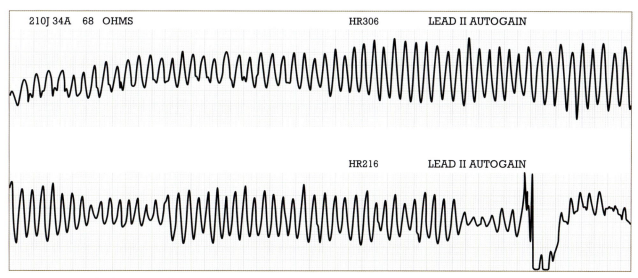

FIGURE 17.7. Rhythm strip of torsades de pointes (ie, polymorphic ventricular tachycardia).

Toxicity is associated with both tachyarrhythmias and bradyarrhythmias. An increase in intracellular calcium can cause increased automaticity; an increase in vagal tone can cause decreased automaticity. Atrial, junctional, and ventricular premature beats and tachycardia, sinus bradycardia, bundle-branch blocks, and varying degrees of AV nodal blocks can occur and co-occur in digoxin toxicity (Figure 17.8). The most common arrhythmia is frequent premature ventricular beats. Paroxysmal atrial tachycardia with variable block is highly indicative of cardiac glycoside toxicity, as are accelerated junctional rhythms (Figure 17.9). Bidirectional ventricular tachycardia is described almost exclusively in the context of cardiac glycoside toxicity.[36]

Acute poisoning of the Na-K ATPase pump by cardiac glycosides can acutely raise serum potassium concentrations, and the added effects of hyperkalemia on the ECG can be detected. Hyperkalemia causes spiked T waves, lengthening of the PR interval, and widening of the QRS. Conversely, *chronic* inhibition of the Na-K ATPase pump causes a much more gradual, time-dependent increase in serum potassium concentrations that is not usually associated with hyperkalemia because the potassium is eliminated by the renal system.

CALCIUM CHANNEL BLOCKERS

Cardioactive calcium channel blockers inhibit the high voltage L-type calcium channels found in myocardium and smooth muscle.[5] Inhibition of these channels prevents the inward movement of calcium into cells. Depletion of intracellular calcium slows conduction and decreases contractility. Antagonism of calcium channels at the sinoatrial and AV nodes produces bradycardia and conduction blocks. Calcium channel blockers are negative inotropes and chronotropes and cause peripheral vasodilation.[5] Calcium channel blockers are divided into three pharmacologic subclasses:

- dihydropyridines,
- phenylalkylamines, and
- benzothiazepines.

The dihydropyridine subclass (nifedipine, amlodipine, nicardipine) has an increased affinity for peripheral smooth muscle receptors. Overdoses with these agents often result in hypotension with reflex tachycardia. The most common electrocardiographic manifestation of dihydropyridine calcium channel blocker toxicity is reflex tachycardia. More profound dihydropyridine toxicity will be associated with bradycardia and AV nodal block

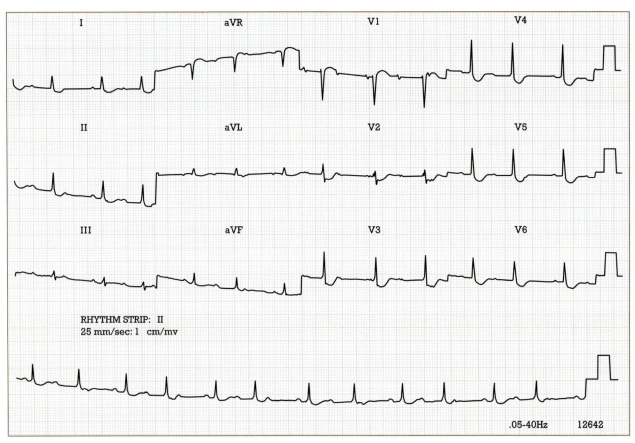

FIGURE 17.8. ECG in a digoxin overdose. Rate 90/min, Wenckebach 3:2 conduction, scooping of ST segments. Digoxin concentration 7.6 ng/mL. The scooping pattern is termed "digoxin effect" and is not necessarily a manifestation of toxicity.

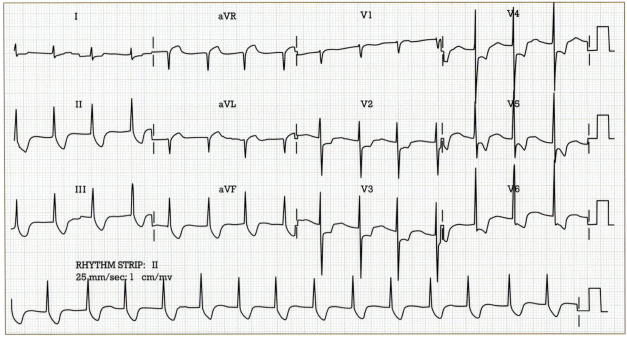

FIGURE 17.9. ECG in a digoxin overdose. Rate 80/min, junctional rhythm, scooping of ST segments. Digoxin concentration 7.8 ng/mL. The scooping pattern is termed "digoxin effect" and is not necessarily a manifestation of toxicity.

and junctional and ventricular bradyarrhythmias.

The phenylalkylamine (verapamil) and benzothiazepine (diltiazem) subclasses of calcium channel blockers possess a strong affinity for the myocardium calcium channels resulting in hypotension and bradycardia that can result in myocardial ischemia. Interestingly, verapamil has exhibited some calcium channel blockade effects both in vitro and in vivo.[4] The most common electrocardiographic finding in verapamil and diltiazem overdoses is bradycardia. Severe overdoses will be associated with AV nodal block and junctional and ventricular bradyarrhythmias (Figure 17.10). A widening of the QRS can be present, although the significance of this finding is unknown. In life-threatening overdoses, asystole will occur. Electrocardiographic changes indicative of myocardial ischemia can be present.

BETA BLOCKERS

Beta blockers, like calcium channel blockers, are seen in an increasing number of exposures. Beta blockers competitively inhibit beta$_1$ and beta$_2$-adrenergic receptors, decreasing intracellular cAMP and ultimately decreasing intracellular calcium.[5] Inhibition of beta$_1$ receptors results in a decrease in force and rate of myocardial contraction (negative inotropy) and a decrease in AV nodal conduction (negative chronotropy).[5] Inhibition of beta$_2$ receptors results in a relaxation of smooth muscle in the vasculature, bronchi, and gastrointestinal tract.

Beta blockers are a class of agents that do not necessarily share the "class effect." Propranolol nonselectively inhibits beta$_1$ and beta$_2$ receptors. Metoprolol selectively inhibits beta$_1$ receptors. In addition to their effects on beta-adrenergic channels, beta blockers have a number of properties that modify their effects and their electrocardiographic manifestations. Labetalol and carvedilol, for example, inhibit alpha receptors. The ratio of beta-to-alpha inhibition in the case of labetalol is 7:1 when administered intravenously and 5:1 when administered orally. Acebutolol, oxprenolol, penbutolol, and pindolol have intrinsic sympathomimetic activity, also termed partial agonist activity. In theory, these agents would appear safer in overdose situations. Pindolol is associated with hypertension and tachycardia in overdose, but data are insufficient to state that pindolol is safer in overdose. Propranolol, betaxolol, oxprenolol, and acebutolol cause Na$_v$ blockade. Sotalol, and possibly acebutolol, inhibit

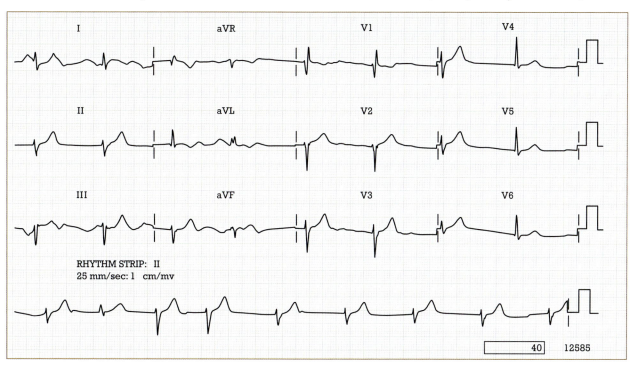

FIGURE 17.10. ECG in a calcium channel blocker overdose. Rate 50/min, junctional rhythm.

I_{Kr}. Finally, propranolol causes hypoglycemia in overdose situations.

The most common electrocardiographic manifestation of beta-blocker toxicity is AV block followed by bradycardia. In one small case series, first-degree AV block (PR interval prolongation of 216 milliseconds) was the most common electrocardiographic finding.[37] Bradycardia was infrequent in this case series, but this could reflect confounding variables such as administration of sympathomimetic agents. QRS prolongation (>100 milliseconds) was found in 8 of 13 symptomatic overdose victims and was most pronounced with overdoses of acebutolol, raising the question of whether propranolol truly possesses more Na_v blockade effects than acebutolol.[37] Sotalol is unique among beta blockers because it inhibits I_{Kr}, prolongs the action potential duration, and lengthens the QT interval. This, in turn, predisposes to torsades de pointes and ventricular arrhythmias.

GAP JUNCTION INHIBITION

Gap junctions, also known as connexins, are specialized intercellular channels found in all tissues except skeletal muscle. Contrary to traditional receptors, which allow communication between the cytoplasm and the extracellular space, gap junctions allow direct communication between the cytoplasm of two adjacent cells via a connexin. Inhibition and uncoupling of gap junctions in cardiomyocytes will slow cardiac conduction and cause QRS prolongation. Aconitine (monkshood plant), bupropion, and MDMA are known gap junction inhibitors.[38,39] It is important to recognize this new toxicologic mechanism because QRS prolongation induced by uncoupling of connexins might respond to hydrogen influx into cells more so than to sodium administration.[40]

SPECIAL CASES

Potassium

Drug-induced hypokalemia can occur following overdoses of beta agonists (albuterol), methylxanthines (caffeine, theophylline), and chloroquine (Table 17.6). It is manifested by muscle weakness, areflexic paralysis, and respiratory failure. Electrocardiographic changes are common and include sagging of the ST segment, decreased T-wave amplitude, and increased U-wave amplitude.

Drug-induced hyperkalemia can occur following overdoses of, among others, cardiac glycosides (digoxin,) and beta blockers (Table 17.2). Hyperkalemia presents with nausea and vomiting, muscle weakness, ascending paralysis, and

TABLE 17.6. Drugs that cause hyperkalemia and hypokalemia.

Hyperkalemia
Amiloride
Angiotensin-converting enzyme inhibitors
Beta blockers
Cardiac glycosides
Fluoride
Heparin
NSAIDs
Penicillin (potassium)
Potassium supplements
Succinylcholine
Triamterene
Trimethoprim
Hypokalemia
Beta-adrenergic agonists
Bicarbonate
Carbonic anhydrase inhibitors
Chloroquine, hydroxychloroquine, quinine
Diuretics
Insulin
Licorice
Methylxanthines (caffeine, theophylline)
Oral hypoglycemics
Sympathomimetics
Toluene

respiratory failure. Electrocardiographic changes include the presence of tall peaked T waves, QRS prolongation, loss of amplitude of the P wave, and prolongation of the PR interval. As the hyperkalemia progresses, a sine wave configuration is possible.

Calcium

Drug-induced hypocalcemia occurs with therapeutic uses of antiepileptics and aminoglycosides. It can occur following severe life-threatening overdoses of ethylene glycol, sodium fluoride, sodium bifluoride, hydrofluoric acid, bisphosphonates, sodium phosphate (Fleet enema), and phosphate-containing fire extinguisher contents. Symptoms of hypocalcemia include paresthesias, carpopedal spasms, tetany, and seizures. Electrocardiographic changes associated with hypocalcemia include prolongation of the QRS and QT intervals[41,42] (Figure 17.11).

Drug-induced hypercalcemia occurs rarely but can result from (usually chronic) overdose of antacids or vitamin D or from thiazide diuretic therapy. Ingestion of cholecalciferol, an ingredient in some rodenticides, can increase calcium enough to make the patient symptomatic. Symptoms of hypercalcemia include lethargy, constipation, nausea, and mental status changes. A shortened QT interval is the classic electrocardiographic abnormality found in patients with hypercalcemia.

Lithium

Lithium overdoses are fairly common. Lithium can cause shifts and depletion of intracellular potassium and also affect intracellular pools of calcium causing electrocardiographic changes. It can cause diffuse T-wave inversion, QTc prolongation, ventricular arrhythmias, AV nodal conduction defects, sinoatrial nodal dysfunction, and even myocarditis. In one small case series, 55% of patients with supratherapeutic lithium concentrations had a QTc of more than 440 milliseconds.[43] Furthermore, the combination of T-wave inversion in lateral precordial leads together with a QTc prolongation of 440 milliseconds or longer yielded a sensitivity of 64% and a specificity of 97% in predicting supratherapeutic lithium concentration.[43]

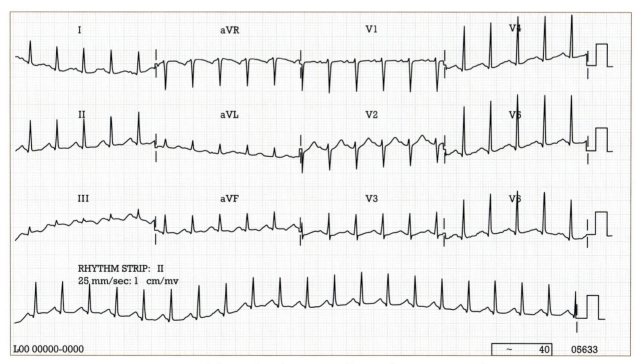

FIGURE 17.11. ECG in a patient with hyperphosphatemia and hypocalcemia. Rate 120/min, sinus rhythm, QTc 500 milliseconds. Serum phosphorus 9.5 mg/dL, calcium 4.5 mg/dL.

Halogenated Hydrocarbons

Halogenated hydrocarbons include chloroform, chloral hydrate, carbon tetrachloride, trichloroethanol, and trichloroethylene. Halogenated hydrocarbon overdoses are also associated with varied electrocardiographic manifestations stemming from the fact that they sensitize the myocardium to catecholamines.[44] Sinus tachycardia, ventricular ectopy, ventricular tachycardia, ventricular fibrillation, and sudden death are reported.[45,46] The mechanism of arrhythmias appears to be related to endogenous catecholamine release causing extrasystoles in the setting of altered repolarization, usually prolonged QTc interval. In one case series, 11 of 12 patients admitted to an intensive care unit with chloral hydrate overdoses had ventricular ectopic activity.[45] Halogenated hydrocarbon-induced ventricular tachyarrhythmias are usually resistant to standard antiarrhythmic agents but respond to the administration of beta blockers such as propranolol or esmolol.[46]

Ethanol

Acute ethanol intoxication has been associated with a number of different cardiac arrhythmias. The basic electrophysiologic effects of ethanol on the heart are not well described. But hyperadrenergic states, electrolyte abnormalities, impaired vagal tone, and repolarization abnormalities occur following ethanol consumption. The term *holiday heart* generally refers to de novo atrial fibrillation following a period of heavy ethanol consumption. Ventricular tachyarrhythmias are also associated with heavy ethanol intake. Also, heavy ethanol consumption in healthy human volunteers has been associated with increased QT dispersion. QT dispersion is the interlead difference in the QT interval. It is a marker for ventricular inhomogeneity and electrical instability.[35]

In conclusion, overdose patients can present with a wide array of electrocardiographic changes. (Tables 17.5, 17.6) In many instances, a common mechanism affecting a particular component of the cardiac action potential accounts for the electrocardiographic manifestations. Knowledge and understanding of these mechanisms is helpful in the management of overdose victims. Sodium channel blocker overdoses are quite common and are usually manifested by QRS prolongation, a tall R wave in aVR, or the Brugada pattern. Potassium channel blocker overdoses are manifested by prolongation of the QTc. Cardiac glycosides cause a wide assortment of electrocardiographic abnormalities, including bradycardia, AV nodal block, and bidirectional ventricular tachycardia. Multiple medications cause electrolyte changes. Lithium causes reversible nonspecific T-wave changes and QTc prolongation. Finally, halogenated hydrocarbons, like chloral hydrate, can cause resistant ventricular ectopy in overdose situations. In all instances, defining the cause of the electrocardiographic abnormality will guide therapy.

REFERENCES

1. Manini AF, Nelson LS, Stimmel B, et al. Incidence of adverse cardiovascular events in adults following drug overdose. *Acad Emerg Med*. 2012;19:843-849.
2. Stein EM, Gennuso KP, Ugoaja DC, Remington P. The epidemic of despair among white Americans: trends in the leading causes of premature death, 1999-2015. *Am J Public Health*. 2017;107(10):1541-1547.
3. Katz A, Grossestreuer AV, Gaieski DF, et al. Outcomes of patients resuscitated from cardiac arrest in the setting of drug overdose. *Resuscitation*. 2015;94:23-27.
4. Holstege CP, Elderidge DL, Rowden AK. ECG manifestations: the poisoned patient. *Emerg Med Clin North Am*. 2006;24:159-177.
5. Yates C, Manini AF. Utility of the electrocardiogram in drug overdose and poisoning: theoretical considerations and clinical implications. *Curr Cardiol Rev*. 2012;8:137-151.
6. Neher H, Sakmann B. Single-channel currents recorded from membranes of denervated frog muscle fibers. *Nature*. 1976,260:799-802.
7. Nattel S, Keable H, Sasyniuk BI. Experimental amitriptyline intoxication: electrophysiologic manifestations and management. *J Cardiovasc Pharmacol*. 1984;6:83-89.
8. Neimann JT, Bessen HA, Rothstein RJ, et al. Electrocardiographic criteria for tricyclic antidepressant cardiotoxicity. *Am J Cardiol*. 1986;57:1154-1159.
9. Liebelt EL, Francis PD, Woolf AD. ECG lead aVR versus QRS interval in predicting seizures and arrhythmias in acute tricyclic antidepressant toxicity. *Ann Emerg Med*. 1995;26:195-201.

10. Wolfe TR, Caravati EM, Rollins DE, et al. Terminal 40-ms frontal plane QRS axis as a marker for tricyclic antidepressant overdose. *Ann Emerg Med.* 1989;18:348-351.
11. Brugada P, Brugada J, Mont L, et al. A new approach to the differential diagnosis of a regular tachycardia with a wide QRS complex. *Circulation.* 1991;83:1649-1659.
12. Monteban-Kooistra WE, van de Berg MP, Tulleken JE, et al. Brugada electrocardiographic pattern elicited by cyclic antidepressant overdose. *Intensive Care Med.* 2006;32:281-285.
13. Goldgran-Toledano D, Sideris G, Kevorkian JP, et al. Overdose of cyclic antidepressant and the Brugada syndrome. *N Engl J Med.* 2002;346:1591-1592.
14. Lopez-Barbeito B, Lluis M, Delgado V, et al. Diphenhydramine overdose and the Brugada sign. *Pacing Clin Electrophysiol.* 2005;27:730-732.
15. Littmann L, Monroe MH, Kerns II WP, et al. Brugada syndrome and "Brugada sign": clinical spectrum with a guide for the clinician. *Am J Heart.* 2003;145:768-778.
16. Banta TA, St Jean A. The effect of phenothiazines on the electrocardiogram. *Can Med Assoc J.* 1964;91:537.
17. Boehnert M, Lovejoy FH. Value of the QRS duration versus the serum drug level in predicting seizures and ventricular arrhythmias after acute overdose of tricyclic antidepressant. *N Engl J Med.* 1985;313:203-109.
18. Kolecki PF, Curry SC. Poisoning by sodium channel blocking agents. *Crit Care Clin.* 1997;13:830-848.
19. Liebelt EL, Ulrich A, Francis PD, et al. Serial electrocardiogram changes in acute tricyclic antidepressant overdoses. *Crit Care Med.* 1997;25:1721-1726.
20. Shannon M. Duration of QRS disturbances after severe tricyclic antidepressant intoxication. *J Toxicol Clin Toxicol.* 1992;30:377-386.
21. Ozhan H, Akdemir R, Yazici M, et al. Cardiac emergencies caused by honey ingestion: a single centre experience. *Emerg Med J.* 2004;21:742-744.
22. Drolet B, Khalifa M, Daleau P, et al. Block of the rapid component of the delayed rectifier potassium current by the prokinetic agent cisapride underlies the drug-related lengthening of the QT interval. *Circulation.* 1998;97:204-210.
23. Wang W, MacKinnon R. Cryo-EM structure of the open ether-a-go-go related K$^+$ channel hERG. *Cell.* 2017;169(3):422-430.
24. Beckman KJ, Bauman JS, Pimental PA, et al. Arsenic-induced torsade de pointes. *Crit Care Med.* 1991;19:290-292.
25. Isbister GK, Brown AL, Gill A, et al. QT interval prolongation in opioid agonist treatment: analysis of continuous 12-lead electrocardiogram recordings. *British J Clin Pharmacol.* 2017;83(10):2274-2282.
26. De Ponti F, Poluzzi E, Montanaro N, et al. QTc and psychotropic drugs. *Lancet.* 2000;356:75-76.
27. US Food and Drug Administration. E14 Clinical evaluation of QT/QTc interval prolongation and proarrhythmic potential for non-antiarrhythmic drugs — questions and answers (R3): guidance for industry. Updated June 2017. Available at: https://www.fda.gov/downloads/Drugs/GuidanceCompliance-RegulatoryInformation/Guidances/UCM073161.pdf. Accessed October 2017.
28. Mehvar R, Brock DR, Vakily M. Impact of stereoselectivity on the pharmacokinetics and pharmacodynamics of antiarrhythmic drugs. *Clin Pharmacokinet.* 2002;41:533.
29. Smith S. Chiral toxicology: it's the same thing...only different. *Toxicol Sci.* 2009;110(1):4-30.
30. Bazett HC. An analysis of the time-relations of electrocardiograms. *Heart.* 1920;7:353-370.
31. Fridericia LS. The duration of systole in the electrocardiogram of normal subjects and of patients with heart disease. *Acta Medica Scand.* 1920;53:469-486.
32. Carceller-Sindreu M, Diego-Adelino J, Portella MJ, et al. Lack of relationship between plasma levels of escitalopram and QTc interval length. *Eur Arch Psychiatry Clin Neurosci.* 2017;267(8):815-822.
33. Frommeyer G, Fischer C, Ellermann C, et al. Additive proarrhythmic effect of combined treatment with QT prolonging agents. *Cardiovasc Toxicol.* 2018;18(1):84-90.
34. Schwartz PJ, Woosley RL. Predicting the unpredictable. Drug induced QT prolongation and torsades de pointes. *J Am Coll Cardiol.* 2016;67(13):1639-1650.
35. Uyarel H, Ozdol C, Gender AM, et al. Acute alcohol intake and QT dispersion in healthy subjects. *J Stud Alcohol.* 2005;66:555-558.
36. Valent S, Kelly P. Images in clinical medicine. Digoxin-induced bidirectional ventricular tachycardia. *N Engl J Med.* 1997;336(8):550.
37. Love JN, Enlow B, Howell JM, et al. Electrocardiographic changes associated with beta-blocker toxicity. *Ann Emerg Med.* 2002;40:603-610.
38. Caillier B, Pilote S, Castonguay A, et al. QRS widening and QT prolongation under bupropion: a unique cardiac electrophysiological profile. *Fundam Clin Pharmacol.* 2012;26(5):599-608.
39. Zhang SW, Liu Y, Huang JZ, Liu L. Aconitine alters connexin43 phosphorylation status and calcium oscillation patterns in cultured ventricular myocytes of neonatal rats. *Toxicol In Vitro.* 2007;21(8);1476-1485.

40. Garciarena CD, Youm JB, Swietach P, Vaughan-Jones RD. H$^+$-activated Na$^+$ influx in the ventricular myocyte couples Ca$^+$ signaling to intracellular pH. *J Mol Cell Cardiol*. 2013;61:51-59.
41. Holstege CP, Baer A, Brady WJ. The electrocardiographic toxidrome: the ECG presentation of hydrofluoric acid ingestion. *Am J of Emerg Med*. 2005;23:171-176.
42. Doyon S, McGrath JM. Hyperphosphatemia and cardiac arrest after insufflation of dry chemical fire extinguisher. *Clin Toxicol*. 2003;41:38 (abstract).
43. Chih-Hsin Hsu, Ping-Yen Liu, Jyh-Hong Chen, et al. Electrocardiographic abnormalities as predictors of over-the-range lithium levels. *Cardiology*. 2005;103:101-106.
44. Bowyer K, Glasser SP. Chloral hydrate overdose and cardiac arrhythmias. *Chest*. 1980;77:232-235.
45. Graham SR, Day RO, Lee R. Overdose with chloral hydrate: a pharmacologic and therapeutic review. *Med J Aust*. 1988;149:686-688.
46. Zahedi A, Grant MH, Wong DT. Successful treatment of chloral hydrate cardiac toxicity with propranolol. *Am J Emerg Med*. 1999;17:490-491.

CHAPTER EIGHTEEN

The Pediatric ECG

STEPHANIE J. DONIGER AND GHAZALA Q. SHARIEFF

KEY POINTS

- Right axis deviation is normal in neonates and young infants; the axis assumes a leftward direction as the child grows and the left ventricle enlarges.
- For children younger than 8 years, the upper limit of normal for the QRS duration is 80 milliseconds. Therefore, ventricular tachycardia can present in young children with QRS durations as low as 80 to 90 milliseconds.
- A practical tip is to count the heart rate using a stethoscope rather than trying to palpate a very rapid pulse.
- Newborns and infants can manifest sinus tachycardia with heart rates as high as 200 to 220 beats/min.
- T-wave inversions in leads V_1 through V_3 are common and normal from infancy through adolescence.
- To assess for prolonged QT syndrome, which is a cause of syncope, the Bazett formula should be used to calculate the corrected interval $QTc = QT/\sqrt{R\text{-}R}$ interval.
- Tachycardia faster than expected for the degree of fever is classic in myocarditis, although it also can be seen in ventricular arrhythmias, advanced atrioventricular blocks, and low-voltage QRS complexes.
- Supraventricular tachycardia is the most common symptomatic arrhythmia in infants and children. The delta wave associated with Wolff-Parkinson-White syndrome is often identified only after the rhythm is converted to sinus rhythm.
- Right bundle-branch block is more common than left bundle-branch block in children. It is commonly seen in children after operative repair of congenital heart disease and can be mistaken for a wide complex tachycardia if P waves are not carefully sought.
- All degrees of atrioventricular block can be seen in pediatric patients.

A *recent review* of pediatric emergency department utilization revealed that the most common reasons for obtaining ECGs in children are chest pain, suspected arrhythmias, seizures, syncope, drug exposure, electrical burns, electrolyte abnormalities, and abnormal physical examination findings.[1] Of the 71 pediatric ECGs reviewed over a 15-month period, 14 (20%) had clinical significance such as prolonged QT syndrome, ventricular hypertrophy, or premature ventricular beats.[1] In the largest pediatric series outside the intensive care unit, pediatric arrhythmias had an incidence of 11.5 per 10,000 patients, with a median age at presentation of 10.4 years. The most common arrhythmia was supraventricular tachycardia (detected in 56% of the study group), with a low overall mortality rate.[2]

A systematic approach to interpretation, with special attention to age-dependent rate, rhythm, axis, and intervals, is crucial to the interpretation of pediatric ECGs. It is important to evaluate for the presence of ventricular and atrial hypertrophy and for ischemia or repolarization abnormalities.

TABLE 18.1. Pediatric electrocardiography: normal intervals.								
AGE	HEART RATE (BEATS/MIN)	QRS AXIS (DEGREES)	PR INTERVAL (SEC)	QRS INTERVAL (SEC)	R IN V$_1$ (MM)	S IN V$_1$ (MM)	R IN V$_6$ (MM)	S IN V$_6$ (MM)
1st week	90–160	60–180	0.08–0.15	0.03–0.08	5–26	0–23	0–12	0–10
1–3 weeks	100–180	45–160	0.08–0.15	0.03–0.08	3–21	0–16	2–16	0–10
1–2 months	120–180	30–135	0.08–0.15	0.03–0.08	3–18	0–15	5–21	0–10
3–5 months	105–185	0–135	0.08–0.15	0.03–0.08	3–20	0–15	6–22	0–10
6–11 months	110–170	0–135	0.07–0.16	0.03–0.08	2–20	0.5–20	6–23	0–7
1–2 years	90–165	0–110	0.08–0.16	0.03–0.08	2–18	0.5–21	6–23	0–7
3–4 years	70–140	0–110	0.09–0.17	0.04–0.08	1–18	0.5–21	4–24	0–5
5–7 years	65–140	0–110	0.09–0.17	0.04–0.08	0.5–14	0.5–24	4–26	0–4
8–11 years	60–130	−15–110	0.09–0.17	0.04–0.09	0–14	0.5–25	4–25	0–4
12–15 years	65–130	−15–110	0.09–0.18	0.04–0.09	0–14	0.5–21	4–25	0–4
>16 years	50–120	−15–110	0.12–0.20	0.05–0.10	0–14	0.5–23	4–21	0–4

Reproduced with permission from: Sharieff GQ, Rao SO. The pediatric ECG. *Emerg Med Clin North Am.* 2006; 24:195-208. Copyright 2006 Elsevier Inc.

THE NORMAL PEDIATRIC ECG

Many systematic techniques may be used to interpret ECGs, and no one method is particularly better than another. The electronic interpretation provided by many electrocardiographic machines is likely to be inaccurate in children because the machines are generally calibrated with adult values. However, the interpretations are reasonably accurate in calculating intervals, which are averaged over the entire recording period. The settings of the ECG must be at full standard, defined as 10 mm/mV, with a standard paper speed of 25 mm/sec. These settings may be changed to elucidate certain features, but a standard ECG is the only one that should be referenced to normal values. Frequently, additional right ventricular and posterior left ventricular precordial leads (V$_3$R, V$_4$R, and V$_7$) are included with pediatric ECGs to provide additional information about cardiac physiology in patients with complex congenital abnormalities. These leads may be ignored when evaluating most pediatric patients.

Many subtleties in the pediatric ECG are age related. For example, fetal circulation relies heavily on the right side of the heart; therefore, at birth, the right ventricle is larger than the left ventricle and there is a normal right axis deviation. Rapid changes occur over the first year of life as a result of the dramatic changes in circulation and cardiac physiology. During infancy, increased physiologic stress and work of the left ventricle lead to its enlargement. By 6 months of age, the infant's left ventricle is approximately double the thickness of the right ventricle. After this time, changes are more gradual until late adolescence and adulthood.

Normal electrocardiographic values in the newborn, infant, child, and adolescent are listed in Table 18.1.[3-5] Normal ranges for these values are categorized by age for heart rate, QRS axis, PR and QRS intervals, and R- and S-wave amplitudes.

Heart Rate

In children, the cardiac output is determined primarily by heart rate, as opposed to stroke volume. With age, the heart rate decreases as the ventricles mature and stroke volume has a larger role in cardiac output. Hence, it is important to recognize heart rates specific for a patient's age. The average resting heart rate varies with age: in newborns, it can range from 90 to 160 beats/min and in adolescents from 50 to 120 beats/min (Table 18.1).

Axis

In utero, blood is shunted away from the lungs by the patent ductus arteriosus, and the right ventricle provides the vast majority of the systemic blood flow. As a result, in the newborn period, the right ventricle is the dominant chamber. In the neonate and young infant (up to 2 months of age), the ECG shows right ventricular dominance and right axis deviation (Figure 18.1). Most of the QRS complex consists of right ventricular mass. Across the precordium, the QRS complex demonstrates a large-amplitude R wave (increased R:S ratio) in leads V_1 and V_2 and a small-amplitude R wave (decreased R:S ratio) in leads V_5 and V_6. Over time, as the cardiac and circulatory physiology matures, the left ventricle becomes increasingly dominant. As a result, the QRS axis shifts from a rightward axis to a more normal position; the R-wave amplitude decreases in V_1 and V_2 and increases in V_5 and V_6.

QRS Duration

The QRS complex duration varies with age. In children, it is shorter, presumably due to the smaller muscle mass, and gradually increases with age. In neonates, the QRS complex duration is between 30 and 80 milliseconds and, in adolescents, between 50 and 100 milliseconds. In children younger than 8 years, a QRS duration of more than 80 milliseconds can be pathologic. In older children, a QRS duration longer than 100 milliseconds can be pathologic.

PR Interval

The PR interval (measured as the time from the onset of the P wave to the onset of the QRS complex) also varies with age and gradually increases with cardiac maturity and muscle mass. In neonates, the PR interval ranges from 80 to 150 milliseconds and, in adolescents, from 120 to 200 milliseconds.[4]

QT Interval

The QT interval (measured as the time from the beginning of the QRS complex to the end of the T wave) varies greatly with heart rate. As a result,

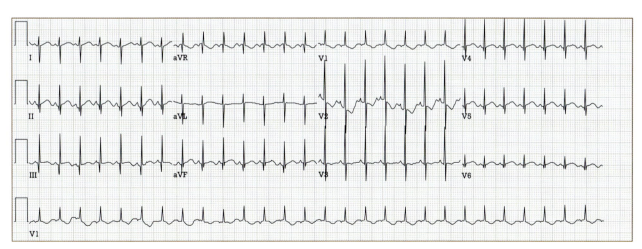

FIGURE 18.1. Normal newborn ECG. This ECG from a 2-day-old child shows characteristic findings of right axis deviation and inverted T waves in V_1. Reproduced with permission from: Pierangelo Renella, MD.

the QT interval is corrected (QTc), usually according to the Bazett formula:

$$QTc = QT/\sqrt{R\text{-}R} \text{ interval}$$

During the first 6 months of life, the normal upper limit of the QTc interval is 490 milliseconds. Beyond this period, the QT interval is relatively constant; it is one of the few intervals that does not vary with age outside the period of infancy. In children and adults, a borderline QTc interval is between 440 and 460 milliseconds, and a QTc of more than 460 milliseconds is considered prolonged. A prolonged QTc is a common cause of syncope. Prolonged QT syndrome can be hereditary, as seen with the genetic syndromes Jervell and Lange-Nielsen and Romano-Ward. Of note, Jervell Lange-Nielsen syndrome is associated with familiar hearing loss. It can also be drug induced and associated with electrolyte disturbances[6] (Figure 18.2). A commonly used medication, ondansetron, has been linked to prolongation of the QT interval. This association is more likely to be seen in children with underlying cardiac abnormalities or in conjunction with coadministration of other QT-prolonging drugs.[7] May and colleagues reported an association between prolonged QTc interval and migraine headaches.[8]

T Waves

In pediatric patients, T-wave changes on the ECG tend to be nonspecific and are often a source of confusion and controversy. What is agreed on is that flat or inverted T waves are normal in the newborn period. In fact, the T waves in leads V_1 through V_3 are usually inverted after the first week of life; this "juvenile" T-wave pattern usually persists through 8 years of age and can continue into early adolescence. The presence of upright T waves in lead V_1 after 3 days of age can be a sign of right ventricular hypertrophy.

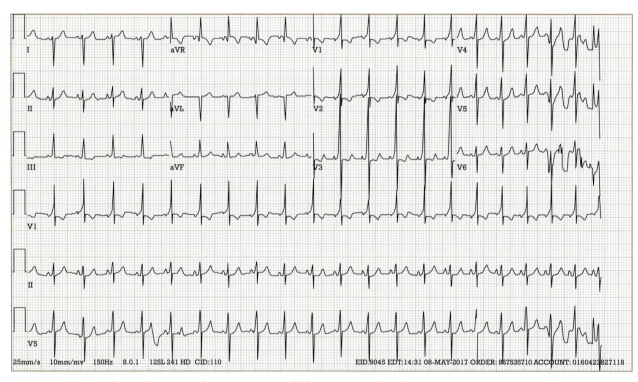

FIGURE 18.2. Prolonged QT complex. An 11-year-old boy presented with severe gastroenteritis. His ECG showed prolongation of the QTc interval and flattened T waves. These abnormalities were caused by electrolyte abnormalities (K = 1.8 mEq/L). They resolved with correction of the electrolyte concentrations. Reproduced with permission from: Sriram Ramgopal, MD.

Chamber Size

Assessment of chamber size is important when analyzing the pediatric ECG for underlying signs of congenital heart abnormalities. The size of the P waves can indicate atrial enlargement: P waves larger than 2 mm in infants and larger than 3 mm in adolescents can indicate right atrial enlargement. Because the right atrium depolarizes before the left atrium, a P-wave duration longer than 80 milliseconds in infants and 120 milliseconds in adolescents could indicate left atrial enlargement.

To assess the size of the ventricles, the QRS complex should be evaluated. Right ventricular hypertrophy (RVH) is best seen in leads V_1 and V_2 with an rSR´ pattern, QR (no S), or a pure R (no Q or S). Right ventricular hypertrophy is also suggested by the presence of a large S wave in lead V_6, upright T waves in leads V_1 through V_3 after the first week of life, or persistence of the right ventricular dominance pattern of the neonate. Similarly, left

TABLE 18.2. Electrocardiographic criteria for ventricular and atrial hypertrophy.

The presence of any of the following is suspicious for hypertrophy. It is not necessary for all criteria to be met.

Right ventricular hypertrophy

- R wave >98th percentile in lead V_1 (see Table 18.1)*
- S wave >98th percentile in either lead I or lead V_6 (see Table 18.1 for upper limits)
- RSR´ pattern in leads V_1, with the R´ height being >15 mm in infants younger than 1 year of age or >10 mm in children over 1 year of age
- Q wave in V_1

Left ventricular hypertrophy

- R-wave amplitude >98th percentile in lead V_5 or V_6 (see Table 18.1)
- R wave <5th percentile in lead V_1 or V_2 (see Table 18.1)
- S-wave amplitude >98th percentile in lead V_1 (see Table 18.1)
- Q wave >4 mm in lead V_5 or V_6
- Inverted T wave in V_6

Right atrial enlargement

- P wave in leads II and V_1 that is >3 mm in infants older than 6 months of age and >2.5 mm in infants younger than 6 months of age

Left atrial enlargement

- P-wave duration is >0.08 seconds in a child younger than 12 months of age or >0.1 second in children 1 year of age or older
- Terminal or deeply inverted P wave in V_1 or V_3R

*qR wave pattern in V_1 is seen in 10% of normal newborns.

Reproduced with permission from: Sharieff GQ, Rao SO. The pediatric ECG. *Emerg Med Clin North Am.* 2006; 24:195-208. Copyright 2006 Elsevier Inc.

ventricular hypertrophy (LVH) is suggested by the presence of tall R waves in lead V_6, large S waves in lead V_1, a left ventricular "strain" pattern in leads V_5 and V_6, and a mature precordial R-wave progression in the newborn period. Evidence of biventricular enlargement on the ECG indicates biventricular hypertrophy (Table 18.2).

THE ABNORMAL PEDIATRIC ECG

Tachycardias

Tachycardias can be classified broadly according to their site of origination. Those that originate from loci above the atrioventricular (AV) node are supraventricular tachycardias, those that originate from the AV node are AV node reentrant tachycardias, and those that are ventricular in origin, ventricular tachycardias. The AV node reentrant tachycardias are more common in the adult population, and the vast majority of tachycardias in children are supraventricular in origin. When tachycardia is identified, a systematic review is crucial in interpreting the ECG. Is the rhythm regular or irregular? Is the QRS complex narrow or wide? Does every P wave result in a single QRS complex?

Sinus tachycardia can be differentiated from other tachycardias by the presence of a P wave preceding every narrow QRS complex. Sinus tachycardia is a normal rhythm and can be a normal physiologic response to stresses such as fever, dehydration, volume loss, anxiety, and pain. It is important to keep in mind that the normal range for heart rate is higher in children than in adults and varies according to age (Table 18.1). Particularly in younger children, it is often difficult to palpate a very rapid pulse; it might be more helpful to count the heart rate using a stethoscope. A resting sinus tachycardia that is not associated with fever, agitation, or medications could be a sign of sinus node dysfunction. Sinus tachycardia can also be a presenting sign of noncardiac pathologies such as dehydration. A recent study showed that children discharged with tachycardia are more likely to return to the emergency department and receive clinically important interventions.[9]

Supraventricular tachycardia (SVT) is the most common symptomatic arrhythmia in infants and children. Infants with SVT typically present with nonspecific complaints such as "fussiness," poor feeding, pallor, or lethargy. Older children might complain of chest pain, palpitations, dizziness, or shortness of breath. Those with severe or unstable SVT can present with an altered level of consciousness and hypotension. The diagnosis often begins in triage with the nurse reporting that "the heart rate is too fast to count."

Newborns and infants with SVT can present with heart rates between 220 and 280 beats/min,[10] whereas, in older children, SVT is defined as a heart rate faster than 180 beats/min. On the ECG, SVT is characterized by a narrow QRS complex tachycardia without discernible preceding P waves. There is little beat-to-beat variability, with the heart rate remaining relatively constant throughout an event (Figure 18.3). It is important to note that the initial ECG can be normal, so a 24-hour rhythm recording (Holter monitor) or an event monitor may be necessary to document the arrhythmia, particularly if the patient is experiencing intermittent episodes.

In children younger than 12 years of age, the most common cause of SVT is an accessory AV pathway; in adolescents, an AV node reentry tachycardia is more likely.[5] Wolff-Parkinson-White (WPW) syndrome is one type of SVT. Episodes of SVT in children with WPW syndrome usually occur early in the first year of life.[11] They usually resolve during infancy but can recur later in life, usually between 6 and 8 years of age.[11] In patients with WPW syndrome, SVT is generally initiated by premature atrial depolarization that travels to the ventricles via the normal AV pathway, moves retrograde through the accessory pathway, and reenters the AV node to start a reentrant type of tachycardia.[10,12] Antegrade conduction through the AV node followed by retrograde conduction through the accessory pathway produces a narrow complex tachycardia (orthodromic tachycardia)—the most common form of SVT found in patients with WPW syndrome.[10,12] Less commonly, reentry occurs with antegrade conduction through an accessory pathway and retrograde conduction through the AV node (antidromic tachycardia) to

THE PEDIATRIC ECG

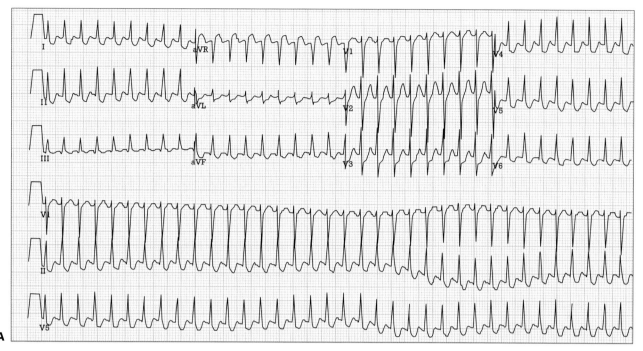

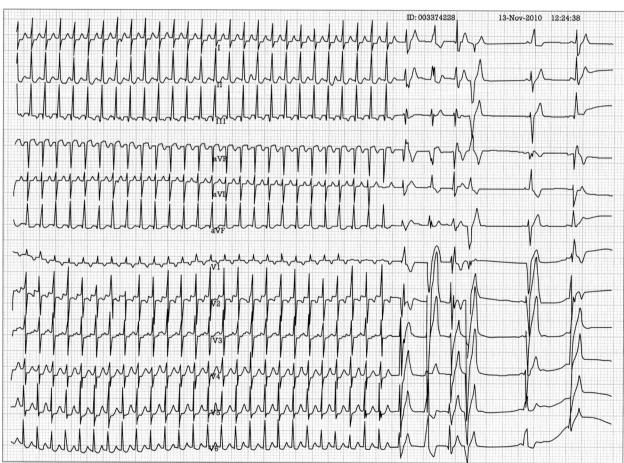

FIGURE 18.3. Supraventricular tachycardia. **A.** Child presented with palpitations and tachycardia. No P waves preceding QRS complexes. **B.** Adenosine-induced pause followed by conversion to sinus rhythm. Reproduced with permission from: Pierangelo Renella, MD.

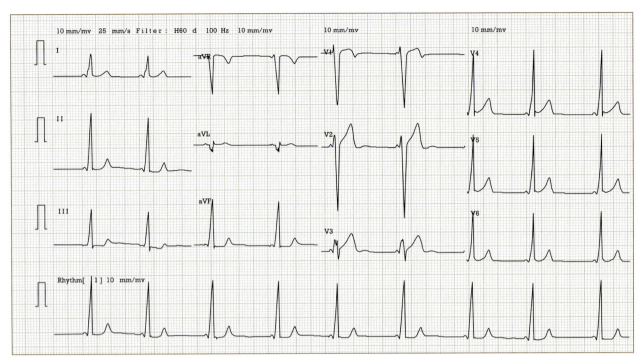

FIGURE 18.4. Wolff-Parkinson-White syndrome. A child presented with a narrow complex tachycardia. After conversion to sinus rhythm, the delta waves became apparent. The delta wave is a positive inflection in the upstroke of the QRS complex. Reproduced with permission from: Pierangelo Renella, MD.

produce a wide complex tachycardia.[11] Typical electrocardiographic findings of WPW syndrome are a short PR interval, a wide QRS complex, and a slurring in the upstroke of the QRS complex, known as a delta wave. The ECG in patients with SVT will not show the delta wave because tachycardia is mediated through the accessory pathway only; the delta wave becomes apparent after conversion to sinus rhythm (Figure 18.4).

In most cases, stable SVT can be converted with intravenous adenosine (0.1 mg/kg IV, may repeat 0.2 mg/kg IV, max 12 mg). It is important to record continuous electrocardiographic or rhythm strips under specific conditions: when the child is exhibiting tachycardia, while adenosine is being administered, and after conversion to sinus rhythm. In the rare cases of unstable or refractory SVT, synchronized cardioversion can be necessary (0.5-1.0 J/kg, if not effective increase to 2 J/kg).[13,14]

Atrial ectopic tachycardia can be differentiated from SVT by the presence of P waves preceding the QRS complexes. Each P wave is conducted to the ventricle but has an abnormal wave morphology. Since the ectopic atrial focus is faster than the sinoatrial node, it determines the ventricular rate.

Ventricular tachycardias (VTs) are much less common in children than in adults. Since the QRS complex is shorter in children than in adults, a QRS complex width of 90 milliseconds can appear normal on the ECG but might actually represent an abnormally wide QRS complex tachycardia in an infant. The differential diagnosis of wide complex tachycardia includes sinus/supraventricular tachycardia with bundle-branch block or aberrancy, antidromic AV reentry tachycardia, VT, and coarse ventricular fibrillation.[15] Findings of VT on the ECG include:

- AV dissociation with the ventricular rate exceeding the atrial rate,
- a significantly prolonged QRS interval, or
- the presence of fusion or capture beats (Figure 18.5).

If a right bundle-branch (RBBB) block is present, the presence of VT is supported by a monophasic qR

THE PEDIATRIC ECG

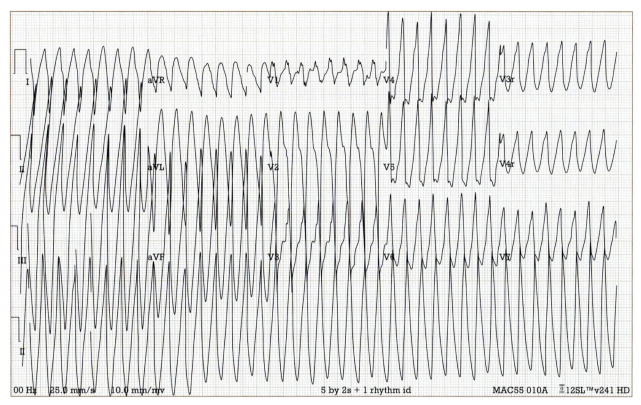

FIGURE 18.5. An adolescent male with stable ventricular tachycardia that was successfully cardioverted to sinus rhythm. Reproduced with permission from: Jerry P. George, MD, MSE.

in V_1 and a deep S wave in V_6. If a left bundle-branch block (LBBB) is present, then the presence of VT is supported by a notched S wave and an R-wave duration of more than 30 milliseconds in V_1 and V_2 and a Q wave in V_6.[15]

Conduction Abnormalities

All degrees of AV block can occur in pediatric patients. Conduction disorders are uncommon during childhood; they are most likely to occur following surgical repair of structural congenital heart disease.[16] It is important to remember that the normal PR interval in infants is shorter and lengthens as cardiac tissue matures with age. Thus, a "normal appearing" PR interval of 200 milliseconds can, in fact, represent a pathologic first-degree AV block in an infant or a young child.

Complete heart block is a common cause of significant bradycardia in pediatric patients and can be congenital or acquired (Figure 18.6). Causes of congenital heart block include structural lesions such as transposition of the great arteries and maternal connective tissue disorders. Acquired heart block can result from disorders such as Lyme disease, systemic lupus erythematosus, muscular dystrophies, Kawasaki disease, and rheumatic fever.[17]

Bundle-branch blocks can be present when QRS complex prolongation is abnormal for a given age. Right bundle-branch block occurs with abnormal rightward and anterior terminal forces, frequently manifesting on the ECG as an rSR' pattern in leads V_1 and V_2 (Figure 18.7.) Right bundle-branch block is more common than LBBB and can be seen after surgical repair of congenital heart defects, particularly after ventricular septal defect repairs. Similarly, LBBB is exhibited by abnormal leftward and posterior forces and is best appreciated in leads V_5 and V_6. However, because LBBB is rare in children, its presence should raise the possibility of WPW syndrome, which can mimic the LBBB pattern.

ELECTROCARDIOGRAPHY IN EMERGENCY, ACUTE, AND CRITICAL CARE

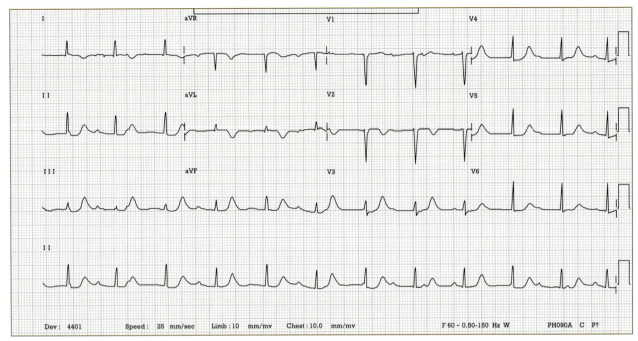

FIGURE 18.6. Complete heart block. A 15-year-old boy's ECG revealed complete heart block. Note the complete dissociation of P waves from QRS complexes. Reproduced with permission from: Ella Cameron, MD.

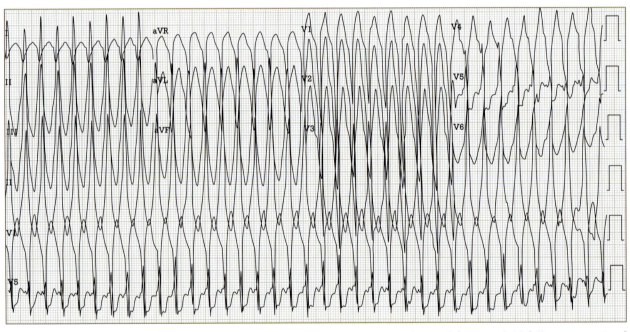

FIGURE 18.7. Sinus tachycardia with bundle-branch block. This ECG was obtained from a child following repair of congenital heart disease. A supraventricularr tachycardia, in this case sinus tachycardia, with bundle-branch block can be easily confused with ventricular tachycardia. On careful examination, the P waves can be appreciated preceding the QRS complexes. Reproduced with permission from: Pierangelo Renella, MD.

Congenital Heart Disease

Congenital heart disease occurs in 8 of 1,000 live births. Many of the structural congenital heart diseases manifest during the neonatal period.[18] The signs and symptoms of congenital heart disease can be nonspecific, such as tachypnea, cyanosis, or pallor that worsens with crying, sweating with feeds, lethargy, and failure to thrive.[19]

Congenital heart disease lesions that present in the first 2 to 3 weeks of life are typically ductal dependent. The ductus arteriosus has been sustaining blood flow for these infants, and when it closes anatomically at 2 to 3 weeks of life, these infants suddenly become ill. Depending on the underlying structural abnormality, these neonates can present with either sudden cyanosis or signs of cardiovascular collapse. The ductal-dependent congenital heart lesions include hypoplastic left heart syndrome, critical aortic stenosis, tricuspid atresia, pulmonary atresia, and transposition of the great arteries. It is important to note that administering 100% oxygen fails to raise the partial pressure of oxygen to normal levels in these infants. Prostaglandin should be given immediately to keep the ductus arteriosus open until definitive surgical correction can be performed. The time of presentation of cyanotic and acyanotic congenital heart diseases and their common associated electrocardiographic findings are listed in Tables 18.3 and 18.4.[20-22]

Left-to-right intracardiac shunts such as ventricular septal or AV canal defects constitute the other

TABLE 18.3. Cyanotic congenital heart disease: time to presentation and typical electrocardiographic findings.

DISORDER	AGE AT PRESENTATION	FINDING
Transposition of the great arteries	Birth–1 week	RVH
Total anomalous pulmonary venous return	1 week	RVH
Severe pulmonic stenosis	1–4 weeks	RVH
Tricuspid atresia	1–4 weeks	LVH
Tetralogy of Fallot	1–12 weeks	RVH
Truncus arteriosus	Any time in infancy	BVH

RVH, right ventricular hypertrophy; LVH, left ventricular hypertrophy; BVH, biventricular hypertrophy.

TABLE 18.4. Acyanotic congenital heart disease resulting in acute heart failure: time to presentation and typical electrocardiographic findings.

DISORDER	AGE AT PRESENTATION	FINDING
Coarctation of the aorta	Within first week	RVH/LVH
Hypoplastic left heart	Within first week	RVH
Complete AV canal	2–3 weeks	BVH or LVH
Patent ductus arteriosus	2–3 weeks	LVH
Ventricular septal defect	2–12 weeks	LVH

RVH, right ventricular hypertrophy; LVH, left ventricular hypertrophy; BVH, biventricular hypertrophy.

class of congenital cardiac lesions that present very early in life. As the normal pulmonary vascular resistance falls during the first month of life, any preexisting left-to-right shunt will see a gradual increase in flow across the shunt, resulting in acute heart failure. The differential diagnosis of acute heart diseases that cause acute heart failure includes not only the left-to-right intracardiac shunts but also hypoplastic left heart syndrome, coarctation of the aorta, tricuspid atresia, endocardial cushion defect, patent ductus arteriosus, aortic stenosis, interrupted aortic arch, aortic atresia, and mitral valve atresia.[23,24]

An ECG should be obtained in all infants suspected of having a congenital heart disease. Although the ECG will not make the diagnosis, it can show evidence of conduction abnormalities or chamber enlargement as a result of the congenital defect. Table 18.5 lists the common electrocardiographic findings associated with specific congenital heart diseases.

Hypertrophic Cardiomyopathy

Most cases of hypertrophic cardiomyopathy are diagnosed in patients between 30 and 40 years of age, but 2% of cases occur in children younger than 5 years of age and 7% in children younger than 10 years of age.[25] The clinical presentation varies, with patients experiencing chest pain, palpitations, shortness of breath, syncopal or near syncopal episodes, or sudden death. Children with hypertrophic cardiomyopathy who experience syncope are at significant risk for sudden death. The hallmark anatomic finding in these patients is an asymmetric, hypertrophied, nondilated left ventricle with greater involvement of the septum than the ventricle itself. This can also be seen on focused cardiac ultrasonography, where there is thickening of the left ventricular walls without associated dilation (Figure 18.8).

Electrocardiographic findings of hypertrophic cardiomyopathy include left atrial enlargement and LVH, ST-segment abnormalities, T-wave inversions, Q waves, and diminished or absent R waves in the lateral leads. Premature atrial and ventricular contractions, SVT, multifocal ventricular arrhythmias, and new-onset atrial fibrillation can also be present.

Myocarditis

Myocarditis is an inflammatory condition involving the myocardium. Although it has numerous causes, including infectious, drug-induced, endocrine, radiation-induced, and collagen vascular diseases, the most common in North America is viral (coxsackievirus A and B, ECHO viruses, and influenza viruses).[26,27] The clinical presentation varies, depending on multiple factors, including the underlying cause and the age of the patient. Neonates and infants can present with symptoms such as lethargy, poor feeding, irritability, pallor, fever, and failure to thrive. Symptoms suggestive of heart failure (ie, diaphoresis with feeding, rapid breathing, and respiratory distress) can also be present. Older children and adolescents might present similarly, complaining of weakness and fatigue, particularly on exertion. With viral myocarditis, the patient could have a recent history of a nonspecific viral-syndrome-type illness. Signs of poor cardiac function, including signs of acute heart failure, can be present on physical examination.

Multiple electrocardiographic findings are possible with myocarditis. The most common arrhythmia is sinus tachycardia. A tachycardia faster than expected for the degree of fever (10 beats/min for each degree of temperature elevation) can indicate myocarditis. Many other arrhythmias are associated with myocarditis, including junctional tachycardias, ventricular ectopy, ventricular tachycardias, and even second- and third-degree AV blocks. Morphologically, T-wave flattening or inversion and low QRS complex voltage (<5 mm) can be present in all limb leads.

REFERENCES

1. Horton L, Mosee S, Brenner J. Use of the electrocardiogram in a pediatric emergency department. *Arch Pediatr Adolesc Med.* 1994;148:184-188.
2. Clausen H, Theophilos T, Jackno K, et al. Paediatric arrhythmias in the emergency department. *Emerg Med J.* 2012;29:732-737.
3. Park M. *Pediatric Cardiology for Practitioners.* 6th ed. Philadelphia: Mosby; 2014.
4. Park M, Guntheroth W. *How to Read Pediatric ECGs.* 4th ed. Philadelphia: Mosby; 2007.
5. Robinson B, Anisman P, Eshagh E. A primer on pediatric ECGs. *Contemp Pediatr.* 1994;11:69.

THE PEDIATRIC ECG

TABLE 18.5. Common electrocardiographic findings associated with specific congenital heart diseases.

	RVH	LVH	RIGHT ATRIAL ENLARGE-MENT	LEFT ATRIAL ENLARGE-MENT	RIGHT AXIS DEVIATION	LEFT AXIS DEVIATION	RIGHT BUNDLE-BRANCH BLOCK
Patent ductus arteriosus		+					
Atrial septal defect	+		+		+		+
Ventricular septal defect	+	+				+	+
Coarctation of the aorta	+ (newborn)	+ (older child)			+ (newborn)		
Tetralogy of Fallot	+				+		+ (after repair)
Transposition of the great arteries	+				+	+	
Tricuspid atresia	+	+	+			+	
Pulmonary atresia		+					
Hypoplastic left heart syndrome	+						
Aortic stenosis		+					
Pulmonary stenosis	+		+		+		

Reproduced with permission from: Sharieff GQ, Rao SO. The pediatric ECG. *Emerg Med Clin North Am.* 2006; 24:195-208. Copyright 2006 Elsevier Inc.

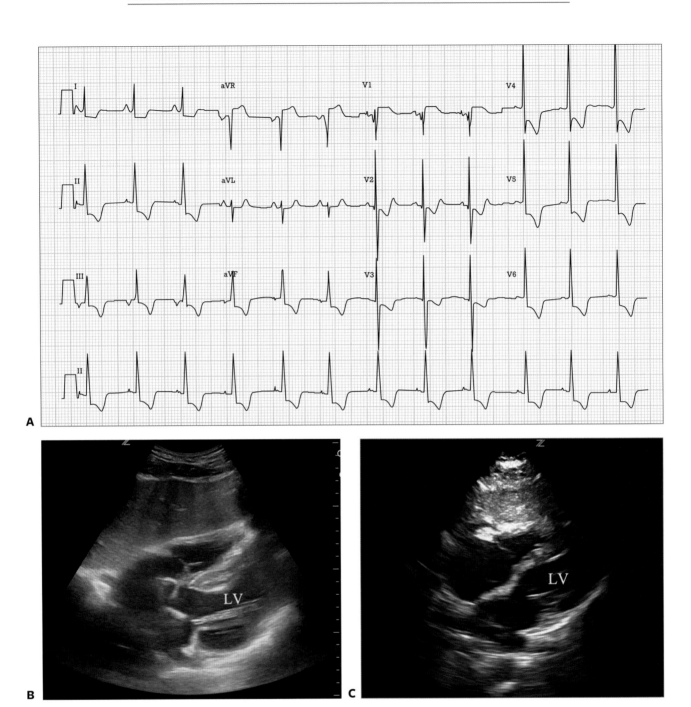

FIGURE 18.8. Hypertrophic cardiomyopathy. **A.** ECG of a patient with hypertrophic cardiomyopathy. Note LVH, which can also be seen on point-of-care ultrasound. This child also has evidence of ischemia with ST-segment depression. **B.** Point-of-care ultrasound imaging of a different child with hypertrophic cardiomyopathy caused by Pompe disease. The subxiphoid view of the heart shows the left ventricle with asymmetrically thickened walls. **C.** Normal subxiphoid view of a child's heart.

6. Marzuillo P, Benettoni A, Germani C, et al. Acquired long QT syndrome: a focus for the general pediatrician. *Pediatr Emerg Care.* 2014;30:257-261.
7. Moeller J, Gummin D, Nelson T, et al. Risk of ventricular arrhythmias and association with ondansetron. *J Pediatr.* 2016;179:118-123.e1.
8. May L, Millar K, Barlow K, et al. QTc prolongation in acute pediatric migraine. *Pediatr Emerg Care.* 2015;31:409-411.
9. Wilson P, Florin T, Huang G, et al. Is tachycardia at discharge from the pediatric emergency department a cause for conern? A nonconcurrent cohort study. *Ann Emerg Med.* 2017;70:286-276.e2.
10. Perry J. Supraventricular tachycardia. In: Garson A Jr, Bricker JT, Fisher DJ, et al., eds. *The Science and Practice of Pediatric Cardiology.* 2nd ed. Baltimore, MD: Lippincott Williams & Wilkins; 1998.
11. Quinones C, Bubolz B. Cardiac emergencies. In: Fleisher G, Ludwig S, eds. *Textbook of Pediatric Emergency Medicine.* Philadelphia, PA: Lippincott Williams & Wilkins; 2016:638-49.
12. O'Laughlin M. Congestive heart failure in children. *Pediatr Clin North Am.* 1999;46:263-273.
13. Diaz-Parra S, Sanchez-Yanez P, Zabala-Arguelles I, et al. Use of adenosine in the treatment of supraventricular tachycardia in a pediatric emergency department. *Pediatr Emerg Care.* 2014;30:388-393.
14. Lewis J, Arora G, Tudorascu D, et al. Acute management of refractory and unstable pediatric supraventricular tachycardia. *J Pediatr.* 2016;181:177-182.e2.
15. Silka M. Emergency management of arrhythmias. *Current Concepts in Diagnosis and Management of Arrhythmias in Infants and Children.* New York, NY: Futura Publishing; 1998:319-322.
16. Saleh F, Greene E, Mathison D. Evaluation and management of atrioventricular block in children. *Curr Opin Pediatr.* 2014;26:279-285.
17. Fitzmaurice L, Condra C. Cardiovascular system. In: Fuchs S, Yamamoto L, eds. *APLS: The Pediatric Emergency Medicine Resource.* Burlington, MA: Jones & Bartlett Learning; 2012:130-167.
18. McCollough M, Sharieff G. Common complaints in the first month of life. *Pediatr Emerg Med Clin North Am.* 2002;20:27-48.
19. Savitsky E, Alejos J, Votey S. Emergency department preentations of pediatric congenital heart disease. *J Emerg Med.* 2003;24:239-245.
20. Flynn P, Engle M, Ehlers K, et al. Cardiac issues in the pediatric emergency. *Pediatr Clin North Am.* 1992;39:955-983.
21. Sharieff G, Wylie T. Pediatric cardiac disorders. *J Emerg Med.* 2004;26:65-79.
22. Woolridge D, Love J. Congenital heart disease in the pediatric emergency department: pathopysiology and clinical characteristics. *Pediatr Emerg Med Rep.* 2002;7:69-80.
23. DiMaio A, Singh J. The infant with cyanosis in the emergency room. *Pediatr Clin North Am.* 1992;39:987-1006.
24. Wigle E, Rakowski H, Kimball B, et al. Hypertrophic cardiomyopathy: clinical spectrum and treatment. *Circulation.* 1995;92:1680-1692.
25. Jouriles N. Pericardial and myocardial disease. In: Walls R, Hockberger R, Gausche-Hill M, et al. eds. *Rosen's Emergency Medicine: Concepts and Clinical Practice.* 9th ed. Philadephia, PA: Elsevier; 2018:987-999.
26. Kopeck S, Gersh B. Dilated cardiomyopathy and myocarditis: natural history, etiology, clinical manifestations, and management. *Curr Probl Cardiol.* 1987;12:569-647.
27. Li M, Klassen T, Watters L. Cardiovascular disorders. In: Barkin R, Caputo G, Jaffe D, et al. eds. *Pediatric Emergency Medicine: Concepts and Clinical Practice.* 2nd ed. St Louis, MO: Mosby; 1997.

Index

Please note that page numbers provided in *italics* indicate figures.
Page numbers in **bold** indicate tables.

A

accelerated AV junctional tachycardia, 54
accelerated idiopathic ventricular rhythm, 75
accessory pathway syndromes. *See* preexcitation and accessory pathway syndromes
acute coronary ischemia and infarction.
   See also sudden cardiac death (SCD)
   cardiac blood supply and areas of infarction, 92
   differentiating from myocarditis, 179
   differentiating from pericarditis, 177, *178*
   evolution of STEMI, 94
   hyperacute T waves in, 95, *96*
   incidence of acute coronary syndrome, 91
   key points, 91
   left bundle-branch block with MI, *111*, 112
   left ventricular aneurysm, 107–112
   loss of precordial T-wave balance, 101
   normal and nondiagnostic ECGs in, 93
   posterior infarctions, 107–112, *108*
   prehospital ECG and, 92
   Q waves in, 101–105
   reperfusion and, 104–108, *106*, *108*
   right bundle-branch block with MI, *110*, 111
   right ventricular infarction, 107–112, *109*
   ST-segment depression, 98, *102*
   ST-segment elevation and current of injury, 95–97, *97*
   T-wave inversions, 98, *104*
   Wellens syndrome, 100, *105*
acute coronary syndrome (ACS)
   distinguishing from common mimics
      non-ACE causes of ST-segment elevation, 141–156
      non-ACE causes of T-wave abnormalities, 162–167
      non-ACS causes of ST-segment depression, 159–162
   ECG goals in, 129
   ECG interpretation in, 2
   ECG limitations in, 10, 11, 22
   ECG recommendations for, 93
   management of, 50
   pediatric differential diagnosis, 292
   risk stratification for, 5
   spectrum of, 91
acute cor pulmonale, 7, 250
acute heart failure (AHF)
   arrhythmogenic right ventricular cardiomyopathy and, 206
   congenital heart disease and, **201**, **291**, 292
   differentiating between VT and SVT, 76
   left ventricular aneurysms and, 111
   left ventricular hypertrophy and, 6
   management of bradycardia in, 50
   multifocal atrial tachycardia and, 58
   myocarditis and, 292
   odds ratio suggestive of poor outcomes, 8
   risk stratification and, 5
acute myocardial infarction (acute MI)
   AV block progression in, 46
   benefits of fibrinolytic therapy in, 5
   differentiating from mimics, 141
   distinguishing from pericarditis, 141, *178*
   ECG limitations in, 10
   in-hospital mortality with, 93
   left anterior fascicular block and, 24

left posterior fascicular block and, 26
in patient with RBBB, 16
acute myopericarditis
diagnosis, 5
differential diagnosis, 95
key points, 171
PR-segment depression in, **180**
acute posterior myocardial infarction
12-lead ECG results in, 120
15-lead ECG results in, 120, 122
benefits of additional-lead testing for, 117
incidence of, 119
leads V1 and V2 and their posterior correlates, 121
acute reperfusion therapy
de Winter T-wave pattern and, 135, 136
hyperacute T waves and, 95
indications for, 5
key points, 129
left bundle-branch block and, 129–132, 132
Q wave disappearance with, 103
right ventricular-paced electrocardiographic pattern, 132–134, 133
Sgarbossa criteria for MI in LBBB, 131
ST-segment elevation in lead aVR, 134, 135
ST-segment in LBBB, 130
ST-segment recovery following, 104
Wellens syndrome and, 137
acyanotic congenital heart disease, **291**
additional-lead testing
benefits of, 117, 125
drawbacks of 12-lead ECGs, 117
indications for, 122–124, 123
key points, 117
leads V1 and V2 and their posterior correlates, 121
Lewis lead, 122, 124
limitations of, 124
obtaining 15-lead ECGs, 125
posterior leads, 119–122, 122
right ventricular leads, 117–119, 119
agonal idioventricular rhythms, 35, 36
altered mentation, 10
anterior acute myocardial infarction
complications compared to right ventricular involvement, 118
fibrinolytic therapy for, 5

resolution of ST-segment elevation following, 95
antidromic AVRT, 192, 195
aortic dissection. *See also* thoracic aortic dissection
as cause of pericarditis, **173**
focal reciprocal ST-segment changes in, 162
ST-segment depression in, **160**
ST-segment elevation in, 134, **142**
arrhythmogenic right ventricular cardiomyopathy (ARVC)
diagnostic criteria, 206, **207**
electrocardiographic findings in, 206, 208
functional changes with, 206
heart failure associated with, 206
invasive testing for, 206
key points, 199
overview of, **201**, 206
prevalence of, 206
treatment, 206
atrial fibrillation (AF)
acute pericarditis and, 175
bradycardic ventricular response with, 35, 36
causes of, **59**
electrocardiographic characteristics, 59, 60, **61**
wide complex tachycardia due to, 78
with an accessory pathway, 77
with Wolff-Parkinson-White syndrome, 77, 82, 197
atrial flutter, 61, 62, 85
atrial tachycardias, 53, 58, 72, 288
atrioventricular (AV) asynchrony, 221
atrioventricular (AV) dissociation
additional-lead testing for, 122
AV dissociation by usurpation, 47
AV heart block and, 30, 47
electrocardiographic findings in, 49, 80, 81, 82, 123
ventriculoatrial conduction and, 80
atrioventricular (AV) heart blocks
2:1 conduction, 42
causes of clinically significant, **39**
differentiating from AV dissociation, 47
electrocardiographic findings in, **38**
first-degree, 37, 40
first-degree with wide QRS complexes, 39
high-grade second degree, 43

key points, 29
management of, 50–52
pediatric patients and, 289
prognosis, 30
risk of progression to third-degree, 46
second-degree, 39, **41**
second-degree Mobitz type I, 39
second-degree Mobitz type II, 41
third-degree, **47**
third-degree (complete), 44–46, 289
treatment, 30
types of, 36, **37**
atrioventricular junctional (nodal) escape rhythm, 33, 35
atrioventricular node reentrant tachycardia (AVNRT)
electrocardiographic characteristics of, 63, 64, **65**, 66
illustrations of, 72
mechanisms of, 56
overview of, 53
pediatric patients and, 286
atrioventricular reentrant tachycardia via an accessory pathway (AVRT), 53
electrocardiographic characteristics of, **65**
mechanisms of, 56
orthodromic vs. antidromic AVRT, 192, 195
atrioventricular reentry tachycardia, 63
atropine
bradycardic patients and, 50, 52
heart block differentiation using, 43
Mobitz type II heart blocks and, 42
sinus bradycardias and, 31
third-degree heart blocks and, 46
automatic junctional tachycardia, 54
AV canal defects, 291

B

battery depletion, in pacemakers, 231
Bazett formula, 199, 209, 270, 281, 284
Beck triad, 180, 183
beta blockers
electrocardiographic findings, 276
glucagon administration in toxicity, 52
method of action, 275

bidirectional VT, 74
bifid T waves, 167
bigeminy, 32
blocked premature atrial complexes (PACs), 32, 33
blunt cardiac injury, ST-segment elevation in, 149, 150
blunt chest trauma, 10
bradycardias
agonal idioventricular rhythms, 35, 36
atrial fibrillation with bradycardic ventricular response, 35, 36
blocked premature atrial complexes mimicking, 32, 33
electrocardiographic clues, 30
escape pacemaker rhythms and, 32–34, **33**
key points, 29
management of, 50–52
Mobitz type II, 30
QRS complex in, 30
sinus bradycardias, 31
symptoms, 30
toxicologic causes and treatment, 52, 269
types of, 30
broad complex tachycardias, 69
Brugada syndrome
diagnosis, 200
differentiating from hypothermia, 249
electrocardiographic characteristics of, 146, 148, 203, 267
genetic predisposition to, 200
key points, 199
overview of,
risk stratification, 200
secondary ST-T wave repolarization abnormalities in, 165
symptoms, 200
types of by ECG analysis, **202**
bundle-branch blocks. *See also* right bundle-branch block (RBBB); *See also* left bundle-branch block (LBBB)
ECG limitations in, 11
pediatric patients and, 289
with prolonged and distorted QRS complexes, 41
QRS complex changes in, 16

C

calcium channel blockers
    electrocardiographic findings, 275
    glucagon administration in toxicity, 52
    method of action, 273
    subclasses of, 273
camel-hump wave, 248
Cannon A (atrial) waves, 76
capture beats, 48, 79, 80, 81, 288
capture thresholds, in pacemakers, 231, **232**, 233
cardiac blood supply, 92, 93
cardiac glycosides, 271–273, **272**, 276, 278
cardiac memory, T-wave inversions in, 165
cardiac resynchronization therapy (CRT)
    devices, 213
cardiac rhythm management devices (CRMDs), 222.
    See also pacemakers and pacemaker dysfunction
cardiac tamponade. *See* pericardial effusion and
    cardiac tamponade
cardiac transplant
    denervation following, 31
    wide complex tachycardias in, 86
cardiorespiratory arrest, evaluation of, 10
cardiotoxicity
    predicting, 10
    primary electrocardiographic determinants of, 8
central nervous system events
    electrocardiographic changes
        associated with, 257
    epilepsy, 259
    increased intracranial pressure, 259
    key points, 247
    subarachnoid hemorrhage, 257
cerebral T waves, 166
chest pain
    ECG limitations in, 11
    role of ECG in, 5–6
cholecystitis, **259**, 260
chronic obstructive pulmonary disease (COPD)
    electrocardiographic findings in, **255**, 255–257, 256
    key points, 247
clinical decision tools
    HEART score, 6
    value of, 5

clinical presentation, components of, 2
clinical scenarios for ECG use
    altered mentation, 10
    blunt chest trauma, 10
    cardiorespiratory arrest, 10
    chest pain, 5–6
    dyspnea, 6
    metabolic abnormality, 10
    renal failure, 10
    syncope, 7
    toxic ingestion, 8–10
cocaine, ST-segment elevation with, 151
complete SA block, 50, 51
concealed accessory pathways, 190.
    See also preexcitation and accessory
    pathway syndromes
concertina effect, 190, 191
congenital heart disease, 289, **291**
connexins, 276
coronary artery dissection, focal reciprocal
    ST-segment depression in, 162
coronary vasospasm
    cocaine-induced, 138, 151
    compared to STEMI, 156
    focal reciprocal ST-segment depression in, 162
    subarachnoid hemorrhage and, 257
    transient ischemia due to, 156
crosstalk, preventing in pacemakers, 219
current of injury, 95
cyanotic congenital heart disease, **291**

D

de Winter T-wave pattern, 129, 135, 136, 163
diagnosis-based indications for ECGs, 4
digitalis effect, 161, 166, 265, 272, 274
digoxin
    AV heart blocks due to, 29
    bidirectional VT in toxicity, 74
    bradycardia and, 52, **269**
    cardiac glycosides and, 276
    classic signs of toxicity, 53
    digitalis effect and, 272
    ECG findings in overdose, 9, 274
    enhanced automaticity and, **54**, **59**, 63
    sodium-potassium pump inhibition

INDEX

with, 271, **272**
tachyarrhythmias associated with, **54**, 55
third-degree AV heart block and, **47**
dopamine
    bradycardic patients and, 51
    cocaine exposure and, 151
    increasing heart rate with, 74
    third-degree heart block treatment and, 46
    Wenckebach block treatment and, 42
ductal-dependent congenital heart lesions, 291

E

early repolarization
    differential diagnosis of hyperacute T waves, 95
    differentiating from pericarditis, 174
    effect on T waves, 163
    electrocardiographic findings, 146
    key points, 141
    overview of, 145
echo probe sign, 172
electrical alternans, 182
electrical injuries, 247, **260**
electrocardiographic rhythm monitoring, 8
    value of, 4
electrocardiographs (ECGs)
    applications for, 1, **2**, 4
    clinical scenarios for use
        altered mentation, 10
        blunt chest trauma, 10
        cardiorespiratory arrest, 10
        chest pain, 5–6
        dyspnea, 6
        metabolic abnormality, 10
        renal failure, 10
        syncope, 7
        toxic ingestion, 8–10
    impact on ED population, 1, 3
    interpretation within clinical presentation, 2–4, 10
    key points, 1
    limitations of, 10–11
    P waves, PR interval, and QRS complex in, 15
    reasons for obtaining, 1, 2, 4
    risk assessment strategy and, 5
electrolyte imbalances
    hypercalcemia, 241, 277
    hyperkalemia, 237–238, **238**, 239, 240, 241
    hypocalcemia, 242, 243, 277
    hypokalemia, **238**, 238–241, 242, 276
    key points, 237
    magnesium abnormalities, 243
    prolonged QT complex in, 284
    ST-segment depression in, 162
    ST-segment elevation in, 151
    T-wave inversion with, 166
elevated intracranial pressure
    focal reciprocal ST-segment changes in, 162
    sinus bradycardia and, 259
    ST-segment elevation in, 154
    T-wave inversion with, 166
epilepsy, 259
epinephrine, bradycardic patients and, 31, 51
escape pacemaker rhythms
    atrioventricular junctional (nodal), 33, 35
    AV dissociation by usurpation and, 47
    fatal ventricular asystole, 32, 34
    idioventricular escape rhythms, 33, 35
    slow idioventricular rhythms, 33, 34
    types of, **33**
ethanol intoxication, 278
excessively discordant ST-segment elevation, 111

F

fascicular blocks. *See also* left posterior fascicular block; *See also* left anterior fascicular block
    bifascicular blocks, 26
    diagnosis, 23
    differential diagnosis of QRS prolongation, 269
    idioventricular escape rhythms caused by, 45
    importance of recognizing, 22
    trifascicular blocks, 26
    types of, 15, 16
fibrinolysis
    electrocardiographic findings before and after, 253
    indications for, 5
    prehospital ECGs and, 92
Fibrinolytic Therapy Trialists Collaborative Group, 5
first-degree AV blocks

acute MI with, 40
ECG interpretation in, 2, 4
electrocardiographic findings in, 38, 44
risk of progression to third-degree, 46
sinus bradycardia with, 40
treatment, 36
wide QRS complexes and, 39
fishhook pattern, 145
flutter waves, 61
focal atrial tachycardia
electrocardiographic characteristics of, 58, 59
enhanced automaticity and, **54**, 55
mechanisms of, 56
overview of, 58
focal junctional tachycardia, 54, 63, **67**
full-standard recordings, 21
fusion beats, 48, 78, 80, 288

G

gap junction inhibition, 276
gastrointestinal disorders, **259**
German military spiked helmet, 151, 153

H

half-standard recordings, 21
halogenated hydrocarbon, 278
heart blocks
atrioventricular blocks, 36–48
sinoatrial blocks, 48–50
types of, 36, **37**
HEART score, 6
hemiblocks, 16, 22
hemodynamic collapse, causes of, 10
hemorrhagic pericardial effusion, 172
high-grade AV heart blocks, 37, 43, 46
holiday heart, 278
hyperacute T waves, 95, 96, 163, 164
hypercalcemia
drug-induced, 277
ST-segment depression in, 162
ST-segment elevation in, 151, 154
symptoms, 277
hyperkalemia
clinical presentation, 276
diagnosis, 10, 237

drug-induced, 276
drugs causing, **276**
ECG changes in mild, 237, **238**, 240
ECG changes in moderate, 237, 239
ECG changes in severe, 238, 241
renal insufficiency and, 238
ST-segment depression in, 162
ST-segment elevation in, 151, 154
tall T waves in, 164
hyperthyroidism, 55, **164**, 189, 237, 243
hypertrophic cardiomyopathy (HCM)
diagnosis, 204
electrocardiographic characteristics in, 204, 205
key points, 199
overview of, **201**
pathophysiologic changes associated with, 204
pediatric patients and, 292, 294
symptoms, 202
treatment, 204
hyperventilation
ST-segment depression in, 162
T-wave inversion with, 166
hypocalcemia
drug-induced, 277
ECG changes in, 243, 277
ST-segment depression in, 162
symptoms, 277
hypoglycemia
ST-segment depression in, 162
T-wave inversion with, 166
hypokalemia
clinical presentation, 276
drug-induced, **276**
ECG changes in, **238**, 242
ST-segment depression in, 162
hypothermia
arrhythmia reversibility, 248
Brugada pattern in, 249
electrocardiographic findings in, 248, 249, 252
key points, 247
Osborn wave (J wave), 248, 253
ST-segment depression in, 162
ST-segment elevation in, 154
hypothyroidism, 244
hysteresis function, 221

INDEX

I

idioventricular escape rhythms, 33, *34*, 35
implantable cardiac devices. *See also* pacemakers and pacemaker dysfunction
    cardiac resynchronization therapy (CRT) devices, 213
    cardiac resynchronization therapy device with defibrillator (CRT-D), 213
    ECG interpretation with, 132–134
    implantable cardioverter-defibrillators (ICDs), 213
inappropriate sinus tachycardia, 55
incessant VT, 73, 78
incomplete LBBB, 22, 23
incomplete RBBB, 18
incomplete SA block, 50, *51*
inferior acute MI
    additional-lead testing and, 5, 121
    benefits of fibrinolytic therapy in, 5
inherited syndromes. *See* sudden cardiac death (SCD)
intermittent preexcitation, 190, *191*
intestinal obstruction, **259**, 260
intraventricular conduction abnormalities
    causes of, 16, **17**
    electrocardiographic manifestations of, 15–16
    interpretation of, 16
    key points, 15
    left anterior fascicular block, **23**, 23–26, *26*, *27*
    left bundle-branch block (LBBB), **19**, 19–21, *21*, *22*, *23*
    left posterior fascicular block, 24–25, **25**, *26*
    most common types of, 244
    multifascicular blocks, 26–27
    nonspecific intraventricular conduction delay, 27–28
    pediatric patients and, 289
    plus RBBB, 27
    right bundle-branch block (RBBB), 16, 17–19, *18*, *19*, *20*
isorhythmic AV dissociation, 47, *49*

J

Jervell and Lange-Nielsen syndrome (JLNS), 284
junctional ectopic tachycardia, 54
junctional tachycardia, 54
juvenile T-wave pattern, 165
J wave, 155, 248, 253

L

late delta wave, 248
left anterior descending (LAD) artery
    diagram of, *93*
    ECG representing occlusion, 16
    function of, 92
    stenosis in Wellens syndrome, 100
left anterior fascicular block
    differential diagnosis, 24
    ECG criteria for, 23
    key result of presence of, 24, 26
    overview of, 23–24
    trigger for recognition, 23
left bundle-branch block (LBBB)
    acute MI with, 132
    acute reperfusion therapy in, 129–132
    differential diagnosis, **19**
    ECG recorded at half-standard, *21*
    electrocardiographic criteria for, **21**
    fibrinolytic therapy in,
    incomplete LBBB, 22, *23*
    infarct diagnosis with, 111
    key morphologic findings in, 19
    left QRS axis deviation and, *22*
    pediatric patients and, 289
    Sgarbossa criteria for MI with, 130–134, *131*, 149
    ST-segment changes with, 21, *112*, 130, 147
    ST-T wave repolarization abnormality in, *161*
    variations of typical pattern, 20
left circumflex (LCx) artery, 92, *93*
left main coronary artery (LMCA)
    diagnosis and evaluation of occlusion, 134
    diagram of, *93*
    function of, 92
left posterior fascicular block
    conditions associated with, 26
    differential diagnosis, 25
    ECG trigger for, 25
    electrocardiographic criteria for, **25**
    key morphologic findings, 25

RBBB and, 26
right axis deviation and, 26
left-sided conduction delay, 22
left-to-right intracardiac shunts, 291
left ventricular aneurysm (LVA)
    electrocardiographic features of, 107, 110
    ST-segment elevation in, 143, 144
left ventricular hypertrophy (LVH)
    ECG criteria for, **285**
    ECG findings in, 27
    ECG limitations in, 11
    pediatric patients and, 285
    risks associated with, 6
    secondary ST-T wave repolarization abnormalities and, 160, *161*
    ST-segment elevation in, 141–143
Lewis lead
    additional-lead testing using, 122, *124*
    demonstrating P waves, *123*
lightening injuries, 260
lithium, **70**, **271**, 277
long QT syndrome
    clinical manifestation of, 208
    congenital LQTS, 208, 284
    diagnosis, 209
    differential diagnosis, 270
    electrocardiographic findings in, 209, **210**
    gene-specific therapies for, 210
    key points, 199
    management of, 210
    nongenetic causes of, 208, **209**
    overview of, **201**
    pharmacologic causes of, 269
Lown-Ganong-Levine syndrome, 190
low-voltage ECGs, 181, 244, *245*

M

magnet exams for pacemakers, 223, 225, 227, 229
metabolic conditions
    affecting pacemakers, 213, **232**
    hypercalcemia, 241, 277
    hyperkalemia, 237–238, **238**, *239*, *240*, *241*
    hypocalcemia, 242, 243, 277
    hypokalemia, **238**, 238–241, *242*, 276
    key points, 237
    magnesium abnormalities, 243
    ST-segment depression in, 162
    T-wave inversion with, 166
mitral valve prolapse
    focal ST-segment depression in, 162
    T-wave inversion in, 165
Mobitz type II (non-Wenckebach) block
    causes of, **39**
    clinical significance of, 36
    electrocardiographic findings, **38**, *43*, *44*, *46*
    electrocardiographic findings in, 30
    overview of, **41**, 41–42
    QRS complex in, 43
    treatment, 41
Mobitz type I (Wenckebach) block
    electrocardiographic findings, **38**, *42*, *45*
    electrocardiographic findings in, 39
    overview of, **41**
    QRS complex in, 43
    treatment, 36, 41
monomorphic VT, 73, 78, 79
multifascicular blocks, 26
multifocal atrial tachycardia (MAT), 58, **59**, 60
multifocal VT, 74
myocardial contusion
    diagnosis, 10
    ST-segment elevation in, 149, *150*
Myocardial Infarction category 3 (TIMI-3), 104
myocardial injury
    causing third-degree heart block, **47**
    de Winter pattern and, 136
    diagnosis, 150
    electrocardiographic findings in, 18
    sinus bradycardia in, 31, 32
    sudden cardiac death due to, 199
myocarditis
    conditions associated with, 179
    differentiating from true myocardial ischemia, 179
    electrocardiographic characteristics of, 156, 165, **179**, *180*, *181*
    key points, 171
    pediatric patients and, 292
    symptoms of, **179**

INDEX

N

narrow complex tachycardias, 53–68
    atrial fibrillation, 59–61
    atrial flutter, 61
    atrioventricular node reentry tachycardia, 63
    atrioventricular reentry tachycardia via an accessory pathway, 63
    definition of, 53
    differential diagnosis, 61
    evaluation and diagnosis, 65–68, **67**
    focal atrial tachycardia, 58
    key points, 53
    mechanisms of, **54**, 54–55, **56**
    multifocal atrial tachycardia (MAT), 58
    nonparoxysmal junctional tachycardia, 62
    overview of, 53–55
    paroxysmal supraventricular tachycardia (PSVT), 53
    sinus tachycardia, 55–57
    supraventricular tachycardia (SVT), 53
    terminology used, 53
    types of, **54**
negative biphasic T waves, 167
noncardiac conditions affecting ECGs
    central nervous system events, **257**, 257–259, **258**
    chronic obstructive pulmonary disease, **255**, 255–257, **256**
    electrical injuries, 260
    hypothermia, 248, 249, 252
    key points, 247
    pneumothorax, 254
    pulmonary embolism (PE), 249–252, **250**, 251, 252
    selected gastrointestinal disorders, 259
    thoracic aortic dissection, 253–256, **254**
nonparoxysmal junctional tachycardia
    electrocardiographic characteristics of, 63
    mechanisms of, 56
    overview of, 62–63
    synonyms for, 54
nonspecific intraventricular conduction delay, 16, 27, 28
non-ST-elevation ACS (NSTE-ACS)
    ST-segment depression in, 98
    terminology used, 91
    T waves in, 101
non-ST-segment elevation MI, 91
normal variant ST-segment elevation, 145
NSTEMI (non–ST-segment elevation MI)
    diagnosis, 5, 100
    terminology, 91

O

odds ratio (OR), 8
orthodromic AVRT, 192, *195*
Osborn wave (J wave), 155, 248, 253
oversensing, in pacemakers, 229

P

pacemakers and pacemaker dysfunction
    causes of circuit disruptions, 213
    DDD pacemakers, 216, 217
    dysfunction workup
        device manufacturer phone numbers, **222**
        first steps, 222
        identifying patient devices, 222
        magnet exams, 223, *225*, 229
        paced ECG appearance, 222, 224, 225
        pacemaker interrogation, 222
    electrocardiographic artifacts caused by, 216
    indications for pacemaker placement, 214
    key points, 213
    nomenclature used for, 216, **217**
    overview of, 213
    paced ECGs with heart rate too fast, 223–229, 226
        ventricular rate below upper rate limit,
        ventricular rate over upper rate limit, 225
    paced ECGs with heart rate too slow or normal, 229–233, 230
    pacemaker parts and function, 215
    programming features, 219–224
    timing cycles, 217, **218**, 220
pacemaker syndrome, 221
pancreatitis, **163**, 259, **260**
paroxysmal junctional tachycardia, 54
paroxysmal supraventricular tachycardia (PSVT), 53, 63
pathologic Q waves
    acute MI and, 102
    description of, 101
    differential diagnosis of, 103
    electrocardiographic findings, 105
    potential for adverse events with, 6

relationship between leads V1 and V2, *121*
subarachnoid hemorrhage and, **257**
pediatric patients
    abnormal ECGs
        conduction abnormalities, 289–290, *290*
        congenital heart disease, **291**, *291*–292, **293**
        hypertrophic cardiomyopathy, 292–294, *294*
        myocarditis, 292–293
        tachycardias, 286–288, *287*, *288*, *289*
    age-related ECG subtleties, 282
    bifid T waves in, *167*
    juvenile T-wave pattern in, *165*
    key points, 281
    normal ECGs
        axis, 283
        chamber size, 285
        criteria for ventricular and atrial hypertrophy, **285**
        electrocardiographic findings, 283
        heart rates, 283
        overview of, 282
        PR interval, 283
        QRS duration, 283
        QT interval, 283, *284*
        T waves, 284
    reasons for obtaining ECGs in, 281
    systematic approach to ECG interpretation in, 281
    wide complex tachycardias in, 86
percutaneous coronary intervention (PCI)
    indications for, 5
    prehospital ECGs and, 92
pericardial adhesions, 172
pericardial effusion and cardiac tamponade
    diagnosis, 180
    echo probe sign and, 172
    electrocardiographic characteristics of, *181*, *182*, *183*
    incidence of, 172
    key points, 171
pericarditis
    arrhythmias and, 175
    causes of, **173**
    diagnosis, 172
    distinguishing from acute MI, 141, 177, *178*

ECG limitations in, 11
echo probe sign, 172
electrocardiographic characteristics of, 172, *174*, **175**, *176*
key points, 171
localized to specific regions, 172, 177
stages of, *175*, **176**
ST-segment elevation in, 144, *145*
symptoms of, **174**
T-wave inversions in, *165*
pharmacologic agents, ST-segment elevation with, 150, **151**. *See also* toxic ingestion
physiologic J-junctional depression with sinus rhythm, 159, *160*
physiologic pacing
    automatic mode switching, 221
    minimizing right ventricular pacing, 220
    rate-responsive pacemakers, 219, 227
    rest, sleep, and hysteresis modes, 221
pneumomediastinum, ST-segment elevation in, 153
pneumothorax
    definition of, 254
    electrocardiographic findings in, 254, **255**
    key points, 247
    ST-segment elevation in, 153
poisoning. *See* toxic ingestion
polymorphic ventricular tachycardia, 73, 270, 273
positive biphasic T waves, *167*
posterior wall MI
    diagnosis, 107
    electrocardiographic characteristics of, *107*
postoperative pericarditis, 172, 177
potassium. *See* hyperkalemia; *See* hypokalemia
potassium rectifier current inhibition, 269–271, **271**, *272*
precordial concordance, 80, 83, 85, 101
preexcitation alternans, 190, *191*
preexcitation and accessory pathway syndromes
    anatomic substrates and accessory pathways, 187, *188*
    associated abnormalities and epidemiology, 188
    clinical significance
        tachyarrhythmias, 192
        tachycardias requiring an accessory pathway, 192, *195*, *196*

tachycardias where accessory pathway
    facilitates rapid transmission, 193, *197*
  electrocardiographic pattern of, 189
  key points, 187
  overview of, 187
  pediatric patients and, 286
  related electrocardiographic
      phenomena, 190–192
    concealed accessory pathways, 190
    concertina effect, 190, *191*
    intermittent preexcitation, 190, *191*
    Lown-Ganong-Levine syndrome, 190
    MI diagnosis in WPW, 192, 194
    preexcitation alternans, 190, *191*
    pseudoinfarction pattern, 192, *193*
    type A and type B WPW syndromes, 190
  secondary ST-T wave repolarization
      abnormality in, 161
prehospital ECGs, mortality reduction
    associated with, 92
premature atrial complexes (PACs), 32, *33*
Prinzmetal angina, 156
PR-segment
  depression with pericarditis, 172
  as manifestation of cardiac impulse, 15
pseudoinfarction pattern, 192, *193*
pseudo-Wellens syndrome, 167
psychotropic medications, 9. *See also* toxic ingestion
pulmonary embolism (PE)
  diagnosis, 7
  ECG evaluation in, 7
  ECG limitations in, 10, 11
  electrocardiographic findings in, 250, *251*, *252*
  focal reciprocal ST-segment changes in, 162
  key points, 247
  low sensitivities of ECG presentations in, 7, 249
  ST-segment elevation in, 152
  T-wave inversion with, 166, 167
pulsus paradoxus, 180
purulent pericarditis, 175

Q

QRS complex
  bradycardias and, 30
  bundle-branch blocks and, 16, 17
  left bundle-branch blocks and, 19
  leftward axis deviation in left anterior
      fascicular block, 23
  as manifestation of cardiac impulse, 15
  Mobitz type II AV blocks and, 43
  nonspecific intraventricular conduction
      delays and, 27
  right bundle-branch blocks and, 17, 27
  rightward axis deviation in left posterior
      fascicular block, 25
  TCA toxic ingestion and, 9
  Wenckebach-type AV blocks and, 43
qR variant, of RBBB, 17
QR waves, 102
QS waves, 101
QT dispersion, 271, 278
Q waves
  acute coronary ischemia and, 101–104
  differential diagnosis of pathologic, **103**
  Q-wave equivalents in precordial leads, **103**

R

rabbit ear rSR pattern, 17
rate-responsive pacemakers, 219, 227
rectifier potassium current, 269–271, **271**, 272
renal failure, 10
reperfusion therapy. *See* acute reperfusion therapy
repolarization
  abnormalities in arrhythmogenic right
      ventricular cardiomyopathy, **207**
  abnormalities in central nervous system
      events, 257
  digitalis effect on, 272
  ECG limitations in, 11
  effect of hyperkalemia on, 237
  effect of hypocalcemia on, 243
  electrocardiographic findings in LBBB, 23
  ethanol ingestion and, 278
  halogenated hydrocarbons and, 278
  HEART score and, 6
  in WPW, 192
  masked by QRS depolarization, 159
  potassium rectifier current inhibition and, 269
  role of electrolytes in, 151
  secondary ST-T wave abnormalities, 160, 165, 190

right bundle-branch block (RBBB)
    acute MI in, 16
    ECG representing, 16, 44, 85
    electrocardiographic criteria for, 19
    incomplete RBBB, 18, 20
    key morphologic changes in, 17
    key to ECG evaluation in, 110, 111
    left anterior fascicular block and, 27, 78
    pediatric patients and, 289
    pulmonary embolism and, 251
    qR variant of, 17, 18
    R-wave variant, 19
    STEMI and, 20
    ST-segment and T-wave changes in, 18
right coronary artery (RCA), 92, 93
right QRS complex axis deviation, differential diagnosis, 25
right ventricular hypertrophy (RVH), 285
right ventricular MI (RVMI)
    12-lead ECG results in, 118
    additional-lead testing benefits and drawbacks, 117, 118, 124
    complications and mortality associated with, 118
    electrocardiographic characteristics of, 107
    treatment, 119
    true incidence of, 117
right ventricular (RV) pacing, 220
risk stratification
    ACS-related complaints and, 92
    ARVC diagnosis and, 208
    HEART score, 6
    important factors in, 202
    noninvasive methods for Brugada syndrome, 200
    risks associated with left ventricular hypertrophy, 6
    role in emergency medicine, 5
    role of clinical decision tools, 5
    standardized electrocardiographic classification systems for, 6
    syncope and, 8
    using initial 12-lead ECGs, 6
Romano-Ward syndrome, 208, 284
rule-out MI protocol, 1, 4
runaway pacemaker, 227

S

San Francisco Syncope Rule, 8
scenario-based ECG interpretations, 2
secondary ST-T wave repolarization abnormalities, 160, 165
second-degree AV blocks
    2:1 conduction, 44
    electrocardiographic findings in, 46
    Mobitz type I, 39, **41**
    Mobitz type II, 41
    risk of progression to third-degree, 46
sedative-hypnotics, 9. *See also* toxic ingestion
seizure, ECGs predictive of, 9
sensor-driven tachycardia, 227
sepsis, tachycardia due to, 79
Sgarbossa criteria, 111, 129, 130–134, **131**, 149
sick sinus syndrome, **37**, 50, 52
sinoatrial (SA) blocks
    electrocardiographic findings in, 48, 50
    identifying, 48
    key points, 29
    management of, 50–52
    mechanisms of, 48
    PACs mimicking, 32
    symptoms, 48
    types of, **37**
sinus bradycardias
    conditions associated with, 32
    ECG presentation of, 31
    key points, 32
    myocardial injury and, 31, 32
    situations occurring in, 31
sinus tachycardia
    causes of, 55
    diagnosis, 55
    differentiation in pediatric patients, 286
    electrocardiographic findings in, 55, 57
    illustrations of, 72
    mechanisms of, 56
    TCA toxic ingestion and, 9
Smith-modified Sgarbossa criteria, 131, 132, 134
sodium channel blockers
    agents, 265, **266**
    Brugada pattern and, 267

INDEX

intraventricular conduction and, 265–269
    ST-segment elevation with, 150
    T-wave inversion with, 166
sodium-potassium pump inhibition, 271
spiked helmet sign, 151, 153
Spodick sign, 175
standardized electrocardiographic classification systems, 6
Standardized Reporting Criteria Working Group of the Emergency Medicine Cardiovascular Research and Education Group, 6
early repolarization, **142**
STEMI equivalent, 149
STEMI (ST-elevation myocardial infarction)
    acute reperfusion in, 5, 104–109
    current of injury in, 95
    diagnosis, 5, **92**, 141
    diagnosis in presence of LBBB, 111
    ECG limitations in, 10
    evolution of, 94, **95**
    fibrinolytic therapy in, 5
    RBBB with, 20
    ST-segment depression in, 98, 108
    ST-segment elevation in, 98, 99, 106, 109
Stokes-Adams syncope, 37, 41
stress-induced (takotsubo) cardiomyopathy, 155
ST-segment depression
    according to area of infarction, 100
    acute subendocardial ischemia and, 98, 102, 108
    common causes of, **160**
    excessively discordant, 111
    high lateral STEMI and, 99
    LBBB pattern and, 112
    measurement of, 159
    mortality associated with, 98
    non-ACS causes of, 159–162
ST-segment elevation
    acute reperfusion therapy and, 134, 135
    acute STEMI and, 95, 97, 98, 99, 102, 106, 109
    final diagnosis in, 11
    LBBB and, 112
    non-ACS causes of
        Afro-Caribbean pattern, 146, 147
        Brugada syndrome, 146, 148
        early repolarization, 145, 146

        electrolyte imbalances, 151, 154
        elevated intracranial pressure, 154
        global cardiac injury, 149, 150
        hypothermia, 154, 155
        key points, 141
        left bundle-branch block and paced rhythms, 147–150, 149
        left ventricular aneurysm, 143, 144
        left ventricular hypertrophy, 141–143, 143
        myocarditis, 156
        pericarditis, 144, 145
        pharmacologic agents, 150, **151**, 152
        Prinzmetal angina, 156
        pulmonary conditions, 152
        spiked helmet sign, 151, 153
        ST ELEVATION mnemonic,
        stress-induced cardiomyopathy, 155
    RBBB and, 18
    STEMI location, **92**
    transmural MI and, 105
subarachnoid hemorrhage (SAH), 257, 258
sudden cardiac death (SCD)
    arrhythmogenic right ventricular cardiomyopathy, 206–208, **207**, 208
    Brugada syndrome, 200–202, **202**, 203
    early repolarization and, 145
    hypertrophic cardiomyopathy, 202–205, **204**, 205
    key points, 199
    long QT syndrome, 208–211, **209**, 210
    overview of, 199, **201**
    prevention with ICDs, 213
sudden unexplained nocturnal death syndrome, 200
supraventricular tachycardia (SVT)
    differentiating between VT and SVT, 76–82
    pediatric patients and, 286
    use of term, 53
    WCTs of supraventricular origin, 71–73
symptom-based indications, 4
syncope,
    appropriate electrocardiographic approach to, 8
    evaluation of, 7
    risk stratification in, 8

T

tachyarrhythmias
- associated with accessory pathway syndromes, 192
- AVRT via accessory pathway, 65
- common types of, 179
- COPD patients and, 247
- digitalis effect and, 273
- ethanol ingestions and, 278
- halogenated hydrocarbons and, 278
- hypertrophic cardiomyopathy and, 204
- key points, 187
- magnet exam and, 223
- mechanisms of, **54**, 55
- pacemakers and, 213, 219
- subarachnoid hemorrhage and, 258
- syncope patients and, 8
- toxic ingestion and, 265

tachy-brady syndrome, **37**, 50, 52

tachycardias
- drugs causing, **270**
- narrow complex, 53–68
- pacemaker-mediated, 227, 228
- pediatric patients and, **286**, 286–288
- requiring an accessory pathway, 192
- sensor-driven, 227
- where accessory pathway facilitates rapid transmission, 193
- wide complex, 69–86

tall T waves, 163

tamponade. *See* pericardial effusion and cardiac tamponade

third-degree (complete) AV blocks
- causes of, 45, **47**
- electrocardiographic findings in, 38, 48
- hallmark findings of, 44
- pediatric patients and, 289, 290
- risk of progression to, 46
- treatment, 46

thoracic aortic dissection
- conditions associated with, 253
- differential diagnosis, 253
- electrocardiographic findings in, **254**
- key points, 247
- Stanford classification for, 253
- symptoms, 253

thyroid disorders
- hyperthyroidism, 243
- hypothyroidism, 244

torsades de pointes
- causes of, 270
- electrocardiographic characteristics of, 75, 273
- illustration of, 74
- treatment, 74

toxic ingestion
- beta blockers, 52, 275
- calcium, 277
- calcium channel blockers, 52, 273–274, 275
- diagnosis, 8
- digoxin, 9, 52, 74
- ECG abnormalities in, 9–11
- ECG limitations in, 10
- ECGs interpreted within clinical presentation, 10
- ethanol, 278
- gap junction inhibition, 276
- halogenated hydrocarbons, 278
- intraventricular conduction and, 266, 267, 268
- key points, 265
- lithium, 277
- potassium, 276
- potassium rectifier current inhibition, 269–271, **271**, 272, 273
- psychotropic medications, 9
- sedative-hypnotics, 9
- sodium channel blockers
  - agents, 265, **266**
  - bradyarrhythmias, 269, **270**
  - intraventricular conduction and, 265–269
  - ventricular arrhythmias, 269
- sodium-potassium pump inhibition, 271–273, **272**, 274
- tricyclic antidepressants (TCAs), 8–10, 26, 150, 152

transesophageal atrial "pill" electrodes, 83

transthoracic echocardiography (TTE), 83

triad of electrical alternans, low voltage, and PR-segment depression, 181, 183

tricyclic antidepressants (TCAs)
- common agents, **266**

ECG less than reliable in toxic ingestion, 9
ECG limitations in, 10
screening asymptomatic toxic ingestions, 10
ST-segment elevation with, 150, 152
toxic ingestion, 8–10, 26, 266, 267, 268

T waves
    bifid T waves, **167**
    causes of biphasic T waves, **164**, 167
    causes of tall T waves, **165**
    causes of T-wave flattening, **162**, 164
    causes of T-wave inversions, **163**, 164–166
    deeply inverted or biphasic, 100, 137
    de Winter pattern, 135, 136
    hyperacute in acute coronary ischemia, 95, 96
    inverted in acute coronary ischemia, 98, 104, 138
    loss of precordial T-wave balance, 101
    non-ACS causes of abnormalities, 159, 162–167
    potential for adverse events with inversion, 6
    RBBB and, 18

U

undersensing, in pacemakers, 232, 233
unstable angina
    current terminology for, 91
    diagnosis, 5
    treatment, 138

V

ventricular aneurysms, conditions associated with, 111
ventricular arrhythmias
    ECG presentation predictive of, 9
    odds ratio suggestive of poor outcomes, 8
    sodium channel blockers and, 269
ventricular assist devices, 86
ventricular asystole
    ECG presentation of, 34
    escape pacemaker rhythms and, 32
ventricular-paced rhythms
    suggestive of acute MI, 133
    WCT and, 75
    wide complex tachycardia and, **70**
ventricular repolarization. *See* repolarization
ventricular safety pacing, 219
ventricular septal defects, 291

ventricular tachycardia (VT)
    additional-lead testing for, 122, 124
    bidirectional VT, 74
    differentiating between VT and SVT, 76–82
    electrocardiographic findings in, 81, 123
    monomorphic VT, 73, 74
    morphological criteria favoring, **84**
    multifocal VT, 74
    pediatric patients and, 288
    polymorphic VT, 73, 74, 75
    sodium channel blockers and, 269
    sustained vs. nonsustained (intermittent), 73, 74
    ventricular-paced rhythms, 75, 111
ventriculoatrial (VA) conduction, 80
viral pericarditis, 172, 182

W

Wellens syndrome
    Afro-Caribbean pattern mimicking, 146
    electrocardiographic criteria for, **101**
    electrocardiographic findings in, 105
    key points, 91, 159
    overview of, 100, 137
    pseudo-Wellens syndrome, 167
    Wellens T waves, 107, 129, 137, 163, 167
wide complex tachycardias (WCT)
    additional-lead testing in, 122, 123
    algorithms for treatment, 86
    algorithms to determine origin of, 83
    approach to, 70
    causes of, **70**
    differentiation between VT and SVT
        challenges of, 76
        clinical features, 76
        ECG findings, 77–82
        morphological criteria favoring VT, **84**
        patient history, 76
        WCT by QRS regularity, **77**
    illustrations of, 72
    key points, 69
    monomorphic VT, 71, 73, 78, 79
    overview of, 69–70
    pediatric patients and, 288, 291
    special patient populations
        cardiac transplant or implantable devices, 86

pediatric patients, 86
therapy, 83
TTE and pill electrodes, 83
WCTs of supraventricular origin, 71–73, **73**
WCTs of ventricular origin, **73**, 73–76
wide QRS complex tachycardia, 69
Wolff-Parkinson-White (WPW) syndrome
  anatomic substrates and, 187, 188
  associated abnormalities and epidemiology, 188
  atrial fibrillation in, 61, 77, 82, 197
  clinical significance of, 192–194
  distinguishing type B from LBBB, 22
  electrocardiographic pattern of, 189
  key points, 187
  narrow complex tachycardia in, 63
  overview of, 187
  pediatric patients and, 286, 288
  related electrocardiographic phenomena
    concealed accessory pathways, 190
    concertina effect, 190, *191*
    intermittent preexcitation, 190, *191*
    MI diagnosis in WPW, 192, *194*
    preexcitation alternans, 190, *191*
    pseudoinfarction pattern, 192, *193*
  secondary ST-T wave repolarization abnormality in, 161
  type A and type B classification scheme, 190